Politics
of the
Heart

Politics
of the
Heart

A
LESBIAN PARENTING
ANTHOLOGY
edited by
Sandra Pollack
and Jeanne Vaughn

Firebrand
Books
Ithaca, New York

Selections from this book have appeared previously in the following periodicals: *Common Lives/Lesbian Lives, Conditions, Matrix, N.Y.U. Review of Law and Social Change, off our backs, Plexus, Quest, Toronto Lesbian Mothers Defence Fund Newsletter, Sinister Wisdom, Washington Blade,* and *Womanews.*

Permission from the following authors and publishers is gratefully ackowledged:

"A Birthday Remebered" by Ann Allen Shockley from *The Black And White Of It* (Naiad Press, Tallahassee, FL: 1981)

"Diatribe Of The Deserted Poet" and "Your Kids Have Germs" by Martha Shelley from *Mothers And Lovers* (Safir Publishing, Oakland, CA: 1981)

"Legacy" by Pat Parker from *Jonestown & Other Madness* (Firebrand Books, Ithaca, NY: 1985)

"Lesbian/Grandmother" by Faith Reboin from *Long Time Passing: Lives Of Older Lesbians* edited by Marcy Adelman (Alyson Publications, Boston, MA: 1986)

"A Long Story" by Beth Brant from *Mohawk Trail* (Firebrand Books, Ithaca, NY: 1985)

"Man Child: A Black Lesbian-Feminist's Response" by Audre Lorde from *Sister Outsider* (Crossing Press, Freedom, CA: 1984)

"Open Windows" (II and V) by Marilyn Hacker from *Assumptions* (Alfred P. Knopf, New York, NY: 1985)

"The Survivors" by Caeia March from *The Reach And Other Stories* edited by Lilian Mohin and Sheila Shulman (Onlywomen Press, London: 1984)

Politics Of The Heart, A Lesbian Parenting Anthology
copyright © 1987 by Sandra Pollack and Jeanne Vaughn

Individual selections copyright © by their respective author(s).

Book and cover design by Mary A. Scott
Typesetting by Bets Ltd.

Printed in the United States by McNaughton & Gunn

This publication is made possible, in part, with support from the Literature Panel, New York State Council on the Arts.

Library of Congress Cataloging-in-Publication Data

Politics of the heart.

    Bibliography: p.
    1. Lesbian mothers—United States.   I. Pollack,
Sandra, 1937–   .   II. Vaughn, Jeanne, 1954–
HQ75.53.P64 1987   306.8'743   87–27250
ISBN 0-932379-36-2
ISBN 0-932379-35-4 (pbk.)

Contents

Preface

During the fall of 1982 I was asked to become part of a group of women who would bring to life the stories, songs, prayers—the very lives of lesbian mothers. I agreed.

Together we named the work *And The Thick Ones Are Comforters: A Lesbian Mother's Anthology*. We bonded to each other in the names of our children and mothers and committed the following two years to the work before us. We worked together as sisters, friends, political and cultural allies. We met with, talked to, and corresponded with hundreds of women about the anthology. We made family together and were constantly confronted with our fears, our differences, and our self-limitations. Always we were mothers who loved women.

We were rich in diversity: a welfare mother of immigrant working-class background with one son; a Black Southern feminist writer with one daughter; a white working-class native Californian community activist with two daughters; a Puerto Rican community worker and activist mother of five, a Black native of New Mexico and mother of one son. We believed that our differences were our most valuable natural resources.

The two years passed quickly, and this work demanded still more time, more file cabinets, more meetings, more child care, more manuscripts, more long-distance phone calls, more fund-raising, more of everything! By the summer of 1984, only Jeanne Vaughn and I could commit to further work on the anthology, and I was moving three thousand miles away. What we did not know as we parted was that I, too, would be unable to continue as an editor of this work.

For an entire year Jeanne worked alone. Unable to find a coeditor, and no longer able to stand the frustration and isolation, she was at the point of giving up. Celine-Marie Pascale, a lesbian who is not a mother, offered to help with the editing and administrative duties until Jeanne could locate another coeditor. With Celine-Marie's support and many hours of work, along with Bettina Aptheker's suggestion of a prospective publisher, Jeanne was able to get the original manuscript completed and mailed to Firebrand Books.

In February 1986, Sandra Pollack, a Jewish lesbian mother of two who teaches and resides in Ithaca, New York, became coeditor of the anthology at Nancy K. Bereano's suggestion. Sandra, who with Charlotte Bunch coedited *Learning Our Way: Essays In Feminist Education*, was able to provide the steady, dependable, and experienced hand needed to bring this work to full term. When Sandra had turned forty-four years old in 1981 and felt she had lived half her life, she had made a list of all of the things she wanted to accomplish in the second half: editing a book about lesbian parenting was on that list.

Jeanne and Sandra worked four thousand miles apart, Jeanne on the West Coast and Sandra on the East. Although having never met face to face for almost a year, the partnership flourished. With the support of Firebrand, they were finally able to meet together in Ithaca and work through to the final stages of preparation for publication.

Five years from its inception, Jeanne Vaughn is the only one of our original group to see this work to actual publication as coeditor. *Politics Of The Heart* is a tribute to her tenacity and need, the kind which comes when to create something means to save your own life. *Politics Of The Heart* has become what Jeanne envisioned in a letter to me in November 1982: "For me the anthology is about making connections between women across time, class, race, and political position. I want to open a dialogue between parents and nonparents, lesbian and nonlesbian women, and to address the issues of who raises our children, how we raise our children, and what our individual and collective responsibilities to our children, ourselves, each other, and the planet are. I want the words of poor women, Third World women, welfare mothers like myself, to be foremost. It is these women, I believe, who have the most to say. It is our vision and counsel which has most often been ignored, and it is through our struggle and survival that the body of wisdom we have to share has grown."

For Sandra, this anthology has moved her to a new level of self-awareness. She writes: "I just came back from the National Women's Studies Conference at Spelman College in Atlanta. Minnie Bruce Pratt read and spoke of her struggle to write about being a lesbian mother. After the reading I returned to my room thinking about how much anger I still have not allowed to surface. It was over ten years ago, and still I feel anger at the three years in court—anger at my ex-husband and his lawyer asking me if I was a lesbian; anger at my knowing that I could not answer yes, anger at how my journals were stolen and then presented in court, anger at my fear of letting myself feel. It's been more than ten years since the court decision awarding joint custody—a victory in spite of the exposed lesbianism. But it was a short-lived victory when my daughters' father punished them by refusing to see them. In silence for many years I carried my sorrow for their pain, also never voiced. Like Minnie Bruce, I, too, was finally finding a voice to begin speaking of my life as a lesbian mother, searching for beginning words to share my pride in who I actually am. This book is my contribution to the ways we are breaking the silence. It is a celebration that I ask others to join with me in recognizing. It is my 50th birthday present to myself."

Politics Of The Heart pays tribute to the voices of Lesbian Mothers, the women whose work appears here, the lives and times that are spoken of here. *Politics Of The Heart* is a tribute to the women who read this work and weep, laugh, shake their heads nodding, saying, "Yes, this is me, this tells my story, speaks my pain, my truth, my joy, my dream."

I began to write when I was pregnant with my daughter. I wanted to put down on paper the things it would be years before I could communicate with her about. She is now eleven and often asks me to tell her about my childhood, her early childhood, or to trace this memory or that one. I truly believe that *Politics Of The Heart* is a legacy and a guidebook for my daughter, for lesbian parents, for nonparents, and for the young people we are all responsible for.

Welcome to another precious piece of our lives as we work to make them whole again. Here we are speaking and singing, raising our voices in passionate discourse, healing, confronting, demanding, praying, awakening, remembering that which we have always known; and telling and telling and telling the whole of that which is our truth, our lives.

Andrea R. Canaan
June 27, 1987
New Orleans, Louisiana

Introduction

There have always been lesbians who were mothers, lesbians who struggled with the decision to have children, lesbians who have gotten pregnant against their will, lesbians who have adopted and/or been foster parents, lesbians who have had children in heterosexual marriages, lesbians who have raised the children of relatives and friends, lesbians who have lost their children, who have had their children taken from them, or who have felt the necessity to give them up, lesbians who have been open, and lesbians who have hidden their lifestyles from their children.

In 1976, Adrienne Rich in *Of Woman Born* provided insight into, and a language to talk about, the institution of motherhood. Although dealing primarily with white middle-class norms, Rich demonstrated how the experience of motherhood is tied to patriarchal institutions that, in turn, affect all women—mothers, women without children, daughters, sons, lesbians, and heterosexuals. As Rich suggests in the Introduction to the recent tenth anniversary edition, women's voices should point us toward future analysis and action—toward "a collective movement to empower women." It is in this spirit that we present the words of lesbian parents in 1987.

The history, experience, and issues that have confronted lesbian mothers have changed over the years. Prior to the Civil Rights movement in the 1960s, and the women's and gay liberation movements in the late '60s and early '70s, lesbian mothers lived in a much greater degree of secrecy and isolation, particularly with regard to the legal system. Support gained from the social movements of the time helped lesbian parenting to enter a new phase. Lesbians began to confront the legal system, challenging the courts, and to a very limited extent, winning custody. We started to emerge from invisibility and demand the right to our children and our families. As lesbians, we articulated our concerns and began to organize as welfare mothers, as women of color, as poor and working-class women, as Jewish women, as differently abled women. These years also saw the growth of lesbian mother support and legal advocacy groups, and a sense of pride in one's life as a lesbian.

Although lesbians still face the very real threat of losing their children in the 1980s, the issues have expanded beyond the initial struggles for custody. Increasingly, lesbians are choosing to openly conceive as lesbians, bear children, parent, and create distinctively lesbian families. There is an entire generation of children growing to adulthood who have been raised by out lesbians.

These gains not withstanding, there are many questions continuing to confront us. What makes lesbian parenting special? Does it offer a radical alternative to traditional socialization, or is it only a slight variation on an old theme? Can we develop a lesbian-feminist theory of family that includes the elements of race and class to counter traditional family theories? How do poverty, racism, and age affect our parenting situations? What about the values that people from various threatened/decimated groups—Black, Jewish, Native American—place on having children? How do we deal with homophobia, racism, classism, etc., in ourselves, our children, our community? How do the issues change as the children grow from infancy to childhood, from adolescence to adulthood? What are the needs of biological/nonbiological lesbian parents? What is the role of the comother? Are lesbian mothers just like heterosexual mothers as some current comparison studies imply? Or does the status of lesbians in our culture insure that, to one degree or another, lesbian mothers *will* experience motherhood differently? What similarites do we share with straight mothers that could be the basis of political action? How much influence do we really have on our children? How do lesbian families deal with issues of disability? How is lesbian child-rearing affected by alcoholism and/or substance abuse? Why do we choose to parent or not to parent? What are the politics of our choices? How do children affect our relationships? What happens when our relationships break up? How do we deal with health, legal, education, and social service institutions? Do we treat boy and girl children differently? Should we?

Growing political repression in the '80s, and the movement toward the reestablishment of traditional patriarchal family values, affect all mothers, both lesbian and heterosexual. Attacks on female-headed households are attacks on all of us: three out of five people living below the poverty level are women; two out of three older people living in poverty are women; one-third of all poor in the U.S. are children, and the fastest growing and poorest family form is the single-parent household headed by a woman.[1] The situation for people of color, especially women and children in female-headed households, is much worse than the general statistics reflect. While 30% of all households in the U.S. are female-headed, 45.8% of all Black households are headed by women. Infant mortality rates for Black children continue to be double that of white children, and maternal deaths are almost four times higher.[2]

Racism, classism, and economic exploitation, both in the U.S. and worldwide, are not abstract issues for many lesbian (or other) mothers. Oppression in its various forms is a constant, daily presence that denies women not just the luxury of "choice," but of basic necessities for their own and their children's survival. As lesbians, we have a unique opportunity to develop and maintain environments in which having and raising children is a revolutionary experience. How we use this opportunity will have much to say about our future.

Too few of us, for example, speak of demanding adequate child care as an issue larger than having, or not having, the women's community care for the children on a regular basis. American women are far behind other industrialized countries in terms of maternity benefits, child care, and job protection while on leave. Less than half of all working women in the U.S. have any maternity coverage, and most of what does exist is inadequate. Poverty and the lack of child care are crucial issues for all mothers. It seems clear that our political demands must include legal and economic supports through social programs, health insurance, programs for adequate housing, and a welfare system that does not ask about sexuality in determining economic need. "Welfare policies confuse the economic issue of how to support a family with the personal issues of sexuality and procreation, and this confusion shapes the perception of Black female-headed households as lacking men rather than money."[3] This misconception also extends into the legal system where the problem for lesbians is perceived as the lack of a male presence rather than the lack of income.

This book has taken much longer to complete than anyone imagined, and reflects the realities of our daily lives as parents: the interruptions, the fragmentation, the contradictory demands between the public and the private spheres of our lives. Working as parents, and with parents, has meant that the process has been punctuated by school work, births, children's illnesses, and financial crisis. It is a tribute to the persistence and courage of the contributors that *Politics Of The Heart* exists at all. After the pressures of work and children, it is something of a miracle to find/make a few hours to sit down and write. This time often comes at the sacrifice of sleep, solitude, being with a lover or friend, or simply relaxing. For many lesbian parents, the reality of our material conditions, poverty, and the lack of institutional support takes its toll. The contributions to this anthology are affirmations of our strengths and our ability to grow and create in the face of oppression. They are portraits of how we survive and pass on those lessons to our children.

In *Politics Of The Heart*, some writers use the terms *parent* and *parenting* rather than *mother* and *mothering*. The former are more inclusive and incorporate the role of persons who are not the biological mothers, such as coparents, step and adoptive parents, and others who are bringing up children. The term mother too often tends to imply only the biological mother and to reinforce potentially inaccurate distinctions. Some of the contributors to the anthology write under their own names; others, reflecting the oppression we encounter, have chosen to use a pseudonym.

Politics Of The Heart is divided into eight sections. It moves from our struggles with the outside world to our growth as individuals and a community.

Survival deals with the external pressures that weigh upon the lesbian family—primarily court and state intervention. From Jeanne Vaughn's appraisal of the lesbian community seen through the lens of personal experience, to Minnie Bruce Pratt's loss of custody of her sons, to Rosalie G. Davies and Minna F. Weinstein's recounting of the formation of CALM (Custody Action For Lesbian Mothers), contributors share their pain, loss, separations, and actions of strength and survival.

Choices addresses the social and political economy of motherhood. Nancy D. Polikoff examines the implications of the choice to parent and what this means within the context of our relationships, our community, and the larger society. Elly Bulkin and Blue Lunden depict lesbian existence during the 1950s and the lack of options lesbian mothers often faced. Irena Klepfisz shares the decision not to have children; Susan J. Wolfe, the personal contradictions decisions often entail. Rocky Gámez and others explore the creation of specifically lesbian families.

Coparenting focuses on the concerns of the "other mother." Toni Tortorilla describes that experience as life "on a creative edge which celebrates a commitment born of love rather than biological imperative." This section considers our celebrations, our tragedies; our position as nonbiological parents; the struggle to find our own definitions and meanings for family; our relationships to our children and our partners; and the creative ways in which we are meeting these challenges. How conflicts are resolved becomes an important issue as lesbians turn to the courts in the absence of alternative structures to resolve our own custody battles.

Conflict looks at the fragmentation of our lives as lesbian parents and the search for integration. This section expresses the contradiction between the roles and expectations imposed on us from the outside and our own needs and desires. Sometimes collisions arise between our creative selves and our obligations as mothers. Other times it is the juxtaposition of our politics and our families, as evidenced in Marilyn Murphy's "no-win mother dilemma" and Faith Reboin's search for a "model for new possibilities." More than one writer has likened the situation to that of a soap opera, as Martha Shelley suggests: "Tune in next week/for another thrilling episode/can two happily married lesbians/survive motherhood?"

Growing Up scrutinizes the issues of growth, separation, connection, and our hopes for our children. Many of the pieces lament the lack of models—as lesbian mothers, as women of color and interracial lesbian couples raising children in a racist and sexist sociey, as mothers of boy children, as lesbian mothers of lesbian daughters. In a powerful piece recognizing the positive aspects of lesbian parenting, Black poet Pat Parker moves from society's expectations of us—"They think/that instead of getting up/in the middle of the night/for a 2 AM and 6 AM feeding/we rise up and chant/'you're gonna be a dyke/you're gonna be a dyke' "—to the legacy of spirit and her people which she leaves her daughter—"If this is the result of perversion/let the world stand screaming./You will mute their voices/with your life."

Working It Out shows how we explore issues with our children. Some of the selections concern homophobia and the positive ways we attempt to deal with it in our homes. Others chronicle the sometimes long and difficult process of coming out and gaining acceptance—both our own and our children's. As Baylah Wolfe states, "It is likely that lesbian mothers will feel the painful effects of homophobia acted out by their children, and like night follows day, feminist mothers will feel the sexism that their sons have absorbed." Other writers deal with our children's perceptions of lesbianism, sexuality, love, and day-to-day life.

Community probes the experience of mothering in the lesbian/women's community, the development of community and family. This section investigates our differences and our similarities, the places where we meet and support each other, and where we do not. Ivette Merced recognizes that we must give birth to ourselves in forging community: "Es ahora la hora/a ser la madre/mi'ja de todas/y de nadie/pero de mí misma." ("Now is the time/to be the mother/the child of all women/and of none/but myself.") Andrea Canaan's article touches on the interactions between mothers and child-free women: "How do I survive the critical scrutiny of myself and the other women in my life, recognizing we have wide and varying capabilities, desires, inclinations, and choices concerning young people and motherhood, that come out of complex and often painful experiences?"

Into The Future is a search for directions. Sandra Pollack and Nancy D. Polikoff chart social science/courtroom/legal research strategies and their implications for feminism's development. Jan Clausen talks about the specific ways in which we must be willing to explore our differences in building a lesbian parenting community. Audre Lorde asks what it means that lesbians and gays of color are having babies, given the worldwide system of racism, and she articulates the need to provide children of color with an accurate picture of this world as a weapon for their survival and growth.

Politics Of The Heart has been five years in the making. Jeanne Vaughn worked with a number of women over that time, and our thanks go to Andrea Canaan, Wendy Culter, Celine-Marie Pascale, Yasmin Sayyed, Robin Song, Peggy Sullivan, Lenore Willard, and Rosamara Zayas for various contributions to earlier stages of the book. Sandra Pollack came on as coeditor in February of 1986 when Nancy K. Bereano of Firebrand Books expressed interest in the manuscript. Sandy and Jeanne reevaluated the old material, then solicited and edited additional writing.

Special appreciation is due for Sue Gambill, who gave up the title of her original manuscript so that we could use *Politics Of The Heart* as the name of this anthology. We wanted a title that would reflect the intricacies of the lesbian family, one that would express, as Robyn Roberts says, "How complicated...the theories and politics can be when they mix with matters of the heart."

We are grateful to the insights provided by Marcy Alancraig, Elly Bulkin, Jan Clausen, Janis Kelly, Biddy Martin, Kate Miller, Paula Ross, and Barbara Smith. Our thanks to the Lesbian Herstory Archives for help in tracking down addresses, and to Bettina Aptheker for suggesting the publisher. Jeanne would like to thank her companion Vanessa Valdez for her understanding, her encouragement, and for being the wonderful woman that she is. Sandy's special thanks go to Ba Stopha for her love and care, and to her daughters—two women she has learned much from. We would also like to thank our publisher Nancy K. Bereano for her support, hard work, and critical advice during the course of this project.

The pieces included in *Politics Of The Heart* describe numerous family configurations and various viewpoints and perspectives—at times seemingly contradictory. We intentionally avoid presenting any one view advocated as "correct" so that we can listen to many of the things lesbians are saying about their families. Referring to her children in the classic piece "Man Child: A Black Lesbian Feminist's Response," Audre Lorde tells us: "Both Beth and Jonathan need to know what they can share, and what they cannot, how they are joined, and how they are not. And we, as grown women and lesbians coming more and more into our power, need to learn that difference does not have to be threatening." We have to separate romanticism from reality, fact from myth, and to do this we must be able to hear ourselves and one another.

Sandra Pollack (Ithaca, New York)
Jeanne Vaughn (Santa Cruz, California)
July 1987

Notes

1. Zillah R. Eisenstein. *Feminism And Sexual Equality* (New York: Monthly Review Press, 1984), p. 115.

2. *Statistical Abstract of the United States* (Washington, DC, U.S. Bureau of the Census, 106th edition, 1985).

3. Barbara Omolade. *It's A Family Affair: The Real Lives Of Black Single Mothers* (Kitchen Table: Women Of Color Press, P.O. Box 908, Latham, NY 12110, 1987). She goes on to note: "Recently the Human Resources Administration in New York City began requiring women applying for welfare to provide explicit sexual information about themselves and the fathers of their children, but backed off under protest from community groups and civil libertarians."

Survival

The Rock Will Wear Away

A Question Of Survival

Jeanne Vaughn

Slightly over three years ago, I relinquished the daily obligations of parenting and embarked on a journey which has prompted me to question the very foundations of who I am, my role as a mother, my feminism, and the lesbian community.

Motherhood came at a terrible price for me—a price no woman should have to pay, and one which many women are still paying. It came at the sacrifice of a large part of myself and was also at a cost to my child. As I look back at my own experience, I have concerns for us as lesbian mothers, for our futures, for our daughters and our sons.

I was a child myself when I gave birth. I was seventeen years old, alone, and living on my own. I was also strung out on heroin. Several months before I discovered I was pregnant, my housemates busted me. I was seated in the bathroom with a needle in my arm. I had forgotten to lock the door.

Although well-meaning friends sent me to San Francisco to clean up, I returned two months later completely intending to start shooting dope again. Somewhere along the line, someone commented that I should get a pregnancy test, as I was gaining weight and it was all in one place. The possibility of pregnancy had never occurred to me; due to the heroin, I hadn't been having regular periods anyhow. A few days later I went down to the Free Clinic in Mission Beach for the verdict.

"I'm sorry to have to tell you this," said the woman with the Good Intentions, "but the test was positive." This is how I was introduced to the idea of motherhood.

In 1970, therapeutic abortions were still illegal. I did not know anyone who had had one. I had neither money nor resources, and the thought simply never entered my head.

The father was someone I barely knew, someone I had been sleeping with for a few months. He was a substitute for my first boyfriend, the one who introduced me to heroin. The first one told me he would never play second fiddle to a drug; that if I got strung out he'd leave me. I did, and he left.

"Is it mine?" this second one asked, and we made plans to set up housekeeping. Two months later, he was picked up for armed robbery, assault with a deadly weapon, and probably a host of other things as well. We wrote a few letters, I went to visit him once or twice, and I kept in touch with his mother. When it came time to sign the forms so that I could receive welfare payments, he refused. I cried. It was my only hope of escape from an intolerable family situation. In those days, a woman couldn't just be pregnant; she had to name the father in order to be eligible for state funds. In the end he recanted. I have rarely felt such hatred for anyone.

Midway through my pregnancy, I was walking down the street clutching those precious welfare forms when I was stopped by a police officer who wanted to know why I wasn't in school. I had graduated early the year before from a continuation school, and I tried to explain the situation. Nevertheless, he took me to Juvenile Hall after talking to the eligibility worker whom I had just, moments ago, spoken with. She assured me there would be no problem. To him, she said, "It might speed things up a little to take her in."

The humiliation of being handcuffed and put in the back of the police car was beyond comprehension, and it echoed the lack of dignity and power which I felt so acutely in my life. It was a premonition of my experience in the juvenile courts, the hospital birth, and the years I was to spend in the welfare system. Those handcuffs closed around my wrists as tightly as the facts of my childhood, the incest, the alcoholism in my family. As tightly as the "maternity ties" and the metal stirrups, as the State of California, the eligibility workers, the income reports, the diapers, the bills, and the endless round of minimum wage jobs. They were a symbol of my hopelessness, of pain and determination, of persistence and struggle in the face of impossibility. And, of ultimate powerlessness. Pregnant teenagers didn't have a chance.

A few weeks later, I hitchhiked back up to San Francisco to the home of the woman with whom I was currently infatuated. I sat around depressed, day after endless day, eating saltine crackers and reading Zap Comics. I felt like a burden on the people I was staying with, like some sort of mindless growth planted in front of a window on Dolores Street, whose sole purpose in life was watching the thin, grey San Francisco rain. The rain in that alien place fell on streets of grey concrete broken only by dog shit, oil stains, and an occasional blade of grass pushing up between the cracks in the pavement, unable to find its way home into the welcoming soil under the asphalt. I felt related to that rain, kin to the water; we were both prisoners in a sad, lonely world which neither of us had created.

It took me a long time to actively begin creating my own world, to start picking up the pieces, to learn to speak from the authority of my own survival. Much of that ability began with the absence of my child. The freedom to no longer be the sole person responsible for another human being's needs gave me the room to examine my own life in a way never before possible. It gave me a quality of time which I believe is available to very few mothers.

As a young mother, I lived for years shut off from the pain of my past, a woman in an hermetically sealed limbo from which there appeared no hope of escape. Ironically, without a past one can have no real future. Without examining my experience in detail, there was no freedom from it. Without the space, the time to myself, the ability to get up in the morning and answer only to my own needs, I seriously doubt that I would have had the emotional, physical, financial, or psychic energy to confront my life head on. I doubt if I would have been able to take myself seriously enough to push beyond mere survival into a full and meaningful existence, to examine the scars from my childhood that prevented me not only from being the adult woman I wanted to be, but the mother my child needed. My child's absence enabled me to move past my own working-class expectations and eventually into graduate school, to find the time for self-reflection, and the intellectual stamina to make the connections between my private life and the political/economic system we live in.

The decision to send my son to live with his grandmother was one of the most painful ones I ever made, and also one of the best. I love my son, and I love myself. His leaving was my gift to both of us. I literally found myself at a point where I had nothing more to give either of us. The situation reached a crisis after my father died, and I started to explore in therapy the meaning of the alcoholism in my family. Slowly, images of incest and molestation emerged—my father, a neighbor, a cousin. Although I was gaining a new understanding of my own inner workings and motivations, the hold I had was tenuous; the more time I took for myself, the more my son rebelled. A few months later, he boarded the airplane to his grandmother's.

Although my personal situation may appear extreme to some, it is one which is not foreign to many mothers. It is a reality which is distinguished by a brutal lack of choices.

This issue of choice is one which continues to plague me. We need a word which describes a decision made in a seemingly conscious manner which looks like a choice but isn't, like the choice to be heterosexual, or the choice to have children. "Compulsory Heterosexuality and Lesbian Existence" by Adrienne Rich[1] is still one of the most brilliantly articulated pieces dealing with partriarchal cultural assumptions and the illusion of choice. We must begin to look at motherhood in the same light. Especially now. Especially as lesbians.

I see around me what appears to be a romanticization of motherhood operating in the lesbian/women's community. During the '70s, I witnessed a similar (and from my working-class perspective, offensive) romanticization of poverty. For a brief while, downward mobility was "in," and it was chic to be working-class, or at least to look that way. There was a time a few years ago when it was fashionable to be Third World, to be "ethnic." Right now it is "in" to be Native American. Literally hundreds of Southwestern restaurants have opened in Manhattan, the work of artists like Gorman and Peña are prominent in frame shops and galleries around the country, and Sunday supplements and travel magazines discuss how to best plan your travel experience in the "Land of Enchantment." All of this is happening at exactly the same moment in history that Congress votes unanimously in favor of relocation at Big Mountain.

There is a warning in this.

Lesbians are having babies. We are having babies at a time when statistics show that the Great Middle Class is slipping, making less money, postponing its births. There is a move to force women back into the home: family protection bills have been introduced, the Right-to-Life is in full force, and single mothers and women over forty are the largest and fastest growing pool of urban poor.

The hard-won gains made over the past twenty years are being challenged and eroded, as evidenced in the attempts to dismantle welfare, affirmative action, and other social programs. Female poverty, racism, and homophobia are on the rise. The New Right sees the welfare state and women's equality in the market as a threat to male authority and the traditional patriarchal family; the National Organization for Women, Planned Parenthood, Gay Rights National Lobby, National Abortion Rights Action League, and Women Strike for Peace have been identified as the leading single-issue political groups responsible for the liberal takeover of the family.[2] In the neoconservative analysis, social programs and sexual equality are seen as an excess of democracy. "Equality of opportunity. . . is all that the individual should expect. To demand that as individuals we have the right not to marry, or not to bear children, or to be lesbian or homosexual is an excess of equality and sexual freedom. For the neoconservative sexual equality and sexual freedom pose the dilemma of liberalism because once sexual equality is promised and is interpreted to mean *a real equality of conditions*, heterosexuality, marriage, and family life along with the legitimacy of the state are challenged."[3]

In spite of the media hype, things aren't getting better for women. We live in an age where armchair activists believe they are being political and can save the hungry or stop apartheid by buying a record or a video. The media message is clear: "We've made it," "You've come a long way baby." In contrast, material reality for the majority of women is quite different. Nationally, a woman (lesbian) on her own is twice as likely to live in poverty as a man, and children are six times more likely to be living in poverty with their mothers than their fathers. Statistics for women of color are even more frightening. There are an estimated eleven thousand homeless children and their mothers living in welfare hotels in New York City, in addition to those living on the streets. The mortality rate for infants in these hotels is more than double the national average.[4]

Motherhood continues to be marketed as a personalized experience. We're led to believe that in raising *our* children, "this time it's going to be different," that through *our* children, "we can make a difference in the world." What we are not told is that motherhood is the great leveler. Although the institution of motherhood manifests itself differently—like all other institutions, depending on what social class, race, or ethnic group you happen to belong to—in one way the core experience is still pretty much the same. Presented with what we are taught is the opportunity of a lifetime to express our individuality, we become faceless mommies who spend our days doing things that nobody else wants to hear about.

My argument is not that we shouldn't be having children. My fear is that we are overlooking something, that there are issues we should be seriously addressing. I know from my own experience that the unexamined is frequently repeated—what is not worked through often comes back to haunt us.

As a young mother, my world was shaped and defined by my past. I had no models outside of the alcoholic family I was raised in, no experience in coping other than through my own drug abuse. I passed a mode of behavior on to my son, the basic tenets of the alcoholic family: don't talk, don't trust, don't feel. I passed on a way of being in the world that perpetuates its own illness.

Similarly, I am concerned about what we, as lesbian mothers, unconsciously pass on to our children. All of us have grown up as the unwilling participants in a system that has negated our very existence. Unless we shake ourselves free of dominant cultural values and assumptions about The Family, we are almost bound to recreate something which not only doesn't work, but which oppresses us.

What does it mean to choose to have or not have children? A set of consequences beyond our own creation or control comes with each decision. How much is truly choice, and how much is a kind of cultural romanticism that serves as a substitute for real power?

The decision to become a mother (provided there is a choice in the first place) is one which affects all areas of our lives and the lives of those around us. Unfortunately in this society, motherhood severely limits the options for most of us, especially the poor, the Third World, the working-class, the young. Mothers become responsible for the lifelong needs of another human being(s). If we are lucky, another person or persons come along to pick up (some of) the slack, but the responsibility still falls heavily on one person. Motherhood under these terms is an impossible job and one that is doomed to failure. The private property outlook toward children keeps mothers tied into *our* children, *our* families, *our* homes. It divides us—our resources and our attention. This conception of the family prevents us from looking too far beyond the front porch, from learning how to ask for help (assuming there is help available if we do ask), or how to even recognize it when it's sitting on our doorstep. It keeps us inside our individual homes with our individual children, TVs, telephones, bills, diapers, cars, and family problems. It doesn't allow us to envision other possibilities.

We live in a nation that posits nuclear and small family units as the ideal. Yet, as Rayna Rapp points out, there are many different kinds of family experiences. "Many of us have been to the archetypical meeting in which someone stands up and asserts that the nuclear family ought to be abolished because it is degrading and constraining to women. Usually, someone else (often representing a Third World position) follows on her heels, pointing out that the attack on the family represents a white middle-class position and that other women need their families for support and survival. Evidently both speakers are, in some senses, right. And just as evidently they aren't talking about the same families. We need to explore those different notions of family if we are to heal an important split in our movement. To do so, we must take seriously the things women say about their experiences in their families, especially as they vary by class."[5]

The ideal American family configuration—mother, father, and children—that is accepted without question by most as natural and normal simply does not exist in other cultures outside our own.[6] "It is now clear that our form of raising children is historically specific, a product of advanced capitalist society, which idealizes mother*hood* while isolating and marginalizing mother*ing*, in a classic demonstration of the mystifying function of ideology."[7]

I bought that ideology, unconsciously, for many years. Even as an out political lesbian, deep down inside I felt guilty for having needs, guilty for being angry at a community in which I felt unsupported, a community from which I wanted/expected more. I was entrenched in the predominant child-as-private-property view of the world. What right did I have to ask for/expect help—after all, he was *my* child. I was implicitly encouraged to take this view by the same community I wanted to turn to for help. It has taken me a long time, and the absence of my son, to (painfully) reverse these ideas.

Although I have chosen to be childfree and do not want to be involved in the daily world of children, I realize I still must actively challenge the marginalization and oppression of women with children, to raise the concerns of parents, and to insure that child care and other supports are available. I must not lose sight of the needs of other lesbians whose lives are different from mine, for we all have a responsibility to mothers and to children.

The politicization of motherhood in a specifically lesbian context has vast implications. It is not enough just to *be* lesbian mothers. We must begin to ask the really hard questions, to examine our cultural assumptions, beginning with our assumptions about The Family.

As lesbian mothers our position in society is tenuous at best. We are not legally sanctioned in our partnerships. In many states our relationships are illegal, and it is not against the law to discriminate against us on the basis of our sexual orientation.[8] I worry when we start looking too "normal," when we think that we have, or can attain, some kind of social respectability. Our position in society is not going to change until the entire social order changes.

"Women have been so historically exploited and their oppression so institutionalized that for us to have power necessitates a culture radically different than the one in existence. Our exploitation is an integral part of social, economic, political, emotional, intellectual and religious life, beginning on the level of the family—with compulsory heterosexuality and male privilege in the home resulting in the division of labor and authority that is the model of male-female relationships in the rest of society."[9]

In other words, revolution begins at home.

We have an opportunity for radical social change beginning in our homes, change that requires rethinking our views of family, of kinship, of work, of social organization. We need to develop some specifically lesbian-feminist theories of family. How would/did/could we mother our children without the institution of compulsory heterosexuality? Where can we look for other examples? For most white middle-class women who have never seen anything else than the nuclear family, this may be a particularly difficult challenge. For others who have lived in extended and other family configurations, it is a little easier to imagine. And imagine we must.

The lack of a cohesive theory of lesbian mothering often shows itself in the way the lesbian/women's community deals with (or doesn't deal with) children. It is reflected in the absence of feminist child care (or child care at all) and in the neglect of child-care issues in general. It is reflected in our inability to meaningfully engage our sons as well as our daughters, in our indifference or intolerance of young people and their needs.

Where is the political analysis of The Family in the context of compulsory heterosexuality? How do lesbians, especially lesbian mothers, fit into this analysis? How are things going to be different for the new generation of lesbians with children than it was for those of us with teen-agers and grown children? Lesbian mothers still continue to be isolated in their homes with their children, still responsible for needs which they can't possibly fill, still open to blame and derision for the way their children turn out. We live, for the most part, as though we existed in a vacuum. As though intending to raise our children (especially our sons) to be feminist and nonviolent could be enough. As though the all-pervasive culture leaves our homes, our hearts, our psyches untouched.

There is an unarticulated assumption that somehow things are going to be different for lesbians now choosing to have children, that our having children as lesbians is enough to change things. In the long run, it makes no real difference if we are lesbians or straight women raising our children if we unconsciously pass on the same unexamined beliefs. "We romanticize at our peril what it means to love and act against the grain, and under heavy penalties; lesbian existence has been lived (unlike, say, Jewish or Catholic existence) without access to any knowledge of a tradition, a continuity, a social underpinning."[10]

The lack of the kind of continuity Rich talks about takes its toll on us. We have no specifically lesbian traditions, no lesbian customs to guide us in our daily lives. We have no time-honored way of formalizing our unions, our separations, our births, our deaths, our comings and goings, no social services geared to our needs.

This reality has an impact on our families, and one of the most painful ways this operates is in our break-ups. We have no language yet to be able to talk about what happens when children are involved as relationships end, children who are frequently abandoned on a variety of levels. What responsibility does the birth mother have to the comother, the comother to the children? How can visitation and time-sharing be handled? What do our break-ups say to our children about the value of our relationships, of the "other" mother, of who and how we see ourselves to be? So often there is only a painful silence, a gap left unbridged. Frequently, nonbiological mothers are not encouraged to continue the bonds they have established, especially after the birth mother has become involved in another relationship. At what point does one move from being someone's lover to being the comother of her children? How is this decided? What formalizes it? How is it talked about? How are the day-to-day arrangements, the division of labor, arrived at? How many mothers can a child have? Is comother number one still a mother after the break-up when comother number two or three moves in? How do we decide these issues? What guides and motivates the choices? The answers tend to seem so individual, so personal, to be worked out and decided upon in each lesbian family, in each particular situation. We need to be discussing these issues on a larger scale, looking closely at our beliefs to see how they reflect the heterosexual norms.

In every society, the economy (political, sexual, emotional, or material) institutionalizes and sustains the value system of the society it is founded on.[11] Each makes certain assumptions about human nature, and those assumptions, in turn, affect all of our choices: where we live, what we eat, our health, education, work, how we view ourselves, our families, our friends.

As lesbians, it is essential that we look at our beliefs about our families and our relationships in light of the social and material conditions of the value system(s) within which we live. We must take our ideas, beliefs, and assumptions to their logical conclusions. Perhaps we will find that many of our attitudes and actions regarding the family echo and reflect a belief system we say we want no part of.

Without some real dialogue, some clear thinking and sharp analysis, without a willingness to move beyond our differences, I fear we may be repeating a cycle I have seen and experienced so painfully in my own life as a mother—the unquestioning replaying of what went before. "We probably have no cause to fear (or hope) that The Family will dissolve. What we can begin to ask is what we want our families to do. Then, distinguishing our hopes from what we have, we can begin to analyze the social forces that enhance or undermine the realization of the kinds of human bonds we need."[12]

Here is where we must start. Having children is a political act because it occurs in a political context where the idea of choice is nonexistent for many of us. As Audre Lorde writes, "But giving in to the fear of feeling and working to capacity is a luxury only the unintentional can afford, and the unintentional are those who do not wish to guide their own destinies."[13] It is imperative that we guide our own destinies and the destinies of our children. It is a question of survival.

Notes

1. Adrienne Rich, "Compulsory Heterosexuality And Lesbian Existence," *Signs: A Journal Of Woman In Culture And Society* 5.4 (1980), pp. 631-60.

2. Zillah Eisenstein, *Feminism And Sexual Equality* (New York: Monthly Review Press, 1984), p. 43.

3. Eisenstein, p. 80. (emphasis added)

4. *The Guardian*, February 4, 1987, p. 10.

5. Rayna Rapp, "Family and Class in Contemporary America: Notes Toward an Understanding of Theology," *Science And Society* 42 (1978), pp. 278-300.

6. According to Collier, Rosaldo, and Yanagisako, "An outside observer, for example, may be able to delimit family boundaries in any and all societies by identifying the children of one woman and that woman's associated mate, but natives (of that culture) may not be interested in making such distinctions.... Many languages...have no word to identify the unit of parents and children that English speakers call a 'family.'" In "Is There a Family: New Anthropological Views," *Rethinking The Family*, ed. Barrie Thorne (New York: Longman, 1982), pp. 25-39.

7. Renate Bridenthal, "The Family: The View From a Room of Her Own" in Thorne, p. 232.

8. Several rather pronounced recent examples of this can be found in *Lesbian Connection*, Jan./Feb. 1986.

9. Lisa Leghorn and Katherine Parker, *Woman's Worth: Sexual Economics And The World Of Women* (Boston: Routledge & Kegan Paul, 1981), pp. 19-20.

10. Rich, p. 649.

11. Leghorn and Parker, pp. 10-11.

12. Collier, Rosaldo, and Yanagisako, p. 38.

13. Audre Lorde, "Uses of the Erotic: The Erotic as Power," *Sister Outsider* (New York: Crossing Press, 1984), p. 54.

The Child Taken From The Mother

Minnie Bruce Pratt

I could do nothing: nothing. Do you
understand? Women ask: *Why didn't you—?*
like they do of women who've been raped.
And I ask myself: Why didn't I? Why
didn't I run away with them? Or face
him in court? Or—

                    ten years ago I
answered myself: No way for children to live.
Or: The chance of absolute loss. Or:

I did the best I could. It was not
enough. It was about terror and power.
I did everything I could: not enough.

This is not the voice of the guilty mother.

Clumsy with anger even now, it is a voice
from the woman shoved outside, one night, as words
clack into place like bricks, poker chips.

Like the lawyer: *It's a card game. You were too
candid. They know what's in your hand.*
I look down. My hands dangle open and empty
in the harsh yellow light. Strange men,
familiar, laugh and curse in the kitchen, whiskey,
bending over cards. Or is it something held down
on the table? Someone says: *Bull Dog Bend.*
Someone says: *The place of the father in the home.*

My mother's voice: *Those women have never held
a little baby in their arms.* In the old window,
a shadow. Two hands, brick and mortar, seal
the house, my children somewhere inside. The youngest
has lost his baby fat, navel flattened, last
of my stomach's nourishing.

You say: *Do something.*
You say: *Why is this happening?*

My body. My womb.
My body of a woman, a mother, a lesbian.
And here,
perhaps, you say: *That last word doesn't belong.*

Woman, mother: those can stay. Lesbian: no.
Put that outside the place of the poem. Too
slangy, prosy, obvious, just doesn't belong.
*Why don't you: Why didn't you: Can't you
say it some other way?*

The beautiful place
we stand arguing, after the movie, under blue-white
fluorescence: two middle-aged women in jeans,
two grown boys, the lanky one, the tactful one,
bundled in a pause before cold outside, to argue
the significances: bloody birth, the man cursing
a woman in the kitchen, dirt, prayer, the place
of the father, the master, the beatings, black and
white, home lost, continents, two women
lovers glimpsed, the child taken from the mother
who returns.

No one says: *This is about us.* But
in the narrow corridor, stark cement block walls,
we become huge, holding up the harsh images,
the four of us loud, familiar.

Other movie-
goers sqeeze past, light their cigarettes,
glance, do not say even to themselves: *Children
and women, lovers, mothers, lesbians. Yes.*

A Long Story
Beth Brant

Dedicated to my Great-Grandmothers
Eliza Powless and Catherine Brant

"About 40 Indian children took the train at this depot for the Philadel-phia Indian School last Friday. They were accompanied by the govern-ment agent, and seemed a bright looking lot."

The Northern Observer
(Massena, New York, July 20, 1892)

"I am only beginning to understand what it means for a mother to lose a child."

Anna Demeter, *Legal Kidnapping*
(Beacon Press, Boston, 1977)

1890

It has been two days since they came and took the children away. My body is greatly chilled. All our blankets have been used to bring me warmth. The women keep the fire blazing. The men sit. They talk among themselves. We are frightened by this sudden child-stealing. We signed papers, the agent said. This gave them rights to take our babies. It is good for them, the agent said. It will make them civilized, the agent said. I do not know *civilized*.

I hold myself tight in fear of flying apart in the air. The others try to feed me. Can they feed a dead woman? I have stopped talking. When my mouth opens, only air escapes. I have used up my sound screaming their names— She Sees Deer! He Catches The Leaves! My eyes stare at the room, the walls of scrubbed wood, the floor of dirt. I know there are people here, but I cannot see them. I see a darkness, like the lake at New Moon. Black, unmoving. In the center, a picture of my son and daughter being lifted onto the train. My daughter wearing the dark blue, heavy dress. All of the girls dressed alike. Never have I seen such eyes! They burn into my head even now. My son. His hair cut. Dressed as the white men, his arms and legs covered by cloth that made him sweat. His face, streaked with tears. So many children crying, screaming. The sun on our bodies, our heads. The train screeching like a crow, sounding like laughter. Smoke and dirt pumping out the insides of the train. So many people. So many children. The women, standing as if in prayer, our hands lifted, reaching. The dust sifting down on our palms. Our palms making motions at the sky. Our fingers closing like the claws of the bear.

I see this now. The hair of my son held in my hands. I rub the strands, the heavy braids coming alive as the fire flares and casts a bright light on the black hair. They slip from my fingers and lie coiled on the ground. I see this. My husband picks up the braids, wraps them in cloth; he takes the pieces of our son away. He walks outside, the eyes of the people on him. I see this. He will find a bottle and drink with the men. Some of the women will join him. They will end the night by singing or crying. It is all the same. I see this. No sounds of children playing games and laughing. Even the dogs have ceased their noise. They lay outside each doorway, waiting. I hear this. The voices of children. They cry. They pray. They call me. *Nisten ha.* I hear this. *Nisten ha.**

1978

I am wakened by the dream. In the dream my daughter is dead. Her father is returning her body to me in pieces. He keeps her heart. I thought I screamed...*Patricia!* I sit up in bed, swallowing air as if for nourishment. The dream remains in the air. I rise to go to her room. Ellen tries to lead me back to bed, but I have to see once again. I open her door. She is gone. The room empty, lonely. They said it was in her best interests. How can that be? She is only six, a baby who needs her mothers. She loves us. This has not happened. I will not believe this. Oh god, I think I have died.

Night after night, Ellen holds me as I shake. Our sobs stifling the air in our room. We lie in our bed and try to give comfort. My mind can't think beyond last week when she left. I would have killed him if I'd had the chance! He took her hand and pulled her to the car. The look in his eyes of triumph. It was a contest to him, Patricia the prize. He will teach her to hate us. He will! I see her dear face. That face looking out the back window of his car. Her mouth forming the words *Mommy, Mama.* Her dark braids tied with red yarn. Her front teeth missing. Her overalls with the yellow flower on the pocket, embroidered by Ellen's hands. So lovingly she sewed the yellow wool. Patricia waiting quietly until she was finished. Ellen promising to teach her designs—chain stitch, french knot, split stitch. How Patricia told everyone that Ellen made the flower just for her. So proud of her overalls.

I open the closet door. Almost everything is gone. A few things hang there limp, abandoned. I pull a blue dress from the hanger and take it back to

---

*mother

my room. Ellen tries to take it from me, but I hold on, the soft blue cotton smelling of my daughter. How is it possible to feel such pain and live? "Ellen?!" She croons my name. "Mary, Mary, I love you." She sings me to sleep.

1890

The agent was here to deliver a letter. I screamed at him and sent curses his way. I threw dirt in his face as he mounted his horse. He thinks I'm a crazy woman and warns me, "You better settle down Annie." What can they do to me? I am a crazy woman. This letter hurts my hand. It is written in their hateful language. It is evil, but there is a message for me.

I start the walk up the road to my brother. He works for the whites and understands their meanings. I think about my brother as I pull the shawl closer to my body. It is cold now. Soon there will be snow. The corn has been dried and hangs from our cabin, waiting to be used. The corn never changes. My brother is changed. He says that *I* have changed and bring shame to our clan. He says I should accept the fate. But I do not believe in the fate of child-stealing. There is evil here. There is much wrong in our village. My brother says I am a crazy woman because I howl at the sky every evening. He is a fool. I am calling the children. He says the people are becoming afraid of me because I talk to the air and laugh like the raven overhead. But I am talking to the children. They need to hear the sound of me. I laugh to cheer them. They cry for us.

This letter burns my hands. I hurry to my brother. He has taken the sign of the wolf from over the doorway. He pretends to be like those who hate us. He gets more and more like the child-stealers. His eyes move away from mine. He takes the letter from me and begins the reading of it. I am confused. This letter is from two strangers with the names Martha and Daniel. They say they are learning civilized ways. Daniel works in the fields, growing food for the school. Martha cooks and is being taught to sew aprons. She will be going to live with the schoolmaster's wife. She will be a live-in girl. What is a *live-in girl?* I shake my head. The words sound the same to me. I am afraid of Martha and Daniel, these strangers who know my name. My hands and arms are becoming numb.

I tear the letter from my brother's fingers. He stares at me, his eyes traitors in his face. He calls after me, "Annie! Annie!" That is not my name! I run to the road. That is not my name! There is no Martha! There is no Daniel! This is witch work. The paper burns and burns. At my cabin, I quickly dig a hole in the field. The earth is hard and cold, but I dig with my nails. I dig, my hands feeling weaker. I tear the paper and bury the scraps.

As the earth drifts and settles, the names Martha and Daniel are covered. I look to the sky and find nothing but endless blue. My eyes are blinded by the color. I begin the howling.

1978

When I get home from work, there is a letter from Patricia. I make coffee and wait for Ellen, pacing the rooms of our apartment. My back is sore from the line, bending over and down, screwing the handles on the doors of the flashy cars moving by. My work protects me from questions, the guys making jokes at my expense. But some of them touch my shoulder lightly and briefly as a sign of understanding. The few women, eyes averted or smiling in sympathy. No one talks. There is no time to talk. No room to talk, the noise taking up all space and breath.

I carry the letter with me as I move from room to room. Finally I sit at the kitchen table, turning the paper around in my hands. Patricia's printing is large and uneven. The stamp has been glued on halfheartedly and is coming loose. Each time a letter arrives, I dread it, even as I long to hear from my child. I hear Ellen's key in the door. She walks into the kitchen, bringing the smell of the hospital with her. She comes toward me, her face set in new lines, her uniform crumpled and stained, her brown hair pulled back in an imitation of a french twist. She knows there is a letter. I kiss her and bring mugs of coffee to the table. We look at each other. She reaches for my hand, bringing it to her lips. Her hazel eyes are steady in her round face.

I open the letter. *Dear Mommy. I am fine. Daddy got me a new bike. My big teeth are coming in. We are going to see Grandma for my birthday. Daddy got me new shoes. Love, Patricia.* She doesn't ask about Ellen. I imagine her father standing over her, coaxing her, coaching her. The letter becomes ugly. I tear it in bits and scatter them out the window. The wind scoops the pieces into a tight fist before strewing them in the street. A car drives over the paper, shredding it to garbage and mud.

Ellen makes a garbled sound. "I'll leave. If it will make it better, I'll leave." I quickly hold her as the dusk moves into the room and covers us. "Don't leave. Don't leave." I feel her sturdy back shiver against my hands. She kisses my throat, and her arms tighten as we move closer. "Ah Mary, I love you so much." As the tears threaten our eyes, the taste of salt is on our lips and tongues. We stare into ourselves, touching the place of pain, reaching past the fear, the guilt, the anger, the loneliness.

We go to our room. It is beautiful again. I am seeing it new. The sun is barely there. The colors of cream, brown, green mixing with the wood floor. The rug with its design of wild birds. The black ash basket glowing on the dresser, holding a bouquet of dried flowers bought at a vendor's stand. I remember the old woman, laughing and speaking rapidly in Polish as she wrapped the blossoms in newspaper. Ellen undresses me as I cry. My desire for her breaking through the heartbreak we share. She pulls the covers back, smoothing the white sheets, her hands repeating the gestures done at work. She guides me onto the cool material. I watch her remove the uniform of work. An aide to nurses. A healer of spirit.

She comes to me full in flesh. My hands are taken with the curves and soft roundness of her. She covers me with the beating of her heart. The rhythm steadies me. Her heat is centering me. I am grounded by the peace between us. I smile at her face above me, round like a moon, her long hair loose and touching my breasts. I take her breast in my hand, bring it to my mouth, suck her as a woman—in desire, in faith. Our bodies join. Our hair braids together on the pillow. Brown, black, silver, catching the last light of the sun. We kiss, touch, move to our place of power. Her mouth, moving over my body, stopping at curves and swells of skin, kissing, removing pain. Closer, close, together, woven, my legs are heat, the center of my soul is speaking to her, I am sliding into her, her mouth is medicine, her heart is the earth, we are dancing with flying arms, I shout, I sing, I weep salty liquid, sweet and warm it coats her throat. This is my life. I love you Ellen, I love you Mary, I love, we love.

1891

The moon is full. The air is cold. This cold strikes at my flesh as I re-move my clothes and set them on fire in the withered corn field. I cut my hair, the knife sawing through the heavy mass. I bring the sharp blade to my arms, legs, and breasts. The blood trickles like small red rivers down my body. I feel nothing. I throw the tangled webs of my hair into the flames. The smell, like a burning animal, fills my nostrils. As the fire stretches to touch the stars, the people come out to watch me—the crazy woman. The ice in the air touches me.

They caught me as I tried to board the train and search for my babies. The white men tell my husband to watch me. I am dangerous. I laugh and laugh. My husband is good only for tipping bottles and swallowing anger. He looks at me, opening his mouth and making no sound. His eyes are dead. He wanders from the cabin and looks out on the corn. He whispers our names. He calls after the children. He is a dead man.

Where have they taken the children? I ask the question of each one who travels the road past our door. The women come and we talk. We ask and ask. They say there is nothing we can do. The white man is like a ghost.

He slips in and out where we cannot see. Even in our dreams he comes to take away our questions. He works magic that resists our medicine. This magic has made us weak. What is the secret about them? Why do they want our children? They sent the Blackrobes many years ago to teach us new magic. It was evil! They lied and tricked us. They spoke of gods who would forgive us if we believed as they do. They brought the rum with the cross. This god is ugly! He killed our masks. He killed our men. He sends the women screaming at the moon in terror. They want our power. They take our children to remove the inside of them. Our power. They steal our food, our sacred rattle, the stories, our names. What is left?

I am a crazy woman. I look to the fire that consumes my hair and see their faces. My daughter. My son. They still cry for me, though the sound grows fainter. The wind picks up their keening and brings it to me. The sound has bored into my brain. I begin howling. At night I dare not sleep. I fear the dreams. It is too terrible, the things that happen there. In my dream there is wind and blood moving as a stream. Red, dark blood in my dream. Rushing for our village. The blood moves faster. There are screams of wounded people. Animals are dead, thrown in the blood stream. There is nothing left. Only the air echoing nothing. Only the earth soaking up blood, spreading it in the four directions, becoming a thing there is no name for. I stand in the field watching the fire, The People watching me. We are waiting, but the answer is not clear yet. A crazy woman. That is what they call me.

1979

After taking a morning off work to see my lawyer, I come home, not caring if I call in. Not caring, for once, at the loss in pay. Not caring. My lawyer says there is nothing more we can do. I must wait. As if there has been something other than waiting. He has custody and calls the shots. We must wait and see how long it takes for him to get tired of being a mommy and a daddy. So, I wait.

I open the door to Patricia's room. Ellen and I keep it dusted and cleaned in case my baby will be allowed to visit us. The yellow and blue walls feel like a mockery. I walk to the windows, begin to systematically tear down the curtains. I slowly start to rip the cloth apart. I enjoy hearing the sounds of destruction. Faster, I tear the material into strips. What won't come apart with my hands, I pull at with my teeth. Looking for more to destroy, I gather the sheets and bedspread in my arms and wildly shred them to pieces. Grunting and sweating, I am pushed by rage and the searing wound in my soul. Like a wolf, caught in a trap, gnawing at her own leg to set herself free, I begin to beat my breasts to deaden the pain inside. A noise gathers in my throat and finds the way out. I begin a scream that turns to howling, then becomes hoarse choking. I want to take my fists, my strong fists, my brown fists, and smash the world until it bleeds. Bleeds! And all the judges in their flapping robes, and the fathers who look for revenge, are ground, ground into dust and disappear with the wind. The word *lesbian*. Lesbian. The word that makes them panic, makes them afraid, makes them destroy children. The word that dares them. Lesbian. *I am one.* Even for Patricia, even for her, *I will not cease to be!* As I kneel amidst the colorful scraps, Raggedy Anns smiling up at me, my chest gives a sigh. My heart slows to its normal speech. I feel the blood pumping outward to my veins, carrying nourishment and life. I strip the room naked. I close the door.

No Apology Offered

Sue Overstreet

Watching the children in our community, I am struck by how important they are to us individually and collectively—what enthusiasm and wisdom they offer all of us. I can't forget the fights so many of us have fought to have them with us, and the cost to those who struggled.

As I watch my own daughters, it is difficult to imagine them not living with me; yet, there was a time when they didn't. Telling the story of that time in our lives uncovers my rage and fear, the pain and the strengths that dominated then, that are still just beneath the surface. It was a time of struggle and challenge, and a time upon which I reflect when I need to remember just how strong I am and can be.

For fifteen months after separation from my former husband, my two young daughters (then two and six years old) lived with him. During that period, he and I negotiated, fought, and threatened one another, while two young children were left stranded in the hostility. It wasn't my lesbianism that kept me from my children, he claimed, but rather my politics—my strident inflexibility. It was because of my lesbianism that *I* was certain no court battle would return my children to me. So on August 2, 1982, I stood before the Superior Court Judge and relinquished custodial rights of my children to my husband. The "generous" visitation rights were not a comfort; the knowledge that a prolonged court battle would have ended similarly, if not worse, was not a comfort. I felt I had succumbed to the almighty male power again and lost myself.

It was in a busy court corridor that I signed the settlement agreement. Footsteps rang impersonally on the cold floor, and unknown faces passed in a blur, as a single signature denied my right to care for my children. I left alone, went home alone, and sat alone all night, unable to fathom the finality of what had occurred. A shaky signature ended my primary caretaking role and stamped it indelibly in the courts as my former husband's domain.

Eleven days later, on Friday, August 13, I was in the same corridor, in front of the same judge, with much the same feeling: this can't be real. Three days before, I had learned of my former husband's sexual abuse of my oldest daughter. I had returned to court for an emergency hearing to remove the children from his home.

But there is more to the story. Immediately after learning of the sexual abuse charges, I arranged the escape of my daughters through a ploy to have them spend the night with their aunt. When we went to the police head-quarters for the mandatory investigation, I was told by the investigating officer after a three-minute interview with my daughter, that she was greatly disturbed and needed a psychiatrist because he was certain no abuse had taken place. He then gave a sucker to a child who had been forced to fellate her father.

He felt it necessary to interview me and question me at length about my personal life, which I deftly danced around, not yet knowing that my husband had told him both that I am a lesbian and that I was on my way to a music festival where, he said, we throw penises into a bonfire. The officer took my crying children from me and returned them to their father, threatening to lock me up if I did not immediately stop my "hysterical" rantings. Having been clued by that time that the issue was my lesbianism, the anger swelled from previously unrecognized depths and, to this day, I can recall the power I felt as I yelled with passion and pride in police headquarters, *I am a lesbian, I am a mother,* and no male system would keep me from my daughters. I threatened, screamed, cried, and raged, at that moment feeling the pain and fury of all women. Undoubtedly the most empowering moment of my life, I refused their intimidation and platitudes. I refused to behave.

It was with that strength, and the strength of the women who came to support me, that I testified for hours about my personal life, not flinching as I "admitted" my sexual proclivity that seemed to everyone else somehow relevant to my parenting. It was a circus from which I sat back and watched with amazement and disgust. My husband, knowing the judge would temporarily remove the children from his home, argued in favor of foster placement for them rather than placement with me. The male judge, surprisingly, asked me questions relevant to the children's welfare about the home I shared with my lover, while the attorney asked me incredibly insensitive questions about my personal practices and relationships. At the end of the circus, I had temporary custody of my children and had been court-ordered to joint counseling with my former husband to resolve the custody issue.

After four months of counseling, my former husband capitulated to the strength he was amazed to see in me—strength and power I had never known before and which he had certainly never seen. During those months I was the relentless warrior I had always wanted to be, collapsing under the weight only in the safe dark of the night, alone. Now, when I am described as an angry woman, I remember how empowering that anger is, and how critical it was in the protection of my daughters and in my own growth.

I am still often told that I am a furious, intense woman. I wonder how any woman cannot be. Yes, I am angry, and I am angry with a passion, and I don't apologize for it anymore.

And When I Die

Auguste Elliott

I, Elizabeth Holland Simmons, also known as Elizabeth Simmons Martinez, Lizzy, Holly, Bones, Moon Blossom Womon, being of full age and
sound and disposing mind, memory and understanding, do make, publish
and declare this to be my Last Will and Testament.

"Are you sure we've got all the names now?"
"Yes, I'm sure."
"Martinez, that was your married name?"
"Yes."
"How long were you married?"
"Is that relevant?"
"Yes."
"Three years."
"And now you're single."
"I am unmarried, if that's what you mean."
"You have one child?"
"Yes."
"Full name?"
"Wade Forest."
"Forest? Is that the boy's father's name?"
"No."
"Where is the boy's father?"
"His father is not in the picture."
(You know, the picture that's supposed to be on everybody's mantle, the
one in the readers and textbooks, the one in the church bulletin, the con-
sumer handbook, and on the cereal box.)
(*In the picture* sounds so much softer than *unknown.*)
"Father's name?"
"Unknown." (Well, you asked.)
"Unknown, are you serious?"
(This is a consultation, not a custody hearing. And you were recommended
to me as the most open, sensitive lawyer in this town, and so help me, I'm
going to get through this, so our son doesn't end up in some homophobic
foster home.)

"Yes, I'm serious."

"Well, on to your estate. Are there specific valuables for which you wish to designate the beneficiary?"

"I would like my grandmother's diaries kept for my son."

"Your grandmother's diamonds? Yes, very important."

"Not *diamonds, diaries,* you see my grandmother wrote something in her diary every day for seventy years."

"Yes, well, what other valuables?"

"There are several things: the trunk Grandpa Peat came to California with, the birdseye maple vanity that belonged to Great Aunt Liz, the spoon (that's all that's left of Grandma's side of the family—a silver spoon, by God), and three cords of human hair woven by my great-grandmother."

"Let's just put down *heirlooms,* shall we? What about jewelry?"

"Well, my wedding ring was probably worth something, but it's lost."

(Put it in the secret compartment of my desk when I left it with a friend in San Francisco. Didn't even want to look at it for two or three years. Went back to check and—poof—it was gone.)

"Real estate?"

"Nope, I've been a renter all my life."

"Personal automobile?"

"Well, with the way the Volkswagen's been smoking, I can't say it's worth much. Let's face it, my property in this life doesn't amount to much. I'm here to be certain my son is properly cared for if something should happen to me."

(Properly cared for, my foot. My son has another mother, a mother that none of your annotated codes would recognize. A mother who held him and me before that first day and will be there on the last. She's changed his poop, spelled his words, tied his shoes, and answered his questions, and I'm gonna do everything in my power, including lie, to see that they're together when I'm gone.)

"And whom do you wish to be your son's guardian?"

"Jenna Harris."

"Relationship?"

"She's his...(Don't risk it. Remember the day-care worker who left the conference room and never came back?)...she's my...friend."

"Friend? Doesn't the child have any other relatives—grandmother, aunt, uncle? The court will not look favorably on turning a child over to a mere friend of the mother's."

"But, they are very close."

(I'm struggling for control. Breathe, damn it, breathe, think, be creative, think!)

"Well, actually, she's...his godmother. That's it, she's his godmother!"

(Is godmother a legal term. . . is there really a separation of Christian church and state? Something tells me the only way to get this guy to write down what I want on legal-size paper with pink-lined margins is to use the word *god*.)

"Well now, *that's* a different story."

(Isn't it always.)

Confronting The Courts

Rosalie G. Davies and Minna F. Weinstein

Rosalie arrived at the courthouse a few minutes past 10:00 a.m. to find her attorney waiting at the top of the marble staircase. It was fall of 1974, Montgomery County, Pennsylvania, and this was the day in court that every man in America can count on.

Rosalie sat at a table on one side of the bar, and her former husband at the other. He and his wife of two weeks had decided to leave the United States and were determined that Rosalie's two children would go with them. In her favor was a millenium of sexism that said children should be with their mother; against her was the documented fact of her lesbianism. Rosalie had been a public lesbian activist for many years, had put her name to manifestos and petitions, had testified before City Council on behalf of a gay rights ordinance. It was too late to pretend heterosexuality, too late to promise to be good.

To be a lesbian is to violate sexual standards, but to be a public lesbian is a challenge to society. She had gone beyond any debate over sexual preference vs. sexual orientation, claiming lesbianism to be a good thing, a positive behavior that demanded recognition and equality. The male power structure, in microcosm in the courtroom, could not and would not tolerate this, and she was to be punished for her arrogance. Her access to her children was limited to one day a month in Nova Scotia—noncumulative, one phone call a week, and two weeks visitation at her parents' home in Montreal.

As bad as this decree was, it was better than what her former husband had attempted. After nearly five years of shared custody, his intention was to spirit the children into Canada without her knowing, thereby cutting her off totally. She had learned of his plan from the children and had taken legal action through the courts and the immigration service to prevent it. The moment of loss, however, was irreparable.

The preparation for the case was hurried and more than a little frantic, but turned up several important issues. Rosalie's research seemed to reveal that there were no lesbian custody cases; certainly no one was *admitting* to being a lesbian. The litigation that presented any clues at all was difficult to find, obscured by initials in place of names and references to ungendered paramours, leaving behind no body of decisions and opinions to build on or work against. Women were being advised to conceal their lesbianism. Cases were being heard in chambers "to protect" families. Lovers and lifestyles were being denied. Lesbian women, already virtually powerless within a construct erected by centuries of male jurists, were pressed into even greater passivity and feebleness by the threat of the loss of their children. But an important truth emerged: acquiescence did not achieve custody. Lesbian women lost their children in court battles whether they acknowledged their lesbianism or not.

In the face of this assault, three responses surfaced. Some women capitulated entirely by pretending to be what they were not. Probably the largest group, they attempted to assimilate into the mainstream of heterosexuality at a cost that cannot be estimated. Others went underground, taking their children with them. A network of safe places was put together to provide asylum to those women seeking to take on new identities and begin new lives. A third route was to challenge the law, an arduous and potentially painful option.

Women choosing to confront the law faced loss of jobs, homes, and family support due to the publicity frequently attending lesbian custody cases. Further, it is a rare relationship that can survive the accompanying atmosphere of anger, frustration, and helplessness engendered by litigation. The woman who lives with the mother, her life partner, is helpless in the litigation situation. She often is seen as the root cause of the problem, but for her there is no lawsuit. The mother, helpless and angry, can find it easier to direct those feelings at her partner rather than at the court whose negative judgment of her is frequently internalized for years to come.

Choosing this third alternative led to the creation of CALM (Custody Action for Lesbian Mothers)*, established by Rosalie Davies in 1974 as an advocacy and litigation support service for lesbians threatened with the loss of their children. The task that CALM undertook was enormous, since the very notion of *lesbian* and *mother* was a contradiction in terms to the average judge. For him, lesbian mother was semantically, physically, and ideologically impossible; he was likely to believe that the lesbian standing before him was the only one he had ever seen.

CALM, along with a number of civil rights attorneys and the Lesbian Mothers' National Defense Fund, has struggled to devise strategies to combat the sexual label that inevitably connotes a devastating array of stereotypes and conceals the real woman in the courtroom.

CALM has also worked to establish a base of support in the lesbian community. That was a remarkably difficult assignment a decade ago. Women with children were not often welcomed, especially if the children were male. Motherhood seemed an anachronism, a reminder of a troubled time best forgotten. The primary support group has consisted of other lesbian mothers, and women in relationships with mothers and their children.

---

* CALM, P.O. Box 281, Narberth, PA 19072, (215) 667-7508

Today, some things have changed and others have remained the same. Rosalie's personal story had a happy ending. Her children voluntarily returned to her less than a year after the judge's decree was entered, a familiar scenario in such cases. Custody granted to a father invariably translates to custody granted to a stepmother or a grandmother. Children who are mature enough to make choices appear to choose their mothers over a substitute parent. Rosalie is now a lawyer in private practice serving primarily women clients and remains involved in the on-going work of CALM.

CALM itself is strong in its internal structure and sophisticated in its approach. Funding comes mainly from several small foundations and the community support which was so elusive earlier is now more easily available. Attitudes toward parenting have changed with the accessibility of artificial and self-insemination, as more lesbian women choose to be mothers. Clearly, the issue had not been one of mothering, but of a tendency to link motherhood with heterosexuality.

The larger political scene, though, is grim. Homophobia is back in fashion, made respectable and strong by a newly invigorated conservatism. Custody cases which would have been won a few years ago are today being lost; values previously affirmed are again being repudiated.

Nonetheless, the courts have been confronted and challenged; our lives are now part of the record, visible within the canon. The lesbian mother is a reality. Her name has been spoken.

Choices

Turning
It
Over

Lesbians Choosing Children:
The Personal Is Political Revisited

Nancy D. Polikoff

Five years passed from the time I decided I wanted to have a child until I adopted my daughter. During those years I had dozens, maybe hundreds, of conversations about having a child—as a lesbian—with friends, acquaintances, and men who were possible fathers. I watched close lesbian friends have children: one got pregnant in a one-night stand, one adopted after many miscarriages, one got married to a man. I joined a group of lesbians considering motherhood which now, more than two years later, has seven children and one on the way.

There were several dominant themes in those discussions: how to get pregnant; whether to have an involved father and, if so, how involved; how to deal with family and work. Looking back, I am struck by the extent to which virtually all of these discussions had as their basic premise the *personal* nature of the issues and concomitant decisions involved. For example, I do not believe that anyone ever pushed me to examine, from a feminist perspective, my adherence to a belief in a known and involved father. For a movement that was built on the premise that the personal is political, there was, and there continues to be, surprisingly little political analysis of our choices to have children and all the decisions that flow from that choice.

There is a difference between doing political analysis and making judgments. As I have begun to raise these issues in my immediate circle of friends, I have met resistance from those who believe these decisions are so personal that no one else can or should say that there is a "correct" answer. Such a response misses the point. Our choices have political implications; they are made in a political context. If we are to build a stronger movement for radical social change and pass down to our children a sense of what is possible, a vision of a world less dominated by patriarchy and other oppression, and a desire to continue to struggle, we have to understand the political dimensions of all of our apparently personal choices.

This is not a new idea. Consider the "choice" to be heterosexual or lesbian. The feminist movement has produced volumes on the subject of the politics of sexual orientation. At its core is an awareness that the issues are not purely personal because the world does not make heterosexuality and lesbianism equally available and attractive options, and because there are social, economic, and political consequences of one's sexual orientation.

In the same way it is essential that the discussions of choices surrounding lesbian motherhood include the political context and ramifications of each of our decisions. This will, of course, produce divisions between us. It is easier not to ask each other the hard questions, and not to see the differences. We mothers need a lot of help and support in our work of raising children, and other mothers are our easiest and most logical allies. It is hard to jeopardize that support by raising difficult political issues. I am convinced, however, that the failure to address these issues is destructive to the goals of building a strong women's movement and ending all oppression.

Being a mother in this society is in fact no more a free choice than being a heterosexual. The cultural pressure is enormous, the propaganda overwhelming. Women who never have children are considered empty ("barren"), selfish, peculiar. Until they reach their mid-thirties or so, others will tell them they will change their minds; that it's just a stage; that, as soon as other aspects of their lives are established, they will want children. As the "biological clock" ticks, women without children are told they will be sorry, sorry, sorry.

Turn the pages of popular magazines. You will find successful career women extolling motherhood, saying they never realized how little meaning their lives had before their children were born.

Listen to the rhetoric about abortion. Politicians talk only about rape and incest victims; feminists talk about married women with several children already who can't afford more, or about teen-agers too young to be expected to bear the responsibilities of motherhood. Who is talking about women who don't ever want to be mothers? No one.

Examine the burgeoning industry of reproductive technology. There is now always something else that can be done to facilitate pregnancy. One more dangerous drug. One more invasive surgical procedure. The time. The money. The energy. The obsession. Literally years out of a woman's life devoted to producing a biological child. Where is the room to say *no*, to say *enough?* Where is the room not to try?

Are lesbians immune to a culture of compulsory motherhood? Of course not. We were girls before we were aware lesbians, and we were raised by families that expected us to become mothers. We read the same books and saw the same movies as our heterosexual sisters. And today we live in the same world, one which purports to value motherhood above anything else a woman can do.[1] We rarely ask each other why we want children, and when we do, we are satisfied with personal answers. (Mine was that I liked kids and looked forward to a relationship with an adult child which would be as positive as my relationship with my father.) My own introspection has forced me to recognize that I wanted a child in part because I wanted to be "normal," because I wanted to have more in common with other women, and because I didn't want a life that seemed so clearly on the fringe of society. I also wanted a relationship I could depend upon, a product that would survive my death, and a focus for my life at a time when organized political activism seemed either too amorphous or too rigidly sectarian for me.

It is rare to hear a lesbian say she wants a child because she wants to put her politics into practice, and childrearing is one way to do that. I am not sure I have ever heard a lesbian say she wanted a child because she wanted to make a public statement that there was another model for childrearing, and that it was better than the traditional model. The practice of lesbian childrearing as an avenue for political action and change is not a prominent part of lesbian discussions about whether to have children.

Many lesbians feel defensive about their decision to have children. Motherhood alters a women's lifestyle drastically, and nonmother friends are not always anxious to adapt. It is easy to feel, as a mother, that old friends no longer understand your needs.

But how do those lesbians who don't want children feel? In a culture that values childbearing and childrearing as much as ours does, there is no easy way to talk about not wanting children or about valuing other activities more. Rarely does anyone challenge making a baby the focus of one's life and one's reason for doing or not doing just about everything. Women without children who question this prioritizing are dismissed as not understanding what it means to be a mother. What does this mean for the full-time political activist who can no longer get enough help sending out mailings? For the feminist candidate with fewer campaign workers? For lesbians who are not mothers but who have pressing responsibilities and get little sleep—like the lesbian photographer recording days and nights of political demonstrations; or the legal worker in the middle of a political trial, staying up all night preparing for the next day? Who nurtures them? Who sympathizes with their fatigue? Not their parents, not their coworkers at straight jobs, and, too often, not their lesbian friends. No wonder they are hostile, or at least skeptical.

These thoughts have not led me to conclude that lesbians should remain childless. They have, however, led me to believe that a lesbian who chooses motherhood has a concomitant obligation to defend the right of others not to have children, and especially to support those women who make feminism their full-time work. No one else will say that their choices are as valuable as ours. No one else will say that it's strong, positive and self-affirming not to have children, that it's more than just "all right." What's more, our decisions to have children will be used to reinforce the isolation of lesbians without children from mainstream society. We who are raising children are in the best position to make it clear that we fully support a decision not to have children.

I am also concerned about the impact of lesbians choosing motherhood on another group of lesbians—those who had children within marriage and voluntarily gave up custody of them. Although many lesbians have lost custody of their children against their wishes, others have decided not to assume primary responsibility for the ongoing care of their children. For those who have turned away from the day-to-day work of mothering as part of a process of embracing a lesbian lifestyle, the choice of motherhood by significant numbers of lesbians must at least appear puzzling and may seem to be an implicit judgment. All of society views women who give up custody of their children with suspicion, disapproval, and disbelief. If we who have children as lesbians do not explicitly support our sisters who have decided to stop the daily tasks of raising their children, we become part of their oppression and contribute to divisiveness in our community.

In practical terms, this translates into a need for lesbians who choose motherhood to affirm in all relevant public forums—conferences, meetings, publications—the decisions of other lesbians not to mother or to withdraw from being mothers.

It is important to analyze why we want children because the reasons reflect larger truths about our community. For some, having a child signals a retreat from the political to the personal, from the public to the private. Why? And why now? On a more intimate level, lesbian couples may be having children to keep their relationships together, or to avoid confronting issues within their relationships, such as no longer making love. What are the ramifications of deflecting attention from the root issues of our relationships or from the crucial task of building a more positive vision of lesbian sexuality?

Although some of the reasons lesbians are having children stem from aspects of their personal, intimate lives, others seem to be more connected to the current climate of options for political work. For me, the one or two-year period before I adopted was characterized by political inaction, almost lethargy. I thought, I read, but I didn't do much because there was no focused political action which seemed to have any likelihood of meaningful success. During a time of increasing political repression, with the mainstream moving farther and farther to the right, it is hard to feel that any radical political work will be effective. The sense of isolation overwhelmed and immobilized me. I felt in my gut that my involvement in political action would make no difference, so I saw raising a child as a concrete, creative, focused activity.

Naturally, I now wonder how many other lesbians look to motherhood to get them out of this rut. To the extent that motherhood drains the available pool of lesbians engaging in ongoing political work, its long-term significance is overwhelming. Additionally, these motivations are bound to aggravate the tensions between nonmothers and mothers, as mothers take on society's most acceptable excuse for not doing anything in the public sphere.

Certainly, childrearing itself is subject to political analysis and can be guided by positive political principles. But childrearing probably should not become the total focus of one's political energy anymore than other important, intimate endeavors, such as coming out to parents and working on homophobia. There is a lot of work to do. And all of us who don't do it must ask ourselves why, must try to understand the nature of these times, and must struggle to find a way for more people to resume the larger fights. Mothers cannot let themselves off the hook. I am afraid also that this particular motivation to have children has an impact on childrearing practices, allowing less clarity, understanding, and questioning about the political ramifications of our childrearing choices. If this is true, then having a child becomes not a way to focus political activity but a way to avoid it.

The other motivation to have a child I felt, which I believe is common and needs to be more fully discussed, is the desire to be more normal and have more in common with most women. Political isolation and personal isolation are related. It is easy to get tired of political work which appears to have minimal impact. We are all worn down by the personal truamas we experienced with lovers and friends that shattered our naive beliefs in building one large lesbian community. Once I was no longer energized by the feeling of being different, I began to seek ways of fitting in. Having a baby because of this motivation is the same kind of defeat as returning to heterosexuality. It is testimony to the power of the most repressive parts of our society. And it is a larger defeat as well, as it makes the road harder for all those who continue to resist society's prescribed roles for women.

A realignment according to motherhood or childfreeness means that a lesbian mother believes she has more in common with a heterosexual, usually married, mother than with a lesbian who has no children. I have seen lesbians whose social lives have come to revolve around families, usually straight, with other children close in age to their own. I have seen child-care plans made with heterosexual families of unknown politics because it was the most convenient arrangement. As the mother of a two-year old, I understand the difficulties of arranging child care. But I also believe the perception that one's interest as a mother supercedes one's interest as a lesbian is politically devastating. I am especially troubled when alliances with straight mothers do not include explicit openness about being lesbian.

Few lesbians are always out. With various coworkers, colleagues, customers, clients, family members, etc., we may choose to say little about our personal lives so that our lesbianism remains hidden, or at least unspoken. Having a child, however, is a principal indicator of heterosexuality. To most of the world, a mother is by definition a heterosexual, and one who embraces the social norm. I have never felt that lesbians should always come out in all situations; survival sometimes demands otherwise. But to not come out as a lesbian mother is to assume a public position of heterosexuality. I have done it myself. I have chatted with colleagues about disciplining and birthday parties; I have told potential employers about the connections between my child-care arrangements and my work commitments; I have been able to make small talk with just about anyone on the universal subject of our children. Every time I do it, I separate myself from my lesbian sisters. Unless I also identify myself as a lesbian, which is sometimes impractical and sometimes unwise, I put myself in an implicitly heterosexual woman's place and accept it as natural. On a larger scale, this makes it harder for lesbians to come out and is not neutral but incredibly destructive to building a lesbian and feminist movement.

Interestingly enough, even when someone knows I am a lesbian my motherhood makes me seem more normal. It is amazingly easy for people to put difficult information in the back of their minds. The ability to talk about preschool programs as two mothers virtually eclipses my differences from a married woman, unless I say I am specifically looking for a program that will foster my daughter's pride in being part of a lesbian family, which I do not always do. My experience is that straight women clearly feel that my choice to have a child *balances* my choice to be a lesbian and makes me more normal, easier to understand, woman, less of a challenge to their lives.

When I have put out this analysis to other lesbian mothers or mothers-to-be, I have been challenged by some who say that having a child forces them out of the closet, thereby making them *less* normal, especially when two women raise a child coequally and the child calls them both *mommy*. There is certainly truth to this, although I believe it is limited to situations involving equal comothering. The *family unit* will not appear normal anywhere it functions as a unit, with schoolteachers, storekeepers, or family members. But the individual mother, and even the nonlegally recognized mother, will be more normal in her life as an individual. And she will have many times in her life when she will be put to the test of explicitly disclosing her lesbianism or accepting the presumption of heterosexuality that makes the "deviant" choices of lesbianism and childfreeness less possible for others.

It might well be asked why I inquire so intently into the reasons lesbians have children, as though we need better, or even different, reasons than our heterosexual sisters have. After all, our right to have children can be seen, almost on a civil rights level, as a right to the same opportunities that heterosexuals have. It is especially tempting to take this approach in the face of recent moves in Massachusetts and New Hampshire to bar lesbians and gay men from foster parenting and adoption.

Certainly it is critical to assert and defend our right to have and care for children. Those who would deny us this right are profoundly antigay and antilesbian, and this manifestation of homophobia, like all others, must be vigorously opposed. But while we fight for the ability to make the same choices as our heterosexual sisters, we must nonetheless critique those very choices.

Many lesbians have taken this precise posture with respect to the legal ability to get married. While most would agree that as long as marriage is available to heterosexuals it should also be available to lesbians, many lesbians have profoundly questioned the institution of marriage, have expressed reservations about our ability to transform that institution even if we were allowed access to it, and have concluded that they would not marry even if legally permitted to do so.

I find this a compelling analogy to childbearing and childrearing. Motherhood is an institution.[2] It functions as an integral part of patriarchal society to maintain and promote patriarchy. Our lesbianism does not negate or transform the institution of motherhood. Motherhood, like marriage, is too loaded with this patriarchal history and function to be an entirely different phenomenon just because lesbians are doing it. If we fail to ask ourselves the kinds of questions I have raised here, and many more, we essentially embrace not only the personal experience of mothering but the institution of motherhood as well.

The great challenge of lesbians choosing motherhood and the possibilities opened by it lie precisely in asking questions, a lot of questions, a lot of hard questions. This article has principally addressed the issues of choosing whether to have a child. In future articles, I would like to go farther and examine how we have our children and how we raise them. The dialogue we can have about these questions, the answers we come up with, and the process of developing those answers are a great gift which we have to offer to our community and to our children.

Notes

1. There have been, of course, historical periods when motherhood has not been encouraged because economics dictated the need for use of women as a "reserve labor force." This is often associated with a nation being at war. At the moment, dominant economic ideology (as opposed to reality, which mandates the employment of women for the survival of many families) dictates just the opposite, that high unemployment rates are at least in part a function of the number of women in the labor market.

Furthermore, it is beyond the scope of this article to examine the different pressures upon women and girls of different races and classes to become mothers. It is unquestionable that differences in status and options in the larger society impact upon the circumstances under which women become mothers.

2. Adrienne Rich's *Of Woman Born* is probably still the most eloquent analysis of motherhood as an institution.

Women Without Children/ Women Without Families/ Women Alone

Irena Klepfisz

This article has grown out of my need to express some of my feelings and conflicts about being a woman who has chosen to remain childless, as well as to break the silence surrounding the general issue of women without children.

That the silence has persisted despite the presence of the women's movement is both appalling and enigmatic, since the decision not to have a child shapes both a woman's view of herself and society's view of her. I have read a great deal about woman as mother, but virtually nothing about woman as nonmother, as if her choice should be taken for granted and her life were not an issue. And though I have heard strong support for the right of women to have choices and options, I have not seen any exploration of how the decision to remain childless is to be made, how one is to come to terms with it, how one is to learn to live with its consequences. If what follows seems at moments somewhat bleak, it is because I feel very strongly that in celebrating a woman's liberation from compulsory motherhood, we have neither recognized nor dealt with the pain that often accompanies such a decision.

My intent is to be neither objective nor exhaustive. I am aware that this issue evokes many other feelings than those expressed on the following pages, the feelings of women whose lives differ drastically from mine. I hope that they too will break the silence.

1. The Fantasy

At the center of my bleakest fantasy is the shopping-bag lady. I see her sitting on the subway, trudging along the highway, or crouched in a doorway at dusk. Invariably she clutches her paper shopping bags close to her. From a distance, her face looks blank, her skin grey. She is oblivious to the things around her, unresponsive to sounds and movements. She is particularly indifferent to people. Periodically she makes a quick motion, like an animal automatically brushing itself free from an irritation, a tic. Her gesture is loose, flabby, hardly aimed. It is, perhaps, the tremor of a muscle.

I keep my distance from her, though at times in my imagination I venture closer, detecting a faint stale odor, an odor distinctly communicating stagnation. In reality, however, I have moved only close enough to discern the discolored skin, the broken blood vessels on her legs, stained purple bruises, barely healed wounds. I have eyed her socks and stockings, her shoes, her faded dress, the safety pins which hold her coat together. I have studied the surface content of her bags, seen the bits of material (clothing, perhaps), newspapers. I always want to know more, to know if the entire bag is filled with rags and papers, or if deep inside, wrapped neatly and carefully in a clean cloth, lies an object from the past, a momento from a life like mine. But my desire to know has never overcome my real terror of her. So I have never ventured closer.

I have a distinct fear of contagion. But it is not necessarily of disease—though there is that too, the physical fear of being touched by such a creature. My greater fear is that she carries another kind of disease. On a subway, I watch as this creature sits, harmless, self-contained, oblivious to the other people in the car, while an invisible circle seems to form around her. No one will come near her, no one will sit close to her, no one will risk being touched by her. If she has succeeded in excluding us from her world, we must remember that our response to her reflects our equal determination to keep her out of ours. It is almost as if I, as if everyone else in the subway car, were determined to classify her as a species apart, to establish firmly that there is no connection between her and us. By keeping my distance, I affirm she is not of my world, reassure myself that I could never be like her, that there is nothing she and I have in common—in short, that her disease is not communicable.

It is, I think, the most comfortable way of looking at her, for it deems her irrelevant to my life. Of course, if I were totally convinced, I would lose my fear of contagion. But this is not the case. More and more, I sense my connection to her, allow myself to absorb the fact that her world and mine overlap. More and more I dismiss as romantic the notion that some great, swift calamity, some sudden shock must have overtaken her and reduced her to her present condition. It is far more probable that her separateness, her isolation, resulted not from fire, nor from sudden death, nor from unexpected loss, but rather from a low erosion, an imperceptible loosening of common connections and relations—a process to which I too am subject. Her disease is one to which I am and will remain vulnerable. She is not an anomaly, nor is her isolation from the rest of us a freak accident. She came from the same world I did, underwent the same life processes: she was born, grew up, lives.

So I remain in a state of terror and keep myself separate from her. I fear that I will not build up the proper immunity to resist the erosion; I am afraid

I too will end up alone, disconnected, relating to no one, having no one to care for, being in turn forgotten, unwanted and insignificant, my life a waste. In the grip of this terror, I can only anticipate a lonely, painful old age, an uncomforted death.

It is difficult to own up to this fantasy. I do so both because it is true that I have it, but also because I know I am not unique in having it. I have heard many other women express it, perhaps not always in terms of shopping-bag ladies, but in terms of old age, insecurity. And it is not surprising because among my friends, many in their late thirties and early forties, these issues are becoming increasingly important. It is not surprising because we are living in a period of depression (1977) when everyone is worried about money and jobs, about the possibility of surviving in some decent way. For me, the shopping-bag lady epitomizes these fears, and though I often tell myself that she is an exaggerated example, equally often I think that she is not.

2. The Myths

For a long time I believed (and on some nonrational level still believe) that I could acquire immunity to the shopping-bag lady's disease by having a child. When depressed about the fragility and transiency of friendships, or the inconstancies of lovers, it was the myth of a child, a blood relation and what it could bring me, which seemed to me the only guarantee against loneliness and isolation, the only way of maintaining a connection to the rest of society. And certainly one of the difficulties for me, a woman who now knows that she will never bear children, is to let go of that myth without sinking into total despair.

That the myth is powerful is not surprising, since it is nurtured by everything around us, fostered by the media, by popular literature, by parents, by the questionnaires we fill out for jobs: *Are you married?* No. *Do you have children?* No. *Do you live alone?* Yes. *How many members in your household?* One. It is a myth perpetually reinforced by the assumption that only family and children provide us with a purpose and place, bestow upon us honor, respect, love, and comfort. We are taught very early that blood relations, and only blood relations, can be a perpetual, unfluctuating source of affection, can be the foolproof guarantee that we will not be forgotten. This myth, and many others surrounding the traditional family, often make it both frightening and painful for women to think of themselves as remaining childless.

In reality, of course, I know that many shopping-bag ladies are mothers, have families, have children. What is obvious to any mature, rational woman is that children are not a medicine or a vaccine which stamps out loneliness or isolation, but rather that they are people, subject to the same weaknesses as friends and lovers. I have talked to many women whose ties to their families seem to be irrevocably broken. It is common to hear stories of the prodigal daughter going cross-country, returning home after fourteen, fifteen years to parents who are strangers. Expecting a traumatic, painful reunion, the woman returns numbed by her lack of connection, by her indifference to strangers. They are people with no special relation. They follow the accepted and expected rules, in a dire crisis write dutiful checks, and, upon their death, bequeath china to their unmarried daughters. But the emotional pull is not there from either side. There is no exchange of love, of comfort. Blood might indeed be thicker than water, but it, too, is capable of evaporating and drying up.

Yet despite this, despite having read Shakespeare's *King Lear* and Tillie Olsen's *Tell Me A Riddle*, despite having been taught by experience that children often come to love their ideals more than their parents (and vice versa), that children may take different roads, rejecting all ties to the past, despite all this, the myth retains its power and dominates my fantasy life. And there are important reasons why it does.

First, what I have just described is what I would like to believe is an extreme, an exception. There are, after all, many warm, loving relationships between parent and child. In these relationships, one can recognize genuine affection and ties among members of the family, even if often the very same relationships are fraught with tensions and painful encounters.

Once when talking with a woman about our feelings about being childless, she began to tell me about her relationship with her mother, a relationship which for years had been filled with anger and pain. But I could sense that on some level the woman felt a deep attachment, had genuine concern and responsibility toward her mother, despite the fact that the relationship remained problematic, and many painful conflicts were still unresolved. While she was describing this to me, she suddenly revealed that her mother was on welfare and was receiving $180 a month. When I asked her how her mother could possibly manage on such an absurd amount, the woman laughed and said that, of course, she helped her out financially. We continued talking more generally about the issue, but then the woman suddenly said: "You know it scares me. Being alone, without family. I think about my mother and what she would be doing now without me. I keep trying to think of her as just a woman, like me, trying to cope with world. But there is a difference, a major difference between us. She has a daughter."

A second reason for the myth's ability to retain its hold on my fantasy life is that I have found no adequate substitute for it. To discard it is to be left with nothing, to be faced with the void (or so I think in my most depressed moments). I admit this with some hesitancy, because certainly one aim of the lesbian/feminist movement has been to expose the superficiality of the family myth. The movement has consciously struggled to develop new alternatives for women, has, in a certain sense, offered itself as a new and better "home," a source of the support, affection, security that many of us seek. I think, however, that for women who at one time or another were involved in various movement activities, support groups, collectives, business projects, experimental communes, for those women who as a result of these activities and groups experienced the first flush of excitement in their discovery of other women and in the sharing of feelings and goals, for those women who thought that they had indeed found new and permanent homes, alternate families—for them the disappointment has been quite keen. Too often, instead of providing a new and supportive home, the collective experiments ended in frustration, bitter anger, a hard silence that severed what everyone had hoped would be permanent ties. That this occurred, is repeatedly occurring, is not surprising. Because expectations were so high, because we wanted these groups to fulfill so many divergent needs, they were destined to disappoint. For me and for many other women it was a sobering kind of experience, to say the least.

I do not mean to imply that nothing has worked or that we are standing in the midst of ruins. What I wish to emphasize is rather the sense of disillusionment and disappointment experienced by me and by many women with whom I have spoken, a sense which has contributed to a feeling of insecurity and, to some degree, pessimism. It is when these feelings become acute that I am most vulnerable, that my fantasy returns again to the concept of family and children. The old images resurface. But the difference between envisioning them now and envisioning them years ago is that now they hold no solace, they remain empty. Their uselessness in my life creates further pain, for I am without the alternatives which a few years ago, when I first became involved in the lesbian/feminist movement, I thought I had. I find the community's present and future only vaguely delineated; whatever community exists is still very young and rather shaky. The emptiness of the past, the vagueness of the future, leave me fearful, hesitant about my decision not to have a child.

Many women have had to face a similar issue on a more personal and more immediate level. They have had to face the fact that lesbian relationships are not instantly more stable, more secure, more permanent, than heterosexual ones. And because of this, the myth of motherhood takes on added power. A woman who thought she was about to break up with her lover told me: "For the first time in a really long time, I thought about having a child. I won't do it of course. But I did think about it." She was clearly expressing the idea that somehow a child would guarantee her a permanent relationship.

The emphasis, is of course, on *guarantee* and on *permanent*. If the parent is good, so the logic of the fantasy goes, then the relationship with the child will withstand shock, change, growth, poverty, differences in temperament and ideals: in short, anything and everything. The woman who dreams this way may acknowledge that such a relationship has yet to be realized, but she may be quick to add that she has learned a great deal from her own experience as a daughter, that with *her* child, she will avoid all the mistakes that her parents made with her. By learning from their errors, the woman now fantasizes, she will establish a far more perfect, loving, supportive relationship with her child and, thereby, guarantee for herself a permanent connection during her lifetime.

My fantasy of being a mother and my desire to have a child have been with me for a long time. It has taken me years to realize, however, that both the fantasy and the desire were to a great degree expressions of my dissatisfaction with my relationship with my own mother. It seems clear to me now that by becoming the calm, loving, patient, supportive mother I have so often envisioned, I have hoped in effect to annihilate the impatient, critical voice within myself, the voice that has kept me insecure and dissatisfied. Thus my desire to become the perfect mother, to act out that fantasy, has in reality nothing to do with having a child, but rather with my desire to experience something I wish I had experienced. It is not a child I wish to mother, it is myself.

In my fantasy, of course, the understanding, the patience, the support are always outwardly directed, because the myth of motherhood demands that they be so. According to the myth, if I do not have a child I will never experience that caring, that uncritical peace, that completely understanding sensibility. Only the role of mother will allow me that. This is clearly a wrong reason for having a child—one which can be ultimately disastrous.

This kind of thinking, however, points up another aspect of the myth about having children, i.e., that certain qualities can only be expressed through a relationship with a child. I am not saying that a relationship with a child is not unique. It is. But some of the qualities which we attribute to it are not limited to child-parent relationships. I would like to discuss just one of these qualities. Women expressing a desire to have a child often explain that they want their values and beliefs to be passed on. They feel that by having a child they can have some measure of control, some input into the future. A child, after all, can be molded and influenced; to a child can be passed on a whole way of life. That parents have tremendous influence over their children is, of course, self-evident. But the myth excludes the fact that they do not have total influence over their children, that they can never exert total control. As a woman once said to me about her child who was going to a day-care center: "Oh yes, I have great influence. I send her off in the morning looking like a human being, and she comes back in the evening with green nailpolish because green nailpolish is some teacher's idea of femininity."

There is something extraordinary in the idea of being able to participate so immediately in the shaping of another life, no matter how much other factors attempt to undermine that influence. Nevertheless, it is not only through a growing child that a woman can influence the world around her, though in the interest of the traditional family, women are taught to believe that it is the most direct and most meaningful way for them. Obviously, a woman taught to think this way will think that her life, her work, are totally useless and ineffectual if she does not have a child, an heir to her ideals and values. This is another real impasse for many women who decide to remain childless. I was interested in a conversation I had with a woman who told me she was considering adopting a child. One of her main reasons was the one I have just discussed. Later in the conversation, she told me about a talk she had had with a friend. Sometime after the talk, her friend told her that she had had a tremendous impact on her, that the talk had helped her in making certain basic decisions about her life. The woman told me, "I was really stunned. I always consider conversations with friends just talk. It never occurs to me that anyone really listens to me, or that what I say has any effect on anyone."

This is not to say that for every aspect of a relationship with a child we can find a substitute, and women who decide not to have children can somehow "make up for it" by looking elsewhere. I believe a relationship with a child is as unique as a relationship with a friend or a lover. Each has its own special qualities. But myths about having children do prevent women from seeing just what it is they want from having a child and from participating in such an intimate way in another life. It is something which needs closer examination, so that when a woman decides not to have children, she knows what she is giving up—both the negative and positive aspects of being a mother—knows it in a real, concrete way, and not in the foggy, idealized, sticky-sentimentalized version with which we all are so familiar.

3. The Consequences

Myths and private fantasies are not the only obstacles in the way of women coming to terms with their childlessness. There are also the very real, and often harsh, circumstances of living in a society where a woman who does not marry and, above all, who does not have a child, is stigmatized, characterized as cold, as unwomanly and unfeminine, as unnatural in some essential way. I wince when I recall how throughout my twenties, when I

was certain that I was destined to marry and to have children, I would assume with total confidence that a married woman who did not have children must either have physical problems or deep psychological ones. And
I remember with some shame the freedom with which I would mouth these
opinions.

Today, many of us know better. But although we may understand that a
woman has a right to choose to remain childless, the society in which we
live still does not, and most of the time it is extremely difficult to be a woman who is deliberately not a mother. On the most immediate level, a childless woman must deal with the painful confrontations and equally painful
silences between her family and herself. Let me use myself as an example.
I am an only child, a survivor of World War II. My father was killed during
the war, as was his whole family; my mother was the only family I had.
Most of her friends were, like us, surviving members of families which had
been wiped out. It was an unstated aim of the individuals of this circle to
regenerate the traditional family, thereby making themselves "whole." And
over the years, most of them were quite successful. Some remarried; those
who did not had the satisfaction of watching their children grow up and of
knowing that they would take the normal route. Soon there were in-laws,
then grandchildren. The nuclear family seemed to reassert itself.

It has been extremely difficult as well as painful for me to live with the
knowledge that I willingly, deliberately, never produced the child who could
have continued "my father's line"; that I never provided my mother with
the new family and the grandchildren she was sure would appear, which
she thought were her right to expect. I know that other women, coming out
of different circumstances, have experienced similar difficulties and pain—
women who were raised as only children, who were given the burden of
providing their parents with the stereotypical props of old age. These wom-
en have complained bitterly about how their parents' disappointment in them
(as if they had failed at something) has affected them. The "you're-the-last-
of-the-line" argument always makes the woman who chooses not to have
children appear perverse, stubborn, ungiving, selfish. Equally painful can
be the excitement of parents when they inform the childless daughter of the
birth of a friend's grandchild. I have heard this kind of excitement in my
mother's voice, and have often resented the fact that nothing that I could
achieve could elicit that tone of voice, that kind of lasting, enduring satisfaction. Her envy of her friend is clear; and underneath it, I know, lies a
silent, unstated criticism of me: I have held back.

A woman who was not an only child is often relieved of this kind of burden and pressure when one of her siblings marries and gives birth. But this,
too, creates its own problems; often the childless woman feels resentment
and jealousy because the parents seem so pleased with the other sibling for

making them grandparents. A woman once told me how her sister, who had recently given birth, said to her that she was glad she had been able to provide their mother with the pleasure of seeing her first grandchild. The mother was dying. The woman felt deeply hurt, not only because of her sister's insensitivity to her feelings, but also because she felt she had nothing comparable to offer her mother.

At moments like these, women often yearn for the perfect excuse which will relieve them of the burden of having chosen to remain childless, which will convert them back into "warm, loving women." The choice seems too great a responsibility, seems too much against the values of our society. I remember a few years ago, when I had to have surgery on my uterus, how frightened I was at the prospect of having a hysterectomy. I told the doctor that, if at all possible, I wanted to keep my ability to have children. What I did not express to anyone, and barely to myself, was that a part of me wished that in fact a hysterectomy would be necessary. By becoming sterile, I would be relieved of having to make an agonizing decision. Remaining childless would no longer be a result of my "perverseness." I would be childless because I could not bear children. What could anyone possibly say to me after I had had my hysterectomy? I have heard other women reluctantly confess similar secret thoughts, women with raised, feminist consciousnesses, who nevertheless find it difficult to make the decision not to have children, and also to take full responsibility for it without feeling defensive and to some degree unjustified.

In the end, I did not have a hysterectomy, and my childlessness is a result of my own decision. The process by which that decision was made is in large measure difficult for me to trace or reconstruct. To a certain degree, I think I made it over a long period of years, during many of which, on the surface at least, I was not consciously thinking about the issue. Certainly, for a long time I thought there was no decision to be made; I was sure that I would marry and have a family. Furthermore, I never doubted my intense desire to have a large family, never stopped to question whether I really wanted this, or whether it was something I thought I should want. Looking back, I find that often, in order to appear normal to myself, I adopted attitudes and values which were clearly not my own. In this particular case the unconscious argument went as follows: A normal woman wants children; I am a normal woman; I want children. This kind of short-circuiting of real feelings is quite common with many women, women who cling to fantasies created by others. These fantasies, many women think, will keep them in the mainstream, will prevent them from appearing different or conspicuous.

I fantasized about my future family for a long, long time, though in my actual life there was nothing to indicate that I was moving in that direction, that the fantasy would become a reality. I never married, never became pregnant. Yet I continued to assume that it was simply a question of time, that of course *it* would happen. It did not.

At the age of thirty, I was finally able to admit to myself that I did not want to marry. That realization, however, did not resolve the question of whether or not I should have children, and so I began to think about the issue in more real, more concrete terms. Two years later I became involved with a woman, and a year later I had to have my operation. At that point I was already thirty-three, was beginning to realize that I had to make a clear decision. And I made it by doing nothing about it. I thought a good deal about children, my need for them, my intense longing for them, my fears about being without them. But I did nothing.

The long years during which I was making my decision were extremely difficult. Most of the time I felt inadequate and incomplete. I was conscious that many people around me thought it was peculiar that I was not being swept away by "a normal woman's instinct" to bear and rear children, an instinct which should have overridden any of my qualms about marriage. The message communicated to me was that I—a woman alone, without a partner, without children—was enigmatic at best, superfluous at worst. In those years, I was unable to articulate to myself or to others that I was following other instincts. The best defense that I could muster was to say, "I'm too *selfish* for that life." Nevertheless, I evolved my decision and stuck to it.

4. Conclusion

This past April I became thirty-six and I think it is not accidental it was about that time I began thinking about writing this article. Though most of the time I really do not know what to make of my age, what to think of its significance, it is around the issue of having a child that my age becomes real to me. For if I do not feel thirty-six (whatever feeling that is supposed to be), I certainly know that biologically my body is thirty-six, that the time for bearing children is almost over for me, and that once I pass a certain point, the decision not to bear a child is irrevocable. That the decision has already been made is very clear to me, though I cannot pinpoint the exact moment when I made it. No matter what my age, the issue is closed.

Often, of course, I wish I had done it, done it in those unconscious years when so many women I knew were doing it. They are now mothers whose children are almost real adults—eight, ten, twelve years of age. Frequently I find myself envying those mothers for having gotten it over with in those early years. That certainly seems to be the perfect solution: have the child in the past, so you can have it now. Fantasizing in this way, I can easily skip over all the hardships and frustrations that many of these women have experienced in the past ten or twelve years of raising their children under extremely difficult circumstances, hardships which they continue to experience, and which I can only partially understand.

Still, there are moments when I can actually assert a certain amount of pride in the way I have chosen to lead my life, when I can feel extremely good about the fact that I did not succumb and did not keep myself in line. I am pleased that I withstood the pressures, that I kept my independence, that I did not give in to the myths which surrounded me. I know, of course, that there are various reasons why I did not and others did, which include conditions over which none of us had very much control. Nevertheless, I do experience momentary delight in the fact that I escaped and did what I wanted to do (even when that was somewhat unclear), that I did not give in to the temptation to please my mother, did not give in to the pleas of my father's ghost to keep him alive, did not conform with the rest of my friends, but instead kept myself apart and independent in some essential way. In moments like these, I can easily take responsibility for my life and say it is the life that I have chosen.

None of this is ever very simple. There are pleasures that one gives up when one decides not to have children. But as I keep telling myself: you can't have everything. Choices have to be made, and consequences have to be lived with. The act of choosing inevitably brings loss. It is a difficult lesson to understand and accept. I keep trying to relearn it.

While writing this article, I visited my mother who had just discovered, stuck away somewhere in a closet, my favorite doll. I was surprised by my instant sadness at seeing and then holding it. The sweetness of the face, the smallness of the head against the palm of my hand. I felt as if I wanted to cry. But in touching it, it was not a baby I envisioned, but rather myself, five or six years old, cradling the doll in her arms and rocking it gently to sleep.

from
An Old Dyke's Tale:
An Interview With Blue Lunden
Elly Bulkin

Elly: I thought we could start with talking about your coming out and with your experiences of being a lesbian in the fifties.

Blue: I started coming out when I was thirteen, when I fell in love with Gloria, the girl down the block. I wasn't really conscious that this was a taboo until my aunt began to react to my being so open about my feelings. It was just after that time that I heard the word *lesbian*, and I went to the library to do the research that I think has been done by so many lesbians throughout history. From that time, I realized I should be quiet about my feelings. It was just after that I found *The Well Of Loneliness* on the drug-store bookracks—of course I went back to that bookrack. I haunted it, and I found other books, perhaps half a dozen. Before that time I had no inkling how many lesbians there might be. Then at least I got the idea there were probably some more in my city.

I lived with an awful lot of people after my mother died when I was about ten. I lived primarily with my godmother, a woman who had also been a friend of my mother's. Traditionally in French families, godmothers really do take responsibility for the children if something happens to the mother. My godmother and I had an incredible struggle about power and control and independence and so on. So I ran away. I guess two weeks was the most that I managed to avoid the cops. They'd find me. But once you've been in reform school, it's very easy to go back. Next time I got into trouble I was sent back to reform school. We were stealing license plates from wrecked cars and selling them. It was a little racket. But because I had already been there, I just got sent back. It was in reform school I first heard about the Goldenrod, which was a lesbian bar.

Elly: What year was that?

Blue: Probably '52 or '53. I was there with a girl I had been in reform school with. I was sixteen; she was fifteen. All of a sudden the lights went on, the jukebox stopped, the police came in and said it was a raid and everyone was under arrest. Poor Pat! She gave her real age, and I never saw her again; I'm sure she was sent back to the House of the Good Shepherd. I didn't lie about my name. Somehow I thought they'd know I was lying about my name, so I gave them my real name and I gave them my real address, but

I lied about my age—I said I was eighteen. They took us all to the precinct and booked us and put us in a cell. Then, late that night or early in the morning, the owner got us out on bond, and they set the court date for the next night. Some women were saying there'd been reporters outside and they were really scared.

The next morning I went down to the drugstore (the same one where I had found *The Well Of Loneliness*) to get a cup of coffee and bought the newspaper and started looking for the police reports, where most arrests were reported in the paper. My father religiously read the police reports, so I knew he was going to find out about it if it was in the police report. It wasn't there, and I was so relieved. Then I turned back to see what the news of the day was, and the headline said, "64 Women, 1 Man Arrested." There were all kinds of remarks about what kind of bar it was, about the sign saying "No Males Allowed."

That night we had to go to court, and I discovered they had raided every gay bar in New Orleans. It was like a big cleanup. I had never seen so many gay people in my whole life. I had no idea there were so many gay people. It was really exciting! I almost forgot to be scared about whether I would be convicted or not. My case was dismissed, but I think that set me free in some way.

Elly: Were the other cases dismissed?

Blue: I think they were. There may have been instances where people were found guilty of something; usually the charges were things like "wearing the clothes of the opposite sex" for drag queens and for butch lesbians, or "no honest, visible means of support." It was true, most of us didn't have any honest visible means of support. If you chose to dress in such a way that clearly identified you as gay, it was impossible to get any kind of straight job, assuming you would want one. Most often all of those charges were dismissed when you came before a judge. I don't know why, particularly, except that I believe the arrests were intended as a kind of harrassment— when it was intense enough, it drove people away.

Some of us didn't have any other place to go. We were caught every time they happened to walk in when we were there. Whereas for other people, just being there in that bar was one of the riskiest things they'd ever done in their lives. If they even witnessed an arrest, even if they didn't get taken in, it was usually sufficient to scare them away for years to come. You see how this kind of stuff works to limit what kinds of risks people take. When I look back at that now, I am really amazed people were persistent. I wonder why I was unconscious that I was part of a resistance.

We were going to all these bars and I was observing. I was learning—it was like school for me. I saw that a lot of butches had *old ladies* who were prostitutes. Some of them had several old ladies and that was called *sister-*

in-lawing; they actually lived together—two or three old ladies and a butch. That was very admired, a pimp par excellence. But I was coming from too square a place to relate to that at the time, so the only option for me was prostitution. I didn't even expect to get a job in a bar at that time. I wasn't even of age, but nobody knew it.

One night, Virginia and I were at the bar, and this guy propositioned me, and I went with him. I'd never been in bed with a man in my life so I thought I'd find out. . .God, it was really, really awful. But I got the $20. I came back, and I tried to buy a drink for Virginia. She wouldn't let me. A lot of people were upset because they knew I had never done anything like that before. And that was the end of it. Except that in a few months I realized I was pregnant. Once I was pregnant, I figured I can't get any more pregnant, and I needed money, so during that period, until I was too pregnant, I was a prostitute. I didn't do anything different—I didn't dress up or do anything like that—but there were plenty of people coming into those bars looking for sex and there were a lot of men who, I think, felt more like men if they could get a lesbian to go to bed with them.

Elly: They thought they were going to change your life.

Blue: It seemed really important to them that you said you enjoyed it. I just saw it as an acting job basically. Lila and I were buddies—she was a drag butch like I was. We used to do shows together, and we thought this was hysterical because we were both stone butches so we would never have anything to do with each other sexually, but we would just put on these great shows that we'd make a lot of money on. And I can just remember laughing in her cunt while all these guys would think we were sexually excited.

Between living with Virginia and being on my own, I spent the next four years in those bars. I went from being a prostitute to learning to be a pimp, although we didn't call them pimps. I had a lot of lovers who were strippers. Strippers make money not so much by dancing but by B-drinking. I did B-drinking too, looking to roll somebody if they were flashing a lot of money. After Linda was born, I was really careful. I didn't want to get pregnant again. But I did a lot of other stuff like sex shows. A lot of people did. Eventually I was driven out of New Orleans by the police.

Elly: How did they do that?

Blue: The charges began to get more serious and they began to do things like break the door down and tear the whole apartment apart looking for drugs. And I was using some drugs, and the chances were that sooner or later they would catch me—I wasn't any big drug dealer and I wasn't a junkie, but everybody fooled around with some drugs in that kind of situation at that time. They arrested my lover for prostitution. She was convicted and given a suspended sentence, probably because she was white and had no record. They picked her up at our house, where she had brought a john.

They offered to make a deal that if we'd pay them $250, they wouldn't show up at court to testify. We paid them, and they showed up anyway. We knew it was going to be really bad from there on out. We had a chance to get out, so we did. We were in Corpus Christi, Texas for a year and a half before coming to New York. About that time (in New York), I began to get involved with Jeanie, who lived on the top floor, and up till then had been straight. All of our friends were gay or knew lots of gay people, but were freaked out about us. She was also very reluctant to get involved with me because she didn't want to be a lesbian. In the midst of all this, I got word about my daughter. I had given her up for adoption when she was a year old although I had a lot of guilt about it. There was an agreement that I would be able to see her, and when she was older she would know I was her mother. Instead they just disappeared after the papers were signed.

Elly: You knew the people who adopted her?

Blue: Yes, a guy who was the manager of one of the bars that I hung out in and his wife. In fact, she took off with Linda and left him. This was some three years later. My godmother was calling to say that she was going to adopt my daughter, that the woman was no longer able to take care of Linda. Everybody got involved. We got money together, and I flew down there to get her. There was this big scene. Nobody wanted to give her to me because I was a lesbian; I went down there pretending that I wasn't a lesbian anymore and was on the verge of getting married.

Elly: So she had been legally adopted.

Blue: Yes, she had. I never did get her back legally. But I got her up here and once I did I changed addresses and disappeared. She was four and one-half then. Jeanie and I moved in together, and we became like this little family. I would never have made it without Jeanie. We were very isolated because none of our friends could accept that we were lovers; it made them all uncomfortable, perhaps because we were in such obvious roles.

Elly: Did you know any other lesbians who had kids?

Blue: No. I was very careful to keep Linda separated from my social life, so that we would only invite over trusted friends when Linda was at home. When we had a party, I would arrange for Linda to spend the night with my brother. If anybody ever made remarks about how she was really a cute kid and she'd make a nice little lesbian when she got older, I was really upset. I guess I was pretty self-hating.

Elly: Did she ask questions at all about it when she got a little older?

Blue: Not really, but she used to make remarks that would flip me out. I remember one night Jeanie and I were getting dressed to go out to a dance and she came over and said, "Gee, mommy, you look so handsome," and then she said to Jeanie something about how she "looked beautiful." I remember being amused on the one hand and a little unnerved on the other. I'd go to PTA meetings and make efforts to look as straight as possible. I always felt guilty because I didn't encourage her to bring friends home, but encouraging her to bring friends home meant such a trip for me in order to play the role that I thought a mother was supposed to play. Because I didn't have any friends who had children, she didn't really have many kids to play with.

I guess I came out to her when she was ten or eleven. In fact, I just checked it out with her. We were talking about prejudice, and I talked about prejudice against lesbians, and I said, "You know, Aunt Jeanie and I were more than just friends." (By this time, Jeanie and I had split up.) She said, "Yeah, I knew that." She used to have this timing, finding a way to quietly walk into the bedroom when we were necking or something like that. That was really difficult because I thought we shouldn't show any affection in front of her.

Self-Contradictions
Susan J. Wolfe

When I was sixteen, I knew what it meant to be a mother. My mother told me. I had just given birth to an eight-pound-fifteen-ounce baby boy, and I was not married. In six weeks, I would sign papers relinquishing any right to him, putting him up for adoption. My mother's definition was supposed to console me. "Having a baby doesn't make you a mother," she said. "Raising it makes you a mother."

I didn't tell her the social worker insisted that each unwed mother in her caseload hold and feed her baby during the daytime, each day for six days, in order to be sure she wanted to "give the baby up." I didn't tell her, or my father, anything much at all. They had said that it was over, and there was no point in discussing it.

I did tell other people. I told my lover of a year and a half, the woman who had married the man who got me pregnant. Two years later, I also told my new boyfriend, who sounded a lot like my parents when he told me he didn't want to hear about it again. I did not tell my younger brother, who had been told I was in a mental institution; I did not tell him until after my mother's death, twenty years later. Newly married, he was relieved to hear I had only been pregnant. He has been concerned that mental instability might run in the family. My parents' neighbors never knew. They had been told I was caring for an ailing grandparent.

I got very good at secrets. I never told anyone, anyone at all, that I was worried I was a lesbian. My husband and I had shared a good many secrets about our past, but somehow I knew enough not to bring up my relationship with a best girlfriend.

He and I had shared a mutual secret, the abortion I had had in my sophomore year of college when abortions were still illegal. (Rather than tell my parents, I remained in my dormitory room when I began to hemorrhage, with my meals delivered by an anxious boyfriend. I felt that I "owed it" to my parents not to burden them further; I had "done enough" already. Paradoxically, I concealed the fact of this abortion from parents who had suggested one in order to terminate my first pregnancy. That first time, I couldn't bring myself to take the life of the fetus; the second time, I couldn't bear to go through a term birth without keeping the baby, and couldn't envision marriage to someone still eighteen and unemployed.)

For twelve years, I was not a lesbian in my own eyes, since I was having no sexual relationships with women nor, indeed, any very close friendships. I married and, two years later, "perfectly timed," had my son—less than seven years since the first, only four since the abortion. I remember thinking, cradling his head in my hand as we drove from the hospital, *I get to keep this one. I get to take this one home.* I was a mother.

I was not worried I was a lesbian. I did not even have the word. I had once worried about *it*, a pronoun which stood for emotional and sexual attraction toward women. For years, however, I didn't worry about *it* at all. College, marriage, household tasks, and having a baby occupied me until 1973. I didn't even get out much, and when I did, the women I saw were like myself—married to salesmen, living in the suburbs, raising a family.

I knew, by the way, what a lesbian was. My mother had shown me. She had shown me a taxicab driver in full drag, derisively mentioning that her sister was a "tramp," too. "The whole family is mixed up," she said. When I was in grade school, she had pointed to a woman who had been expelled from high school for connecting with a swift uppercut to the vice principal's jaw. In both cases, she alluded to the outcast status of the woman and her family. The message was clear: if you want to be normal, if you want to stay in school, if you don't want to drive a cab, you can't be a lesbian. And, conversely, if you are married, if you have a college education, if you have children, you are, by definition, not a lesbian.

I did not move from New York to South Dakota in order to rediscover my feelings for women and discover a lesbian identity, but that's the way it turned out. A new professor, I first discovered myself attracted to some of the graduate students about my own age. Within three years, while kissing one, I realized with horror that *it* was back.

For three months I juggled my new relationship with Cathy with other responsibilities, assuming that one of us would leave the other and I could suffer silently, but maintain my carefully constructed world. I had been married for seven years. My son was five. I had been a professor for less than three years. I had known I was a lesbian for three months. Three short months, but everything had changed. Like a crustacean, I had shed one shell, emerging new, unprotected, and vulnerable. Frightened.

I felt as if I was trying to cram two entire existences into one life, every day. I commuted ninety miles a day to write my dissertation on campus so I could spend time with Cathy. Later, for nearly a year we would both drive 350 miles round trip to Nebraska; there, I could do collaborative research with Julia Stanley. And Cathy and I could spend a weekend together, with other lesbians, in women's space. But before I left, I made roasts and meat-loaf, washed and folded all the laundry, cleaned—and felt guilty. I kept this up for fifteen months. I saw very little of my son Jeffrey, but convinced myself that it would be all right because we would soon be able to spend all our time together, when I no longer lived with his father. In the meantime, I fought with Cathy, who had long since run out of patience with my role as the lesbian Hamlet, unable to decide, unable to act.

The divorce papers which arrived at 9:30 p.m. one evening in March 1977 took matters out of my hands. In them, my husband claimed to have custo-dy of Jeffrey, although we were still living under the same roof—still sleep-ing, in fact, in the same bed. I forget what he said when I questioned him. I know he had virtually caught Cathy and me making love twice, but the word *lesbian* was never said, never mentioned in the document. Nor was my fitness as a mother questioned. In fact, he said he was confident I made a better parent when I "put in the effort," but that I hadn't worked at it late-ly.... My "loyalties had shifted."

Cathy and I had discussed custody on and off for a year. She had taken care of Jeffrey, living with all of us after my husband had had surgery and I a sprained ankle which left tendons and ligaments stretched. She had driven him back and forth to day care and fixed his meals; she was better at dis-cipline than I, and enjoyed showing children how to do things—how to fish, how to pitch a tent, how to bank a pool shot. But custody was my decision, and I couldn't make it.

I had always played Supermom in the past. As an infant, Jeffrey had not been left to cry. I picked him up at the first whimper for six months. (Once, a neighbor queried me when I suddenly leapt up from a chair and ran to get him from his crib. She, a mother of four, had heard nothing. "That's crying?" she asked. "He hasn't even learned to cry.") He was breast-fed on demand and sometimes slept next to me when I dozed off in the middle of a feeding. I walked the floor with him up to six hours a day because he seemed to like the position better. I ate with him in an infant sling, nursing, until the evening he vomited in my lap. I rejected a teaching assistantship because I was breast-feeding. When he was two, I "deserted" him for one afternoon a week, leaving him in day care; I cried when I saw him proudly carrying his lunchbox, feeling he was being torn from me by forces beyond our control.

Later, with a ninety mile daily commute, I taught, the sole support of the family for six months. I felt guilty—guilty that I was not home for Jeffrey, guilty that my husband was. When I was home, I fussed over Jeffrey and tried to keep him at home, over my husband's protests, because I wanted to have him with me. Jeffrey always protested day care on the days I did not teach, and his protests fed my guilt at being a working mother. I enrolled him in ceramics and in swimming classes, took him to the library, picked out gifts for him on birthdays and holidays. I brought home the pets my husband invariably objected to, and was responsible for them too. I tried to be a model parent.

But I always knew my husband would "fill in" as he had while I wrote my dissertation, taking Jeffrey bowling, watching TV with him—considering it part of his duty, considering Jeffrey part of him. If Cathy assumed child-care responsibilities, it would not be central to her existence. Jeffrey might be integral to our lives, but they would never love each other in the same way. We both assumed Jeffrey would ignore her, as he had seemed to do when she had taken care of us all before. Moving in with Cathy and Jeffrey, I would have become a supermom *and* the head of the household. I couldn't imagine how I would do it. I couldn't imagine being any other kind of mother, either.

The divorce papers seemed to take the decision out of my hands. I should have been relieved. Instead, I went wild, screaming, "You bastard! I gave up one baby, I had one torn from my guts, and now you want to take the only one I have?" and charged my husband. I threw a drink in his face and flung myself at him. He was about 290 pounds and six-foot-seven. He pinned me to the sofa while I tried to bite him, but I couldn't move my head enough to get a purchase. When he let me up, I slammed a large, antique china clock he'd bought himself on the floor and stomped on the pieces. Later I remember walking down the paved alley outside the house without shoes on, noticing absently that there was some broken glass. When I came in, I crawled upstairs to Jeffrey's bedroom and curled up at the foot of his bed—I wanted to be close to him. I was to do that more than once during the next month.

My husband tried—gently, I think—to get me off the floor of the bedroom. I think he asked if it was a good idea for me to be there. (A good deal of this period is mercifully blank, or hazy, hence the constant iteration of the phrase *I think*.) I responded by curling up on the living room floor, next to a chair, like a dog. He panicked and raced to Vermillion to get Cathy, sensing, though he had not yet labeled the relationship, that she would be more help than he. When she woke me up, she remembers I said, "The house is his, Jeffrey is his, everything is his, but I figure nobody owns the ground." I suppose she had asked why I was on the floor.

I had to break the news to Jeffrey. Though allegedly uncaring, I could still communicate better with him than his father. Jeffrey was in the bathtub when I told him. By the time we were done, we were both wet with tears and bath water. His father stood near the door of the adjoining room. At the time, this intruded only slightly on my consciousness, annoying me very little. Now, I feel a sense of pity, recalling how often in the last years of our marriage he stood on threshholds, an observer but not a participant in my life.

To say I *thought* about custody is a misnomer. I *felt* about custody. A lesbian existence, a relationship with Cathy, felt like freedom. The surge of emotion and intellect which followed in the wake of my love for her had made it possible to research and create, to return to music, art, literature, nature. Marriage was security—acceptance by family and society, a comfortable income, roles with which I was familiar—and my son Jeffrey.

I had a lesbian-feminist lawyer who would have defended my right to custody if I pressed for it. But she thought I ought to know, and told me, that no lesbian mother whose lesbianism was known to the court had ever been awarded custody in Iowa. She also told me that under Iowa law, Jeffrey would have to have his own lawyer, and would have to be in the courtroom with his lawyer while the case was tried. I reasoned and stated at the time I did not want to see Jeffrey undergo that ordeal; he was hurt enough by the imminent divorce.

That is what I told my lawyer. That is what I told my husband. That is what I also told myself. I had done what was best for my first baby by allowing him to be placed with a "good family." Now I was doing what was best for my second, since I had no doubt my husband would shortly remarry and provide Jeffrey with a "normal," "stable" home, and, in earning more than I ever would, also ensure that he "would have the best of everything."

All of this made perfect sense to everyone I consulted. I was acting "in the best interests of the child." Some were attempting to comfort me; others, undoubtedly as homophobic as I, probably regarded the term *lesbian mother* as I did—an oxymoron.

At the time, the thought of leaving Jeffrey was gut-wrenching. I vacillated between accusing myself of unconscionable cowardice and congratulating myself for self-sacrifice, the ultimate maternal instinct. I was not being an unnatural mother; I was simply protecting my child from the horror of a courtroom drama in which we would all be actors—his the only part completely unrehearsed—and the horror I did not identify as such, the discovery that his mother was a lesbian. All the while I was tortured by his father, who kept insisting that if Jeffrey was important to me, I should want to stay married to him. They were a "package deal." For my part, I kept insisting that I could want my son without wanting his father, never acknowledging that our views on roles within the family differed very little, if at all.

I have never reconciled being a lesbian with being a mother, not to this day nearly ten years after the divorce. I am still with Cathy in a committed relationship. But when Jeffrey is here, I scarcely touch her in the privacy of our bedroom. One summer, we had no sexual contact during his five-and-one-half week visit. In his presence, we do not even hug or hold hands. Coeditor of *The Coming Out Stories*, I have been praised and admired by lesbians and others across the country for my personal courage, but I cannot bring myself to come out to my son. I have assumed, rightly or wrongly, that he will reject me, and I have chosen to be rejected for having deserted him rather than for my love for women.

Once I came close to telling him, but it was only about a year and a half ago. I felt almost secure, believing that he must have figured out I am a lesbian. He was arguing I should have gotten custody because "most kids, when their parents are divorced, live with their mothers." I felt pushed, pushed to defend my apparent abandonment, and said, "Jeffrey, are their mothers gay?" I knew he understood the word. "What?" he asked with irritation. "I said, 'Are their mothers gay?' " "What's that supposed to mean?" he asked, for all the world as if I had *not* been living with Cathy for over seven years, as if I had not traveled with her, moved with her, slept in the same bed with her.

I could not process his question. I asked if he knew what the word meant, though I knew full well he did, and he assented. He simply couldn't understand the relevance of the question to the conversation we had been having.

I had achieved my goal perfectly: I had a perfectly normal son, one whose definitions of *lesbian* and *mother* were identical to my own—in short, a homophobe. His mother simply could not be a lesbian. His question registered not as denial but as simple bewilderment. He seemed even to have forgotten the statement he had made soon after the divorce, a seven-year-old boy, hurting. "Sometimes I think I'm not the most important thing in your life anymore," he had observed. "Why?" "Because when I'm here, Cathy's here, and when I'm not here, she's still here." Hinting, then, that Cathy and I were more than friends, closer even than he and I. But I had forestalled the discussion, not by explaining our relationship, but by stating, "I'm the most important thing in my life, but you will always be important to me." Other, later discussions on our constituting a family had evidently registered only as the half-truths they were. The right words had never been said.

Many of the women who have talked to me about coming out mention someone they simply cannot tell—a parent, a child, someone, strangely enough, who is closer to them than anyone else. I have been able to reassure them we are all in that position. I am not sure that we are, but it has been comforting for me to believe that, because I have still not told my son.

This year, he will be seventeen; it will be ten years since the divorce. He is six-feet-two-inches tall and over 190 pounds, not the baby I held in my arms. Lately, he has learned not to ask penetrating questions; he hardly seems to talk at all. He visits for short periods of time, a weekend here, a day there. I feel I have lost him completely. He has forgiven his father a disastrous second marriage and divorce. They have regrouped, father and son, as they did after our divorce, a tight family unit once again. I no longer fill the role of sounding board and confidante. I seem to have no role at all. Although the terms of the divorce settlement permit me two months' summer visitation and two weeks during winter and spring breaks from school, I have never insisted on adherence to them. At first, Jeffrey's new family seemed to take precedence over our visits, and I wanted him to fit in with his new siblings—after all, I was not providing a family environment for him. I tried not to be jealous when Jeffrey began calling her *Mom* shortly after she moved in, before her marriage to my ex-husband, and when he began to use similar language to describe her entire family, I apologized for my discomfort. It was "my problem, not his." That the All-American Family has since been revealed as a facade is no satisfaction. I had convinced myself I had made a good decision for Jeffrey, only later to discover the marriage had been a failure almost from the beginning, and he had been unhappy almost as long.

In a sense, the willingness to "give him up," the failure to fight for custody (and, yes, I did regard it as a failure—still do, late at night when feelings seem to run high), was a relief. For most of the year, I would be free to pursue career, deal with feminist issues, live the life of an open lesbian. During Jeffrey's visits, I could provide "quality time." I could feel noble about it.

It has, in fact, been the case that I put as much work as possible aside during his visits, creating the artificial atmosphere of a day-care center for an adolescent rather than a home, demanding nothing of Jeffrey but that he be there. I have ensured that no demands have been made upon him, by me or by Cathy, however we may have fought over the years in order to insulate him, always regarding this house as a place he could run to escape reality.

In writing this essay, I promised to tell myself the truth. One truth is that giving him up has allowed me to escape a reality. If his comings and goings have filled me with grief, if I have repeatedly indulged in tears and self-recrimination, I have never had to deal full-time, year-round with either the burdens of the working mother getting little support from her partner, or those of the open, self-assertive lesbian seeking mutual love from a child and acceptance for him. I may have wept to the point of blurring my eyeglasses as I watched his plane take off for his "real home" with his father, but I have had my freedom, freedom I did not feel I could have allowed myself had I been a mother.

Here is a second truth: there is a bedroom in the upstairs of our house referred to as *Jeffrey's room* by both of us, although he now occupies it for a total of two weeks a year. I do not enter it very often. When something must be put away, I ask Cathy to do it.

In writing this essay, I have finally told her how I felt about custody—how I saw the choice as Cathy/lesbian/freedom/profession on the one hand, and Jeffrey/marriage/security/housework on the other. How I made the choice, consciously if painfully. How angry I have been with her during all those years she has said, "I'll tell you something. . .if he ever came to live with us, he'd have to act different. He'd have to act like part of this house, or I'd know the reason why." How secretly I agreed with her but could not force myself to discipline the child I had chosen, and then not chosen. Until now, I have not admitted I made the decision for me, rather than have to change, rather than relinquish stereotypes long since useless.

At a National Women's Studies Association conference eight years ago, I attended a session on lesbian parenting under the guise of gathering data. (I really *thought* that's why I was going.) I had been asked to edit a book on the topic of lesbian parenting, and went with every intention of being objective, listening. Instead, I began to talk, and when I did, I began to cry. I told a room full of women I'd never seen that I had given birth twice, but was raising neither child. "I don't even know whether I belong here," I said. "I don't know if I'm a mother or not. Do you have to be living with your children to be a mother?"

I still don't know the answer to that question.

If All Else Fails, I'm Still A Mother
Lucia Valeska

What I have to say about women and childraising is harsh. I know of no other way to get the message across, so mucked up are we in fear, myth, romance, and historical ignorance of the world's oldest and most significant female vocation—motherhood. The harshness comes from a sense of urgency. Unless we untangle the real features of childraising, the feminist movement will fail to jump its most difficult hurdle.

Three years ago (1972), in the midst of the contemporary lesbian rebellion, as a mother I turned to my lesbian sisters and said: "Mothers will be next and lesbians will look like silly putty in comparison." Mothers outweigh us in numbers, rage, and immobility. When they strike, we will come up with them or they will take us down. That is how I felt. Two years later, in an impatient surge toward individual liberation, I gave up custody of my three children. As a result, I am a mother and then again I am not. Nonmothers, or the childfree, measure their words in my presence, and since I've left the fold, most mothers find me fundamentally suspect. But the view from renegade bridge is enlightening.

I see three distinct but occasionally overlapping political camps: 1) the childraisers, 2) the children, and 3) the childless or childfree. These camps share a common oppression, but they are also in direct conflict with one another. Each situation carries a series of contradictions and concomitant ambivalences, complicated by the separate realities of sex, race, and traditional class divisions. The job of untangling the conflicts, of forging a common struggle, is nearly beyond comprehension, but we must start digging somewhere.

The Childraisers

Mothers are not the only childraisers. Included in this group are lovers; housekeepers; babysitters; nursery, elementary, and secondary school teachers; communal mothers; relatives; friends; feminist aides; and an occasional father. There are what can be broadly defined as primary and secondary childraisers, with much variety and several degrees in between. A primary childraiser is the primary source of emotional and economic support for her children. The secondary childraiser is only one of a group of people who is economically and emotionally responsible for the children.

Whether you are a primary or secondary childraiser, and what else you do with your time, makes a big difference. The myth tells us simply that you are a mother or you are not. But the facts cast the deciding vote, especially regarding the strength or poverty of the self-image you derive from childraising. Ethel Kennedy affords a ready illustration. Tennis, horseback riding, golf, a huge houseful of surrogates, and the Washington cocktail circuit can uniquely influence the self-concept of your basic mother of eleven. The single mother who works a nine-hour shift in order to support her four children will have a different self-image. What we do well tends to create a solid self-concept. What we do poorly results in the opposite. How well we do anything directly depends on the economic and social environment in which we do it. The crunch in childraising comes when you realize that poor mothering and faulty child care are currently built-in givens in the North American social and economic system.

Specific signs of decay are readily apparent. To begin with, we are all familiar with the dreaded question "And what do *you* do?" *(a)* "I'm a mother," *(b)* "I'm a lawyer," or *(c)* "I'm a pig farmer." As a mother, I was always tempted to answer with *c* because there are some interesting historical parallels. The primary difference boils down to the fact that pig farming went out a little earlier than motherhood and so you pick up an extra point or two on its antique value. Not even the middle-class American supermom with the greatest resources at her private command can beat the inevitable failure. As the feminist movement legitimizes rebellion, supermom after supermom throws in the towel of her discontent, and as often as not, returns to school.

If being with children is a joy, why aren't we fighting harder for the privilege? Why is it when you ask for child-care volunteers, everybody in the room contemplates their boot laces? Why is it the mothers and a handful of political stalwarts are inevitably left with the job of consciousness raising (children are human beings too) and organizing child care for meetings, jobs, community, wherever?

The signs are real. The message is clear. If you're looking for a solid self, don't be a mother, or an elementary school teacher, or a child-care center aide at all. Since failure is built into childraising in our society, there is no such thing as a good mother and no such thing as a good self-concept emerging from this work. The situation goes beyond the sole dictates of male supremacy. It has nothing whatever to do with any individual childraiser's advanced skill at maneuvering. There are a number of ingenious, if partial, escape routes that the more privileged work out for themselves. But there you go; it is an escape—something to get away from. That *something* transcends good or bad mothering. What is it?

The Changing Economy Of Motherhood

Early one morning, everybody in the world woke up and decided in unison to hate children. Hence the cure: we all wake up tomorrow morning and decide to love children. Stripped of its rational facade, this is the kind of solution which too often prevails. Many contemporary writers (Jill Johnston, Shulamith Firestone, Germaine Greer, Jane Alpert) talk of returning to the good old days when children were "integrated" into adult society, when they were treated as "small adults" and were a constant presence in the daily life of the community. It's not a bad idea. We could gather up all the children and go marching through the factories, business offices, medical schools, cocktail lounges, libraries, college administrations, board meetings, nuclear laboratories, saying: "Here's three for you and three for you and three for you; keep them safe, happy and intelligent; we'll be back for them in twenty-five years."

The description of an integrated society these writers present resembles an historical truth, which in many parts of the world still prevails. But it is the entire social, technological, and economic fabric of these periods and places that makes the integration of children a viable reality. Many of these integrated children vitally contribute to the economic life of the community. They work from sunup to sundown. Most significantly, their relationship to their mothers is relatively casual.

In any economic setting with an extended family, the mother's relationship to her children is automatically secondary. That is, the children will be raised and *economically supported* by a group of people of which the biological mother is simply one member. This is generally true for all classes, races, and cultures.

The economic settings that maintain a secondary relationship between mothers and children cover an enormous range and variety in lifestyle. They include nomadic communal gathering and hunting peoples, agrarian societies, feudal societies, and early industrial societies. Since these economic forms have prevailed for most of human history, many of the contemporary expressions of motherhood are outgrowths of an economic existence that is now obsolete in most parts of the United States and generally in any advanced industrial setting.

Here's the deal: The nuclear family is the result of an economic system that has come to depend on small, tight, economically autonomous, mobile units. It is essential to capitalism because it not only meets the peculiar production needs of our economy but also fits the requirements of capitalistic consumption. Thus, the ideal nuclear family boasts one producer and several (but not too many, lest the labor force explode) consumers. It is a middle-class ideal and the norm held out for all classes. Even though the working-class family rarely achieves the ideal, it, too, believes this is the way life is supposed to be. In the good family, the man works; the woman is wife, mother, and homemaker.

The nuclear family provided stable family units for the advanced industrial state for a number of years. Now, the very mobility it arose to feed is turning around and killing it. The means of stabilizing and sustaining the old family have progressively disintegrated: neighborhoods, churches, ministers, relatives. New institutional buffers have taken their place: TV, psychiatrists, psychologists, social workers, family counselors, school counselors, and a huge educational system.

By keeping the nuclear family limping along, these adjustments have eased the new primary relationship between mothers and children. But short of total fascistic control (no divorce, no abortion, no child care), the attempt is economically doomed. The U.S. government has failed to salvage an institution that served it well. The stopgap adjustments have not been sufficient. Psychiatrists no longer even attempt to save marriages; they help people through transitions. The divorce rate soars, giving the nation a new choice and women and children a new deal. Either the old nuclear provider supports two, three, or four families, which most men can't or won't afford, or middle-class women join the labor force with unmatched vengeance. All this at a time when the number of jobs is rapidly shrinking.

Meanwhile, back at the homestead, the children are waiting to go to school to make this new deal possible. For a mother of three, that's a minimal wait of nine years on diaper duty before she is free to look for "work." Upon finding that job, she also finds she must be away from home for at least eight hours a day, not including travel time. Most children's school days run two to four hours short of this requirement. Talk about credibility gaps, here we have a possibility gap. Welcome, ladies, to the working class.

But long ago, they moved middle-class women out of the extended family, Mexican, Irish, Italian, Jewish neighborhood. Mother still lives in Pocatello, Aunt Jean is in an institution up in Rhode Island—so who now will watch the kids? Arise the new child-care center: haphazard, unfunded, disorganized, and expensive. A college-educated woman earns less than a male with two years of high school training. If you even find a job, do you grasp the size of the paycheck coming in, minus babysitting, child care, groceries, moving, housing, and medical costs? This is a framework for built-in failure.

Take a good look at the rhetoric surrounding the issue of motherhood. The term *childless* represents our society's traditional perception of the situation. Since motherhood was the primary and often only route to social and economic well-being for women, having children was a material asset, and to be childless was historically negative. Indeed the term was often directly equated with *barrenness*. Few women were autonomous; survival depended on marrying and bearing children. No man wanted a barren woman. Under these circumstances, no sane woman *chose* not to have children. To be childless still carries a negative stigma, even though the social and economic reality has drastically changed. Consequently the question, "must we be childless?" is loaded.

The term *childfree* represents a new perception of reality in the United States. Not only is motherhood no longer the only route to social and economic well-being, it has become a real detriment—a detriment that is clearly visible when a mother looks for a job, a place to live, babysitters, or child care, whenever she tries to take her children any place she goes.

Women must, for the first time in herstory, leave the nest in order to gain an identity and a living wage. Yet a mother cannot leave the nest because she is the children's sole remaining legal, economic, and emotional representative. When children are barred from any productive role until they are twenty-five years old, it makes the job of representative tenfold what it was in the past. To be a good representative, you must be economically solvent, have a solid self-concept (gained elsewhere), and have a great deal of time on your hands.

On another level, the debate between *childless* and *childfree* is purely rhetorical. Clearly, with or without children, women are not free in our society. Even more important, as long as the children exist, it is a delusion to speak of being free of them. They are still all out there, impatiently clamoring for recognition and support.

Meanwhile, the government takes its own stand. It has already paid farmers not to grow food and workers not to work past a certain magical age. It pays students not to join the labor force and fathers to stay away from home. Now the government is implicitly paying women not to have children. Ford follows Nixon in refusing the necessary funds for child care. Like Nixon, he calls it "economizing and preserving the American Family." The new deal for children and mothers amounts to no deal at all. They are being forced into an economic and social transition doomed to failure from the start.

Consequences And Strategies

The situation portrayed presents distinct consequences and strategical possibilities for the three political camps: mothers, children, and the childfree. We must recognize the contemporary condition of women and children as a complex product of economic history. The problem is far more complicated than just the result of bad men in places of power. The grim fact that women in feminist collectives refuse to deal with the dilemma unless mothers literally put them up against the wall is one indication that our situation is not a simple by-product of the ideology of male supremacy.

Think. In general the feminist movement has benefited its members. It has given them a collective identity, which in turn has made them stronger as individuals. Women have given of themselves freely and deeply in order to develop this new strength. Of course we've had our casualties, but, in general, the prize has been worth the cost. In the case of childraising, the prize does not yet equal the cost. We reflect society's perception that mothers, children, and child care are expendable. The expendability is often expressed in statements such as "Child care is a reformist issue." But this expendability of mothers and children is built into the economic system that controls all of us.

Mothers

Mothers must make it militantly clear that they are not expendable. The economic changes that have made motherhood a national disaster area can be changed. National and local budget priorities and consciousness can be rearranged to suit job, educational, and child-care needs. Of course the privileged, be they men in power or your so-called childfree sisters, will *never* give up their advantages out of the goodness of their hearts. They need to know that the price of not dealing with your situation is greater than the cost of dealing with it—that whatever endeavor they are involved in simply cannot proceed without meeting your needs. You are raising their children; they must provide the resources to do the job adequately. Mothers everywhere must caucus, organize unions, and put an end to their isolation through collective action. There is a lesbian mothers union based in California, and mothers should use this as a beginning model for collective effort.

In the meantime, if an individual mother's situation is unbearable, and if the option of custody transfer is remotely feasible, she should give this option serious consideration. It is the surest, quickest, most effective strategy available for personal survival. It is also a political statement. It says in no uncertain terms, "If my community will not provide me with the freedom I need to rebuild my life, then I will take it for myself." For a growing number of women, custody transfer is more than an option. It is a necessity.

The potential tragedy is not that children and mothers are lost to each other, but that the decision is made in a social vacuum. There is virtually no community support. The so-called experts—psychologists, counselors— paint an invariably gloomy future for you. Even the most liberal, nonjudgmental shrink tends to lose her cool at the mention of custody transfer. The one I consulted rose up out of his chair and shouted, "You can't do that."

Fortunately, I disregarded this advice and proceeded. What women need is some one or group to share positively both the decision and the transition with them.

No mother makes this choice easily. Both the social taboo and the mother's entire conditioning conspire to keep it out of the realm of serious possibility. Another obstacle is the false assumption that the decision will be complete and irrevocable—a "here today, gone tomorrow" finality. Such is not usually the case. The details, including psychological consequences for both mothers and children, will vary with the individual situation.

Whether a child is raised by her uncle, her grandmother, two people, or a group of people, and what kind of people they are, makes all the difference in the world. My own three children have two sets of parents (one lesbian, one heterosexual), and four functioning grandmothers. They spend summers with my lover and me, and the school year with their father and another mother. The transition was gradual. My oldest child moved in with his father three years ago. A year later the two younger ones joined him.

In our case the change was a necessity, economically and emotionally. Perhaps we could have scraped by economically, although I had no vocational skills and was still working on a college degree. But emotionally, the situation for me as a single mother was disastrous. My two-year stint in the women's movement had allowed a vast reservoir of rage to surface. The open resentment at being trapped began to far outstrip the pleasures of mothering, and the daily burden was too great for me or my kids to bear. That a healthier situation was available was a stroke of luck and privilege for which I shall be forever grateful.

Children

A key feature of industrialization is that the workplace is far removed from the home, which gradually leads to the segregation of children from the business of the world. As industrialization and technological development proceed, the discrepancy between adult and child spheres grows. Children must be set aside for longer and longer periods of their lives before they can play an integral, responsible role in the life of the community. At the same time, increased mobility combines with supermedia to expose children to a constant flow of new situations and a complex environment that demands they grow up more quickly than ever.

In essence, we have mass-produced a nation of young people who are extremely sophisticated, while we have simultaneously denied that sophistication any serious expression. Because children are segregated and constantly held down, they have developed their own culture, with values, codes of honor, and means of social control that clash with the adult ones. Even though children are packed neatly away in their ghetto—the American public school system—we cannot avoid bumping into them because there is trouble brewing in the ghetto.

Like other oppressed people, children have begun to organize, to demand basic rights and responsibilities commensurate with their abilities. As with other oppressed groups who begin to rebel, society has reacted negatively to these initial efforts. Just as rape has become a national sport, razor blades and arsenic in Halloween treats and armed guards in the corridors of our best middle-class junior highs have become standard. These reinforce the children's own conclusion that they live in a state of siege.

Segregation of children has had one potentially liberating consequence: it significantly dilutes the impact of where they lay their heads at night. It is no longer possible for adults to stamp out pint-sized replicas of themselves through the nuclear or traditional family. The individual child's destiny is increasingly determined by her own community. In this respect, children are in part seeing to their own liberation. But their situation is still unique for two reasons. First, their condition is temporary by definition. Second, they are by nature to some extent dependent on the adult community. That's where we come in.

A well-developed industrial system changes children from an advantage to a deficit. Under other economic systems, children materially contribute to a family's wealth and well-being, and eventually the young take care of the old. Not so today. This change has tremendously influenced both our perception and treatment of children. No amount of sweetness and light, innocence or charm, can outweigh the fact that they are a pain in the ass and cost a lot of money. Since our perception of children comes from a specific social and economic environment, it can be changed only by altering that environment. The cost of childraising can no longer be shouldered by private individuals. Childraising must move from the private to the public sphere, from the individual to the local and national community. *My* children must become *our* children.

We have begun this transition—witness the education industry. But we are dragging our heels all the way. If we compare need with designated resources, the educational establishment today is a mere welfare program. By and large, the treatment of children in it is comparable to the treatment of welfare recipients. Imagine how different funding for education and child care would be if the grandchildren of our national Congresspeople were in public child care from three months of age up!

In making the transition from *my* children to *our* children, we can and must change the consciousness of our sisters first. And then, we change the nation. But society's perception of children will not change until we create a viable role for children and give them the resources to fulfill that new role. In the meantime, child-hating must go. It should not be replaced with old platitudes on the natural virtues of children or life with them. Rather, it should be replaced with a firm understanding of why children are unacceptable in our society, and a concrete strategy to include children in our thoughts and actions.

Any organization or gathering is practicing child-hating if it does not arrange for quality feminist child care by the childfree. Furthermore, any person who says, "But I don't particularly like children," is practicing child-hating. She is letting society's negative stereotype of children take over her mind. There is as much variety among children as there is among individual women. How can you dislike all of them? The statement comes from one who perceives children as an inferior group that is not worthy of her personal recognition or time. Struggles against racism and sexism have set our minds bolt upright on these issues. The casualness with which child-hating statements are made and received is a measure of our lack of consciousness of this issue.

The Childfree

All women who are able to plot their destinies with the relative mobility of the childfree should be encouraged to take on at least one existing child, part-time or full-time. Love that child, teach her something she might otherwise never learn, show her respect she might not find elsewhere. Oh yes, and be consistent. Let one child in your community grow to expect and rely on your coming just as she relies on the air she breathes. You should not do so because the experience will be joyful but because it is politically necessary for the growth of all women and children. Then if joy comes, halleluja!

To have our own biological children today is personally and politically irresponsible. If you have health, strength, energy, and financial assets to give to children, then do so. Who, then, will have children? If the childfree raise existing children, more people than ever will "have" children. The line between biological and nonbiological mothers will begin to disappear. Are we in danger of depleting the population? Are you kidding?

Right now in your community there are hundreds of children and mothers who desperately need individual and community support. It is not enough for feminists to add to this population and then help out in their spare time. A growing number of young women are indeed beginning to resist having their own biological children—mostly from a sense of self-preservation. But the new childfree must not only take conscious control of their reproductive organs, they must also see that true self-preservation depends upon the survival of their entire community—one that includes living children.

We must develop feminist vision and practice that includes children. We must allow mothers and children a way out of the required primary relationships of the nuclear family. This can be done only by forging new relationships, with economic and emotional underpinnings, between children and the childfree. At this historical moment, the goal is a moral imperative only. Moral imperatives have a habit of hanging out there in thin air until hell freezes. It is the responsibility of nonmothers to end the twin tyrannies of motherhood and childhood as they are lived today, but the childfree will not do so until mothers and children light a big fire of their own.

Lesbian Coparenting: Creating Connections
Nancy Zook and Rachel Hallenback

We are a lesbian-feminist couple committed to the growth and change a child brings to our relationship. We are intensely proud of our choice to live our lives fully and completely as lesbians and try to fearlessly confront homophobia in ways that make sense to us. We are aware that raising a child is an option not everyone would choose. We make no judgment on those who decide otherwise, although we believe that the choice to parent should be available to all women, including lesbians. While the numbers of lesbians choosing to raise children is growing, there are still few role models in our culture for us to follow. As we find our own way in the parenting process, we have been supported by many and hope, in return, to touch others.

Our daughter was joyfully welcomed into our loving arms the morning of April 28, 1984, after a well-managed and drug-free labor in the birthing room of our local hospital. Those eighteen hours of altered consciousness required a shared effort, trust, and flexible support which will remain the pivotal point in our new life together as a family.

The decision to become parents was made after great thought and careful examination of our feelings and expectations. We knew that there would be times when we would wish we had chosen otherwise (and there have been times). One of our strengths as lesbians includes the deep-seated belief that neither of us claims "ownership" of this child. She came through Nancy's body, but is coparented by and is developing her own separate relationship with each of us. Rachel's role as coparent is one that has few models. Different from that of a father, yet not a biological mother, she has sometimes been left feeling a stranger. In order to reenforce Rachel's role, she was actively included from the beginning in decision-making and in the conception process itself. For us, this precluded Nancy having sexual intercourse with a man as the route to conception.

We accepted the challenge to conceive with humor, anxiety, and joy, and set about charting Nancy's ovulation and the task of finding a sperm donor. Our daughter was conceived through a process we define as *alternative fertilization*, language which to us reflects a sense of woman-controlled conception rather than the traditional term *artificial insemination*, which calls up images of medically induced plastic babies.

In considering the role of a man in this process, several questions arose. Should he be anonymous to us as well as to our child? Should he be known to us but not to our child? These questions forced us to examine our underlying attitudes about men, our own fathers, male role models for both boy and girl children, what it might mean to raise a boy child, and the ways in which our attitudes could affect a growing child. We felt we could not take the responsibility for denying our child access to the knowledge and company of her/his father if they both so desired in later years. We wanted our child to grow up fully aware of who her/his father was, and why he did not live with us. Like all lesbians examining the issue of parenting, we were concerned abut custody rights, given that the father would probably be granted such rights in a court of law should problems arise that led to court involvement. Clearly, we were looking for a man whose values matched ours and with whom we could feel safe. We were fortunate to find such a man in a heterosexual friend, the single father of a teen-age daughter.

After several meetings, honest sharing, and hysterical laughter over the physical aspects of his involvement, we planned his visits to our home to coincide with three prime times for conception at the end of July 1983. We made no formal written agreement or contract, but did have a clear verbal understanding of his role and felt comfortable with him because of our past relationship. Contracts have been important for some couples but do not always have validity in court. Some women feel more secure with a go-between, a person who collects the jar of sperm from the donor and then brings it to the woman waiting to conceive. We chose to do the entire process together as the extended family we really wanted to create. We laughed nervously as we sterilized a mason jar and welcomed our friend at the door. After hugs and more laughter, he proceeded to our spare room alone to ejaculate into the jar. We prepared ourselves in Nancy's room with a brief conception ritual to clear our minds and focus our energy and hearts on our endeavor. Minutes later, the jar was handed over, hugs exchanged, and he was on his way. With Nancy's hips on pillows at a forty-five-degree angle, Rachel, taking a quick breath, inserted the semen into Nancy's vagina with a sterile syringe. The two of us waited together for forty-five minutes.

No words can truly convey the sense of wonder, joy, fear, and tenderness for the unseen process unfolding within Nancy's body. Rachel's participation in conception was crucial to us, as this was to be her child as well. We did nothing to try to enhance conception of a female child. Instead, we chose to accept what destiny brought us, including a possible inability to conceive. We repeated the process two more times during the next few days, and then waited to see if Nancy's menstrual period would begin. When it did not, we waited until a pregnancy test could confirm what we already suspected--Nancy was pregnant! This quick conception is unusual; the average time is six to eight months and sometimes longer. Sharing the news with friends was wonderful. Dealing with the reactions of family members, finding health care providers who could support our concept of family, and deciding what and when to tell our various coworkers took time, persistence, and a few tears. All was managed successfully, however, and while both our families were initially skeptical, everyone has been supportive and fully involved since our daughter's birth.

· Nancy experienced the normal positive and negative aspects of pregnancy. We were helped immeasurably in this by the Ithaca Birth Group, an organization dedicated to sharing information and support for alternative birthing choices. One of the leaders became our labor coach and stayed with us during labor at the hospital, where we received considerate and respectful care. Our female general practitioner paved the way for Rachel to have all the rights and responsibilities accorded a father. We left the hospital eight hours after our daughter was born and began our new life.

Our daughter is currently two and one-half years old and thriving. It is hard for us to remember there was a time when she wasn't with us. It has been far easier to be lesbian parents than we had imagined, perhaps, in part due to the special community in which we live. Our relationship with our daughter's father has become a source of joy for all of us. Although we initially felt fear and uncertainty, we have been able to discuss our concerns and actively support each other in our varied roles. For the past year, our daughter's father has been spending several hours every Friday afternoon with her. He describes himself as a father, but not a parent. He rarely reveals her identity to anyone except close friends, and names himself a friend of hers when others ask him how he is related. His role looks like that of an intimate family friend, and she calls him by his first name. When we decide to tell her he is her father, it will be after a cohesive plan to answer her questions can be developed, one we can all support. Despite the rational quality of our relationship and the closeness we all feel, we still own a certain amount of nervousness. We are aware that we are charting new territory and remain confident that we will be able to navigate together.

In many ways, our lives as lesbian parents have been accepted by others more easily than we had expected. We were nervous about Rachel's public school colleagues and their reaction to the change in our family, and wondered if Rachel would be accorded the same treatment other members of the department received when their babies were born. Nancy worked briefly at the school, was well-known to the staff, and was regularly invited to social events, so it made sense that she would continue to attend functions during her pregnancy. While no one ever asked directly, people were able to respond to the sense of family we were projecting. Other teachers often asked Rachel how Nancy was doing, and some even sent clothing outgrown by their children. We were delighted when a surprise baby shower was held. Teachers continue to ask Rachel how the family is doing and, again without an explanation from us, we recently received an invitation to another baby shower which included a special note to "please bring your family." We have learned that our easy acceptance and confident projection of family goes a long way in enabling other people to react with the same acceptance.

Our lifestyle as a lesbian family on our traditional family-oriented block was another source of concern. Time has led us to conclude that some people are either unaware of our differences, don't care, or look for the areas where our lives are similar and find topics of conversation that we can easily share. With our next door neighbors, for example, the conversation centers around our young children and how parenting and working for a living affects our lives. To this day, we think they believe we are sisters and that Rachel is the biological mother!

We feel as though our life as a family moves in spirals, ranging from problem-solving beyond any level we have known before to the most exquisite moments of peace and joy. There are times when stroking our daughter's hair evokes deepest sensations of awe and wonder. There are times when one of us knows that if we don't immediately leave the room, the anger and resulting lack of control may cause us to do something we will regret. Parenting is physically and emotionally exhausting work. We live in a culture which provides few real supports in flexible time off from work, adequate and affordable day care, and other services which parents and those close to young people require. We have been able, in lucid moments, to recognize this and attempt to remedy the situation in creative ways.

We have received support from lesbian and straight friends who do not have children and yet want to be involved in the life of a young person. Several women in our community have felt a strong sense of connection with our daughter, and since her birth, five lesbian women have spent weekly time with her. Currently, one lesbian couple spends an evening a week with our daughter; other friends share time occasionally as their schedules allow. While their doing so gives us the freedom to do things either alone or together, it is important to emphasize that they don't spend time with her to help us, but because they feel it is important for their own growth to develop relationships with her.

In addition, she has several wonderfully playful and caring men in her life who see her regularly. While appropriate male models are important for the growth and development of all children, these men are important to her because she chose to accept what they can offer her and not because we orchestrated their involvement.

We are frequently asked our feelings about what her sexual preference will be. The developmental process whereby one becomes aware of sexual preference is complex and not completely understood. We are ourselves daughters of heterosexual parents, which leads us to believe that the orientation of one's parents is not the most important factor in one's sexual choices. What we wish for her are fulfilling, mutually satisfying relationships with anyone she chooses.

While daily life for lesbian parents presents problems not all parents have to face, dealing openly with sexual differences and with the effects of prejudice can bring a closeness to family interactions. We expect to tackle discussions for which there are no precedents or models and hope that we can stay clear of the traditional "parents know best" stance and together be able to discuss possibilities and dilemmas in a spirit of mutual respect. Our daughter will grow up being familiar with a wider range of human expression than either of us knew. This cannot help but enhance the possibilities for her own relationships.

Excitement about language development, toilet training, and elaborate bedtime rituals now occupy a large part of our lives together. At times, we feel torn between two worlds. Many of our contacts are with heterosexual single parents or couples with other small children. We have earnest discussions of appropriate footwear, sleeping patterns, and how long to continue breast feeding. We are clearly not an integral part of that world and find an important element in our lives missing when we are with these straight parents. Gatherings of lesbian friends provide an atmosphere of trust and open sharing, and is certainly the world in which we feel our power as women-identified women. Since most dances and other cultural activities occur too late at night for us to find a sitter (assuming we were not already too exhausted), and the concentration required for an in-depth political discussion is not always possible with a young child present, and the forethought necessary to locate a sitter in order to have such "spontaneous" discussions sometimes eludes us, at times we feel not totally a part of this world we so love.

Even with the added support our family of friends can give to us, we are often exhausted or feel alienated and alone in our choice to parent. Parenting is like that—a completely mixed bag from high to low and back up again. We look forward to a time when we can be spontaneously sexual again, and when we can sleep long into the morning curled around one another. Still, we would never change the choice we made to become parents. Our daughter—a distinct personality all her own, full of unique charm and wonder, intelligence and delight—brings a richness and challenge to our lives that cannot leave us unchanged. Our life together shall continue to grow and expand in ways we have yet to imagine.

Gay Parenting, Or, Look Out, Anita

Pat Parker

Five years ago, my lover Marty and I decided we wanted to raise a child together. This in itself did not seem so earthshaking, and it wasn't. It was complicated by the fact that we are both women. It shouldn't have been, but it was.

The first discussions evolved around the process. How do we get a child? I have long been an advocate of adoption. It seems logical to me that you take a child who needs a parent and a parent who wants a child and make two people happy. However, we had to look at reality. The chances of us getting a healthy infant through the state adoption system, even in the reputedly liberal state of California, was not going to be easy. I had once been warned by a lesbian friend in a position of power in the organization to go into the closet if I wanted to become a "Big Sister." Now my closet door has no key; it's impossible for me to go lock myself in it. We decided that the logical decision was for one of us to become pregnant and have the child.

At the time, I was thirty-eight years old and worked full-time as director of the Oakland Feminist Women's Health Center, as well as being a writer and a performer. Many of the staff at the health center had had children recently. So many, in fact, that we set up a child-care center in the building. That way, our staff could still bring their babies to work but not have them crawling all over the place. Having a baby would clearly not interfere with my job at the clinic. However, the image of myself appearing pregnant on stage did not appeal to me. In fact, the image of me appearing pregnant anywhere did not appeal to me, and the prospect of the childbirth was downright unattractive.

So, it seemed Marty would be the candidate for birthing. Unfortunately, that also presented a problem. Marty is a journeywoman roofer. No way was she going to be climbing ladders with eighty-pound sacks, pregnant. We calculated when the rainy or off-season for roofers would be, and then calculated when she would need to conceive to deliver during that time. Of course, lingering in the back of both of our minds was the realization that with conception, no one has any guarantees.

The next consideration was race. I am Black; Marty is white. I was already coparenting an all-white child with an ex-lover, and I definitely wanted this child to be at least half-Black. At the same time, I had to consider the possibility that if I died, the raising of the child would be left to Marty.

In recent years, I have seen several white women raising half-Black children white. I definitely wanted no part of that phenomenon. Would Marty be able to raise our child and give her a sense not only of culture, but also of identity, without me? Marty is a feminist. She knows and understands oppression, and dealing with racism is a constant part of her political process. She could, and more importantly would, raise our child with political consciousness.

The next question was, "Who's going to be the biological father?" This presented problems. We definitely wanted to raise this child. We did not want to find ourselves in court a year or two later fighting the biological father because he decided he wanted to be a parent. And we were both too feminist to simply have Marty go out and pick up some stranger.

Fortunately, the health center had started the Northern California Sperm Bank, which has a donor insemination program as one of its components. Marty and I would be able to go to the sperm bank as a couple, screen the donor catalog, and pick a donor. I could be present at the insemination or do it myself. This solved the legal problem of having the birth father turn up later in our lives and eliminated the concern about the health of the biological father. The sperm bank extensively screens their donors. A donor being accepted would mean we would not only have a complete past medical history, but current screening for AIDS, gonorrhea, and a host of other illnesses and diseases. Plus we would be able to pick a donor as near as possible to my physical characteristics. The combination of feminism with modern technology is awesome.

All that was needed now was to register with the sperm bank, go through the orientation program, and wait for the right time to begin insemination. While Marty was willing to be the birth mother, she had no overwhelming desire to experience the "miracle of childbirth." It simply seemed the best way to accomplish our goal. But the goddess was watching out for us.

In January 1983, I received a call from a woman who runs a private adoption agency. She had a sixteen-year-old Black woman who was almost seven months pregnant, and she had no Black couples on her waiting list. She wanted to know if our health center knew of any couples. I knew for sure of me. I told the woman I would call her back.

Marty then gets an excited me saying, "There's this sixteen-year-old, pregnant, Black, wants to give the child up but needs to live with the adoptive parents until she delivers because no one knows she's pregnant except her mother and what do you think? Yeah, right."

Marty thought. "Yeah."

I called back the adoption agency and told the counselor to see if the young woman was interested in a single parent adoption. At that time, two people of the same sex couldn't adopt a child in California. The report came back,

"Fine," and arrangements were made for Marty and me to meet with the birth mother (who I'll call Mary) and her mother (who I'll call Jane) to decide if she would be comfortable living with us and if we would be comfortable having her live with us.

Now, if you want to put your house in order, adopt a child. Walls were painted; floors were stripped, stained, and verithaned, and new curtains bought. All the things you say you are going to do someday get done.

Mary and Jane came to our house. My stereotypical fears about the "fast" teen-ager were quickly dismissed. Mary was a sweet kid. She was a quiet, bright girl, who unfortunately succumbed to peer pressure and got caught. When the adoption counselor had told me about them, I admit I was skeptical about Mom. How do you have a six-month pregnant daughter and not notice? Jane worked at night and was unaware of Mary's condition until it was too late for her to have an abortion. This was aided by the fact that at six months pregnant, Jane weighed 105 pounds. I took her to buy maternity clothes, and they practically laughed us out of the store. The smallest size they had hung on her. She went through her entire pregnancy in her regular jeans with the top two buttons undone. Jane was very supportive of her daughter. She allowed her to make the decision whether or not to raise her baby.

Living with Mary was an incredible experience. Marty and I were elated over the fact that we were soon going to have our baby, and yet at the same time we had to be sensitive to Mary's feelings. So things were kept low-keyed for the most part. At the same time, we were living with a teen-ager. I discovered a whole new set of television shows, learned that I hate rap music, and finally put my foot down on going to horror movies. Anastasia (our daughter) is almost four-years old, and Marty still talks about those movies.

Most of our conversations were about Mary's future, her present studies (we had a tutor come in to prevent her from falling behind), how she was going to handle her peer group when she returned to school, and what her plans were for college.

At the same time, we needed to be realistic. In a short amount of time, Mary was going to have a baby. I took her to the obstetrician, had one of the birthing counselors from the health center come over and instruct her in prenatal exercises, labor, and delivery. I also managed to convince her that even though hamburgers, french fries, and Coke tasted good, there were other foods. By the time Mary left our house, she was converted to lobster, crab, and pinochle.

Finally, the time came. After one episode of Braxton-Hicks contractions (false labor), Mary was ready to deliver our baby. The physician (one of our health center doctors) had prearranged everything with the hospital; so off went Mary, Jane, Marty, and I for the delivery. The nurses weren't quite sure how to handle the situation, but they did well.

No matter how much preparation, education, and counseling, sixteen-year-old children are not ready for childbirth. Having babies hurt, and watching Jane watch her baby have a baby, was not easy. Marty coached Jane, and I coached Mary, and Anastasia (Stasia for short) was born. Following the delivery, we moved Mary off the maternity ward to a private room, and for the next three days postdelivery, I went to the hospital and fed Anastasia at 2:00, 6:00, and 10:00 a.m. and p.m. I was tired and bleary-eyed, but very happy.

In three days, Mary went home to Jane, and Anastasia came home to us. Jane brought us flowers and wished us well with our new baby. We were parents.

Even in private adoptions, you must be approved by the State. We had a caseworker come to our home three times (usually it's two visits), and she visited Jane four times (usually it's one home visit and one office visit). This woman wanted to make sure that Jane knew she was giving up her child to a couple of lesbians, even if only my name appeared on the papers. She knew. After nine months of visits, the final papers were signed and the adoption was final.

In raising our child, we have had to do some serious consciousness-raising among family and friends. Anastasia was our child, neither mine alone nor Marty's alone. She has two mothers. One of Marty's sisters-in-law asked us, "What will she call you?" She seemed greatly relieved to know that neither of us would be called Daddy.

The family structure we utilized is not new. Extended families have always existed in Black culture. We simply modified it slightly. Marty's folks are her grandparents. My parents are dead. My ex-lover's parents (remember I'm coparenting another child) are also her grandparents. My other daughter is her sister. All brothers and sisters (Marty's and mine) are uncles and aunts and their siblings are cousins. In addition, she has one godmother (white) and two godfathers (Black).

This was not difficult to accomplish. We simply made it clear that anyone wishing to participate in this child's life had to accept the premise that she has two mothers. In her first three years, Anastasia has been to southern California to see my family several times, met her great-aunt from Texas, made two trips to Ohio (Marty's parents), one being a family reunion, and is watched regularly by her aunt in Berkeley (Marty's sister) and her aunt in Oakland (my ex-lover). Our biggest problem is making sure that we visit everyone fairly equally, given distance and cost considerations.

It's amazing. Relatives may not understand or be comfortable with lesbianism, but they do understand *baby*. A little over two years ago, we decided to buy a home in the suburbs. Stasia's grandfather's (Marty's father) concern was that there might be some racist or homophobe in the neighborhood who would try to cause harm to his grandchild. So to appease her father, Marty went around to all the houses on our block and informed the occupants that we were an interracial couple with two children, one white and one Black, and we were thinking about buying a house in their neighborhood, and if they had any problems with that to say so, please, before we bought the house. None of the neighbors seemed upset about our family structure, but a few did look at Marty strangely for a while.

Raising Stasia has not been uncomplicated, but I know for sure it has been easier than what my friends had to go through twenty years ago. We have the benefit of the civil rights movement, the gay liberation movement, and the feminist movement. We also have the advantage of both being women who spent a lot of time around children. There was no need for lessons to change diapers or prepare bottles. Anastasia's diaper was changed by whoever discovered it needed to be changed. Her late-night feeding was done by whoever was less tired. Since our work was equally important to both of us, it naturally evolved that if I needed to bring work home or was writing, Marty took care of Stasia and I, in turn, do the same. She's taken to the doctor for her check-ups by whoever can most easily get free.

Marty and I come from two different races, classes, and cultures, and we knew that at some point in time, we would disagree about how the other was dealing with Stasia. So we agreed before she was born to never criticize each other about how we were handling a situation with Anastasia in front of her. This was one of the lessons I learned from my ex-lover. It saves us. In addition to minimizing Anastasia's opportunity to play one of us against the other, it also means we constantly talk about rearing our child. She knows my ideas around childrearing. I know her ideas around childrearing.

Thousands of lesbians have reared children before us, and thousands will after us, but one major difference in Anastasia's life is that she is not being raised "heterosexual."

I've seen lesbians with their children who try to "out-straight" the straight folks. I know one woman whose daughter's entire wardrobe is pink. I've seen women allow their male children to go shirtless in hot weather, but not their daughters, with no discussion of male privilege. The girls get dolls; the boys get trucks. In our house, Anastasia gets almost everything. No war toys, guns, racist or sexist books allowed.

Most importantly, she gets positive images. She knows women can work on roofs and at computers. Women can cook and clean houses, cut yards and build fences. Women play chess and Scrabble; they also fish and play softball.

The learning doesn't just occur at home. We had to educate her teachers as well. She attends a Montessori school. We put her there because of their progressive reputation. They got it that she would get picked up by both of us; that the permission slip was signed by whoever remembered to do it; that potluck food was prepared by whoever had time. I still had to go to the school after her first Mother's Day there and make it clear that she came home with two Mother's Day gifts or none at all. They've learned that one, and I must give them credit. At least they had the good sense not to send her home with a Father's Day present.

Anastasia knows she has two mothers, and because of the changing familial structure in this country, she's not at all unusual. She has friends with one parent, two parents, three parents, and four parents. She doesn't have to fear that her playmates will ostracize her because her parents are lesbians. Many of her friends' parents are lesbians and gay men, and those who are not, know who she is and who we are. The only closets in our house hold clothes.

Anastasia will soon be four years old. She knows the difference between boys' bodies and girls' bodies. She knows that Marty is one race and I am another. She has no idea what sexual preference is, but she knows that her godfather Joe loves Julie, and her godfather Charles loves Pablo. She also knows that her mama Pat loves her mama Marty and they both love her. Her friends and loved ones are all races and classes.

We still have a long way to go in eliminating the things that oppress people in this society, but we are trying to change them, and we know that one of the ways to do this is to teach the children. The thing that is exciting about our child's life is that she is not alone in her learnings.

People, get ready! If you are racist, sexist, classist, or homophobic, my child is going to think you are strange.

A Baby For Adela

Rocky Gámez

One would think that after that dreadful episode with Rosita, Gloria would've learned her lesson. But the poor girl was incapable of learning from experience. Without giving her shattered psyche a chance to heal, she wanted to go through the same thing all over again.

I read her letter when I was back on campus the following fall and nearly wept from exasperation. In the sea of life, there was not a tub of hope for her. Right away, I put on my glasses and poised myself in front of the typewriter to tell her so.

"What is the matter with you, grandisíma animal?" I wrote. "Are you possessed or what?"

I couldn't understand, for the life of me, what it was that churned inside that heap of compost between her ears. How could a person spring back so fast from an emotional thrashing like the one she had received from Rosita and contemplate doing it all over again? That to me was not resilience; that was a case of sheer lunacy. But it was all there, spelled out for me in a dozen pages of ruled stationery:

I met a girl named Adela at the bus station in McAllen. She's from Reynosa but has a visa to come shopping in the U.S. It was love at first sight, and we hit it off behind Duffy's tavern which is a skip and a hop from where I met her. We are now living in my little cottage. Remember where I surrendered my virginity to that asshole I married when they kicked me out of junior high? Well, that's our love nest now.

Mother adores Adela, and I know you will love her too when you meet her. She is not anything like that devil Rosa Vásquez. So if you are sucking in your breath right now, forget it. Adela is sincere and honest. A little bit older than I, but who cares about age? She was still a virgin when I met her, but now she's preparing to be the mother of my baby. . . .

She didn't answer my letter. My guess was that she was too busy feathering her new nest to care what I thought about her latest venture. But when I went back to the Valley for the Christmas holidays, I saw her. She came over right away when I called her from the Shrine in San Juan where I had gone to give thanks to the Blessed Mother for helping me heal from the injuries of the accident the year before. I still couldn't get rid of my phobia of riding in a car, but I could walk now.

She was driving a pick-up, a grey affair that belonged to her new boss, the manager of a broom factory. She said she wasn't disemboweling cows at the slaughterhouse anymore; she was climbing up the economic ladder selling brooms door-to-door all over the area, from Rio Grande City to Brownsville, and meeting interesting people along the way. "It's a nice job," she said. "At least it's clean, and I don't have to go around like Dracula's tea bag all the time."

Gloria looked good and healthy, nothing like the old rag I had last seen when she was bemoaning the fact that Rosita had played her for a sucker. And she looked happy, too. Whatever had transpired in those three months had set very well with her. She even looked a little more feminine than her usual butchy self. She was wearing a brown wool cardigan sweater, women's chino pants, and penny loafers. Her hair was a little longer over the ears. Did I like her new look?

"Oh yes, Gloria," I replied. "But you don't look like Sal Mineo anymore. You look like Toña la Negra."

"Helps me sell more brooms though," she chuckled. "At least the housewives won't bolt their doors on me when they see me stomping up their driveway with my load of brooms."

Then I met her new love. She was sweeping dead leaves from the driveway when we pulled in. My estimation was that she was nudging forty, but I have never been a good judge of age, especially when the vestiges of wear and tear are hidden under several layers of make-up. She certainly was attractive, just as Gloria had said in her letter. She was swarthy and willowy, with a provocative walk that made me think she was swaying to the rhythm of a sultry tune only she could hear. If she had been a virgin until she got tangled with Gloria, she must've been wearing concrete calzones since she was five years old. But I kept the observation to myself. She welcomed me in a very friendly manner, and I was not about to embarrass Gloria with an off-the-wall comment. Gloria had already told her I was her best friend in the whole wide world, and I didn't want to shatter that illusion.

Adela had not only done wonders for Gloria, but had also put her magic touch to the cottage. They had renovated the dilapidated place, painted it white with cute blue shutters, seeded the dead lawn, and planted a variety of blooming plants around their little house as well as that of Gloria's mother, which was just across the driveway.

Despite the gusty winds of the first northerns of the season, the plants were still standing at attention, waving their petals under the waning sun. There were yellow calendulas, purple amaranths, vincas, and portulacas everywhere; white petunias, like little old ladies' panties, waving from wooden planters on the porch. I was touched by all the hard work they had put into the place to make it nice. My throat had never known a larger lump.

And right away, I felt ashamed of myself for the letter of reprimand I had sent Gloria from school.

Adela was a real woman, Gloria declared, nothing at all like that ungrateful dog Rosa. "Look at the house," she beamed when we went inside. "Don't all this work tell you something about a person? She even irons my socks!"

Adela sat there, rejoicing and plying a furious needle into a tablecloth she was embroidering in cross-stitches. I walked around the scaled-down rooms, touched by all this display of domesticity, looking at everything. It was nothing like the apartment Gloria had shared with Rosita. There were no mashed potatoes growing vines on the rug, no petrified chicken bones under the chairs or stacks of *True Confession* magazines littering the floors. Adela had the Betty Crocker Homemaking Award, in my estimation.

They even had my old oil paintings, all framed, on the walls: my fruit bowl still life in the kitchen, my Rio Grande Valley landscapes and the portrait of Gloria in her horrendous Eisenhower jacket graced the living room. There were bookshelves lining the walls, with real books on them—my entire collection of lesbian literature that I had not wanted my family to know I read: *Odd Girl Out, Shadow Of A Woman, Beebo Brinker, Journey To A Woman, The Price Of Salt, The Well Of Loneliness, Carol In A Thousand Cities, We, Too, Must Love*—all of them! And lording over all these books was an unfamiliar title which jumped at me as soon as my eye reached it: *How To Bring Up Your New Baby.*

Adela's head went, "Yes! Yes! Yes!" right away.

"All we need now is the pattering of tiny feet on the brand new rug," Gloria chuckled, and snapped her fingers, cuing her sweetheart to run out to her mother's house next door and bring back some beers.

I sank into the chair she had left vacant. "And how are you going to accomplish that?" I was really curious. "Are you two contemplating adoption or kidnapping?"

"I'm going to get Adela pregnant," she chirped, quite sure of herself. When I rolled back my eyes, she added, "Oh, but it's not anything like you're thinking. I'm not stupid anymore. This time, I'm really going to get her pregnant. I have the ammunition all ready to go."

I didn't understand. "Ammunition? What kind of ammunition?"

"You know, goo. What guys carry in their balls."

"Oh! But how. . .?"

"One of those books I stored for you tells about a girl named Laura. . . ." She leaped out of her chair and ran her fingers over several of the titles, but she couldn't remember which it was. "Anyway, this Laura was injected with some of Jack's stuff, and they had a baby. We're thinking of doing it like that."

"That's fiction, Gloria. It's not easy to make a baby that way in real life."

"Why not? You told me once your father did it like that to the cows when he worked at the King Ranch. You said all he did was smear the selected bull's goo into the cow's *virginia*...."

"I said *vaginia* if I recall...," pronouncing it in Spanish.

"Whatever! Adela has one of those, too, I'm sure. And I already have selected the stuff from a guy I met when I was selling brooms in McAllen."

I wanted to explain to her that it took more than selected goo and a willing virginia to make a baby, just so she wouldn't be all brokenhearted later, but the front door opened suddenly and Adela appeared with two bottles of beer.

Gloria hissed an order for me to say no more. "This is no talk for a lady to hear. We'll talk some more when I take you home."

Later when she was driving me home, she said, "Look, it's no different from how my cousin Lola got pregnant. Remember Lola?"

To make the long story short: Lola was this gland case related to Gloria by her ill-fated marriage to the guy we called Balls. Lola was picking cotton one sweltering summer, somewhere in Falfurrias, Texas. On this particular day, Lola was exhausted from stooping over the rows of cotton and decided to go take a dip in a nearby canal. Unbeknown to the innocent girl, several men from the cotton-picking crew had done the same thing a few hours earlier. One had ejaculated into the stagnant water. Lola's contention was that as she took the plunge, the microscopic rascals were still alive and kicking, and the minute they sensed her unsuspecting snatch, they all swam for it. Everyone believed her, and so Lola's parents opted not to throw her out of the house for ruining the family name, but bore the shame of the whole thing like understanding folks.

"Lola was pretty clever, wasn't she? Even *I* believed that when I was younger. But remember, Gloria, she had three other kids before she got married. How do you explain that, huh?"

She couldn't. She laid the blame on God, because it is He who gives babies, and right away changed the subject.

"Do you remember how your dad did it to the cows?" she wanted to know.

"My father assisted the veterinarian; he didn't inseminate cattle all by himself. And he never let me take a peek because I was always very squeamish."

"¡Ay, qué la chingada!" she lamented. "Here I was hoping you'd teach me how. And I've already paid for it. Damn it, Rocky!"

"I'm sorry. But tell me, Gloria, who's this generous soul you're talking about? When can I meet him?"

She turned the truck north on Highway 281, taking the frontage road toward McAllen to avoid the heavy traffic of Christmas shoppers. "His name is

Moctezuma, but I call him Alby for short 'cause he's one of those white albino people. It don't matter though. A baby is a baby, whether it's black, white, chartreuse, or even polka dot. Gimme that lipstick from the glove compartment."

She did a quick job of painting her lips a putrid purple and giggled. "Alby works for his aunt in her restaurant, the Magic Cocina. Guadalupe doesn't know he's queer, so I don't want to show up too butch at her place, know what I mean? Fluff your hair a little and put on some of this lipstick, too. Alby don't want to look guilty by association. A lot of macho men eat in the Cocina."

The evening had turned gustier and colder. We couldn't find a parking space anywhere on 17th Street where the restaurant was located, so we drove back several blocks and parked behind Duffy's tavern, where Gloria pointed out the exact spot Adela had surrendered her virginity to her. Gloria knew the owner well, and said it was a redneck bar but catered to jotos if they weren't too overtly nelly. A few old gringa dykes that passed as rodeo cowgirls went in to play pool regularly, but they were too prejudiced to talk to Mexicans, so it was best to ignore them.

Guadalupe's Magic Cocina was practically deserted. Every other cantina on the block was jumping with Mexican raucous polkas and drunk noises, but the Cocina was as silent and dim as a tomb. Business must've been very slow that day because the minute we set foot inside the cavernous room, a corpulent woman with lots of gold teeth came rushing at us like a tidal wave, sucking us in.

It was Guadalupe herself. "¡Entren mis amigas!" She greeted us in Spanish. "Come on in! This is the place to eat well."

She only had one customer, a wizened old drunk who was trying to harpoon the few beans he had left on his plate but wasn't being very successful. At the far end of the counter, a bored-looking waitress was absorbed in a comic book. She glanced up once and then, dispassionately, returned her attention to the book. Gloria went ape-shit the minute she saw her; started strutting in her shiny penny loafers like a peacock wanting to score, until she remembered that Moctezuma had cautioned her against cruising the place. It was out of respect to his aunt who didn't have the slightest suspicion about him. Gloria stopped dead in her tracks and told Guadalupe we were there to see her nephew.

Guadalupe waddled across the floor and disappeared into the dark kitchen, where a solitary bulb hanging from the ceiling was making a herculean effort to shed light on the place. "I get him for you," she said in English. "You sit down and wait. My place is your place."

It took forever and two extra days of waiting. The old drunk, meanwhile, discontinued piercing his beans and began leering at us. He must've been desperate for companionship and saw Gloria and me as his last chance. The wind had tossed my hair into a bird's nest, and the purple lipstick made me look whory, but the drunk's piggy eyes thought I was positively alluring.

I was trying to change my image on the wall mirror when all of a sudden odd music came from the direction where Guadalupe had disappeared. It took me a few seconds to put it together with what I had learned in my music appreciation class at Pan American College. It was Ravel's *Bolero*.

Out of the darkened cave of the kitchen walked the strangest apparition I had ever seen. Luckily Fellini was nowhere near Guadalupe's Cocina. He would've drooled on the spot at the sight of a gangly albino dressed in white pants and T-shirt, playing a black clarinet, and moving like an upright snake; movements which I thought were very well rehearsed. He slithered in, undulating provocatively, slowly, and went around the tables half a dozen times.

Guadalupe stood behind, leaning against the silent jukebox and glowing with pride at her nephew. The bored waitress looked up and rolled her eyes, as if to say, "Ay Dios de mi vida, do I have to see this shit all over again?"

The old drunk knitted his brow. "¡Maricón! ¡Pinche joto!" he muttered, tossing the fork on the table. He shuffled out the door muttering other obscenities.

I watched the skinny white boy in total fascination. He moved better than Adela and her provocative sway. I couldn't understand how Lupe's alert eyes had missed that beat, how she couldn't see her nephew's persuasion through all that nellyness he was displaying.

When he finished his routine, Gloria introduced him to me, and later, when Guadalupe gave up hoping for customers, Moctezuma changed into a macho cowboy ensemble—Stetson hat and Tony Lamas boots—and we went to Duffy's where Gloria had parked the truck.

He was all in favor of donating his sperm. They talked about it in low whispers in the darkest corner of the bar, where two very sullen gringa dykes in tight blue jeans and cowboy shirts were playing pool and swearing up a hurricane every time they missed a shot.

I was like Alice in Wonderland. It was the first time I had seen other gays besides Gloria. In the Valley, overt homosexuals were as rare as wings on donkeys. I couldn't keep my eyes off Moctezuma and his exaggerated feminine mannerisms, the way he clipped his words and pursed his lips, and the girlish way he squealed at the thought of having a baby. He was like a different species to me, someone from another world.

Gloria said there were thousands like him all over the Valley, but they were all closeted because of the shitty attitude of the people of the area. Anglos and Mexicans were alike in their intolerance of gays. But she had met zillions of them on her broom-selling route, especially in Rio Grande City where Moctezuma came from.

Neither he nor Gloria could stop talking about the advent of the child. By the time we left him, they had already baptized the kid and sent him to school.

"What if it turns out to be a girl?" I dared to ask.

"Oh, shut up your mouth, Agatha!" Moctezuma slapped my shoulder playfully. "Who's talking to *your* ass?"

The auspicious date of the insemination was going to be in a few days, when Adela was finished with her period.

On Christmas Eve, Gloria came honking her grey vehicle in front of the house. It was a very foggy night. The barrio was decorated top to bottom with Christmas decorations. The carillón from the church was playing the "Ave Maria," and the smell of the traditional tamales filled the air.

I ran out of the house with my trench coat flapping behind me before Mama threw a fit because I was seeing Gloria again. She had a bottle of brandy Presidente with her in the truck. We toasted to everything we held sacred.

"I hope it won't take very long, Gloria," I said. "Mama wants me to take her to Midnight Mass tonight."

It was only nine o'clock. "It won't take long," she said. "I'll get you back in time to recite three complete rosaries and then go to Mass."

Moctezuma was going to wait for us in the restaurant. She held up an empty little jar of French's mustard for me to see where we would be transporting the precious cargo. "Adela is all ready for it."

I had never seen Gloria as happy as she was that night except, perhaps, when she came barreling down the street that other time to tell me she had made Rosita pregnant.

On the way to the Magic Cocina in McAllen, she turned on the radio and caught the tail end of "O Holy Night" that the Mormon Tabernacle Choir was singing. She let out a powerful contralto to join them.

Her joy, however, was quickly dissipated. When we sailed into the Cocina hoping to see Moctezuma there, we found Guadalupe instead. She was at the counter, holding her jaw in her hands, and looking dejected. "Moctezuma not here," she said in English. "He say he sick, but maybe he lied."

Gloria's face turned mournful. I ran out the door after her. For someone with such short legs, she could sure move fast. Her penny loafers were a blur under her, like those of a roadrunner in hot pursuit. "He's probably at Duffy's having a drink," she said. The sidewalk was dark and damp. We were the only ones walking. I could hear our footsteps echoing all the way behind us.

Moctezuma was not at Duffy's. Neither the bartender nor anyone she asked had seen him. Gloria suggested sitting there for a couple of drinks, hoping that he'd show up to keep his commitment, but after half an hour, Gloria began to bristle. Her eyes kept darting to the door every time someone came in.

We strode back to the Cocina in silence. Guadalupe was very hesitant about telling us where she and Moctezuma lived. She acted as though she thought we wanted to do him great bodily harm. Gloria had to lie to her and say she wanted to pay him some money she owed him. Finally, Guadalupe gave us some half-assed directions on how to get to El Granjeno.

El Granjeno was a desolate little village in a bend of the river, below McAllen. I thought no one lived there since the days of the dinosaurs. We went out the door, trying to recall the hasty directions. The only thing I could remember later was that there was a Gulf filling station on a corner, and then we were to go around the block, and it was the first house next to an empty lot. Gloria couldn't even remember that. She was so upset that Moctezuma had stood her up.

We couldn't see very well because of the dense fog. The closer we got to the river, the thicker the fog got. We were going so slow, looking for any sign of civilization, that I soon began to worry about the time. It seemed like we had traveled enough miles to get ourselves close to Laredo, but Gloria said we were still skirting McAllen, traveling around in circles trying to find the river road.

"Maybe we should forget the whole thing, Gloria, and turn back. My stomach is beginning to quiver. I'm still afraid of riding in cars for very long."

She didn't respond. She just kept making pissed sounds with her teeth.

"Come on, Gloria, let's turn back!" I grabbed the flashlight from the dashboard and flashed it on my wrist. "It's ten-thirty! I need to get back to take Mama to Mass."

"Shut your snout, man! I'm thinking about that fucking albino. Do you think he might have skipped town on me after I paid him for his white goo?"

How the hell did I know? I didn't even know the boy.

The pick-up suddenly started bobbing up and down on the road. It felt like we were riding over a plowed field, and when I voiced my suspicion, Gloria got out and checked. I was right. Somehow we had come to a dead end and had kept on going into the field. She kicked the front tire with her femmy penny loafers, uttered a few nasty expletives, and jumped back into the truck, banging her fists on the steering wheel.

"Well, why in hell do you want to have a baby for, anyway?" I finally blurted out what I really felt about the whole sordid adventure.

"Why the hell don't you shut your snout like I tell you?"

"Because you're stupid, like I told you in the letter you never answered. Because you don't even know what the fuck you're doing."

"I want to perpetuate my existence just like everyone else. Is there any reason why I shouldn't? Oh, what do *you* know of these things? You don't even know how to love, you're letting your virginity go to seed. I want to perpetuate my life! Make living worthwhile."

"Then why the hell don't you get perpetuated like other women?"

I could feel her bristle, but she said no more. She put the pick-up in reverse, and we shot backward until we came to level land again. I was so angry with her, I could've slapped her silly.

We finally found the Gulf station and circled the block like Guadalupe had instructed. The front house was all dark, but there was a light in the back one. The only problem was that we couldn't get out of the truck because we had awakened a pack of dogs in Lupe's yard, and they were barking and snarling at us. We couldn't see where they were, but we could hear them warning us away.

Gloria rolled down the window and hollered Moctezuma's name several times. When he didn't respond, we crept in the darkness along the chain link fence, going around the house in front like a pair of burglars, stepping on litter and squishy things and God knows what else. "There must be an easier way than this to make a baby," I kept complaining.

"Shhh! Shut your snout, for heaven's sake! You wanna wake up the cows and the donkeys and the goats and the neighbors? Cheesus Criss! Pain in the ass, that's all you are."

We stopped by the window that was flooded with light and stood in the rectangle cast on the ground. Moctezuma was sitting at the table in the kitchen typing furiously. His white head looked like a turban under the bright glowing light. Gloria called out his name softly several times, and when she gave up hope that he would hear her low calling, she picked up a rock or a clod, whatever it was, and hurled it against the side of the house, making Moctezuma jump off the chair. She was so angry, I could feel the fumes rising out of her. "Call the dogs away from the gate, damn you!"

Moctezuma was not very happy to see us. Something was wrong with him. I could sense it the minute he opened the door for us and slammed it quickly after we went in. He was jittery, edgy, as though he had been expecting someone else. He sat back at the table and resumed his typing. Years later I was to learn that we had come in at the time he was typing a suicide letter to Guadalupe, but that's another story. Gloria pulled him up from the chair and tossed him against the kitchen sink.

"Gloria, I can't do it," he said. "I just got back from confession and I can't do it. The priest says this is a sin. Procreation should only be through married love. I'm sorry, I can't do it!"

"¡Ay, qué la chingada!" She raised her hands to her head. "But I paid you, you white sonofabitch. I paid you!"

"I'll pay you back, honest I will!" He kissed the cross he had made with his pink fingers. "As soon as Tia Guadalupe's business gets better. I promise."

"By that time Adela will have reached her menopause, you lying ghost." She grabbed him by the front of the T-shirt and shook him again.

"Leave him alone, Gloria!" I said, feeling sorry for him. "It's eleven o'clock. Let's go!"

Gloria didn't even hear me. She was as determined as a mongoose.

"Listen to what the nice lady says, Gloria," Moctezuma pleaded.

"Fuck the nice lady!" she said with clenched fists. "I want what I came to get and I want it *now*. I paid you for it, you sneaky ghost."

Whatever happened next between the two, I'll never know. The scene was getting too violent for my taste, and I decided to walk out. Gloria began to push Moctezuma into the bedroom, and he retaliated by pushing her back. I went out the back door, braving the dogs, and found my way back to the truck through the empty lot.

I helped myself to the brandy Presidente that was on the seat, smoked three or four of Gloria's Camel cigarettes, and waited in the freezing cold, accepting my responsibility for my half of this lunacy. She had not put a gun to my head to make me accompany her. I had come with her out of sheer boredom at home, as always.

About half an hour later as I was thinking about the funny ways in which life brings us to these situations, I heard the dogs barking again and I straightened myself up quickly.

Gloria came running out of the foggy empty lot and rapped on the window pane, urging me to open it.

"What's the matter?" I asked.

"I got it! I got it!" she said, handing me something in the darkness. "Don't drop it!"

She had left the empty mustard jar on the dashboard, and I couldn't tell what it was she was handing me though the window.

"It's a spoon, goddammit. Hold it! It's got the only goo I could scrape off the sheets."

"Get that thing away from me!"

"You wanna drive while I hold it?"

"You know I can't drive anymore, Gloria."

I ended up holding the spoon because I had no other choice. It was now eleven-thirty, and in half an hour the Mass would be starting. I had visions of Mama pacing the floor, all worried about me.

Gloria backed up the truck and assured me she could make it in thirty minutes. Moctezuma had told her that the sperm had a very short life, so she wanted to get it home before it would be ineffective. She drove down the foggy road like a madwoman, despite the fact that I told her my phobia was creeping all over my spine like an army of fire ants. She had both hands on the steering wheel, guiding the truck like a mechanical phallus on the way to the awaiting Adela, a vision of whose reclining figure, like Goya's naked Maja, passed before my eyes.

I was so scared we would hit some meandering cow on the road and kill ourselves, but there was no way to make her listen to me. She was as determined as a salmon braving the upstream current. "Hold on, Rocks, just hold on! And don't spill a drop or I'll beat you unconscious."

Out of the blanket of fog came the sound of a siren, and we both turned to look at each other right away. There was no other vehicle on the road but Gloria's pick-up. "What am I going to do with this?" I asked her.

"Let me think," she said, making disgusted noises with her teeth.

The highway patrol car was right behind us, the red light blinking and twirling.

"What do I do with it?" I screamed at her. "Tell me you stupid morphidite!"

She swerved off the road abruptly when the patrol car pulled parallel to the truck, and went sliding into an open culvert. I was hurled onto the door and had to grab the door handle to keep from falling out.

"You dropped it, stupid! You dropped it!" she cried, as the goo slid off slowly from the dashboard.

When the big burly policeman approached her window asking what was our hurry, she cleared her throat and said, "Oh, I'm just trying to get my friend here to Midnight Mass, sir, that's all."

"Seems to me you were trying to get the both of you to the morgue," he drawled. "It's too dangerous to be speeding in the fog." He wrote her a speeding ticket and drove behind us until we came to the big highway.

Neither one of us said a word until she asked me if I wanted her to drop me at home or at the church. I chose the church since my house was all dark by now. I rolled up my pants and buttoned the trench coat all the way to my neck and got out of the truck, tying the belt in a knot in front of me.

Halfway across the damp street I heard her call me and I turned around.

"Tell Jesus Merry Christmas for me."

"Why don't you come in too? It'll do you good."

"Naw, I have a feeling God don't love me too much tonight. I'd rather be with Adela. Pray for me!"

I ran into the church, searching the crowd inside for my mother, wondering what excuse I was going to give her for my long delay. And hoping, really, hoping, that God would descend at the consecration of the Host with a wonderful sense of humor.

Mothers By Insemination: Interviews
Kate Hill

*Artificial Insemination by Donor (AID) as a technique for becoming preg-
nant is increasingly popular among lesbians who want to conceive without
having sex with a man. These women question society's assumption that
sex and procreation must necessarily accompany one another. By choosing
when and with whom we experience parenting, we place the power of reproduction in the hands of women and challenge the core of compulsory heterosexuality. Lesbian mothers of inseminated children have made conscious
decisions to become parents. The process involves months of careful planning and coordinating, and when conception occurs there is a commitment
to parenting that may not be present between heterosexual parents who conceive by accident or in order to conform to societal pressure.*

Jackie And Christine

*Jackie and Christine had been together for five years when they decided
to have a child. They both had always wanted children, but did not know
how to get pregnant without having sex with a man, which neither was willing to do. They eventually found information on AID and began inseminat-
ing soon after with sperm from the Cryo Sperm Bank in Los Angeles. Jackie
was pregnant in three months. At the time of this interview, their son, Jonathan, was four months old. Jackie had gone back to work full-time.*

How do your families/parents feel about Jonathan?
Chris: My parents' biggest disappointment about my being gay was that
I would never be able to have children. Now that Jonathan is here, they're
thrilled.
Jackie: I come from a Spanish family, where the roles are very traditional.
Women always stayed home and took care of the kids. But when Jonathan
was born, they were really excited, and they've been closely involved in our
lives ever since.

Does everybody in your family know how Jonathan was conceived?
Jackie: No, only one person outside my immediate family knows.
Chris: They think she just went out and got pregnant by accident. That's

really humiliating for us and especially hard for Jackie.

Jackie: We just wish people knew it wasn't a mistake and that we're not sorry. My mom told me about a friend of hers saying, "Oh, Nancy, I'm really sorry." I asked my mom if she knew how that made me feel, to be portrayed that way, but it's easier for them than telling the whole story, so they don't say anything.

It's been really hard for me to let go of what people are thinking. There is definitely an element of secrecy around Jonathan in my family. But I told my parents they should deal with it in whatever way was most comfortable for them. I don't see the other relatives very much, and even though I'd rather they knew the truth, my parents are the ones who have to deal with them, not me.

What did you think about lesbians having children when you first came out?
Jackie: I thought we couldn't. I remember saying to a pregnant friend of mine at work that I wished Chris and I could have children. She said she'd talk to her OB about it. I thought she was kidding. She came back and said she'd talked to her doctor, who said, "Tell your friends to come in and I'll tell them their options." That's how everything got started.

I always wanted to have children, but I never saw myself married to a man, which I couldn't quite understand at the time. We talked about it for years, and finally I said I'm really tired of talking. I want to start our family. I was ready to have children.

We asked the doctor how we would do it, and she told us about the Oakland Sperm Bank and said we could drive up there. I said no, I wanted to do it here. They were a little ruffled since they'd never done inseminations in their office before. They agreed to do it, and we started immediately. We didn't want a known donor because we didn't want a third party involved in our lives, so we chose the sperm bank.

Chris: We talked about it a lot, wondered whether the child might want a father. It was more important that we not have to deal with a third party intruding on our lives.

How many kids are you thinking about having?
Jackie: We're thinking about three. Chris will have the next one. We are reserving sperm from the same donor for the next insemination. It's important to me that the children be related by blood.

We're wondering when we have the next baby how both sides will react, if my parents will be as excited as they are about Jonathan and as committed to the second child. I feel like if they were to show preference for Jonathan over the next baby, I would back off from them. It's not fair to the kids. We're as much a family as my brothers and their wives and kids.

What do you plan to tell Jonathan about how he got here?
Jackie: We're going to tell him the truth. The main thing is that we wanted him and we love him very much. We went through a lot to have him, and he is a very wanted child.

What are your roles in caring for Jonathan?
Chris: At first, after he was born, I felt a little bit insecure, not being the primary mom. It was hard for me. I'd always thought I'd be the biological mom because I had more experience with kids. I had all of these preconceived ideas that I'd never talked about. It really bothered me, I guess, and I got really critical of everything Jackie was doing. There was some friction there, but I didn't know what was wrong.
Jackie: So I sat her down one day and said, "Something is not right." I thought I was being really negligent with her and that's what she was upset about. After it was out in the open, I put myself in her shoes and I thought I would have felt the same way.
Chris: We've talked about it, and it really feels like we're both moms. We don't want a big distinction between us.
Jackie: Chris spends more time with him now since I've gone back to work full-time. Sometimes I feel like she's actually closer to him than I am. If he's really upset, she can calm him down better than I can.
Chris: That's what she thinks. I always feel like she's better at soothing him than I am.

Chris, do you think that it's because of her biological connection to him? Does that create or reinforce any insecurities you have?
Chris: Yes, I do think it's part of it. I'll be honest about it, I have some doubts/worries about how he'll deal with us both being mom. So it's really important for us that he knows we both love him and that we be caring parents. I don't really know how it will work out.
Jackie: It's harder being two moms than a mother and a father. There's a definite connection with the biological mom. How can there not be? I think I try to deny it because I really don't want there to be a preference. I don't want that kind of split.
Chris: There will be preferences. Kids prefer different people for different things, and that's normal. I think because we (comothers) don't have that biological connection, we're more sensitive to preferences, and it's hard to remember sometimes that it's O.K. It doesn't mean they don't love us.

I think one thing that has helped us keep a balance is that even though Jackie wanted to nurse, it didn't work out for various reasons. So we've both fed him and had that close connection that I would have been excluded from if she had nursed him.

Jackie: We're thinking about doing bottle feedings for the second baby also. Even though I think there's nothing better than breast-feeding for a baby, I really think it was important that she and Jonathan had that time to bond.

Has having a boy child affected your friendships with other lesbians? Have you encountered any issues around separatism?

Jackie: The only comments we've gotten are that we need to incorporate more men in our lives now that we have a boy. Our friends are fine about the fact that we had a boy. We aren't political at all, and we don't have any friends who are separatists. It hasn't been an issue at all.

One of my straight friends at work said something about us raising him to be gay, like because we were gay, Jonathan would also turn out gay. And I said, "Well, both my parents were straight and look how that turned out!"

How has the transition been for you from couple to family of three? Has there been much stress around the transition?

Chris: For me, at the beginning, it felt pretty stressful with school and work and a new baby, but it's gradually worked into a routine.

Jackie: I don't see it as stress, but I don't have the pressures of school with deadlines and homework and a job also. I have deadlines at work, but I'm used to those after so many years. As the responsibility increases, I feel like I adjust to it.

Chris: He's more of a highlight to both of our lives than a stress. We can't wait to get home from work every day. It's so exciting. Sometimes we fight over who gets to play with him! We really complement each other where taking care of Jonathan is concerned. If one of us is exhausted from working, the other steps in. It flows really well.

Jackie: We never had set roles for chores and things. Just recently we sat down and figured out who wanted to do what to take the pressure off a little, but we're pretty flexible.

Chris: Jackie has a ritual with Jonathan at night. She really wants to put him to bed; it's important to her her, since she doesn't get to see him as much during the day. I love to get up first thing in the morning and be with him; that's my ritual. There are some things we each have natural inclinations to do.

How have you dealt with the idea of role models for Jonathan when he gets older?

Jackie: Although people tell us we should incorporate more men into our lives, we think it's not that easy. You can't make a relationship just around the child if you don't have a relationship existing already. What do kids really need?

Chris: I guess I feel like we don't really know how important it is. I think all of us (lesbians raising boys) will have doubts, but we'll just have to help our kids grow up stable and happy and love them the best we can.

Sarah

Sarah had been involved with Jean for just a few months when she realized she wanted to have a child. With Jean's support, they began the process of insemination soon after. They chose to do home inseminations rather than use a sperm bank because they wanted to know their donors and their individual qualities rather than choose from a list of characteristics. They used several donors, alternating them throughout the month to make the identity of the biological father unclear. It took thirteen months for Sarah to become pregnant. At the time of this interview, their daughter, Megan, was three years old.

How do you and Jean share parenting Megan?
Sarah: In the very beginning, when I was trying to recover from a difficult labor and a Caesarian, I think Jean was actually closer to Megan than I was. I was so out of it, trying to recover from the birth. I can remember going into the delivery room, knowing that I was going to have major surgery, and saying to Jean, "Don't worry about me. I'll be fine. I have doctors and nurses to take care of me. Be with the baby." And she was. By the time I came out of the anesthetic and opened my eyes, I was the stranger. Jean was there and had her thing with Megan, and they were already completely with each other. I remember looking up and thinking, "Oh, thank god, they've got it under control. They're fine. I'm going back under the anesthetic and I'll see you later."

The older Megan got, the more I came to rely on Jean's relationship with her to bring balance to the family unit. I needed it. I needed the break. I needed to trust her, and then very quickly it got to be more and more equal. If Megan's really sick, I won't make a decision without Jean, like whether or not she should go to the doctor, get medication, etc.

Did you always want to have children?
Sarah: When I was an adolescent, I really wanted children. I loved to babysit, would pay people to let me babysit. The most exciting thing I could think of was to have a baby in my arms. I always envisioned myself having lots of children. The problem was, I never envisioned myself having a husband. Even when I was seven or eight, there was no husband in my fantasies of grown-up life.

Then when I was nineteen I came out. I didn't think that having children was an option for me anymore. As I began to accept my lifestyle, I think I stuffed the desire to have children.

When did that change?
Sarah: I was twenty-nine when I realized I really wanted to have a child. Jean was forty-two and we were falling in love, beginning to understand ourselves as a couple.

Jean had always thought she would have children, even though she didn't know how she was going to do it. But she didn't feel quite ready. She had the typical "husband" reaction of "That's a great idea, but not yet, honey. We don't have enough money, our house isn't big enough, I'm not quite launched on my career yet. . . ." So I was the driving force behind the initial decision, but the further along we got in the process of trying to conceive, which took us a year, the more committed she became. In fact, in the end she took over that process. After about ten months of trying to conceive, I gave up. I said, "I can't handle this anymore. I'm just hanging around waiting to get pregnant. Every time I get my period, I'm totally devastated. I've got to get on with my life." And Jean said, "O.K., fine. You can feel that way, but will you let me take over? Will you let me inseminate you once a month?" It was a shock to me. All of a sudden I realized how committed she was to the process.

How did you choose the kind of donor you wanted, and what were your reasons behind your choice?
Sarah: When I first acknowledged I wanted to have a child, I felt totally at a loss. It was the biggest problem I'd ever faced. I thought, "How in the world am I going to do that?"

I realized that I had a great deal of guilt, that I thought children should be conceived in the biological fashion. Obviously men have sperm and women have eggs, and the two are supposed to get together and bond and have children, and if you don't do it that way, you don't deserve to have a child. So my initial reaction was that in order to get pregnant, I would have to sleep with a man. And somehow that would make it O.K. if I could open myself to that experience. I discussed it with Jean, and she was willing to have me do that. What I did was approach two men I knew and loved very much, who Jean and I both felt would be suitable donors. Both of them, for two different and very good reasons, said they supported me in what I wanted to do, wished they could help, but didn't feel it would be for them.

In trying to resolve that whole thing of thinking I had to sleep with a man, I started drinking a lot. Jean finally said to me, "Look, you're getting drunk all the time because you think that in order to do what you want most in the world, which is to have a child, you have to do something you can't do, something that isn't right for you. You've always ruled out donor insemination as something that's artificial, that isn't O.K. because it's not in the main, natural biological order of things. Perhaps you should think about it, because that may be the only way you can do what you want."

As soon as she said it, I felt like I'd had thirty thousand pounds lifted off my head. I stopped getting drunk and started to consider how to find a donor. And once I was in the process of insemination, I understod that all my negative judgments about it had been out of ignorance. Once I was doing it, I felt fine about it.

Jean and I used four donors, two of whom were gay and two of whom were straight. I ended up choosing people on a real instinctive level. It's almost like I had a chemical affinity for certain men. We ended up having four men that we felt great about.

What do you plan to tell Megan about her conception? Do you have any thoughts about her not knowing her biological other half?
Sarah: I tell Megan a donor story, which is actually what happened. I tell her there were four donors and how much we all wanted to make a child and how happy they were when I got pregnant. She met one of the donors recently, and I've never seen her so fascinated in all her life. She just kept watching him.

We hang out with a heterosexual couple for whom the daddy is the main caregiver. Whenever the girls are together, Megan starts saying, "Daddy, Daddy." It feels a little like a knife in my heart, but there are always going to be some drawbacks in an alternative family situation like this, and that's one of them. I know it's going to be hard in some cases for Megan, and that I may hurt a lot, and so will Jean, and that's just one of the things we're going to have to face. We're up against a harder situation. I've always planned to be completely honest with her, and we'll let her know who all of the donors were.

I think had I to do it again, I would look harder for a donor to be known as the father. We are in the process of trying to determine which one is the biological dad. If we can determine paternity with a blood test, and if the man is willing, I would like to use him as a known donor if I have another child.

Is it important for you to provide good male role models for Megan?
Sarah: When I was pregnant, I thought I was going to have a boy, and I went through this incredible guilt trip. I thought, "Who's going to teach him carpentry and skiing and fishing and camping?" And then I stopped and

thought, "Wait a minute. I'm a better carpenter, a better fisherman, and just as good a camper as most men I know.

When you were pregnant and thought you were carrying a boy child, did you anticipate any problems around separatism?
Sarah: Once a baby was already in my body, that level of love and commitment was so great that it completely superceded any notion of separatism for me. During my pregnancy, my peer group really shifted. I went back toward friends of mine who had been bisexual and were not married and having children, and heterosexual friends who I hadn't had much contact with. Now I'm coming back to a more gay-based circle of friends.

In some studies I've read, lesbian mothers have said they consider their mothering as more central to their lives than their sexuality, giving them a stronger bond with mothers in general, regardless of their sexual orientation. Do you feel more of an affinity with lesbian mothers, or have you had a more general connection with all mothers?
Sarah: That's a good question. I do think that the mother in me is a stronger identification than the lesbian in me. Mothering is even bigger than being a lesbian. I have to say that being a lesbian is still damn big—it's right up there with being a mother. I try to balance as much as I can. I have heterosexual mother friends, but at the same time I really need a gay identity and being around other lesbian mothers is crucial. We get together far too infrequently, but then it's hard to get together with any mother, let alone such a select group. I can't deny the lesbian part of me, and I have much more in common with other lesbian mothers than I do with other straight mothers.

I've noticed that when straight mothers find out my son has two moms, they are actually envious on some level: there are two people doing the job they often do alone. They seem to appreciate the benefits of two moms in ways I'd never anticipated.
Sarah: That's true. I also feel like I finally belong absolutely to the biggest club on earth. There's a sense of belonging to motherhood that I never thought I'd have. All of a sudden I'm good friends with my sister who's had children for years. I'm a good friend of my mother's. It's a very precious thing, and I value that belonging, but I am also a lesbian. That is still today a very tough minority to belong to, and I have to have a real strong peer group association with lesbians as well, or I would get lost.

Do you have a contract with Jean in the event that your relationship doesn't continue?

Sarah: We don't have a contract. We do have a verbal agreement. I told her when I was pregnant, and I still believe it, that I would honor whatever her real relationship was to this child. The fact of the matter is she's an equal parent like I am. I don't think that I'm the kind of person who could break up with her and not honor that. I mean she's the coparent, and if we divorce, we would have to work out timing and visitation. I think while Megan is small, I would want the bulk of time with her, but certainly Jean would go on being her parent. I think while she's young, I could provide a better home, make sure the meals were ready on time, that I was home and there were fresh cookies. I'm more like that than Jean is. I don't think that means I'm a better parent or Jean shouldn't have equal rights to Megan. It just means that at this point in our relationship, our roles are different.

Do you have will and guardianship papers?
Sarah: We don't have a formal will. We both have handwritten wills saying that in the event of my death, Megan goes to Jean, and in the event of her death, all of Jean's property goes to Megan. We've tried to work it out with our families to take care of any blocks that could arise. My family would only intervene if Megan was being abused, but I expect any family would do that. Where we get stuck is with what happens if both of us die. We don't have anyone else designated to take care of Megan; we need to do that.

How did wanting to have a child effect your being out as a lesbian?
Sarah: If anything, I went back into the closet a little more. Before, I didn't compromise my freedom to be gay and I was really willing to teach other people about gay rights. Then after Megan came, it wasn't just me at stake. I had to think about if I was going to bring down any unnecessary publicity on her, or any kind of hardship. It made me be more careful. I didn't really go back in the closet, but I'm more careful, and I'm not willing to get in trouble or put myself under the public eye or take on conflict that might make her life harder. There is something I love more than my own freedom, and that's her.

Two Moms, Two Kids: An Interview

Sandra Pollack

Beth and Michele had been together for twelve years when they both be-
came pregnant. Their children are eleven weeks apart. They used a gay male
couple as donors who had also been together for over twelve years and whom
they had known for a long time. At the time of this interview their daughter,
Zoe, was one year old, and their son, Sam, was nine months.

How did you decide to both have a child at about the same time?
Michele: Well, for years we had been thinking about having children. We
would work up to it and one of us would say, "I think I'm ready to have
a child and the other would say, "No, no, not now. I'm not ready." This
went on for eight or nine years until I finally decided I wanted to get pregnant and Beth would just have to come along—or just not come along.
Beth: The desire for each of us to have a biological child was very strong.
Michele: Originally we talked about adopting, but once I started thinking
about a biological child, it sort of took over.
Beth: It was really difficult for us to imagine it would be easier for us both
to adopt, not just given that we are lesbians, but because we are not professional women in the traditional sense. We are both artists. Michele is a visual
artist, and I performed improvisational theatre and traveled a lot to elementary schools and colleges. Michele is thirty-six and I'm forty. And it would
only be one of us who could really adopt a child.
Michele: So legally we would be in the same position as only one of us
having a biological child.

Once you decided to use sperm, what were your concerns?
Michele: Personally, I wanted the child to know the father as much for the
child's protection as anything else. I wanted her/him to be able to say on
the playground, "My father does this, my father does that." I also thought
that if I had a boy, I'd possibly like to have the father around. I had a lot
of fears that in the lesbian community, I'd be ostracized if I had a boy, so
I felt a need to have a larger support network. That hasn't happened, but
I had a lot of fear around it, because no one I knew had had a boy.

How did you choose your donors?
Michele: Originally I chose a heterosexual man who was a friend of mine. His wife and I were good friends, and she actually suggested him. I thought it was a good choice because they already had one child, a nine-year-old girl I was close to. Actually, the first time I really started thinking about having a child was when they had their child. I chose him because he seemed healthy, because I knew him personally, and because he didn't seem to have a high stake in being involved with the child. I knew he wasn't a terribly possessive or jealous person. But he and his wife were also trying to get pregnant, and our ovulations started to coincide, so we had to forget about him as a donor. Instead we went to a gay friend of mine.
Beth: You were also concerned about AIDS at the time, weren't you?
Michele: Yes, I was very concerned about AIDS. But when I lost my first donor, I reconsidered and went to what was truly my first choice—a gay donor.

How did you resolve the issue about AIDS then?
Michele: At the time my gay donor had been essentially monogamous for two or three years. It wasn't known how long it took for the (HIV) virus to break down the immune system, and they didn't have a test then. Now I'd never do it without a test. I wouldn't do it with a straight man without a test either, but at the time I wasn't thinking of AIDS in terms of the heterosexual community too.

Did you both use the same donor?
Beth: No. We used two men who are lovers and who had been in a relationship for a little longer than we had been together.

What role did you want the fathers to play in the children's lives?
Beth: Well, I think it is always unclear until you are right in the middle of it. I wanted them to be involved. I wasn't sure how much. I wanted them to be loving and caring. I wanted the children to know who they were, to feel they could always have somebody they could call their father, and to feel good about it.
Michele: At the time, both of our donors lived in New York City, and I pictured them coming up occasionally, but not being as involved as they actually became.

How are they involved now?
Michele: They are fairly actively involved. They see the children probably eight to ten hours a week.

How is that working out for you?

Beth: Well, it is two-sided. It's really wonderful for the children to have loving people in their lives, and they have been helpful to us in terms of giving us some space and some needed time away from the children. But the kids are so terrific that it's real easy for the fathers to want to have as much as they can and to want to have the parental responsibility or power—or whatever you want to call it—because they want to be close to them. That has been a struggle.

Do you have any written agreements on what they should, or could, or could not do?

Beth: When we started out, they specified that they only wanted to be donors, and we left it unwritten for a long time. We were uncertain whether it was desirable to write a contract and see whether it is honored, or whether to acknowledge on paper the fact that they are the fathers. We didn't put their names on the birth certificate. One of the men was concerned about child support, and he wanted an understanding that he wouldn't have to be responsible for child support.

Michele: And I sort of said I'd prefer not to have a written agreement. But then when the children were born—all of a sudden their families were a real presence. We never discussed the fact that they might want their families involved with the children. It just never occurred to me, and it was, and still is, very emotionally difficult. It is an issue that is not resolved. I feel fond of their families, and I've gotten to know some of them, but as far as the general issue goes, it is very scary to me to have their families involved. So at that point we wrote up an agreement. A very basic agreement. We did it without a lawyer. We got some sample contracts and wrote a simple contract that said we would never sue them for child support and that they would never sue us for custody, and that if Beth or I died, they would honor, and never challenge, the surviving member's guardianship of the child. They waived their rights of guardianship. It was very simple, but it was very difficult for them to really see it on paper.

What would you like to see in the next three to five years as far as relationships with the donors?

Michele: Well, right now we are going to a mediator and that's helped somewhat. We had gotten to a point where we weren't even talking. I'd like to get to feel like we were friends again. I think there is a real need to make it clear to them that Beth and I are the family unit; I'm not so sure they have really accepted that.

Did the two of you suggest mediation or did that come from the donors?
Michele: That came from us. We kept trying to get them to do it last year, but they didn't feel it was important then. Things finally got so bad that we had to do it. We weren't able to talk to each other at all, and when we again suggested it, they accepted. I think we should have done it from the beginning. We thought we knew each other and we really didn't. We had our honeymoon period, and it ended in a real mess.

Around what kind of issues—what made it difficult?
Michele: Family. Their wanting their family involved was incredibly emotional. For example, my donor's mother was here for two months after my son was born. Even though I feel very fond of her and got to like her a lot, it was also an immediate insertion of family to a level which I didn't expect. There is a lot of sending of gifts from their families. What do you do? Do you send thank-you notes? What is my relationship to these people? Do they think I'm in a relationship with the father? I have fears that at some point they might want to take the child away. It's hard to balance the two aspects of wanting to let them know that you are a person, especially if your child is going to know the family, and not wanting to know them at all. It's pretty complex to have to deal with all this right after you've had a baby.
Beth: I would like to feel like we can communicate and feel warmly toward each other because I think it is going to be important to the children. I want Michele and me to be able to make decisions about the children and to communicate it in a better way. There have been a lot of mixed messages on both sides because the first year is a very hard year and stressful. As delightful as it is, it is stressful.

How have you been able to combine the responsibilities of work and home?
Beth: Basically, we've tried to divide it fairly equally. In the beginning, one of us could not go away and have the other watch them both; it was just too demanding. There were too many needs the children had, so initially we always tried to have somebody there, a friend or the fathers helping us. And we did that for the first six or eight months of both of their lives. When there was just Zoe, Michele and I did most of the work, but when there were two children, we really needed more help. I work part-time teaching acting. In the beginning I also did performing, but I decided that it was too much to try to rehearse and be out performing.
Michele: In a way, I have the ideal situation because I work at home. I spent a lot of time in the beginning quickly rushing and working for half an hour when the babies were asleep. Luckily, my work can go that way. What I'm living on this year is what I made last year, but I did keep producing all

year long. I wasn't sure I'd be able to, but I have. We've gotten real good at organizing. We ask people for what we need. This past year we've also been doing therapy with an excellent family therapist who has helped us think about structuring our time differently, making schedules, and sharing money, which we had never done before. Essentially, everything has had to change in the sense that when one of us is off doing her work, the other one has to be home watching the children. That's a major change in terms of our independence from each other and our interconnection.

Beth: Both of us felt it was essential that we be able to continue our work, but I think that neither of us realized the extent to which we would have to let go and give it up. As Michele said, she really does have a much more ideal situation where she can work at home, and although I am working and teaching at college, it is not the same sort of creative work I was doing. Even though we do have someone who comes in once a week for eight hours, there is still not time for me to do my work. I can see that in the future, I'm going to have to make a space for it—emotionally and physically—to really make that happen. And I'm hoping the energy I get from the children will foster that creativity. I don't have that now. I get a lot of energy, but it is also very exhausting, and there really isn't the space I need to direct that energy as I'd like. I think it is incredible that even one of us has been able to continue to do her art work.

Michele: The other thing is that both of us did have well-established careers, and even though Beth isn't doing her art work, she was able to shift over to something that was sort of related. The two of us, each working half-time, have been able to support ourselves.

And Baby Makes Two

Marilyn Murphy

For years I've been thinking of writing about motherhood. Now that many lesbians are seriously considering motherhood as an option for themselves, a thoughtful article on that subject by a lesbian who has mothered for thirty-five years seems timely. I have four children, three females and one male, aged twenty-nine to thirty-five at this writing. And, of course, I am a daughter, the eldest child of a mother whose behavior I have been scrutinizing for fifty-four years. I am grandmother to five, going-on-six, grandchildren as well.

Motherhood is an experience so mystified by folklore and superstition, by science and religion, by womb-envy and woman-hating that most women, at least in this culture, become mothers without really knowing what they are getting into. The people who could bring a little light to the subject, mothers ourselves, are silenced or discredited by the very forces which mystified our experience. It is absolutely unacceptable for mothers to question the motherhood imperative or to point out the difficulties inherent in motherhood unless we include the obligatory disclaimer, "Oh, but it was worth it!" To omit the disclaimer is to risk censure as a bad mother, a bitter mother, a cold mother, a mother who does not love her own children. I have never written anything as anxiety-producing as this essay because I know that many readers of this piece will think that of me. And what of my children? Will they be angry with me when they read this? Will they think I do not love them? Will they reject me? The first draft of this article had defensive, "I'm really a good mother" phrases scattered throughout it. Only my commitment to write the truth as I have experienced it has kept me writing about motherhood in spite of my sweaty palms.

I ask lesbians why they are choosing to become mothers. I know why I chose to become a mother. I believed that my "vocation," that is, my calling, my mission from "god," was motherhood, not the convent life which was my original goal. I was only fifteen at the time I came to this realization, so I do not judge myself harshly for not thinking more clearly. But nowadays, women in their thirties, independent women, lesbian women, are choosing to have babies. Why?

It is not surprising, of course, that so many lesbians are choosing to have babies now that artificial insemination is available to unmarried women. Lesbians are always in the forefront of revolutionary societal changes, and motherhood independent of men is one of those changes. Still, after the revolutionary conception, the result is quite commonplace. It is simply one more woman having a baby, and there has been nothing very revolutionary about that event, miraculous as it seems in each case, for millennia. Someone has to produce the next generation's liberated children, some say. I think this is self-delusion. There's many a surprise between the way a mother tries to raise her child and the adult who develops from the interaction of mother, home, heredity, individual temperament, environment, chance and whatever else it is that makes us different from and similar to each other. Women who believe the influence of a mother is primary need to reflect upon the variety of personality and politics among their own sisters and brothers. Are our siblings like us? Are we like our mothers? If we are loving, independent, talented lesbians, and/or want our daughters to be the same, will we raise them like our mothers raised us? Ah-hah! See the problem?

When a woman tells me she wants to have a baby because she "loves children," I feel pity for the child she may have. Her statement reveals her belief in the stereotypes of young human beings that are not likely to be found in individual young persons, including her own. *Loving* children in the abstract, as an identifiable group, is not unlike loving Jews or Asians or gay men for their positive stereotypes. Childfree women frequently do not realize that babies are persons, just like anybody else. They come equipped with their own temperaments and aptitudes which develop into individual personalities while they are still babies. What if the baby develops a personality which doesn't appeal to us? What if the child grows into a toddler we don't particularly like? What if s/he turns out too active or too tidy or too serious or too silly or too loud or too smart or too dumb or too quick or too slow or too uncoordinated or too boring or—goddess forgive us—too homely for our taste? I am speaking heresy, I know; but I am also speaking truth, a truth that mothers seldom admit. Just as our mothers were "stuck" with us (do they ever wish they had some other woman for their daughter?), so we are "stuck" with our children.

Some lesbians are choosing to have babies because they want to love and be loved by someone forever, *no matter what!* This, too, is a delusion. As a love relationship, motherhood bears some resemblance to that of an arranged marriage, wherein a woman chooses, or is forced, to enter a relationship with a person she does not know, but whom she is expected to love and take care of until one of them dies. No one, not even a mother, can promise to feel love always. We can feel and act upon what seem to be unbreakable ties of loyalty and duty to the members of one's blood family, including one's mother or one's child, but that does not mean that we love them. Some of us can even admit to no longer loving a sibling or a parent. Mothers, however, are not likely to confess a lack of love for their child because to not love or to no longer love one's child is supposed to be the ultimate mother sin, worse than any kind of child abuse done in the name of love, and *every mother knows this.* When love is the exchange, however, there are no guarantees. And this is true in spite of vows at a lesbian commitment ceremony or the commingled blood and tears of this most intimate and intense physical act, childbirth.

The belief that mothers love their children unconditionally, unselfishly, undyingly, is a myth, a myth that keeps women trying, trying, trying to "do the right thing" for their children: to please, to understand, to forgive, to rescue them—over and over and over again, no matter what our real feelings might be, even if we are able to sort them out. Unconditional mother-love is the companion of the myth that women "...can't help loving that man of mine."

This reminds me of boy children. Elizabeth Cady Stanton, the influential nineteenth-century feminist and mother of seven children, wrote this: "It is folly to talk of a mother molding the character of her son, when all mankind, backed up by law and public sentiment, conspire to destroy her influence." I can swear to the truth of that. It is too painful to describe what it is like to watch the growing to manhood of a much loved boy child, and to experience his exercise of that manhood in its maturity. Our daughters, at least, are sister sufferers under patriarchy, and their behavior, even when we abhor it, is behavior we understand.

To believe that one's child will love her mother forever is a particularly cruel self-deception. The library is filled with books which flaunt the most virulent mother-hatred, and the culture is rife with antimother jokes. A visit to the neighborhood nursing home or the sight of a bag lady in a doorway should convince anyone that birthing a child is no guarantee there will be someone to take loving care of us in our old age.

The desire to have a child in order to insure some immortality—so there will be something to show you were here, alive on this earth, after you leave it—is a very powerful, atavistic feeling. I don't know if it is enough, however, to fuel a mother's spirits, even for as short a period as the childbirth experience.

I do believe that many lesbians having babies now are doing so in response to that all-pervasive, hard-to-resist, ages-old patriarchal teaching that having a baby is the most fulfilling, most rewarding, most important activity a woman can undertake, and that there is something wrong with those women who don't believe this, or who don't have children if they are able. This is untrue. When we remember all the women whose work fulfilled them, whose work made a difference to others, women who live on in their work, it is no coincidence that most of them were not mothers of children. That some mothers also were achieving women only reminds us of their scarcity in a world full of mothers.

Men love to quote Francis Bacon, who wrote, "Men who have children give hostages to fortune," though his child bride managed the kids and the house while he became famous for his fulfilling, creative, nonreproductive work. No, in a world organized for men, it is the children of women who are hostages to fortune. It is women whose childbearing and childrearing are the beloved obstacles to study, concentration, time, opportunity, and all the rest that goes into nurturing a talent to maturity.

Of course, most people, even most lesbians, are not gifted with great talent that needs nurturing; and most of us are never going to make some enormous difference in the world. And, given the economic oppression of women, we are more likely to have boring, dead-end jobs than exciting, challenging ones. This makes the prospect of becoming a mother very appealing. In the first place, even though it isn't revolutionary in the cosmic sense, having a baby is certainly miraculously creative to the woman having one. And who is more important to a child than her mother? We've all had mothers, and we may love her, hate her, respect, despise or pity her, but all of us know her importance in our lives. That is why so many women, lesbians included, have babies. Being a mother makes a woman feel important.

But choosing motherhood is so. . .so. . .final. When people talk about making a career change, they do not mean giving up motherhood! Motherhood is forever.

Women considering motherhood need to know that whenever something bad happens to one's child, from the sniffles to death by drowning, almost everyone will judge it to be somehow your fault, and you will agree with the judgment. You will be blamed for birth defects, emotional disturbances, learning disabilities, and colic; every accident, no matter where it happens or who was caretaking at the time; poor performance on tests and on the ballfield; talking in school and not talking in school; "early" sexual development, anorexia, incest, alcohol and drug abuse. You will love and/or protect the child "too much" or "too little." And for a lesbian mother, the problem is bound to be worse. Whatever isn't blamed on her faulty mothering can be attributed to her sexual deviance.

Which brings me to the joys of motherhood. When I started analyzing them, I realized that the joys I experienced were at least two-thirds the feeling of a most intense sense of relief, relief that flooded my body, filled my heart, eased my mind, and soothed my spirit. The first time this happened was right after the birth of my first child, when I awoke from an anesthesia-induced sleep to hear my mother say, "You had a boy, and he is *perfectly healthy.*"

This feeling of relief, which passes for joy, came regularly after its first appearance, more or less intensely depending upon the event that triggered it. When a child did not have the suspected leukemia; when, countless times, they were only late coming home, not. . . . ; when a suspected fractured skull was only a concussion; when "she was run over" meant by a bike, not a car; when she was not pregnant, when she was not pregnant, when she was not pregnant; when. . . . Of course, there are the lesser reliefs, when a mother learns the child didn't lie, steal, hit, sneak, or admits a misdeed and is sorry; and the countless times when, whatever the news is, it isn't as awful as what was expected. And this process is never-ending. I don't have the every hour/every day happenings to trigger the joys of relief now that my children are adults, but they come often enough to keep me going. And now I have five grandchildren and one more on the way! Only my death will release me from these kinds of "joys" and from the worry, terror, anguish, and heartache which precedes them.

I will not describe any of the times when the worry, terror, anguish, and heartache were followed by more of the same. I can only say that no other relationship, not even the one with one's own mother, can equal motherhood for opportunities to experience all of the above.

So having said all this, do I think lesbians should not have babies? No, I don't think that either. I cannot think of any "good" reasons for having babies, and can think of many for passing up this "womanly" activity. Still, I must be honest and tell the whole truth of it. I say that in my next life I want to be a sterile female so I can experience the joys of a childfree life. I say *sterile* female because I am afraid, given the opportunity, I might just do it again. Why? Well, I am crazy about my kids, even now, even though I hated being their mother many times and for long periods of time. I love them more or less depending. . . . I respect them more or less depending. . . . Some of my most satisfying life experiences have been mother experiences. However, all of my worst life experiences originated with my children, too. Motherhood can be a joyful, interesting, and satisfying relationship; but it is also terrible, terrible. If I had had the freedom to choose, knowing then what I know now, would I have chosen motherhood? I can't be sure, but I don't think so. It is still too soon for me to know if the satisfactions of being a mother will outweigh the anguish, will make the mothering worth the trouble and pain—and I have been mothering for thirty-five years. That's something to think about, isn't it?

Coparenting

Sisters
Are
Doin'
It
For
Themselves

Annie's First Poem

Mab Segrest

For Annie Elizabeth Culbertson-Jolly Segrest,
born November 11, 1986, 5:25 p.m.

You came in a year of death and birth—
First Carl, my friend
who died of AIDS
a month before your sparks took flame,
his back arched, as yours
is now, your face as beatific.
Now your hands dance before your eyes,
signing *wonder.*

For years we sought
the path to you—
but three centimeters,
I only wanted her not to hurt.
The bones of your head
closed to open her girdle of bone.
You were caught in the sleeve of flesh,
and, mouth to breast, I sucked you free.

I feared I would regret
you are not my daughter.
I find I love you hers.

My heart is open to ten centimeters,
and I can only push.

The Other Mother:
Lesbian Comother's Journal
Pamela Gray

The following are excerpts from two-and-a-half years of journal entries which begin with my becoming lovers with a pregnant woman, and trace my evolving into the role of a comother. Since they are excerpts, they can't fully recreate the entire process, but I have tried to include a sampling of different emotions and experiences.

Wednesday, 2/23/83, 2:00 p.m.

New mother exhaustion. Everything's an effort. I'm in my apartment now, trying to fit my psyche into this life, this reality, trying to force myself to come back to earth—sort of like Kathleen forcing the nipple into Andrew's mouth. I want to fuss and cry too, *Don't make me do it.* Somehow I've got to prepare for tomorrow's class. Torture. The irrelevance of nineteenth-century lesbianism at this very moment. (At least it's not freshman composition.) In a way, I look forward to class tomorrow, getting the reward of human contact, validation, affirmation. *Maybe.* I'm so spaced out: putting the coffee filter into the measuring cup, pouring the milk on my wrist, spilling the spring water on my leg, ordering one small and one large apple*sauce* at the Edible yesterday. (I saw the woman behind the counter say to someone, "So stupid!" and shake her head at me.) I am not in my body; I need a firm grounding cord to connect me to the earth.

It was either during Kathleen's labor or right after the delivery that I heard noise outside her bedroom and really felt the impact of the cliché "life goes on." It's hard to accept though—I feel like I'm on a big holiday. It was even hard to put money in the parking meters yesterday. Parking meters? A baby was born for goddess' sake.

I woke up and cried again this morning. Kathleen was caressing my face and I woke. The baby was between us. I turned around, faced the wall and cried, missing her, missing what we had, mourning the loss of the life we were sharing together. It is such a sudden dramatic thrust into new territory: Kathleen leaking milk all over herself and the bed, the baby crying crying crying crying, the endless chores and errands to be run, the precious moments of silence spent feeling our exhaustion. Kathleen tells me it will get better, easier; she tells me we're only at the beginning of our lives together. She asked me if I believe her and I said no. I think that I don't.

I want to make love so badly. My feelings are all in fragments—contradictory and disconnected from each other. When I hold Andrew and he (sort of) smiles, or stops crying as I rock him, I just feel full of joy and warmth. And hope. I am losing my disappointment over his sex. Kathleen said this is like transition. Take it one day (contraction) at a time. Yes. It's no good when I walk around Safeway and look at grown men and think about the fact that *I'm* going to be raising one. I need to stay in the present with this little baby in his yellow booties.

Friday night, 2/25/83

I splurged on gifts today—an uncontrollable impulse to buy Andrew an adorable outfit—white shirt, shorts and hat with purple hearts on them; plus one fuschia and one purple T-shirt. Then I finally got Kathleen the long-awaited dozen roses—months ago I planned to do that after the baby was born. Gorgeous lavender roses, a big purple bow on the long box, and one of those preprinted florist shop cards saying, *To my darling wife and baby.* (I couldn't resist *that.*)

Sunday, 2/27/83

Kathleen's been crying just about every day. We cried together this morning. This is *hard*, no doubt about that.

Tuesday, 4/5/83

I dreamt we wanted to xerox Andrew's back! I put him on the machine and suddenly he started to shit everywhere. . . .

Tuesday, 4/12/83

I fed the baby tonight. Last night at the lesbian mother's workshop, I realized, as one woman spoke, I felt very left out because I can't feed him. Hurt by Kathleen's seeming unwillingness to share that fundamental task. How can I raise this baby with you if I can't feed him? This feeling went along with the others—wanting more time with her alone, wanting something separate from the baby.

At the same time there is the urge to bond with him even more. She talked of her own reluctance to separate from him—something she hasn't verbalized before. I said I wanted her to express her milk for two reasons: first, so we could be away from him for longer periods of time (longer than our precious two-hour date Friday night, for example) and second, so I could feed him. This afternoon I found her in the bathroom squeezing her milk into a bottle.

Thursday, 5/5/83, 8:25 a.m.
Had a talk with Kim last night re: trying to be Andrew's legal mother. It can't be done. If I adopt him, Kathleen loses her legal right to him. Can't be done. No one's allowed to have two mommies—legally. Kathleen should write a will soon, Kim said, and make sure it's in writing that I'd get custody. As long as no one contests. . . .

Sunday, 5/15/83, 5:00 p.m.
I'm acting/feeling like a little lost sheep. Kathleen and Andrew are off at a family gathering and I am home alone—by choice—although still disturbed about it. It's the *principle* of the thing, knowing if I went I'd be treated like a nonperson. I have a fantasy of being at one of those family gatherings a year from now and Andrew toddling up to me, calling me mama. *He'll* be the one who will speak the truth.

I was hurt in the Berkeley Bowl when a woman came up to us and asked, "Well, whose baby is it?" and Kathleen said, "Mine." I understood why she said that, but it hurt anyway.

Monday, 5/23/83
As I left today, he was sitting in his chair on the washing machine, the thick rainbow-colored tassles from a pair of booties hanging over him for entertainment, his giraffe and a diaper in his arm, and he was smiling and cooing and checking everything out. Every day with him is a gift, every chance to be with him. He smiles when he sees me—he *knows* me, knows my voice, my songs, my touch. Even the new baby book says that at three months they attach themselves to the person (or persons) who does the *mothering*, and it defines mothering as playing, being there when they cry, answering when they talk, "showing pieces of the world to them." I felt pleased because a printed page affirmed my role, even if the world doesn't.

Friday, 6/17/83, 7:02 a.m.
I am up with Andrew. I heard Kathleen grumbling and cursing and I couldn't take the guilt anymore. It was 6:15 and I was lying in bed wondering how I dared call myself a comother, hearing Diana's words from last night, "Do you ever do relief?" I had no excuse today. I didn't have to go to work. I know I have this attitude that it's Kathleen's job to do the hard stuff since she's the one who wanted to have him.

He's throwing around and banging his rattle keys. In the past couple of weeks, he's gotten so many more abilities. After just a week of having the cradle gym, he's now really hitting it and playing with it and pulling up on it. (It is now 8:30. It's taken one-and-a-half hours to finish that sentence.)

Saturday, 6/25/83

Kathleen and I really *are* alone in this. It's as if our place in the world of our friends has broken off, drifted off like a new island, and now water separates us. Me and Kathleen and Andrew on our little island with occasional boat trips to the mainland and occasional visitors from the mainland. After the little boats depart, we are alone.

Tuesday, 7/5/83

I am in the DMV, waiting to duplicate my license, stolen yesterday with my checkbook. As I walked to the phonebooth, strolling Andrew, a woman said, "Ooh, she's got a Black baby." A woman next to me just asked, "Is the baby mixed?" I said, "Yes." I was so taken off-guard. "Yeah," she said, "they make beautiful babies. A girl?" "No, a boy." If I had said no, he's not mixed, that would have totally confused her, or she'd have just assumed I was babysitting for him.

This is my first time out with Andrew—I mean really out, carseat and all. I feel nervous and stumbly, not used to maneuvering the stroller through doors, not used to getting him in and out of my car, not used to dealing with the public. I still feel like I'm a fraud if I act like he's my baby. I'm afraid someone will ask me questions about labor or my husband or something. I have to keep telling myself that he *is* my baby and he will be perceived that way because it's the truth. I don't owe the straight world any explanation. But even yesterday when a lesbian friend was calling me his mama, I felt like I didn't deserve the title.

Friday, 7/9/83

Andrew was *wild* in the restaurant yesterday when I met Kim for lunch. He threw my glass of water off the table. It all landed in the stroller. He was sucking the table, my hand—searching for *something*. I gave him a round sesame cracker which he sucked until soggy and then ate some of. He cried when he swallowed it. Then he "sang" to the table of people behind us. I still feel awkward and nervous in public, and also so aware of my outlaw status. I have an identity that is completely alien to 99.99% of the people who see me with him. Comother.

Wednesday, 12/21/83

Andrew is growing up, saying *naa naa* and sometimes *no*. He pointed Monday night at the stereo. He looks like a tiny little boy, not a baby anymore. I felt closer to him when he was just a baby, but then it was more projection than intimacy—he just wasn't separate, individuated enough to create any boundaries to closeness. Now he is his own person. The little drummer boy—loves music, rocks and claps, touches the speakers for vibrations.

Wednesday, 1/11/84, 11:45 a.m.

A very difficult session in couples therapy last month. Fran said I have to decide: "Do you want a family?" She kept stressing that a lover with a baby was different than a lover without a baby, and I have to accept that. But is this *it?* Is this what it's like with a lover and a baby or can it be different?

Thursday, 1/26/84

Andrew took three steps yesterday, and he's pointing to everything and babbling what I'm sure is "What's this? What's that?" in babytalk. I told Kathleen I have the uncanny feeling he is understanding everything we're saying and is speaking English back to us, only it is going through a baby-talk filter. One of these days the filter will disappear and it *will* be "What's this? What's that?"

Wednesday, 4/4/84, 4:44 p.m.

I woke and worked on a poem about Kevin Collins and fear of losing Andrew. Kathleen called to say Andrew had fallen at day care with Mr. Potato Head's nose in his mouth, and his gum was bruised and turned black. It really frightened me, but she said he's acting fine. Once I get past my fear, I'll let myself laugh about Mr. Potato Head's nose being in his mouth.

Monday, 7/30/84, 9:15 a.m.

The Comother's Choice. Kathleen is angry that I have one. She is angry that I remind her of it. My doubts—"I don't know if I can do my writing and be in This Situation"—all point to the imbalance between us. She can't choose anymore. She *made* the choice. She chose the baby over her other interests, over her old life. Andrew is the new life. That's not the choice I made. That is the choice of the biological mother. I chose parenting without complete sacrifice. And yes, my alarm system starts ringing when the sacrifices feel too big. That's the other difference. I keep accounts of the sacrifices because I came into this unknowingly. Kathleen is aware of hers, but has to accept them. For me, it is something I am still acutely conscious of—sacrificing spontaneity, sex, freedom, energy, romance in the relationship. If I see it spilling into my creative life, I panic. I came home from the writing retreat with fences around me: No Trespassing. This is Private Property. *My* territory. *Mine. Mine.* Echoes of Andrew's new word. He says it in his crib in the morning, in his playpen, in his highchair. *His* territory.

Friday, 8/10/84, 8:10 a.m.

Andrew said bye-bye Mama this morning. A sentence. A real sentence! He's growing. Fear of the day when we can no longer protect him from what's out there. Fear of the day when everything we've done to protect him goes down the drain.

Friday, 10/26/84

When I was on line in Safeway this a.m., Andrew pointed to the man behind us and screamed, "A man! Mama, a man!" I wanted to laugh hysterically and hide under the cart at the same time. He did a similar thing when I was at Jeri's house with him, and two of her gay male friends came over. He had refused to hug Jeri, but when these strangers walked in, he gave them hugs, grabbed their legs, and said, "Hi, man." Jeri looked at me and said, "I think there's something to this role-modeling stuff."

Monday, 10/29/84

I was in all day except for a brief excursion oput with Kathleen and Andrew for "punkins." How cute he looked with his little pumkin. He went over to the Frankenstein monster (rubber mask and hands, clothes mounted on a pole) hanging up in the pumpkin patch, looked up, and said "Hi." Kept repeating it as if waiting for Frankie's response. We told him it was a monster, and he said, "COOKIE MONSTER!" in his cookie monster voice.

Monday, 11/5/84

Andrew feels the stress between me and Kathleen—all day yesterday, after our argument, he clung and hugged and put his head in my lap and Kathleen's lap; last night he banged his highchair tray with his *hanna* (hammer), saying SHIT! SHIT! SHIT! and at one point, BULLSHIT!

Friday, 11/16/84

Judi's in labor. I have found myself desperately wishing I could do it all over, relive Andrew's birth, and this time really be a part of it with Kathleen, really be there for her *after* the birth. I am jealous of the way Alberta and Judi are sharing it, chose it together and are in it together.

Monday, 11/19/84

It hurt to see Andrew's hurt yesterday when he saw his "girlfriend" Judi's new baby, Daniel; he got so quiet and sullen and wanted me to hold him. He tried to smile at the baby, but you could see that behind the smile he wanted to cry. He said "Bye-bye Daniel" when we left, but I felt like his little heart was broken.

Andrew's been incredibly cranky and hard to be with—Terrible Twos energy—although he still has his irresistable moments. Like pointing to the tampon box and saying, "Crackers," and imitating me saying, "Oh Jesus" when he fell yesterday and banged his head on the bedframe.

Monday, 12/17/84, 8 a.m.

It was torture to get out of bed, to leave the warm pink and purple womb of my new wonderful flannel sheets, but I am up early to work on gathering journal entries for the lesbian mothers anthology. I think it says something about my life that I've been trying to do this for a year, and here I am doing it the last week before the deadline. But I think it also speaks to my own resistance to the task itself: I'm not at a gathering point; I'm still in it, living it, experiencing it on a day-to-day basis. Comotherhood isn't a phase I can finish, review, sort out.

There have been changes, that's for sure. Andrew came into my bedroom at 6:45 a.m. saying, "Wake up Mama La-a-la! Hi Honeypie! Kiss?" (kissed me on the lips). "A hug?" (gave me a big hug). This little character is not the same baby I was writing about twenty-two months ago. I can't believe he's almost two. At Alberta and Judi's last night, they looked at him in the highchair and said they just couldn't believe that someday Daniel would ever be in that chair. I remember *that* point. The future was inconceivable. At *this* point, the past is what's hard to imagine. When I picture Andrew as a *baby* baby, I see the still photos from the picture album. It's so hard to think of him being in that state of only eating/excreting/crying/sleeping. Now he's a real person—he screamed "Prince!" when Prince came on the car radio yesterday and began to dance in his carseat saying, "Look at me Mama! I dancing!" Kathleen and I looked at each other wide-eyed. Did he say that? And then at dinner last night, when he started getting rowdy and I got up to be disciplinarian, he said, "Sit *down*, Mama." And I did.

So far, it's been quite a journey. Yesterday, I met Corky's handsome eighteen-year-old son and realized, watching them joke together, that I didn't fear the future the way I used to. True, I was just as disappointed as always when *both* babysitters cancelled at the last minute, and Kathleen and I couldn't be alone (all I had wanted to do was take a Sunday afternoon walk together), but there's a part of me that's begun to see and believe in the doors that have opened/will open, in addition to any doors that may have closed when I became a part of this experience.

In spite of any continuing resistance, ambivalence inside me, there's a deep commitment to Andrew Michael, a thick cord from my heart chakra to that little boy. I love when he calls me Mama La-a-la—not just the adorable attempt at saying Pamela, but the *Mama* part, too.

The One We Lost

Jennifer Meyer

for Kate Hill

The room we are in is the same one I labored in with our first son. The walls are a soft beige with a flowered border. Framed classics hang on them. But the walls soon disappear. The pictures disappear. Even the red-headed nurse expertly roving your full belly disappears. And there is only the swish-shish of your amplified placenta and those pleading eyes of yours.

"Find it. Find it!" your eyes beg. And I beg, too, but I already know. There is no heartbeat. I stop trying to hold back the tears that now rush down my face.

Later, in the darkened sonogram room, you still didn't believe it. "No!" you screamed. "No, they're wrong!" You clutched at my shirt and wailed desperately. "It's not true!" But a look of sorrowful resignation in my eyes answered you, and you began to sob. I held you. Our baby was dead.

They put you back in the maternity ward and started your labor with drugs. They said you could wait, but you were ready now, your shock and disbelief suddenly turning to resolution. They offered you something for the pain, but you refused. "It's still my birth," you said. "It's still my baby. I want to be there."

All night you worked, full of strength and purpose, even though the reward was gone. You sometimes wept between contractions, sometimes roared with rage. I held you. I cried, too. But I couldn't stop the pain, couldn't wake us up from the nightmare.

By morning, our second son was born. I was afraid to see the body you pushed from you. But when the doctor laid him on your breast, I was amazed at how beautiful he was. His long, muscular limbs, his thick brown hair, a dimple in his chin. How could a baby this perfect just stop living, with no explanation?

I cried like I have never cried. The tears just would not stop. But you. . . . A calm serenity settled over you as you held your child. You did not cry or demand to know why. You stroked each tiny finger and stared into his face. "He was not meant to be here," you said softly, incredulously, as if you suddenly understood. You knew then what you have been trying to remember ever since.

Seven months later, your belly is growing again. We are glad, but it is different now. We don't rejoice this time at every sign of growth. We don't eagerly sort through nighties in anticipation. Our innocence has been pierced. We hope, and we wait, and we remember. Because we will never forget our second son.

142 Politics Of The Heart

Happy Birthday From Your Other Mom
Carolyn Kott Washburne

Dear David,

Today is your first birthday, and since you will be getting toys and clothes from other people, I have decided to give you something special—a letter about you. You came into the world under unusual circumstances, and I want to tell you about them.

Your mother Kathleen is a high-energy, joyful person. She has a good sense of humor and a ready smile. As a girl she was a dedicated tomboy, and even now has many tomboy qualities. She is a jock, for example, and loves the challenge of fixing things when they break. She is also energetically tidy. "I am 100 percent German," she says with a laugh. "Give me a broom and I can rule the world." Kathleen is a social worker, and right now she is the program director at a counseling agency in Milwaukee, a city known for its beer and conservatism.

Kathleen and I fell in love during the winter of 1978 and moved in together the following fall. Even though it is easier today than it used to be for lesbians and gay men to be open about their lives, we were both afraid of what it would mean for us to come out—to let our friends and families and coworkers know that we were in love and making a commitment to each other. Happily, with only a few painful exceptions, the people who mattered to us accepted our love for each other although they may not have understood it.

Kathleen probably always wanted to have a baby but was concerned about how a child would change her life. In addition, she had also been married to a man who didn't want children, and when I met her she had resigned herself to the idea of never being a mother. I felt strongly that I could support her having a child if she wanted to. I have an eight-year-old daughter, Jessie, whom I love dearly. Jessie lives with us half the time and with her father half the time. Although he and I separated when she was three, we still have a cordial relationship.

As we discussed the possibility of Kathleen getting pregnant, it became clear she did not want her baby's father to be anonymous. Some lesbians we know are having children by artificial insemination, but it was important to Kathleen that you know about your father, even if he did not play much of a role in your life. She says she has known too many adopted children whose adult lives are spent searching for their biological families. After thinking about which of her men friends might agree to father a child, she asked Larry, your father, and after much discussion he agreed. Larry is also a social worker and lives in West Virginia. He is quiet, with a wry sense of humor. Kathleen did not ask him for financial support, just that she be able to use his name on your birth certificate. She invited him to share, long distance, in your upbringing, and Larry said he was open to the idea.

I was at first apprehensive about involving Larry, whom I didn't know well. What kind of a man would do this, I wondered? Would he turn on us someday and demand custody of you? (Some of our lesbian friends warned us about this.) So far, I have not had reason for concern. Larry is a gentle, thoughtful person, who speaks clearly and directly about his feelings and responds honestly to ours. While no one can predict the future, it is hard for me to imagine that Larry would one day become so unreasonable that we couldn't work things out. I am delighted that he is sharing in your life. He has come to feel like family to me.

You were conceived on a snowy January night in front of the fireplace at our old apartment on Marietta Avenue. Kathleen and Larry made love, and I was there with them, pleased to be a part of your creation. Sounds kinky? It didn't seem so at the time, although I'll admit my frame of reference is different from most people's. When Kathleen began to tell people about her pregnancy, most were surprised but generally supportive. If there were some who were critical, they had the good grace to keep their opinions to themselves. In some ways, this country is not so very far removed from the days of *The Scarlet Letter*, and I appreciated all those people, especially Kathleen's family and my family, who probably had to stretch their own value systems in order to celebrate Kathleen's pregnancy with us.

Kathleen loved being pregnant. She did yoga exercises every day, rarely drank alcohol or smoked marijuana (a big sacrifice for her), and followed a carefully balanced vegetarian eating program so that you could be the healthiest baby possible. One day in her eighth month we were picking vegetables at a pick-it-yourself farm, and Kathleen held up a large, dark purple eggplant. "This is how I feel right now," she said laughing. "Lush and full and ready to burst." We attended a childbirth class, the only two-woman couple there. (There weren't even any unmarried couples.) We walked tall, though, and had a good time practicing the breathing exercises.

Because she was thirty-six when you were conceived, Kathleen underwent a relatively new procedure called amniocentesis, which by the time you read this will probably be commonplace. The procedure, done in the fourth month of pregnancy, indicates whether a fetus has Down's Syndrome or a number of other genetic problems. While I am generally suspicious of the increasing use of high-tech equipment in pregnancy and childbirth, I was thrilled to see your movements on a television monitor. At that moment you became a real person, someone whom I talked to and thought about and cared about.

The amniocentesis results revealed that you were, at least in terms of genetic problems, healthy, and that you were a boy. Kathleen, the jock, was pleased; I was shocked. I come from a family of girls, my child is a girl, I have few men friends, and I was afraid we would be even more open to criticism for trying to raise a son without "appropriate male role models." But within a month of the news I had completely changed my mind and was looking forward to living with you and learning how a boy child would enrich my life.

Every birth is different, and perhaps someday I will write you another letter describing yours in detail. The important information is this: first, you decided to be born three weeks early, messing up our carefully orchestrated plans for a baby shower, acquisition of furniture for your room, etc. Kathleen's labor was long (we went to the hospital at 2:00 a.m. on a Wednesday, and you weren't born until 7:06 that evening) and at times difficult. We were in a Catholic hospital and told the staff we were sisters so they wouldn't get suspicious about the real nature of our relationship. In the midst of the labor, we got our "family" stories mixed up, but if the staff thought we were strange, they didn't let on.

Kathleen managed to go without medication for pain during the whole labor, not because she necessarily wanted to, but because the staff was too busy to check on her progress until it was too late—the time had come to push you out. In the delivery room, I couldn't decide whether to stand by Kathleen's head so I could talk to her, or at the foot of the delivery table to watch you emerge, so I kept scurrying back and forth. What a joy to finally see you! Your face was very red and pinched, but you looked so much like your father, I almost called you Larry. We took you back to Kathleen's room and played with you for what must have been hours. We were both exhausted and excited, Kathleen, of course, more exhausted than I. I can definitely report that it's much more fun being the support person than being the woman in labor.

We decided not to have you circumcised because nobody could give us a convincing reason why we should, and it seemed like such a cruel thing to do to a little guy like you. Even on the delivery table you were mellow, and you have continued to be a delightful baby. Correction: you did cry for one solid hour the day we brought you home. Kathleen said later she was so depressed that day she was beginning to wonder if she hadn't made a big mistake. She and I were a good team in those first weeks. She was enthusiastic—even, believe it or not, about getting up for night feedings. It was as if thirty-seven years of pent-up mothering was finally being allowed to flower. And I prided myself on my know-how about babies from having been through it with Jessie. I'm not opposed to fathers, but I do think every baby should have at least two mothers.

Kathleen nursed you until you were nine months old. Once in awhile, I felt jealous of your closeness with each other, but in time I developed my own closeness to you. If you were fussy but not hungry, I occasionally let you suck on my breasts, which brought back wonderful memories of my nursing days with Jessie.

When you were two months old, Kathleen went back to work, not because she wanted to (she was having too much fun at home with you), but because she needed the money. You went to work with her every day and slept in a small room at her agency which had been converted into a nursery. Soon the other staff, some of whom were at first skeptical about having an infant in the office, started spending their coffee breaks with you. You even helped some of the nonparents overcome their shyness around babies, and because the experiment has worked so well, two other women on the staff have recently brought their infants to the office. Today, at age one, you are outgoing and trusting and very curious about the world. I believe this is because of your early contact with so many caring people.

Larry has stayed in touch with you even though he lives far away. He visited you three times since you were born and sends you presents on holidays. For your birthday today he has sent a giant stuffed panda, bigger than you are. He has recently started living with a woman named Barbara who, instead of being threatened or embarrassed by your existence, has welcomed you into her life. She came with Larry on his last visit and brought you three bibs which she had embroidered with animals and flowers. Some people have said they think all of us are weird. Others say they admire us but could never do it themselves. Some days I do get apprehensive about the future, but that would probably be true even if I were living in a traditional family. Because our relationships to each other are not defined in traditional ways, I am always reminded that I can't take anything for granted, that I must think about my life anew every day. On my bad days that feels very tiring; on my good days it's invigorating.

Soon you will learn to talk (I thought I heard you say *bye-bye* the other day), and your life will change dramatically. So far you have been a very special small person. When you were an infant we jokingly called you Mr. President, and while I suppose all parents hope that their children will go on to accomplish great things, I wouldn't be at all surprised if you do. Sometimes being different can be a handicap, and sometimes it can be a gift. I believe we have given you a gift. I am looking forward to growing along with you.

Love,
Carolyn

The Diatribe Of The Deserted Poet

Martha Shelley

They call me copout, dropout, deserter
behind my back they whisper
whatever happened to Martha
hard to get her to a party
when I call my lover
when I won't get stoned and dance till one
when I go home early
cause the baby crows at dawn.

Some folks say Martha
has become a bore
she changes diapers, washes floors
all she talks about is teething
she never has the time
to keep up with her reading
she's grown as dumb
as all the other mums of kids
who scream and make demands
who don't fit into ideal plans
of miniature amazons.

No, I can't come out to play
and let my lover mind the kids
if a man did that, you'd say
what a louse *he* is
you say I'm being used
they aren't mine
why should I let the man's law define
them as their father's property
by right of love, they
belong to me as well
or maybe only to themselves.

Look at that boy!
Yes, a small *boy*
he has his father's genes and hair
but he sits in *my* typing chair
with my shoes dangling from his feet
and writes about a kid
who grew six feet tall
and played baseball
"and then everybody liked him."

Look at the girl. "Mommy, Martha,
look at me!" She
badgers us constantly
swinging from the gym
climbing trees, doing headstands for hours.
She cries if I bring flowers
for her mom and not for her.

And the howling baby
who will sprout teeth forever
who will never give us a silent night
screeched with delight to see me
at the nursery, and ran past his Mom
and clambered up my knees
diarrhea dripping from his diapers
on my new blue jeans.

These pleasures don't come free.
They can't be shelved
when I need time for myself
and the boss grinds his profit from me
and the taxman and the landlord
must be fed before
the kids get bread.
We pay to take them to the park
for the weekly ration of fresh air.

But sisters, do you remember
when a lesbian wouldn't dare
raise children openly
go to court for custody
when even we believed
we were unfit
how we hid our love from the kids
and how relieved we were
when they grew up straight?
I say we—

      include me
among the older dykes I knew
we stand on their victories
we bend under the chains
they couldn't undo
hissing bitterly over our differences.

Am I being deserted by friends
who feel deserted by me?
(How nasty of them to remind me
of the days when I was free
to dance all night in the lesbian ghetto
avoiding kids like a swarm of mosquitoes
messy little obstacles
to the quest for success.)
Is it crazy to try
to build a matriarchal family
to raise girls to power
to turn boys into brothers
to be lovers and mothers.

A Process Of Naming

Robyn K. Roberts

At first I did not know what to call myself; there were no words. *Parent* seemed too strong, presumptuous even. I had fallen in love with a woman with children. I had fallen in love with her children.

I had a separate relationship with each, and yet, we were creating a family. I cooked meals, washed clothes, drove the kids to soccer practice. I talked with them about guns, surfing, sexuality, and the latest toys. I dried tears, wrestled in the park, gave them time out for fighting. I held my breath when they told me about climbing trees, roller coaster rides, and not being able to talk with their father about me. I felt protective and worried. I was encouraging, sometimes critical, sometimes jealous, and often proud. Still, when someone asked who I was to these two young boys, I did not know what to call myself.

What began three years ago was a process of naming. Similar to coming out—where being a lesbian has much more to it than sexuality—being a parent is more than the ritual and responsibility of having a relationship with children. It affects every aspect of my life. I have changed my expectations of the world, my community, and my adult relationships. Parenting is, like other important commitments in my life, a passion.

But who will understand? I pray I will be with my partner and children if the bomb drops. I anguish over whether or not I have given them enough time, care, and attention, even when I am not busy or overwhelmed with life.

Do I hold them enough? Am I too strict, honest enough, too attached? What about when they begin to experiment with alcohol and drugs, will my stories as a recovering alcoholic tell them enough about the dangers involved?

Sometimes I feel jealous of the time I don't have with my partner because she is their mom. Do I love them enough?

Our family is unique and complex. The boys live with their father every other week. That makes Friday a transition day. Either the boys are coming home, or they are leaving. Every other week my partner and I have to add two soccer games, four soccer practices, one night of karate, eighteen shuttles to and from school, ten more loads of laundry, twenty scheduled meals, and daily homework to our already busy lives.

The difficult part is accommodating and supporting the kids as they adjust to new rules, chores, environments, and expectations. They are kids of the eighties, living in a blended family, sharing parents in different places.

We have the special needs of creating a family where we are building common history, incorporating the old, adding to the rituals, and allowing a place for their mom and her partner to be lesbians.

We began talking about lesbians and gays soon after we all came together. We went to concerts, rallies, and marches to share the culture. We tried explaining homophobia in hopes the boys would recognize it when confronted with it and be able to make decisions accordingly. The basic queer-hating of their society and peers has, so far, been easier to deal with than the silence or illegitimacy placed on us by their grandparents, aunts, uncles, and their father. Nevertheless, each of them has learned the ropes of the schoolyard, though they do not always choose to keep quiet about lesbians when talking to family.

When the oldest boy was in the third grade, the class was studying word-opposites. The teacher wanted to know the opposite of *straight*. He dutifully raised his hand, ready with the answer. Dismayed by not being called on, he came home telling how the student who answered only said *crooked*. This, he informed us, was not the first definition. When I asked what he thought, he was proud of his own answer, "Lesbian." And what is that other one? "Oh, yeah, gay." What is a parent to do? How does one teach reality without hindering the creativity and innocence of a child?

Two years ago when the kids were at camp, my partner and I wrote both of them every day. No small task, believe me. When one of the camp counselors (a lesbian herself) asked the youngest, "Who is Robyn?" he replied, "My mom's friend." "How nice of your mom's friends to write you," she said. "NO!" he exclaimed, "She's my mom's *friend*." After repeating himself three times, she caught on. He was relieved. This is important information.

Coming to terms with social, peer, and even family pressure is one dimension, but being part of a community that does not know how, or refuses, to include boy children is another. I have experienced more pain, dirty looks, rude attitudes, and silence from women in a community I feel should know better, than in the world I expect it from. Explaining women-only space to the boys was easier than I expected. They clearly understood and respected the idea. But their not being accepted, included, or warmly welcomed in mixed space is as difficult for them to understand as why lesbians are snubbed in the society at large. And as painful.

I respect every woman's right to be around who she chooses. If "boy energy" is something they cannot tolerate, I expect them to take care of themselves. If it is something they do not understand, I welcome them to ask questions.

I do not want us, as individuals and members of a community, to condone casting our differences, anger, hatred, or dislike onto our children.

If boy children are not included in a culture that attempts to teach the equality and empowerment of women, where else will they learn it? If they are made to feel bad simply because they were born, and because they act like boys (and will become men), they will be denied the opportunity to find their humanness.

Since having children in my life, the West Coast Women's Music Festival has taken on new meaning. The women of camp "Tell-Me-A-Riddle" have, over the last three years, told my partner and me how wonderful our kids are. I am included, with no strange questions or looks; no one asks me if I am their nanny, or remarks how lucky my partner is to have such a dedicated child-care worker. I simply have a place to be—as a woman, a lesbian, and a parent. I am recognized and respected.

During the final act of the Festival last year, I realized how complicated all of the theories and politics can be when they mix with matters of the heart. Our oldest boy had been under the blanket for a long time. As it was one of the hottest days of the year, I finally figured out he was hiding. I had been rubbing his leg, thinking he was resting. I did not notice his sobs. When my partner lifted his protection, I saw his swollen brown eyes. He had streams on his face from the tears mixing with dust. Whatever traces he had of his impending manhood were gone for now. Though he had reached the final age of acceptance, he was only a little boy. Still, this festival was his last. A rite of passage at age ten.

Our family rallied around him. His mother, younger brother, some special friends. We held him, cried with him, cracked jokes. He was understanding and brave. Reciting the reasons—women needed a place to be with other women, he was becoming a man, it was nothing personal, many of the women here loved him—yet allowing himself the tears and comfort boys and men are taught to deny.

I have not resolved this for myself. I do not want it to be that as my kids— and the many other boy children in our community—grow older, there will be no place for them to be with lesbians. I do not feel bitterness for the decisions of the Festival, for I, too, cherish a place to be with only women. My hope is that our community will come together to discuss the issues of children and parenting. It is not politically incorrect to bear, raise, know, or parent boy children. If we choose to maintain our silence and anger, we will further perpetuate the division between us.

As the children tell us, cooperation is only as difficult as the world around them makes it.

Planting Mary's Garden

Jiivanii J. Dent

Cool. Thick, slow clouds above me—moist, heavy soil still loose from yester-day's cultivation beneath my feet. There are more beds to dig and fertilize in preparation for the seeds, but today, Good Friday, enough soil is ready for planting Mother Mary's garden. María and I have cultivated this plot for five years. Teresita has helped, too, even when she was too young to do much else than get dirty. But a child always puts more into a garden than an adult can understand.

"Whatever you plant on Good Friday will grow." Mama told me that years ago when I was Teresita's age and helping in the garden. And so I always plant on Good Friday. Except the year I had an abortion. That was on Good Friday; I planted on Easter Sunday instead. Of course the moon had changed by Sunday. It wasn't the same. Still, my garden grew countless flowers, sad and deeply colored.

"Nina." The screen door slamming always seems to follow Teresita's call. "¿Katie Nina, podemos sembrar éstas, también?"

"Let's see what they are." Two heads bend over the brown bag crackling open. "They look like zinnia seeds. Let's plant the marigolds by the porch first. It will be our garden for Mother Mary."

I fold the bag closed and stuff it into one of my overalls pockets, already comfortably packed with bags of seed from past seasons—peas, lettuce, rad-ish, cosmos, morning glories, marigolds. The marigold seeds are fifth gener-ation, from the marigold plants I gave María on her first Mother's Day. Five years of loving each other, of struggling, giving, hurting, of defending our-selves against hostility and ignorance, and that ignorance too often our own.

I kneel in the dirt by the porch. My fingers burrow into the richly fed soil of the flower bed. Flecks of bone meal, manure stubbornly clumped, caliche that will never cooperate, rotting leaves and straw mulched in the fall, seed pods from last year's flowers and weeds—all meet and bury my hands, a joining of substances similar and sacred, each to the others. I feel my hands—strong, capable—and then her face and her breasts and thighs slip silently behind my eyes. María, te amo. Five years ago, with no one to give her a gift for Mother's Day except me, a new acquaintance, already falling in love, stopping by the greenhouse on my way to visit her. María, my beloved. Marigolds for you, María. I will give you so many flowers. "Nina, come on, let's plant the seeds." Teresita is impatient with my adult sense of time.

"O.K., but first let's thank Mary our Mother for protecting us and guiding us this year. This garden is in her honor."

A quietness grows, enlarging, filling the garden, as Teresita and I wait, eyes closed, for a feeling large and quiet to establish itself inside us. That done, I begin the familiar work of searching each pocket for the particular bag of seeds. Teresita helps me look, both hands tugging at the corner of a bag peeping from a hip pocket. When the marigolds are located, we each take a handful of pods and crumble them between our fingers, our palms, sprinkling the potential of spring from these hands upon the expectant soil. Sowing, sowing so many seeds. Sowing every part of the bed.

"Now, cover the seeds with soil, hita. Not too deep, not too shallow, but just right." And in the communion of hands and seeds, hearts and earth, joy rushes to my throat to hum, to sing, "I am alive! I am Life!" I know Teresita feels this pleasure too, as she urges me to plant more seeds everywhere in the prepared beds.

"Let's plant the lettuce next. Can we plant it aquí? Oh, Katie, I want to put the peas right next to this part of the fence, O.K., Mama?"

Sometimes she forgets and calls me mama. I like that.

By midmorning, all the beds have been planted, and it is time to dig and fertilize more planting space. This is the part that bores Teresita. She makes up games to play and occasionally asks, "Is it time for Mama to come home?"

"Soon," I say. "It's Good Friday, and she will leave work at noon." The clouds of dawn have dissipated, and I begin to feel the sun making moisture on my forehead, my lip and armpits. I slip my overalls straps off my shoulders, to hang loose about my hips, vowing to live someplace, someday, where I can freely remove my shirt when I'm working on a warm day.

I hear the gate lock clink and look up expecting an early arriving María. My heart freezes. It is Mick, the neighbor. In our yard. We call him El Loco, crazy as jimsonweed, poisoning the quiet barrio. He strides toward the shed, to the territory he claims. He dredges up a key from the pocket of his tight jeans and opens the padlock on the door. The door creaks, slowly swinging on rusty hinges. Rough and angry hands rummage in the dark interior, throwing out warped, rotted planks on the ground. "So, that's the kind of stuff he guards in that shed," I think. "Maybe the landlord finally told him to clean it out and keep his stuff in his own yard." As if he is suddenly aware of the four eyes unblinkingly aimed at his back, he turns, glaring savagely at us. I pick up my shovel in both hands like a weapon.

"¡Apúrele y métete a la casa!" My Spanish is crude, but Teresita understands and, for once, obeys immediately.

I walk slowly toward Mick, ever so slowly, like facing a rattling, alarmed snake. As I approach, I cast a magic circle about the yard, the garden, the house, about Teresita and me. All is encircled with light. Mick stamps madly toward me. He brings his fist to my face, the padlock hooked over the index finger knuckle. His face is purple, veins pop through the flesh of his neck, vicious brown eyes narrow against the glare. His fist and the metal of the padlock are shaking a hair's thickness from my nose. *Mother, I'm in trouble,* I send.

My knees are trembling; my entire being is trembling. From the far corner of my eye, I glimpse Teresita, a fuzzy grey face, staring at us from behind the screen door. I will absolutely not be afraid. I will not teach her to be afraid. Mick would kill me if he thought I was afraid. I see a thin wall of light slide between my face and the heavy, uncontrolled fist. *Mary,* I acknowledge. "Do your business and leave," I say firmly, with no emphasis on any one word.

Like an explosion pushing all life before its force, Mick's voice rages, "You fuckin' bulldykes takin' over everything. I oughta fuckin' kill you 'n that cuntsuckin' spic you live with. You're ruinin' that little girl. I feel sorry for her. I never done anything to you, why do you hate me? Fuck you, goddam bitch, you'd like to hit me—go on 'n hit me 'n see what I do to you."

I see his lips quiver. Curious. Cruel.

"If you forgive him now and talk to him, try to reason, the situation could change. He's your neighbor. Whatever you plant today. . . ."

I know, I know, I interrupt Mary's signal. *But that's for the old days when women forgave and forgave and still they killed us. No! Now, we require that men change. They must change,* I counter. *Mick has to change, 'cause I'm not dying.* Silence. No signal. Just watching me.

Still spewing dense billowing hatred into the atmosphere, Mick turns, spinning dust beneath his cowboy boots, and stomps to the shed. As he throws his wood and broken tools and rusted pipes about, I see that I could raise my shovel over my shoulder. I could raise my shovel up and bring it down with tremendous power on his head. Bring it down hard, crush his skull. His brains would splatter on the ground, against the trees, against my shirt. He turns his head and looks at me over his shoulder. He sees my nipples stuck to my sweatwet T-shirt with Amelia Earhart printed on the front. He stalks toward me. He looks at my body.

"You wanna hit me, I know. You go ahead 'n try it 'n just see what I do to you."

Now, I see his thoughts, how he would knock me down with his fist, my face bloody, how he would rip my clothes and tear my body, how he would ram me with his penis, kick me with his boots, and then turn to Teresita. I block his thoughts. I will not allow this rape to happen. He will not hurt me. He will not hurt my child. Abruptly Mick turns, quieter now, walks back to the shed and picks at his junk.

The magic circle is pulsing light ferociously. I will wait until he turns again to face me. And then I will kill him. I will end this obscenity. He will turn and I will raise my shovel and smash his slimy mouth. I will raise my shovel when he turns. My heart is a sledgehammer beating an anvil loud. I will kill him when he just turns. He will see me raise my weapon and know I am killing him. Kill him now, DOITNOW!

I'm shaking so hard I can't lift my shovel as he turns, loads up a pile of junk, eyes me evilly, knowing we will battle again. And the gate clinks shut behind him, leaving the circle of light. My shovel drops, the sharp metal edge slicing a crust of backyard adobe.

Mother Mary, I signal. She attends me. *Thanks for not letting me do that. It's not what I really want.* The elm and olive nod—true, true, as I quickly check the circle, reinforcing its power to protect. My heartbeat and breathing slow down to normal. Then, I notice that the shed door is still open. I feel a spear of fear penetrate my guts, my heart knocking hard again, wondering if Mick will come back. I will have to watch the gate today, cautious, with my shovel always close, constantly aware of Teresita, anxious for María to come home safe to us. And the seeds, the seeds must be planted today despite my uneasiness.

I walk, shovel still in hand, to the back door where Teresita waits. I stand my tool just inside the door.

"Katie Nina, is Mick gonna come back with his shotgun?"

I breathe a huge breath before answering. "I don't know, honey. But we're all right. We're strong. Don't worry. Hey, let's make some lunch for María, O.K.? With a pot of coffee...maybe a little whiskey, just a wee drop of whiskey in it for me and the fairies, like my mama would say. Well, maybe not. I gotta be very alert, just in case. Sure is nice to have a day off together, you and me. Right, hita?"

"Right!"

Eleven o'clock. Clear, starry, calm night. Teresita sleeps sideways on her bed, her hair a thick bramble slung blackly over her face and shoulders. No place available for a goodnight kiss. She may need another blanket before morning. Spring nights on the high desert are chilly. María will probably wake up later and check her. I pad softly through the shadowy house, the small lamp in the kitchen a sentinel. The circle of light still surrounds our home, illumining the curtained windows. I enter our bedroom. María, exhausted, already sleeps in our bed, breathing her dreams without me. I lift the blankets and slide legs against legs, belly to back, arms wrapping around warm woman.

I wait the few minutes before sleep, blinking in our dark, adobe room. I think of the seeds planted today, cuddling in their dark, adobe room, their skins swelling with moisture, waiting for the time they will burst with tender new life and push faithfully through the hard-packed clay toward the light, the rain—to flower, fruit, and return.

A Life Speckled With Children
Sherri Paris

Sabra had been, as they say, unlucky—meaning foolish—in love. Out of this foolishness had come a life intermittently speckled with children. Now in her continuing role as friend or mother, she identified, in truth, more with the children who clutched at her with moist open hands, than with their cool, ambivalent mothers who came and went. Everyone assumed that Sabra adored children because she was kind, because she played at the beach in a certain way. This assumption had grown into the legend that she was somehow especially adept with children and irrevocably bonded with them. Well, maybe. . . .

Gayle, the first woman she had sworn to spend her entire life with, now arrived twice monthly with a joint in her mouth, a Halston briefcase clamped to her side, and Richard trailing sullenly along behind her. Sabra and Gayle had parted just over four years ago. During those years, Richard had turned from a sly balding three-year-old to a stodgy man of seven-and-one-half. He was certain and systematic in his movements, with a dim-eyed stubbornness which looked—from a great distance—like some sense of purpose. He was not, Sabra felt, all that different from Gayle's husband, Bryan, who had promptly adopted the boy after their marriage three years ago. Since then, Gayle had never alluded to the life she and Sabra had shared, but maintained instead an easy affection for Sabra, kissing her chastely on the cheek and daintily patting her back whenever they hugged.

Sabra's second eternal love, Diana, still an avowed lesbian, had become so politically inspired in the ensuing years that she had cut off all her hair. Now, she and her son Thaddeus both sported bristling crew cuts, and Diana worked relentlessly to shape him into a feminist man, hopefully gay, and earnestly encumbered with the appropriate modes of guilt. Diana consistently needed child care while she attended her weekly co-op meetings, her committee in sympathy with the women of Nicaragua, her incest survivors' support group, and her network for adult children of alcoholics. Thaddeus, at eleven, was as critical of Sabra's lifestyle as her mother had been, pointing out to her that coffee and television were both addictions which Sabra could rid herself of by turning her life over to a higher Power. Sabra was considering it.

And now, Grace, her most recent lover, had left her for their best friend, Lisa, and Sabra found herself picking up Jewel, Grace's five-year-old daughter, for a Sunday afternoon drive in the park.

"Hello," called Grace, smiling fiercely, as she approached the locked car door. Without looking up, Sabra worked on adjusting Jewel's seatbelt. Jewel fidgeted, cheerfully unscrewing the legs from the Barbie doll she had just acquired for her birthday.

Off the tapedeck, Emmy Lou Harris flipped a melodic line, "Lou, you gotta start new and the first thing you gotta do is get some white shoes."

"Are you going to get white shoes?" Jewel asked Sabra.

"Should I?"

"Sure. Why not?"

Grace leaned forward to blow Jewel a kiss. Sabra gunned the engine loudly. As they drove off, Jewel tugged at Sabra's arm. "How come my mommy always pretends to say hello to you when you never answer?"

"She's not pretending exactly," said Sabra. "Not *exactly*."

"Sure she is. When you first moved out, I used to come downstairs with my blanket and pretend to say good morning to you. Now I don't though. Now I can't even see you with my eyes closed. Look what Lisa bought me."

She held up her hand, showing a gold and ruby bracelet.

"That's very petty."

"I know," said Jewel, taking the bracelet and placing it on her head like a tiny crown.

"I think Mama pretends to say hello to you because she misses you. Why don't you answer her?"

"I can't." Sabra stared down the street aware of the passing homes with unfolding families tucked into their living rooms. "Maybe I'm just not a very nice person."

Jewel stroked her arm softly. "Yes," she said, "You are a *very* nice person."

The two rode together in silence for a while.

"I miss you," Sabra finally said.

"I used to miss people. You and papa. But then, my misser broke. Now I don't miss anyone at all."

"Your misser broke?"

"Yes, I used to have a very strong misser, but then it broke. Like the ET clock Grandma bought me on Christmas. My misser just ran down."

Sabra pulled the car to the curb alongside a tiny park with swings.

"Push me, Sabra. I want to go up high."

"I can't push you, because my body is hurt." Sabra had been disabled for years by rheumatoid arthritis, a difficult thing for a sunny-minded five-year-old to grasp. "Remember?"

"Yes. I remember, but I keep thinking that one day you'll be all better. Like my knee. I skinned it last week, but now—look. It's perfect." She offered her pale, bald knee for Sabra's inspection.

Sabra kissed it. "Indeed, a completely perfect knee."

Jewel giggled. "That's not where you kiss, silly. Kissing is like this." She scrunched her eyes shut tightly, grabbed Sabra's head, and kissed her fiercely on the lips.

"Whew! Where'd you learn that?"

"From Mama and Lisa, of course. I learned everything from Mama. Except for about Jesus. Papa teaches me that."

Sabra walked around the car and unbuckled Jewel's seatbelt.

"You're certainly learning a lot these days."

"Yes, about kissing. Only women do it. Men hardly kiss at all. They do like this." She leaned forward and gave Sabra a dry, papery brush on the cheek. "That's what men do. I learned that from Papa."

Sabra lifted her from the car. As she did so, a twisting blade of pain shot down her spine. "How about if you and I go feed the ducks?" Taking Jewel's hand, she reached into her shirt pocket and popped a pain pill.

"Hey, is that candy? Can I have one?"

"I'll buy you candy later. This is medicine."

"Will it make you well?"

"Not exactly. But it makes me feel better."

"Oh," said Jewel, hopping on one foot, "what kind?"

"Huh?"

"What kind of candy will you buy me later?"

"Well, I don't know. That's a very serious question."

"What's serious?"

"It's when you care about something so much you don't even smile." Jewel scowled, "I'm *very* serious. Do you think we could have chocolate?"

"Yes."

"Good." Jewel hugged her and ran down a shallow hill to the duck pond.

Sabra slumped down on the grass and lay on her back, looking up at the clouds which brooded over the playground like anxious and tangible spirits. It seemed that much of her life had been spent looking up at clouds. Shortly, Jewel returned, flushed with exertion. In her hand she gripped an absolutely undistinguished grey stone.

"Sabra. Look what I found. It was just laying there on the ground. Can you *believe* it? Someone must have lost it or something—huh?"

Sabra picked up the rock and peered under it as if looking for what she couldn't see.

"A fine rock."

"I love this playground. You can find incredible stuff here. It's *amazing*, Sabra."

"Yes," said Sabra, "amazing."

By the time they were ready to leave the playground, Jewel had collected eight rocks, one sneaker, and a yellow plastic squeeze-top with the voluptuous odor of slightly spoiled honey.

She assigned Sabra to carry the squeeze top and two of the larger rocks.

"I don't know about the sneaker, honey. The little boy who lost that sneaker might come back to look for it."

"I *want* it, Sabra, I *want* the sneaker."

"But some little boy will be walking around with just one shoe on."

"Yes. He has one and I have one. That's *fair*. My teacher taught us about that. It's called sharing."

Sabra shrugged. Often these days, because she had so little time with Jewel, because she felt their relationship slowly slipping away, she chose not to argue. Chose to give in. Trying to protect a bond between them which seemed incredibly fragile.

Children, Sabra knew, were not creatures of memory. They loved you when you were there. Once Jewel's and Sabra's hearts had joined through daily hugs and hurts, through afternoon baths and far-fetched stories. Now their lives had separated. And Sabra was attempting to hold that heart with trips to the park and pieces of candy.

So Sabra tended to let Jewel have her way. Not that Jewel had ever been easy to say no to. She stuck out her heart-shaped chin and argued with a dead certainty which had always left Sabra feeling awed and hopeless. Jewel had been unshakable—certain of her right to the universe even as a wobbly toddler. How, Sabra had often wondered, could a *child* be so certain. Sabra's own early years had been dim and cramped, permeated with the smells of the Jewish ghetto: a blend of chicken and cabbage cooking, of floor wax and smoke, and old, frayed sheets, ironed again and again. It was a world ruled by old people; grandparents and widowed aunts, so unlike California which was ruled by the sun, the sea, by the young. By children.

"Now Jewel, suppose we put these rocks in the trunk of the car."

"No. I want them where I can see them. Because they are so bee-yew-tee-ful."

"O.K." Sabra piled the rocks and the plastic squeeze-top on the floor of her car and buckled Jewel's seatbelt. Jewel insisted that Sabra tie the gym shoe to her rearview mirror, the way she had seen people do with bronzed baby shoes.

"That looks *good*, Sabra. You know what? I lost my Barbie doll."

"Oh dear. Should we go back to the duck pond and look for her?"

"Uh, uh. I don't like her anymore. Her legs wouldn't come off. They were stuck. It was too much work. I don't want her."

"Oh, O.K. Well, where should we go then?"

"Nowhere."

"Nowhere?"

"Yes, Sabra. I just want to sit in the car and *be* with you."

"Just stay here?"

"Yes, because you're here and my rocks are here now and I can look at them and you too, Sabra. Tell me a story about you and my mama. O.K.?" Sabra stared at the small, dangling gym shoe. Her relationship with other children had always been distant and indulgent. Sabra used their presence as an excuse to do things off the beaten path of adulthood, things she enjoyed, like devouring pizza to the dance of predictable puppets at Chuckie Cheese. Or wading at the beach or rollerskating at the Discorama rink in Scotts Valley. Or watching strange monsters reenact a classic morality fable in the latest *Star Wars* movie. Activities she didn't do with friends, activities that were so sweetly foolish, she would have felt too lonely doing them by herself.

This time spent watching, doing, eating, was not particularly intimate. Sabra knew this and didn't care. She could not handle intimacy with these small alien people who hugged her so fiercely and left gum on the seat of her car.

Jewel was different. She was too fine-tuned and intense for distractions. Only once during their brief weekly visits had Sabra attempted to entertain them, taking Jewel to see Speilberg's popular *ET*. From the time the small monster appeared on the screen, Jewel hunched in Sabra's lap with her hands clamped over her eyelids, faintly trembling.

"Come on," Sabra whispered, stroking her hair, "we can leave, if you don't like this."

"No, Jewel hissed, her eyes tightly closed. "It's *interesting*, Sabra. It's *interesting*."

They remained like that for over an hour, Jewel intermittently peeking at the screen and shutting her eyes whenever ET appeared, but refusing to leave. Sabra kept her nose in the child's fragrant hair, enjoying the feel of her plump thighs, of the small head brushing against her breasts.

She remembered holding Jewel in the night, after her parents had separated and Grace and Jewel had moved in with Sabra. Jewel had begun having nightmares then, sitting up wild-eyed in the dark while Grace, exhausted and grieving herself, slept on. During those nights, Sabra had been the comforter, and she felt oddly guilty at the movies, having carried Jewel into this world of new and unnecessary terror. Halfway into the film, Jewel opened her eyes and seemed to get into it. She clapped her hands when the children on bicycles rose to the sky with ET. But when the movie was over, Jewel began crying inconsolably. "We had our afternoon, Sabra," she said over and over, "But I miss *you*." And even before the tears began, Sabra herself felt oddly lonely and cheated.

A Birthday Remembered

Ann Allen Shockley

"Hello, Aunt El...?"

The familiar voice came over the telephone, young, vivacious, excited, a girlish echo reminding her of the past. "Tobie...."

"Happy birthday!"

"Thank you." Ellen felt a rush of warmth, pleased that Tobie had remembered. But hadn't Tobie always. Besides, her birthday wasn't difficult to remember, falling on Valentine's Day. *A heart born especially for me*, Jackie used to tease.

"May I come over?"

Now Tobie's voice sounded a little strained. Ellen could visualize the puckers of thin lines forming between her wide-spaced eyes. The tightness in her throat delayed an answer. Why shouldn't she? Then again, why *should* she really want to? Tobie no longer belonged to her—*them*. When Jackie died a year ago, Tobie had to go back to her father. A splintering separation, after all their years of living together, belonging together—Tobie, Jackie, and herself.

The three of them had survived through the tumultuous stress of trying to make it, ever since Jackie walked out on Roger and came to live with her. Tobie was just five years old—too small and pale for her age, too nervous from the parental arguments.

Roger had been furious, appalled and angry at his wife's leaving him for a woman. Ellen knew it was more an affront to his male ego than losing Jackie. Particularly when it belonged to one who was striving ruthlessly to become a top business executive, amassing along the way all the exterior garnishments that were supposed to go along with it. He had purchased a large, two-story brick colonial house in the suburbs, replete with swimming pool and a paneled Country Squire station wagon for Jackie to do her errands. When she left him, he had tried to declare her temporarily insane.

Ellen thought that perhaps Jackie *had* been crazy to leave all of that and come to live with her in a cramped apartment on her salary. She wasn't making that much at the time as a staff writer for *Women's Homemaking* magazine's food section. But, somehow, they had made out until Jackie got a job teaching in an elementary school. Jackie loved children, and had a way with them.

"Hey. . .Aunt El. You still with me?"

Tobie was waiting for an answer. One could get so involved in the past. "Of course, dear. Please *do* come over," she invited, thinking it wasn't until later she was to have dinner with Harriet. All she had to do was change from her jumpsuit to a dress.

"I'm bringing a friend who I want you to meet. O.K.?"

Tobie never had an abundance of friends, only special ones who were close, for that was her way. At first, she and Jackie had mistakenly thought Tobie was ashamed of their relationship, what they were to each other. They knew Tobie was aware of it. How could she not have been. Real love can't be hidden. It inevitably is transmitted through a glance, affectionate touch, strong feelings that show.

Then there was the rainy, cold night in November, one month after Jackie had left him, when Roger came to the apartment, hurling threats, shouting obscenities. He was going to take them to court, declare them perverts, unfit to raise a child. Tobie must have heard the words flung out at them through the paper-thin walls.

"Wonderful, darling. I'll look forward to meeting your. . .friend."

The phone clicked, and Tobie wasn't there anymore. Ellen remained seated on the couch, motionless, as if the remembrance of all that had gone by in ten years had risen like a mist to cover her in sadness. There had not been a divorce because of his man-stubbornness and Jackie's woman-fear for Tobie. When she died, he buried her. She hadn't been allowed to do this one last thing for Jackie. To *be* with her during the last rituals, to hold a fourteen-year-old who was, in all but flesh, her daughter, too. The next morning after the funeral, Tobie came by to be with her, to cry her tears, sustain her grief. The sorrow shared as one was their solitary entombment for her. Through the passing days, the biting cruelty of it all slowly healed, leaving only the scar tissue. Jackie had been laid to rest in her heart.

Ellen's eyes fell on the array of birthday cards on the coffee table and the vase of red roses that Harriet had sent. Meeting Harriet had helped her to get over the travail of death's cruel separation. Incurable illnesses are like earthquakes—they swallow quickly. It wasn't too bad now. She could look back and recall without too much pain. All it takes is someone to help, someone who cares, and the eraser of time.

The living room was beginning to become shaded with dark-fingered lances of shadows. She reached over and turned on a table lamp. The day was quickly vanishing into the grayness of night. What she should do was get a drink. A good, stiff celebrating birthday martini. After all, she was forty-four years old. Six more years, if still alive, she would reach the half-century mark.

She got up and went to the kitchen. There she turned on the light which brought into sharp, garish focus the ultra-modern bright chrome and copper, resembling the spacious kitchens featured in her magazine articles where various culinary talents were exhibited. Thankfully, through her writing skills, she had been able to help make their living better before Jackie passed. She had become editor of the food section and had written a cookbook. Her publisher had assured her that cookbooks always sell, and hers had.

A martini called for gin, vermouth, lemon, and an olive. She got out the glass pitcher and stirrer. Jackie preferred sunrises. She made them for her in the evenings, after the lengthy daily struggles of climbing the ladder together. Jackie had become principal of the school, a model for those beneath her, and an in-school parent for the students. Ellen marveled at how she had blossomed, learning to become independent after being a college-trained housewife to Roger. *There's so much to living that I did not know before,* Jackie had told her happily. Yes, indeed, there was a lot to living that neither had known before.

She mixed the drink in the shaker, stirred it slowly, and poured some in a glass, topping it with a round green olive with a small red eye-circle. *Here's to you, Ellen Simms, on your birthday!* She lifted the glass in a toast and the drink went down smoothly. Then the doorbell rang. Tobie must have been just around the corner. As soon as she responded, Tobie sang out cheerfully: "Happy birthday to you, happy birthday to you!"

Tobie hugged her and Ellen found her nose pressed into the cold leather of her jacket. Tobie seemed taller. *They do grow,* she mockingly reminded herself, comparing her own short stockiness to Tobie's height.

"A present for you, Aunt El."

When Tobie thrust the gift into her arms, Ellen protested, "You shouldn't have." The package was neatly store-wrapped and tied with a pink ribbon holding a card.

"You know I never forget your birthday, Aunt El."

At that moment, she saw the boy standing awkwardly behind her. He had a round, friendly face and a mass of dark brown hair parted on the side.

"Hello," she spoke to him.

"Aunt El, this is Warrick."

"Come in and take off your coats. Would you like some hot cocoa to warm you up? I know it's cold outside." Tobie used to love hot cocoa with a marshmallow floating like a full-grown moon on top. This was her favorite on Sunday mornings when they had a leisurely breakfast together.

"Cocoa, you *know* what I like!" Tobie exclaimed, throwing off her coat and curling up on the sofa.

Ellen watched her, noting the girlishness hadn't gone yet in the transitional adolescent stage. She looked older. Her blonde hair was cut short and bangs covered her forehead. Physically, she looked more like her father with the sharp, angular face, but there was her mother where it counted most, in her warmth and quickness of smile. Did her father know that she was here—with her. Like visiting a widowed parent—eight years of child-rearing, child-caring, child-loving.

"Open your present, Aunt El."

"All right." First she read the heart-shaped card with the fringed edges about Valentine birthdays, and then the scribbled message: *To my one and only, Aunt El, with love, always.* She blinked back the tears and made a fanfare out of unwrapping the gift. It was a big, glossy, illustrated, expensive cookbook of ancient Eastern recipes.

"Thank you, my dear." She leaned over to kiss Tobie's cheek. "It's lovely."

"Tobie saved up a week's salary to buy it," Warrick announced proudly, settling in the rocker opposite the sofa. His voice was changing, and there was an inflamed red pimple beside his nose. On the front of his red and white pullover sweater were the words *Terrence Academy.* The right sleeve had a large white *T.*

"Warrick! Shame on you giving my secrets away," Tobie laughed, playfully chastising him.

"Where are you working?" Ellen asked, hanging their coats in the closet. She couldn't imagine Roger Ewing permitting his teen-aged daughter to work.

"I'm a library page after school at the branch near home. I like to have my own money," she added reflectively.

Ellen hesitated, wondering if she should ask. Don't forget the social amenities. Isn't that what they had taught Tobie throughout the years. "How is your. . .father?" she asked, the words sounding like cracked dry ice.

"Oh, Dad's O.K.," she shrugged, kicking off the high wooden-wedge platforms with interlacing straps. "His main object in life seems to be to prove how much money he can make and keep."

Roger's a miser at heart; he wants every cent I spend accounted for, yet he'll go out and buy something outlandishly showy to prove he's got money, Jackie had commented about him.

Why was it that people happen to be in certain places at the right or wrong time? Like the dinner party she had been assigned to write up for the magazine to describe the elegance of the food, drinks, and table settings. There, seated next to her, was Jackie, looking small, frail and lost among the spirited laughter and inane chitchat of the moneyed. Roger was on her other side, appearing to be thoroughly enjoying himself talking to the big-bosomed woman with the glittering necklace and frosted white hair. There was the interest at first sight, hidden hormones clashing while a subtle intuitive knowingness flashed hidden messages above the clamor of the room. *If only we could decide our own fates, what would life then be?*

"I'll make the cocoa," she said, retreating to the kitchen.

The martini pitcher was on the counter where she had left it. Immediately she poured another drink. She had been ruminating too much. Stop the past. Drink and be merry. Chase the haunting memories away.

"Aunt El, need any help?"

Tobie came in. She had put her shoes back on and they made a hard noise against the linoleum. The wedges looked like ancient ships, causing her to wonder if they were comfortable. The bell-bottom blue jeans billowed over them like sails. "No, nothing to making cocoa. After all the times of doing it for you. . . ." The reminder slipped out. She wished it hadn't.

Tobie laughed, and the sound made everything all right again. "What do you think of Warrick?" she asked, reaching into the closet for cups and saucers. Everything was known to her in a place that had once been home.

"He seems like a nice. . . boy." Suppose it had been a girl? People choose who they want. This they had tried to instill in her in their unobtrusive way. "How does your father like him?"

"Dad hasn't met him yet," Tobie said quietly. "I wanted to get *your* opinion *first*. Anyway, Dad stays busy and away so much that we don't have much time to talk. The housekeeper takes care of the house—and me—who, I suppose, goes with the house." She gazed down at the floor, biting her lip, face clouded. "I miss Mom—don't you?"

"Yes," she replied softly. "But we have to get used to living without loved ones. That time must inevitably come, sooner or later, for somebody."

She turned away, pretending to search the refrigerator so Tobie couldn't see her face. Do something else while waiting for the milk to warm. Prepare sandwiches. Young people were always hungry—feeding growth. She had cold chicken and potato salad left over from last night.

"I thought if *you* liked Warrick, Mom would too. He plays on the basketball team," Tobie continued, watching her slice the chicken and take out the jars of pickles and mustard from the refrigerator.

"Are you. . . serious about him?" Ellen asked, praying that she wasn't. Not at this stage of youth, almost fifteen.

"Of course not! We're just friends. He's someone to go places and do things with."

"Good!" Ellen exclaimed, feeling an impending burden lifted. "There's plenty of time for the other. You have to go to college and—" she went on hurriedly about those things which normally fall in place for young lives.

Tobie smiled. "I *knew* you were going to say that, Aunt El." Then she looked directly at her, blue eyes locking Ellen's in a vise. "Anyway, someday, if I ever *do* get serious about someone, I hope it will be as wonderful and beautiful as what you and Mom had together."

God, for the first time, it was out in the open! She felt the shock of the words, unexpected, frank—a blessing. "I do too, dear. Like we had." Her hands trembled from the weight of the moment between them. A bridge had transformed Tobie from girl to woman now to her.

"Aunt El, the milk's boiling over!"

"I've lost my cocoa-making expertise," Ellen laughed, snatching the pan off the burner. The milk had boiled into a bubbling white-coated cascade of foam.

When the tray of food was ready, they went back to the living room where Warrick was watching TV. While they ate hungrily, Ellen finished her drink, feeling light, warm, and happy.

When the telephone rang, it was like a rude interruption into a special cradle of time. Harriet wanted to know if she would be ready around seven-thirty for dinner. She glanced at her watch. It was just six o'clock. Besides, what was more important to her than this?

Later, Tobie said, "We'd better be going. Warrick's taking me to the movies. Thanks for the treat, Aunt El."

"And, thank *you* for the present. I'm glad you came by to make my birthday a happy one. *Both* of you."

"Nice meeting you, Miss Simms," Warrick said, extending his hand. "Tobie talks about you all the time. Now I can see why!"

She liked him. "Come back—anytime."

Tobie kissed her good-bye at the door. When they left, the tears were finally freed—in sadness and happiness too. Tobie was going to make it all right. Jackie would have been proud. They had made good parents.

On A Creative Edge

Toni Tortorilla

Motherhood came through a side door in the form of a daughter born to my lover of twelve years. She had wanted a child since the beginning days of our relationship. When in the fall of 1977 she became pregnant, we each faced the realization of an idea we had held in our minds and fed with our lives for over a decade. For two lesbians who had begun their relationship at a Catholic women's college, the approach of motherhood was the unexpected fulfillment of a dream we barely dared to dream.

The whole of life changed its context when we learned the results of the pregnancy test. Pregnancy does have a way of doing that! My lover and I puzzled over how and when to tell our families. We were overjoyed by the news, but we would be asking them to accept yet another extension of an already unconventional lifestyle. For her mother, sister, and brother, who were already approving of our lifestyle, the announcement was met with joy. My mother, on the other hand, was shocked. While still disapproving of my relationship, how could she be expected to open her arms warmly to receive this child? My brother, who had been supportive until then, seemed more distant in the years that followed. It wasn't until he had his first child that my having a daughter seemed to fall into place for him. During those intervening years, I longed for my family's acceptance of this child my whole being moved to nurture and protect.

That feeling of acceptance came unexpectedly one day six years later, following my brother's call to announce that he and his wife were expecting a baby. I was delighted. I called my mother to get her reaction to the news and found myself asking how she felt now that she was becoming (officially) a grandmother. (My nonsanctioned parenthood had conferred no such recognition I realized.) She seemed surprised by my question and answered that she was already a grandmother. She said she felt no different this time. She continued to speak and, deeply moved, I tried to absorb the change which had obviously occurred without my awareness. I heard her speak a concern that she might not be able to love another grandchild as she loved Kyla. I was near tears. Six years I had waited for words of devotion toward my daughter and now it was difficult to take in, difficult to trust what I was hearing and feeling. Yet my mother is not one to speak idly nor has she ever been capable of playing favorites. What she did that day, I later realized, was claim Kyla as her first-born grandchild. I cannot describe the deep sense of peace and acceptance I felt then. My daughter and I had finally come home.

Many issues have arisen for me, as a nonbiological parent, which seem unique to the lesbian lifestyle. My own family's reluctance to accept Kyla as my daughter has been the most painful one. The oddest, however, occurred during the months of pregnancy when I felt I had more in common with expectant fathers than I did with my expectant lover. I saw very clearly how society all but ignores the father-to-be, leaving him to cope with his fears and his heightened sense of responsibility without support. There is no cultural structure to assist a man to heartfully bond with a child still in the womb. In fact, everything discourages that from happening.

For me, as a woman, I could feel in my own body the process of gestation through the empathy and kinship I had with my lover. A psychic bond began to grow between our child and myself. After four months she would often respond, through kicks, to my touch. At eight months she came to me in a dream, and I knew from that moment what she would look like when she was born.

As I thought of parenthood throughout those months, I felt I would always be between worlds. I wondered where I would fit in this child's life. As a woman, I could not play the role of a father, nor did I want to. My child would have a mother. What would she need with me? I knew I did not want to play "aunt" or "special friend." I felt parental and wanted to be acknowledged as a parent.

A strange thing happened a few days after we all came home from the hospital. I was putting Kyla in her crib one afternoon, when I was overcome with a need to verbalize my commitment to her. Feeling very foolish, I spoke to the tiny infant in my arms, promising solemnly that I would stay with her no matter what happened. At the time I made that promise I felt absolutely sure her mother and I would always be together.

I laughed at myself for giving expression to the heightened emotionality of this tender and exquisitely joyous time in my life. Yet within three months after our daughter's first birthday (after being together for thirteen years), my lover and I went through a very painful separation, and our family unit entered a state of crisis.

I continued to see Kyla regularly, although I was so raw I could not be with her without grieving over the loss of our family. I wondered constantly about the wisdom of continuing to parent her. Few people acknowledged my parental role in regard to her, and most who did seemed to do so more as a way of supporting me than because they saw a valid connection between Kyla and myself. Since I seemed to be the only one holding firm to that connection (or felt I was), I often questioned whether it would be healthier for all of us if I would just let go.

I felt so confused in my grief. I knew I didn't want to place this child in jeopardy while working through my own pain. If I withdrew from the scene right now, would it really affect Kyla? Was she already bonded to me in some deep way that I could barely know? Would something tear inside her life if I simply left? She was only a year old and couldn't tell me how she felt.

Seeing my former lover was excruciating for me, and I wanted to leave town so as to free myself from all contact with her and her new lover. Each time I got close to a decision to run from it all, my promise to a four-day-old infant would replay in my mind, taunting me, and I would break into tears, unable to leave. Often I have wondered whether my intuitive self prompted that oath so that, when the time came, I would not run away from parenthood in my pain.

Though Kyla's mother had as much difficulty seeing me as I had seeing her during those early months, she continued to honor my role in her child's life, arranging and rearranging with me schedules of sharing our daughter. We each took up the task of single parenting (her new partner being unwilling to parent). Barely able to communicate with one another, we continued to deal with the business of childraising, and that became the only area where discussion was even possible.

Throughout those early years, this parental partnership demanded the greatest courage and triggered some of the worst behavior in each of us. We felt used and abused in different ways by the other. She felt tied down, with ultimate responsibility for Kyla resting on her shoulders, while to her, I appeared free and able to do whatever I liked whenever I wanted. To me she seemed secure, the one who could make the decisions I would have to live by, the most feared being that she would move out of town and take our daughter with her.

Communication became easier. With time, we even began to reestablish some measure of trust. Friendship is growing once again, even as I write this, and we are renewing our individual commitments to the family we have created. It took six years to reach the point of being able to join forces—in a whole new way—not as lovers but as loving parents of our child.

The catalyst for renewal of family ties came, as often happens, in the form of a crisis. As Kyla's mother and I sat having lunch one day (which we had begun to do in an attempt to excavate an eighteen-year-old friendship from the ruins of our separation process), she answered a question by telling me there was a possibility she might be moving. This did not come as a surprise. Her lover had been out of work and looking for a job for several months, and she herself had just lost her position to the declining Oregon economy. With tears in her eyes she looked at me that afternoon and said,

"I can't bear the thought of taking Kyla away from you or of taking you away from her." It was the first time I saw how deeply committed she was to preserving that bond between her daughter and me. In seeing the depth of her feeling, I felt secure as coparent for the very first time. Kyla was nearly seven years old.

This was the beginning of another tremendously uprooting period of change. I was in a new and very supportive relationship with a woman who planned to move to the central California coast the following summer to be near her son. As Kyla's mother and her lover wound through the options available to them, my lover and I were doing the same thing. What was different and unique this time around between Kyla's mother and me was that we were going through the changes together, with an eye toward preserving both our individual and joint family commitments as well as our friendship.

Plans developed quickly that spring. By mid-summer, Kyla and her mother had moved to southern California and my lover and I were making plans to move to Santa Cruz. September would find us all settled into our new communities, with me trying to understand why I had uprooted my life only to locate 300 miles *away* from my daughter. I spent the next nine months attempting to orient myself to living apart from my child while commuting to Southern California once every six-to-ten weeks. It was an extremely difficult time for me. My own relationship suffered from the ups and downs of my erratic emotions.

Toward spring, however, Kyla's mother began expressing misgivings about the value system our daughter was being exposed to in her new environment. In March she, her lover, and Kyla came for a visit. During a late evening conversation which lasted through to the first light of morning, Kyla's mother informed me of her plan to move to Santa Cruz when school let out in June. She wondered if she could stay with me and my lover until she found a job and got settled. She wanted our family to be together again and wanted Kyla to have my daily influence in her life. Her lover would be staying in southern California, at least for the time being.

I was excited about them joining me, and the thought of living with my daughter again gave me great joy. I felt ready to experiment with the possibility of blending families. My lover, not surprisingly, was less than enthusiastic about the prospect of sharing space with my ex-lover. Knowing how much it meant to me, she was willing to try out the living arrangement and be as supportive and adaptable as possible. The *possible* for her has been a continuing source of inspiration for me.

I won't say these last few months have been easy. Living with a lover, an ex-lover, and a child in the same small house has proven to be an intensive experience in lesbian family dynamics. Residing at the heart of this configuration is Kyla, who relates to all of the adults with relative ease and seems to experience the unit as a "family." We adults, however, have had to deal with the emotional edges of the triangle we form, and this has been an enormous challenge at times.

Rediscovering the ground for day-to-day coparenting in the history of our relationship has been wonderfully healing for Kyla's mother and me. Old wounds have been assuaged through the very fact of living together in the same house again. Cooking together, washing dishes, reminiscing about good times as well as painful ones, laughing—all of this has created the foundation for a more unified parenting expression in the months and years to come.

This groundwork has often been experienced as an exclusive, threatening, and confusing exchange by my lover. Sometimes she has wondered where my relationship with her fits into my life. Having been together for less than two years when my ex-lover and child moved into our home, she and I have also been in the process of building our own emotional and psychic foundations. We have had little private space in which to do this, and that, of course, has been terribly frustrating and even alienating at times. Perhaps only another mother could manage such patience and fortitude in the midst of her own emotional turbulence.

Though we have not actually blended into one family unit, we have had many warm moments and a remarkable amount of support for our differing needs. I am amazed at how well we have done within this three-sided fish bowl. All of us have made the effort to give space where needed and to take space as required—both essential to maintaining a balance in the energy flow of the household. We have even had fun. There is a wealth of insight still to be plumbed from this venture into extended family, lesbian-style. I look forward to having time to absorb the ins and outs of all that has occurred.

The child in our midst is thriving. Living together with her mother and me seems to have integrated the two basic structures of her life in a subtle yet significant way. Living together with my lover and me in the presence of her mother has neutralized the jealousy which previously ran rampant when only the three of us (Kyla, my lover, and I) were together. My lover has been more than supportive to Kyla. She has picked her up from school, provided projects for earning money upon Kyla's request, listened to her stories, responded to her needs for nonparental adult interaction, joked with her, and basically remained accessible as well as respectful of her incessant demands on me. Her willingness to be involved with Kyla has helped create a home environment which feels both fluid and secure. My daughter's response to this loving attention has been to open her heart and accept my partner as a valued member of her personal extended family.

The central parenting issue for me during this time has revolved around the pragmatics of coparenting in shared space. Kyla's mother and I have been single parents for all practical purposes since the time of our separation. Consulting one another by phone regarding our child's ear infection or the need to buy her a new pair of shoes is worlds apart from codisciplining an infraction of bicycle privileges. I have come face-to-face with the differences in our parenting styles and values and with variations in our expectations around behavior. I have also had firsthand experience of Kyla's responses to each of us as a personality and as a parent. At times I feel more overwhelmed than ever by the demands which attend this coparenting enterprise. Questions arise. How consistent do we need to be with each other around discipline? How can we continue to guide her cooperatively if we live in different houses? How much coordination of rule-setting needs to occur in order to prevent one of us being played against the other?

As I write, we are in the process of creating two separate households. My ex-lover's partner has found a job here and will be joining us all in just a few weeks. The two of them are searching for a house within walking distance from us and from Kyla's school so she will have equal access to both homes and to her neighborhood friends. Ideally, more space will provide additional freedom for everyone, and the family will be able to come together in a whole new way. For there *is* a family here—vibrant, alive, warm, and caring. We have come to realize over time what we intuitively knew in the beginning: this small and socially unrecognizable unit does comprise a very real family, one whose members love, depend on, and nurture each other in countless ways. It is an extended family of intriguing proportions, and it will continue to grow and to evolve in its own way. I feel enriched by my participation in this journey.

In speaking of lesbian family/extended family, I think it is important to say that throughout the early years of child-raising, Kyla's mother and I were each blessed with knowing wonderful women who were supportive of our personal growth and our parenting. These people took a keen interest in Kyla, allowing us time for ourselves when that time was desperately needed. Our daughter knows she is genuinely loved by these women who maintain their connections with her in innumerable ways. The lesbian community has been, for us, a real family.

The schools have asked few questions when both parents have volunteered time in the classroom and come to school events. They have accepted our time and energy with gratitude, conducted parent/teacher conferences with both of us, and tacitly supported our nontraditional family.

My daughter has been very open about having two moms. She knows her lifestyle is different, but she also feels very much loved and accepted for who she is. This seems to give her the courage to be and to express herself with her peers, even though she has told me this year with questioning concern in her voice, "They just don't understand, Mom."

I am so grateful, now, to that part of myself which motivated me to make a promise which felt out of sync with the times. I am glad I had a commitment to stay and to go through the whole painful process of those first few agonizingly searching years. It has all brought me to a place of knowing that my role is the role of neither father nor mother, but of parent. It is a role which ever changes as the needs of my child change, yet it is firm and clear in its substantial reality.

I still don't fit into the comfortable niches other parents (including lesbian moms) take for granted. But I live on a creative edge which celebrates a commitment born of love rather than biological imperative. I believe my daughter is blessed by my presence in her life. It has taken me nearly eight years to validate my role in this way, though I have felt bonded to her from conception.

It is not easy for the nonbiological parent in a lesbian or gay relationship to validate her or his role in a child's life. There is no readily definable slot. The parameters of society's vision are stretched by our very existence.

For the adults who choose to parent on this edge, there is no official recognition, no legal recourse, no hope for visitation rights if the relationship between lovers should end. There can be no formal adoption, unless the biological mother gives up custody or dies. There are financial requirements without tax allowances. The child cannot be claimed as a legal dependent.

And yet, though standing outside the protection and sanction of the system, many adults still choose to enter into a parental role with the children of their lovers. They commit time and energy to loving, nurturing, and supporting these children while risking the changes which could lead to separation from those whose lives they've nourished and formed. It is a risk the biological parent often minimizes or fails to recognize in her own need for support with childrearing. It is a risk I have come to know intimately.

Once Kyla identified me as parent, I entered a sacred trust with her that began to reshape my views of the world and myself. Being faithful to a relationship unacknowledged as such by the larger society is nothing new to a lesbian. I didn't want to play games with my child's mind or emotions. What I did want was for her to have two parents. I felt committed to standing in that place reserved for a second parent. Though she has strongly felt the absence of a father at times, Kyla has never wanted for love from two devoted parents. It is the steady solidness of that unwavering parental devotion I have sought to express by my presence and full participation in her life. It is an enchanting and infinitely challenging place. I am honored to be here.

Conflict

What's Love Got To Do With It

Blackcat, She-bear, Lesbian Mother

Kendall

Moonlight nurses her two kittens on the back porch, panting in the Texas electric July-oven heat, all hair and fleas and hot. The kittens, nearly three months old, knead and suck her sore, swollen breasts. She has begun weaning them. She's in season again, and the hair on her back and neck is matted and stiff from neighborhood tomcats' violence. A bit of her left ear has been torn or bitten off. A flea scuttles over the wound and she flicks the ear, tries to bat it with a front paw, but can't reach it without moving a sucking kitten. She quits trying. Too hot. Too tired. No doubt she's pregnant a second time, little fetuses sucking life from inside while these two still suck outside. We meant to get her spayed before this happened again. Her eyes half-shut, she rocks slightly. I am with her in the insect-humming afternoon. I know how it is.

The kittens, eyes clenched tight, knead and suck, knead and suck. She gives herself to them, rides the waves of their hunger and her own, dozes to the rhythm of knead and suck. It's erotic. Their mouths and paws relieve the pressure in her breasts, massage as they take from her, comfort as they suck. She slides into her own ease, yielding to their rhythm. She lifts herself to lick affectionately once, twice, then rests against the plank porch, giving and taking, knead and suck, lost with them in a mist.

Her people come and go. The tomcats with their hot teeth and spiny pricks come, and go. Her sister, with her own concerns, moved away. The kittens remain.

She escapes at night, slips off alone while they sleep. Last night this cat my son named Moonlight crouched under the light pole, watching moths. I watched her, black and silent, in the spiraling nightsong of cricket and cicada. A grasshopper flashed through the circle of light and she pounced after it into the blackness. She was young again, sleek, leaping, free, nameless. Roaming the wide night alone. Deliciously alone. This morning when I woke I found her curled protectively around the two sleeping bodies of her babies, smiling in her sleep. She had it all. I could see that.

I want it all, too. The relentless demand, the knead and suck, the need. And the comfort, the closeness. Intimacy intense, hypnotizing, obsessive. And freedom of the night. I want to slip away, sleek, leaping, nameless in the night, free; knowing I will return home to the comfort of that need, that continuance. To have it all.

Mary is my lover, my partner—a proud, smart, gentle dyke who never had, nor wanted, a child. To her, mothering is a weakness. She sees my relation to my sons as a pain in the ass, often. She sees me sucked dry, some days, and would protect me. She never fell for the programming, never needed, she says, to be "fulfilled" in motherhood, never needed that kind of dependence, that proof of femininity. Not her. She wants time with me alone. She deserves it. The boys deserve time alone with their mother. The blackcat in me wants time alone. Sometimes I have too much of it all.

My boys are big now, seventeen and ten, weaned long ago. I no longer sleep curled with them. There is Mary I curl with for comfort. And yet there are also the boys. With my second son I have an intimacy no lover has ever entered into, because he has been with me longer than anyone, ever.

My mother wasn't close to me. We didn't stay together. That's another story. I grew up without roots, never lived anywhere very long. Never stayed long enough to see how a friend grew, or turned out. I've know earthshaking loves: first, as a child, for women—four of them; then, as a young woman, for men—seven of them; finally, as an adult woman, for women—eight of them. Perhaps I have a genius for passionate attachment. But I've never held true for the long run. I've given all I had, everything. But was then tired, dry, weary. Worn thin. Used up, given out. Needed to be alone again to find the parts of me I lost that time around. For one, I gave up music; for another, I moved to an ugly place. One was annoyed by the sound of the typewriter, so I quit writing. Another wouldn't tolerate my vegetarianism, so I cooked meat and gagged. I quit smoking for one and started again for another. You compromise to live with someone; pieces of yourself get buried or lost. Then the separation comes. Time to dig all of yourself up and grow strong again until the next love comes, sweeping all in its wake. That's how it has been for me.

But my second son has been with me ten years. Beats all prior records. He's my best friend, confidante, playmate. Before he could speak in sentences, he would hold his arms out insisting, "Hold you, Mama. Hold you." We have rocked each other, crying. He has lied to me and I've spanked him. I've doctored his heat rash, his ringworm, his head lice. We've gone to movies together, told each other ghost stories in my bed on stormy nights under the sheet-tent, my knees the center poles of our world. Once we ate a whole bag of Oreos. We've held each other's hands through pain—his broken leg, my lost lovers. We've watched each other grow. I never saw anyone grow before.

Seth accepts me. Fully and completely accepts me, loves me with that acceptance. Knows me. Knows my bullshit from my sincerity, my irritability from my anger, my joy from my mania. No lover has ever been around long enough to sort out those distinctions.

The frightening fact is this. I am nearly forty. Nearly forty, and the only consistently joyful relationship of my life, the only lasting love, so far, has been with a boychild now ten years old.

My first son came and went too soon. I was twenty-one in Corpus Christi and married to a man who disgusted me. I was working eight to five, too busy to nurse a baby, waxing floors and ironing on weekends, trying to be good. I remember that young wife reading sex books and child-care books, recipe books and books for the working mother. Mixing formula, sterilizing bottles, tending the baby's everlasting colds and allergies. I remember the unremitting drudgery of that suburban life in which I worked so hard. Christopher, my first-born, was hyperactive and whining, not getting what he needed from a mother so overworked I would fall asleep in my chair at night with my eyes open. Tom thought I had epilepsy. The neurologist laughed. "She's just tired, overworked. Needs more sleep." The men laughed. Funny, woman falling asleep with her eyes open, catatonic. I kept Chris fed, safe, and most of all, clean. My house clean. Dinner on the table. Always on time for work, too, competent, reliable. Good credit rating. Even cheerful, smiling. The good wife and good secretary, smiling. Busting ass.

Outside it was 1966. Hippies were freaking out on Haight-Ashbury; people my age who had the good luck to be in college were marching against the war in Viet Nam. I was filing carbon copies and washing diapers and crib sheets. I sneaked moments to play with Chris, kissing his green-blue eyes and clutching his pearly fingers, sucking on his toes the size of garden peas and nuzzling his velvet bald head. It was like masturbating; my secret excess. I should be vacuuming the floor under his bed instead, quick, before his daddy or my mother-in-law came and saw the roll of dust. He would cry, colic-belly, and I would hold him on one hip, gritting my teeth because he was so demanding, so loud, while I pushed the vacuum with my free arm. We lived in the shadow of our keeper, head of our household, prickbearer, inspector-general, the man. It was a lousy goddam setup.

When I left Tom, I tried to hold on to the baby, then two years old. Chris didn't want me. Cried for his father on weekends. Tom snatched him away, carried him off. In another state, Tom divorced me, remarried, gave Chris another mother. Far from me. I hoped she was tender with him. I was alone in New Orleans, finding myself. Single, free—I slept and loved, burned candles, threw an Indian bedspread over my couch, went to night school. Reclaimed my youth. I was harboring a great clumsy she-bear who'd lost a cub, rooting in dark places among bad-smelling memories. The loss of Chris was primal, shattering. The she-bear was restless in my sleep. I searched. I would wake feeling Chris beside me in his yellow terrycloth stretch suit. Could feel his whole body between my chin and navel, curled into my mountains, safe against my landscape of haunch, rib, breast, shoulder. I would open my eyes to the flat spread of empty sheets. Stone in my belly. For years.

When I found myself pregnant after the man moved to Scotland, something in me started to grin. I was twenty-eight, single, part of a feminist CR group, calling myself bisexual. A great yes shouted in me. Yes. I could do it myself. Like a she-bear. Alone in my cave I could bear my own young, bear down, bear it alone, bear me another child. No man's child, no man to run my show or tell me what to do. No one to check for dust balls under the crib. I could bear me a love-child, put my she-bear to rest. I could have it all.

It was even better than I'd hoped. Seth nursed till he was two, kneading and sucking while my womb answered his mouth, contracting. It was erotic. He sucked milk, converted from my blood, sucked life from me and at the same time pleasured me, relieved the pressure in my breasts, caused a womb echo very like orgasm. Maybe it was orgasm. Kneaded and needed me, and I needed him, his mouth, his devout presence. It was my first time to know giving and taking together. That was my first loving, that I took in my she-cave alone with my second infant and no Other.

I'd expected a womanchild, of course. When no daughter but a male baby came innocent out of me, slick, not knowing my preference, I forgave him his wet balls, his thimble-prick. It was nothing to me. We were mother and infant; we became holy in our solitude and perfect. Bone of my bone. Milk of my blood. Mouth to my breast.

I gathered it all in. I watched how Seth discovered light, shadow, color, texture. He found it all wonderful, wonderful. Music. I would play Handel, Bach, or Segovia on the stereo while I nursed him. No colic-belly, he was big, ten pounds at birth. I made plenty of milk and gave it like a great Buddhist cow, serene, my eyes half-shut, rocking to the rhythm of his mouth on me, yielding myself. I'd missed out on childhood and good cheer, had spent my own child-time in a nightmare of mental illness (my mother's) and physical illness (my own). Had vacuumed the floors of my first-born's child-time. But this time I gathered in.

Survival was complicated. I worked three jobs during my pregnancy and saved all I could. Just before Seth was born, I started school full-time so I could nurse him and make a subsistence salary, a student's salary and hours. For a while I lived on welfare and nearly starved—shoplifted when desperate, had fainting spells from hunger, knew poverty and knew there was no idealizing it. No heat one winter; Seth got pneumonia. I blanketed him with my own cold body, pulled the covers over our heads and nearly suffocated us both. I lost a couple of teeth. I couldn't always pay rent. Moved house more times than I can count. But I learned from Seth to play while I learned from poverty how not to fear. And I learned from the New Orleans lesbian community what women can give each other.

All this learning came at the same time. My mothering and my feminism and my lesbianism all came together simultaneously. I think it had to happen as it did for any of it to work for me. I am saying I think I could not have been a lesbian—could not have begun to feel that intense giving and taking, that devouring yes, that ocean of another woman's acceptance—had I not first dared to learn it through Seth. This shocks even me. But my own small truth is simple: I was afraid.

In my twenties, the men I loved were emotionally safe. They loved me but didn't know me; perhaps they loved me because they didn't know me. I was mysterious to them. But one who would not find me mysterious, who might see clear through me, she might, like my mama, find me unacceptable. Repulsive or inadequate. A change came in me when, in Seth's eyes, I was both known, familiar—and accepted, loved. In our private safety I learned that more was possible. Someone could really know me. And really love me. Amazing.

For me, being a mother is the one sure thing. It ties me to my unknown grandmothers, to women in Botswana, to women in Crete before patriarchy. It loops me into communion with she-bears and mama cats: for me it's a necessity. It shouldn't be necessary for a woman to feel her child's love to discover that she is lovable. But it was necessary for me. It shouldn't be necessary for a woman to nurse a baby to learn give-and-take in sexuality. But that's how I learned it. It shouldn't be necessary for a woman to have a second baby if she has lost her first one. But I did, and was satisfied at last. Mothering first put me together; it holds me together still.

I hope I'll learn some other way to hold together before long. Maybe the very flow of days and nights is enough to hold me together, if I let it. Some days are kisses, like the afternoon Mary gave Seth his first softball lesson. Some days are laughter, like the morning I threatened Seth if he didn't finish his homework I'd go tell his teacher I'm queer. Some nights are sweet with Mary after Seth is asleep, when she teaches me the second loving.

I lay myself down by the landscape of her haunch, rib, breast, shoulder; lay myself down in her safety with my load of scars and treasures, and she feeds me, hides me, gives me harbor. At the same time, she lets me shelter her.

Drawing me closer, she tells me society is fucked. Society, she tells me, trying to heal me, makes women think they must have children to be whole, or to prove they are real women. I agree that is fucked. Mary's a real woman, a testament, a tower of what a real woman is, woman-bodied and nurturant, childfree and full in her good self. It isn't fair for her to have to share my attentions with a prepubescent white male. She gives me all she has. It isn't fair that if Chris comes to visit us, her privacy will be invaded by a blue-eyed redneck prick-bearing boy-man, six feet and 180 pounds of bad debts to collect on me. It isn't fair.

A thousand miles away from us Chris sometimes talks to me on the phone. After long and harrowing court battles, I have given up any claim on him. It is two years since he last chose to visit me. His father is divorced from his fourth wife; father and son live alone together again. Chris, on the phone, sounds thirty, not seventeen. He is too serious, too responsible. Each of us feels rejected by the other. The wounds are old but not about to heal. I wish I could comfort him, give him some warmth, take anything good from him. But we are defended against our old pains. Nothing is easy between us. The man, the years, the losses burn us when we try to touch. We keep trying, or anyway I do. It isn't fair.

But what am I besides that? I've been a mother for half my life. The me before that was a battered child, an earnest, rootless girl of twenty whose perfumed corpse I haul around inside me, but whose face I can't quite remember. She died trying to be a perfect woman, to do the right thing, to be pleasing to everyone, to be forgiven for being. Out of my grief for her comes my refusal to accept any prescriptions—feminist, patriarchal, societal—for how a woman should be. Political correctness, laid like bricks against my body, is oppression, too.

The she-bear still prowls in me. Especially when I am preperiod, I growl and would tear flesh. I fear I may rise up defending my cubs, protecting them and my cub-self and losing the woman I love. Then there's the night-cat in me, sleek and dark, dreaming of a time to slip off alone. Dimly I understand if there's a way for me to find lengthening love with a woman, its lessons are in the give-and-take I learned first with a child at my breast. The end of this story isn't written.

There's nothing so awesome as the courage of a woman daring to need another woman. That's more threatening, more fraught with possibilities for soul-crushing failure, than anything I can think of. There's a time when you know that you know how to mother. I don't see how you ever know if you know how to be lesbian.

The story of how I mother and the story of how I lesbian are one story. Sex, mouth on breast, blood and need, knead and suck, acceptance. I couldn't have let myself lesbian if I hadn't yielded control and let myself mother. The energy, the physical bounty, the political force I gather from being lesbian gives me the strength to mother. In every breath I take and let go, I am lesbian, mother.

But I back off from the details to look at my plot. I see it is compact with repetitions, like Greek tragedy. My mother rejected me, and I her. I never knew my father. My stepfather tongue-kissed me in a dark house in Georgia, smelling of Bourbon. My first son rejects me and feels rejected. My second son doesn't know his father; my first son doesn't know me. My lover's uncle raped her. She rocks in the cradle of our bed with me. My first son is over six-feet tall and carries a big prick in his pants. My second son teeters on the edge of puberty. How does anyone hold all this?

In the Texas electric July-oven heat I breathe summer next to Moonlight and her twins. Wide sky over the oak trees blows no breeze. Too hot, too tired to comprehend the plot of my story, I lean back against a yellow farmhouse which was not meant to contain so much. Alone an instant, away from Seth and Mary, suspended, I yield to the wash of life through me and shudder its passing. Like labor pains, I think. Contractions. You lie back and let them pass through you. Events. Memories. A white cloud stretches itself thinner, thinner, strings itself wider till my eyes ache, trying to see where it goes. I stretch myself out of me into that cloud, dispersing. I fly up, sucked out of time into the thin sky. I am no one with no story, no sex, no name. Sky. Forever. Forever. Coming back to my body I find myself rocking next to Moonlight, my heartbeats blending with the rhythm of her kittens' knead and suck. Moonlight and me: we are in this together.

Incessant Rain/Lluvia Incesante
Zulma

> Incessant rain
> Stop!
> Let me wet my eyes
> without you

The Mirror
(a dream written down by my daughter when she was eight—her return to the normal mirror)

I woke up one morning
And found out that I was
No longer a human being

I felt so strange
I moved to the mirror
And there I saw I lost
All my teeth
I didn't know what to do
So I called my mother. . .she screamed
She told my father—she screamed
the next day came and I found
I was myself again

the end

That Mirror—Dayeynu
(changing images from mother/wife to divorced lesbian mother)

I used to be like that   but not now
I used to play the role of woman   oppressed
With strangers' hands I shaped   my life
I would watch the reflection in my environment   false mirror

The day that all died   my life changed
I left that mirror
But today I can look into it
And I see the reflection of tears
Peeking out of the pupil of my eyes
   My mother/My daughter.
And I see the days
under the masculine law
it taught me to be Woman
to know anger
to defy everything
that gets in my way

If I didn't know better
it would have been enough.

It would have been enough.

Lluvia incesante
¡Para!
Deja que moje mis ojos
sin ti

Ese Espejo—Dayeynú

Así era yo
Jugaba el papel de mujer
Con manos ajenas moldeaba
Miraba el reflejo en mi ambiente

pero ahora no
oprimida
mi vida
falso espejo

El día que todo murió
Dejé aquel espejo
pero hoy puedo mirar en él
y veo el reflejo de unas lágrimas
asomadas a la niña de mis ojos
    Mi madre/Mi hija
Y veo en mi mente los días
bajo la ley masculina
que me enseñaron a ser Mujer
a conocer el enojo
a desafiar a todo
lo que se interpone en mi camino

cambió mi vida

Si no me conociera
hubiera sido suficiente.

Incessant rain
Stop!
Let me wet my eyes
without you

Last Names
(my child is born to a name unknown to me)

First I lost it
Then I got a new one
It lasted 17 years
Then when my daughter was born
She got it

Today, I took mine away
But there are still some reminders
here and there
of that last name
a last name
that didn't fit me ever
A last name I couldn't
even pronounce

However
I am so sleepy!
However. . .
I sign it without thinking.
How long will this habit last?

Lluvia incesante
¡Para!
Deja que moje mis ojos
sin ti

Apellidos

Perdí uno y tomé uno nuevo
Ese me duró 17 años
Luego, cuando mi hija nació
se le pegó

Hoy me lo quité
Pero aún quedan rasgos
aquí y allí
de ese nombre
que no me cupo nunca
que ni siquiera sé pronunciar

Sin embargo
¡qué sueño tengo!
Sin embargo. . .
¡cómo lo firmo sin pensar!
¿cuánto me va a durar ese hábito?

                Incessant rain
                Stop!
                Let me wet my eyes
                without you

Empty Room
(first home as a lesbian mother: an unaffordable two-bedroom apartment, with one bedroom reserved for my daughter but never occupied)

A closed room
        Who lives there?
        Is there anybody in?
                The door is closed
                Should I knock?
        No one can knock
        Is anyone alive?
        Who's coming?

The door opens
        two square windows
        large, cold, violent
                look back at me
                in her empty room.

Lluvia incesante
¡Para!
Deja que moje mis ojos
sin ti

Cuarto Vacío

Un cuarto cerrado
    ¿Quién vive ahí?
    ¿Hay alguien?
                            La puerta, cerrada
                            ¿Toco?
        No hay quien toque
        ¿Vive alguien?
        ¿Quièn viene?

La puerta, abierta
        dos ventanales,
        cuadrados, grandes, fríos, violentos
                    me miran
                    de su cuarto vacío.

An Unread Note
(written upon the occasion of my daughter's first overnight visit in my second new home—a room)

....Good morning....

it is so nice to wake up in the
morning and see the sun outside
and you next to me

it feels like sweet foam on top
of a chocolate milkshake.

I love you so much
I feel like crying.

Incessant rain
Stop!
Let me wet my eyes
without you

Where Are You My Daughter?

Before all—woman
Before all women—a friend
Before me, woman—a friend?

Am I my friend?

¿Donde Estás?

Ante todo—mujer
Ante toda mujer—amiga
Ante mí, mujer—¿amiga?

¿Soy mi amiga?

Loneliness gives you strength
Strength to survive what's missing
But, what is missing is a weakness
I don't have to prove or
Show strength, but this loneliness
makes me, pushes me to
continue, not letting me recede
                              or I die

        Where are you my daughter?

                                        Incessant rain
                                        Stop!
                                        Let me wet my eyes
                                        without you

La soledad te da fuerza
Fuerza para sobrevivir la falta
Pero, esa falta es una debilidad
No necesito demostrar o ejercer la fuerza
y sin embargo esta soledad me hace, me empuja
a seguir sin determe
                      o muero
    ¿Dónde estás?

                              Lluvia incesante
                              ¡Para!
                              Deja que moje mis ojos
                              sin ti

L'Havdol

Teya Schaffer

Friday evenings let me tell you how it is:
I am at work in the store
    only a few hours passing bread and money
    across the counter
    but long enough to have the customers pegged
    and they too of course know me:
    the lesbian or the mother, according to their need.
There are these Friday evenings
erev shabbat
ushered in at the bakery
in the peace of familiar work
selling challah to Elmwood families
sweeping floors, covering cookies
ending the day, cleaning up.
My coworkers, who are my bosses, don't like me
we work not so side-by-side
    I could be lesbian, I could be Jew
    but I am worse, a political lesbian Jew, so
on these evenings there is a little more silence
than women wrapping bread, washing glass
should have.
But it's not to complain, only a few hours a week,
and Friday nights are special.
I drive home, I have a car to drive home in
I have a home to imagine in my drive to it,
and I imagine that my housemate
has left for his lover's home
and I imagine that my other housemate
has taken the bib from 'round my child's neck
and is turning to my friend to ask
if he may leave
    Friday night ritual of departure
    the transfer of responsibility
my friend nods, beginning her weekly gift
of child care, erev shabbat till Saturday morning.

When I arrive it is as I've imagined—
the friend and the child
   and the part I'd forgotten to image
   my key in the door turning my son's steps
   mama's home? mommy's home!
   surely I am on a movie set, carrying my lovebundle
   and a loaf of bread?

Friday evening, Friday nights
I make a separation,
in thirty minutes transiting
the weekday and l'havdol the sabbath
and it is with Asher that I do it
sitting down
slowing time
   there is another home I am heading toward
   another drive in which to image
   the opening door of my lover's welcome
   but I make a separation
   even from that longing
to make a little peace with my son.

Friday nights, he knows the way of
makes sure that my jacket is removed
my back firmly settled against couch cushion
himself a fact of my lap—
   there is discord at work and no evening meal
   instead of candles a two-year-old
   and a thirty-minute transit in which we
   read a book   sing a song
   kiss a wound   tell a tale
   as if in thirty minutes
   I will not go flying out the door. . . .
We begin a time-defined eternity,
two points on a clock holding everything between:
peace. love. an interval, like childhood
like sabbath
brief and enduring.

Open Windows
Marilyn Hacker

II

Tonight when I cup my hand beneath your breast
(fountain and pillow of felicity)
your womb shudders with possibility
suctioned from you, and your sigh is pain. Pressed
even gently against me, you ache; the best
choice, made, presses us both. How will it be
held between us, this complicity
in what we can't repeat? Silken, we nest
aloft, sleep curled. Reflected from the snow,
a dawn lamp glints up through your tall window.
Uptown, my child will wake, ask where's her mother.
Promised, I inhale you, descend from you, gather
scattered woolens, gather my wits to go
from one hard choice, love chosen, to the other.

V

"You'll play with *her*, but you won't play with *me!*"
my lover snapped, gathering up her beach-
mat after her as she scuffed angrily
back toward the car. She turned, we glowered at each
other. Play with my child's part of my work:
loved work, but work. I thought she understood,
after our harried winter in New York,
I'd need an afternoon of solitude
precisely when that work was imminent.
She's going to cry again. This isn't real!
"I *have*" (icily) "other things to do
than *play*. This is ridiculous! I've spent
the last forty-eight hours alone with you!"
I've made our idyll sound like an ordeal...

Your Kids Have Germs!

Martha Shelley

This week was hard for us.
every day I typed ugly sentences
said yes to bosses, made xeroxes;
all day and all night too
you wiped the baby's ass
cooked chicken soup, taught class
ferried the older kids to school
fought with me
and we both got flu.

Sex was our magnet and glue
before you left your man
for me, and the promise of freedom and fun
but when we've got the runs
cranky kids and sleepless nights
even the memory of delight
fades behind the need to
haul our lives uphill.

Tune in next week
for another thrilling episode:
can two happily married lesbians
survive motherhood?

Mother Of The Groom
Marilyn Murphy

I did not go to my son's wedding. The decision shattered the trust that had been building between us, and between me and the woman with whom he was sharing his life. Before they married, they treated me and my companion-lover with affection and respect. We could talk with humor and without inhibitions on a wide range of subjects, agreeing and disagreeing without rancor. Work, distance, and finances kept us from seeing each other often, but we kept in touch by letter and phone. While not idyllic, our relationship was a good one, and I was pleased and relieved that his attitude toward my lesbian life was a positive one.

Since the wedding five years ago, we have seen each other only three times. Each time, we came to visit them. My son and I talk on the phone every few months. I write letters; they send cards. In whatever form the communication occurs, it is usually stilted when pleasant, and painful when serious. I am afraid to speak my mind on anything except at the most superficial level. Yet he and his wife both insist my absence from their wedding is not the cause of our deteriorated relationship; it is only a symptom of the problem. They say it's my indifference, my insensitivity, my intellectualizing, my this, my that. They say *her* mother never. . ., *her* mother always. . ., even his *father*. . . .

I did not want to stay away from the ceremony. I did not want to miss an important event in the life of my child. I did not want him to suffer shame or embarrassment on my account, having to explain his mother's absence from his wedding. Even more heartfelt was my desire to avoid another emotional debacle with one of my offspring. Over the years, I had achieved a more or less easy peace with all four of my adult children, and I dreaded any resumption of trouble with my thirty-year-old, eldest child and only son. Yet once again, I was in a no-win "mother dilemma," a not uncommon place for mothers of adult children, especially lesbian mothers. If I went to the wedding, I would not be at peace with myself. If I did not go to the wedding, I would not be at peace with him. And no matter what the decision, I would feel guilty about it. After all, what kind of a mother has to stop and think about whether or not to attend her child's wedding? A lesbian mother does!

My son and his companion-lover are conscious persons. For three years before the wedding they lived together as a nonconforming heterosexual couple in a committed, monogamous relationship. During those years, they paid the price for living an affectional-sexual relationship outside the socially sanctioned, state-licensed, and state-supported affectional-sexual relationship —the institution of marriage. Their life, health, auto insurance, their credit records, tax returns, airline tickets were those of two single persons, not those of a couple. They could not automatically inherit from each other or speak for each other in case of a medical emergency. When visiting family, they had the problem of sleeping arrangements. They lived with the social awkwardness that comes from existing outside the language and therefore having no word, no term which correctly described each other or their relationship to each other or to outsiders. Many of these problems are the problems experienced by lesbian and gay men couples, problems my companion-lover and I shared with them.

Certainly they had their heterosexual privilege. They could be affectionate in public. They could talk about their lives together, even to people who would think they were living in sin. They never feared losing their jobs or being publicly humiliated should their relationship be discovered. They were accepted in most places and by most people as a couple, one who would eventually do the right thing and marry.

They vigorously resisted the pressure to marry. She was afraid she'd turn into a wife, and so was he. He was afraid he'd turn into a husband, and so was she. They disapproved of marriage, said it institutionalized the inequality of women. They said the state exceeded its power over the lives of citizens by licensing marriage, by which it was legalizing the sexual and reproductive activity of certain *licensed* male/female couples only, and legitimating the children resulting from that licensed sexual coupling. They deplored what they saw as the collusion of the state with religion by its licensing of cohabitation/sexual activity between male/female couples only, thus giving all same-sex couples' cohabitation/sexual activity the status of illegal, illicit *sin*, in spite of any consenting adult statutes the state might have passed. They stood with lesbians and gay men in their opposition to institutionalized heterosexuality.

Need I say that I was proud of the male child I had raised, that I approved of his choice of companion-lover, that I supported them in their efforts to live their beliefs? I was shocked when they told me they had decided to get married. They said they were not giving in to pressure. They said they no longer feared becoming a wife or a husband. They were confident the marriage ceremony would not disrupt the habits of equality their lives together had developed. They were tired of the aggravation and the hassle, personal and financial, they suffered because they were an unmarried couple. They said they were sorry for all the distress they were causing other family members by their refusal to marry. What's the harm, really, in saying a few words in public, words they had said to each other privately many times. And yes, since they were going to do it, they might as well get a license. And yes, the ceremony would be performed by a person with the authority to perform legal marriages. And yes, there would be engraved wedding invitations, wedding showers, wedding gifts, and wedding guests. But the bride would not vow obedience, nor would she wear white!

How could the mother of the groom attend such a ceremony, a ceremony which celebrates the institution which is the cornerstone of her past oppression as a married woman and her present oppression as a lesbian? How could I participate in a ceremony by which the child of my body acted out his informed consent to the right of the state to declare his relationship with his companion-lover lawful, legal, and by default, to declare my relationship with my companion-lover out-of-the-law, illegal? I could not.

So here we are four years later. I feel rejected by my first-born; he feels rejected by his mother. I also feel jealousy, guilt, resentment, and a host of other not-so-nice feelings about our present relationship. It does not help to know that I "did the right thing" and they did not. The personal may be political, but when we act politically instead of personally with our children, they usually punish us for it. Mothers are not supposed to have principles that conflict with our mandate to love our children unconditionally.

Yet men who abhor sexism do not join organizations that deny membership to women. White people who abhor racism do not join organizations that deny membership to people of color. Christians, believers and nonbelievers, who abhor anti-Semitism do not join organizations that deny membership to Jews. The refusal to join organizations that deny membership, and the benefits accruing to members, to others because of sex, race, religion, and so on, is the very least that can be expected of those who profess belief in equality and civil rights for all.

What would we think of a man who called himself a feminist, said he supported the Equal Rights Amendment and the concept of comparable worth, and then asked his women friends to attend the ceremony initiating him into a prestigious men-only club? I'm sure we would not only seriously doubt his commitment to women's equality, but would also consider his invitation an insult. And yet the families and friends of lesbians and gay men continue to join the largest social organization in the world—the most prestigious one, the one everyone is expected to join, the one with the greatest amount of government subsidies and supports, the voluntary association which prohibits membership to lesbians and gay men—the institution of marriage. Their disregard of our feelings, as well as our rights, is so profound that they add insult to injury by inviting us to attend those rites which are denied us. They expect us to congratulate them, to throw a party on their behalf, to act as their maid of honor/bridesmaid or best man/usher. . .and in some cases, want us to leave our companion-lovers at home while we do.

The families and friends of lesbians and gay men are asking us to collude in our oppression when they ask, insist, that we participate in their marriage rites. It is in their best interests and in the best interests of partriarchy when we do what they wish. Our part in their marriage rites allows them to deny us our rites/rights with an easy conscience. It allows them to continue to believe that we believe they deserve the pomp and the ceremony, and the privileges, that go with them; that we, the "deviant," are satisfied with the crumbs from their tables, with our broomstick weddings.* It is way past the time for lesbians and gay men to begin disturbing the consciences of our families and friends, especially those of our children. As long as we are denied participation in what is called the honorable state of matrimony, it is no honor to be called Mother of the Groom.

---

* During the time of legal Black slavery in the U.S., individual slaveowners made the rules governing the lives of their human property, including those for marriage. Many slaveowners, who thought of themselves as "good Christians," did not want to be responsible for "putting asunder" a Christian couple. The solution they devised was not to discontinue the sale of slave couples to separate and distant plantations. Instead, they denied slaves a lawful (i.e. Christian) wedding, and instituted their own ceremony for slaves during which the lucky couple who had received permission to marry was expected to "legalize" the relationship by jumping over a broomstick. Only heterosexual couples received permission to jump over the broomstick, of course.

Lesbian/Grandmother
Faith Reboin

Three years ago my daughter had a baby, and as a result, I became one of those people the world calls a grandmother. Grandmother? Me? Being a grandmother was alien both because of my personal feelings about motherhood and because of my image of myself as a radical lesbian. The process of accepting my new status has meant reconciling these conflicting images and exploring my feelings about my own experience of motherhood. It has led to fundamental and wonderful changes in my life, changes encompassing my feelings about myself as a mother, a lesbian, and an aging woman.

When Debbie called me long distance to tell me she was pregnant, my initial reaction was shock and horror. All my old unresolved issues about motherhood rose up to haunt me, and I was sure that she would find the experience as overwhelming and oppressive as I had. Like a dying person, I saw my life flashing before my eyes. It was impossible for me to separate her future from my past.

I reluctantly entered the world of motherhood at age eighteen after getting pregnant in my last year of high school and hastily marrying my boyfriend of eight months. My parents were crushed at my early marriage, and I took their disappointment in me as a serious indictment. I felt guilty for having been sexual before marriage, for having gotten pregnant, and finally, for not wanting to be a mother. By the time Debbie was born, I was convinced I must compensate for all my wrongs by never allowing her to know she was not a wanted child, and by being a good wife and perfect mother.

After ten years of a chaotic and unhappy marriage, I divorced my husband. Two years later I came out as a lesbian. I was excited, terrified, and very confused, and my confusion and mixed feelings manifested themselves in months of erratic and irresponsible behavior. Debbie's initial cautious acceptance of my lesbian choice soon changed to resentment at my inattention to her needs. Within six months, she decided to live with her father.

In the years after Debbie left, I learned to accept myself as a lesbian, but I could never seem to banish the nagging pain and guilt at having allowed my daughter, to whom I had committed myself to being the perfect mother, to leave me. When she became pregnant, I began to identify with her in a new way as a woman; but as a dyke, I often felt uncomfortable with the memories of unhappy marriage and too-early mothering which this identification revived.

Imagining Debbie, my child, as a mother was frightening and depressing to me, but the reality of seeing her as a mother has proved immensely reassuring and healing. Seeing her with her own baby, I have felt a reassurance no words could have given me about the kind of mother I had been. I recognized her absorption, her patience, and her very loving mothering style immediately and knew that through it she was recapitulating her experience with me—her own mother. Being with my grandchild, I feel again the special uniqueness and pleasure children bring into our lives. When I am with the two of them, I am aware of the almost tangible bond between them, and I remember the glorious, imperative, absoluteness which that bond/love gave to my life twenty years ago.

Since becoming a grandmother, age is another issue which has come up for me. I was forced to a recognition that I am getting older—that I am an *older* lesbian. For me that was fraught with fearful and mostly unexamined possibilities. Although age is an issue for all women, I believe it has a particular significance for me as a lesbian.

Economically it is more threatening since, as a woman without a man, I can expect more than my share of poverty in old age. As part of a subculture which has only in recent years become visible, I have few models of aging lesbians to guide me. The most visible and immediately accessible aspect of lesbian life is still the bar scene, which no longer appeals to me because it reinforces associations of lesbianism and youth, and lesbianism and alcohol, that I am no longer willing to accept.

The issue of age has also challenged my image of myself as a lesbian. There is a conflict of images inherent in the very words *lesbian* and *grandmother*. Our culture defines lesbians as sexual beings, which implies youth and activity. Grandmother means an old woman, and aging in our culture connotes asexuality and passivity. As a lesbian struggling to create for myself new images of strength and beauty, it has been painful for me to discover how much of my own self-image was still based on these outmoded rigid definitions.

Little Golden books say that grandmother has grey or white hair, is plump and matronly, wears aprons and dowdy print dresses, and sits by the fire knitting baby booties and comforters while she waits for the children, the doers of the family, to return to her. In real life, grandmother often looks tired and worn, has a matter-of-fact attitude toward her children and their offspring who surround her like weeds popping up here and there, turning to her when they are in need, always tied to her by the bonds of family. It was difficult to reconcile either of those images with the grandmother me who goes out with my lesbian lover and slow dances with my leg between her thighs, stands up to my boss who treats me disrespectfully, and changes my own engine oil.

It was equally difficult for me to reconcile my image of myself as a grand-mother and as a *political* lesbian. Having come out on the crest of the women's movement, I was convinced that this patriarchal world was desperately sick and oppressive and was always aware of the political implications of lesbianism. I separated myself from men in every way possible, resolved not to participate in this culture they had created, and worked actively to destroy it through the education and agitation of other women. *Reform* was a dirty word to me, since I felt that only when men were forced to give up their power could we women form a sane and egalitarian society. I rejected as opportunistic those women, straight or lesbian, who sought power or privilege within the existing system because I feared they would be co-opted by material success into believing in the political status quo. After years of political action, I became tired and discouraged at the slow rate of change. My response to this frustration was to resign even further from the world through the use of drugs and alcohol.

The birth of my grandchild reminded me dramatically that I am part of the continuum of life, and I began to want to be in the world again, however imperfect it might be. Once again I felt, as I had when my own daughter was young, that my responsibility to the next generation does not end with changing their diapers and keeping Gerber's in the cupboard, but extends to making the world a better place for them to live. I have accepted the reality that the vision I have cherished of a world in which "women's" values are predominant is a goal toward which to struggle; it is not a world which will magically appear in my lifetime or for which I can afford to wait.

When I learned that my new grandbaby was a boy, I was surprised and disappointed. Having decided years before that men were my enemy—the bearers of privilege and the oppressors of women—it was disturbing to have this male child suddenly thrust into the middle of my tidy analysis. Becoming Nathan's grandmother forced me to begin reexamining my attitudes and feelings about men. These old fears and resentments I had clung to from my childhood and my marriage were interfering with this new relationship in my life in very real ways.

My feelings about men and my lesbian political ideology dovetailed perfectly to convince me that the nuclear family is an inefficient and unjust social organization which is particularly oppressive to women and children, and with which I chose not to be associated. It isolates them from the rest of the world, places too much responsibility on individual women, and provides them with far too little compensation in money, security, power, or prestige. Further, since no one woman can possibly fill all the physical and emotional needs of a child, much less several children, it creates for children a model of human relationships based on scarcity. With Nathan's birth, I found myself emotionally invested in just such a family.

Facing my feelings toward men, I have recognized I am no longer a power-less child or a frightened wife and need no longer fear or hate those men who once dominated me. Letting go of my fear and anger, I can afford now to make room in my life for my grandson and his father, and to respect them as the family my daughter has chosen for herself.

With all the adjustments I've made, the grandmothering part has been sur-prisingly easy. I am a traditionally doting grandmother in a way I would never have imagined, and yet the role fits like a comfortable old shoe. An entry from my journal shortly after my first visit after his birth reminds me how I felt when Nathan was a newborn:

When he woke from his nap, I beat Debbi up the stairs to get him out of his crib. As I entered the room, he was letting out little trial yelps, still half asleep, rubbing his fists in his eyes, staring sleepily at me as I picked him up—warm, damp, and relaxed. I think it's know-ing that I have "rights," sort of an instant emotional investment in this relationship, that allows me to let all this out when I am with him. All those tender, motherly, loving, protective feelings well up inside me in a way that is exciting to feel/remember.

Shortly after his birth, I toasted the event with several friends. I vaguely recalled a childhood fairy tale in which the newborn baby was blessed by different witches with wishes for her future health, beauty, happiness, and other desirable attributes. As I named their wishes, I made my own special wish for my grandson: that he would always know and understand what the women in his life had given him, that he would respect the uniqueness of that gift, and through that knowledge he could relate to all women in a respectful and caring way. It was my way of expressing the hope that I could keep this child in my life forever. At five weeks of age, I consciously memo-rized each part of him: the feel of his skin against my cheek, his weight in my arms, his baby aroma, his plump square feet, and his docile good humor. I knew then the time might come when I could no longer like the person he had become, but I would always love this infant grandchild and be grateful for his presence in my life.

The rediscovery of joy has been one of the most pleasant changes I have experienced since becoming a grandmother. I recall myself as being a hap-py, eager, and very energetic child. During my ten years of marriage, I lost some of my eager ebullience, and I lost as much in my decade as a lesbian. I was a guilt-ridden mother who had given up her child and I tended to re-late to all issues of responsibility in terms of guilt, blame, and sacrifice. These attitudes infused all my feelings about myself, and I became increas-ingly dour and joyless. These feelings were also tied to my experience of lesbian oppression. Although aware of my oppression as a woman and a mother before I came out, I was still an acceptable person to the rest of the world. It was as a lesbian I felt unacceptable for the first time, and in my fear and anger, I was so grimly attached to the concept of my own oppression that it became the defining fact of my life. I could not move past it to recall the joy I had known as a mother.

Seeing my daughter as a mother has reminded me of the very special joy of mothering and has allowed me to get back in touch with that part of myself that was at once loving, tender, and protective.

Accepting myself as a lesbian grandmother has required me to look closely at my own self-image and develop a willingness to change it. I discovered within myself depths of self-hatred, misogyny, and homophobia I had not realized existed. These ugly attitudes, fed by four decades of messages from the outside world that old women and lesbian women and mother women are not desirable, normal, interesting, active, and acceptable human beings, were part of me—an aging, lesbian mother. I had to acknowledge these untruths as part of my beliefs about myself first in order to let go of them. Even letting go of such destructive attitudes is difficult, strange as it may seem, when change feels so risky and the status quo is, if nothing else, familiar.

But the rewards for this effort have been incalculable. Most important among them is that I have learned to know and love myself in ways I never dreamed possible. This process for me has meant getting clean and sober, one of the greatest acts of self-love I have ever committed. My relationship with my daughter has grown strong, healthy, respectful, and mutually supportive. After an emotional estrangement of eight years, stemming mainly from my inability to accept myself and therefore not wanting to face her, I have gotten Debbie back into my life. My grandson (and his baby sister) have given me tremendous pleasure and inspiration.

Gradually I have come to incorporate all the conflicting messages about *grandmother* into my own self-image. Now when someone expresses surprise that someone like me (youthful? attractive? active?) could be a grandmother, I am able to respond, "But this is what a grandmother looks like!" It feels important to me to communicate this new reality to other lesbians. Only in this way can we demolish the stereotypes about us, recast the role in our own image, and help create the model of possibilities for other women.

Growing Up

We All . . . Every One Of Us

Legacy
Pat Parker

for Anastasia Jean

Anything handed down
from, or as from an
ancestor to a descendant.

Prologue

There are those who think
or perhaps don't think
that children and lesbians
together can't make a family
that we create an extension
of perversion.

They think
or perhaps don't think
that we have different relationships
with our children
that instead of getting up
in the middle of the night
for a 2 AM and 6 AM feeding
we rise up and chant
you're gonna be a dyke
you're gonna be a dyke

That we feed our children
lavender Similac
and by breathing our air
the children's genitals distort
and they become hermaphrodites.

They ask
'What will you say to them
what will you teach them?'

Child
that would be mine
I bring you my world
and bid it be yours.

I
Addie And George

He was a small man
son of an African slave
his father came chained
in a boat
long after the boats
had 'stopped' coming
his skin was ebony
shone like new piano keys.

He was a carpenter
worked long in the trade
of the Christ he chose
six days a week
his hands plied the wood
gave birth to houses
and cabinets and tables
on the seventh day
he lay down his hammer
and picked up his bible
and preached the gospel
to his brethren
led his flock in prayer

when he was seventy-nine years old
he lay down
in the presence of his wife
and children
and died.

Her father too was a slave
common law wed to an Indian squaw
Addie came colored caramel
long black hair
high cheek bones.

She was a christian woman
her religion a daily occurrence
her allegiance was to God,
her husband, her children
in that order
together she and George
had twenty-two children
many never survived
the first year of life
a fact not unusual
for the time.

When she was seventy-six
George died
she began to travel
to the homes of her children
to make sure they led
a christian life
the children hid
their beer and bourbon
the grandchildren hid
she would come for two months
then move on
leave the words of Jehovah
sweating from the walls
when she was ninety-four years old
she lay down
and died.

II
Ernest And Marie

He came from the earth, they say,
an expression meaning *orphan*
parents in the hands of poverty
best give the boy away
and so he came to live
in a good christian home
with a good christian minister
and his wife
he was a man of many trades
roofer in the summer
tire retreader in the winter
earned far beyond
his four years of education
he wanted to see
all of his children
get educated
he lived long enough to see
his children gone and grown
and then
he lay down
and died.

She was the youngest of the twenty-two
quiet woman
tall for her time
she bore eight children
five survived the early years
she raised them in a christian way
by day she cleaned houses
by night she cleaned her own
she was sixty-two when her husband died
took her first plane trip that same year
when her third daughter was killed
she cremated her child and went home
willed herself sick and weary
she took three years to complete the task
then she lay down
and died.

III

It is from this past that I come
surrounded by sisters in blood
and in spirit
it is this past
that I bequeath
a history of work and struggle.

Each generation improves the world
for the next.
My grandparents willed me strength.
My parents willed me pride.
I will to you rage.
I give you a world incomplete
a world
where
women still
are property and chattel
where
color still
shuts doors
where
sexual choice still
threatens
but I give you
a legacy
of doers
of people who take risks
to chisel the crack wider.

Take the strength that you may
wage a long battle.
Take the pride that you can
never stand small.
Take the rage that you can
never settle for less.

These be the things I pass
to you my daughter
if this is the result of perversion
let the world stand screaming.
You will mute their voices
with your life.

In Response To Reading Children's Book Announcements In *Publishers Weekly*, February 12, 1982

Becky Birtha

They say that children should have books
in which they can see themselves

>So I see they've got a line called
>*Baby's First Books*:
>page after page of
>little fat smiling
>rosy-cheeked white babies
>
>And then they've got
>the *Mister* books:
>Mr. Happy
>Mr. Funny
>Mr. Strong. . . .
>
>This week's picture books are starring
>Ferdinand Fox
>Roger, the cat boy
>and Honey Rabbit (also male).
>
>There is one happy family saga
>about a family of
>mice—no doubt complete with
>mother and sister
>all conveniently colored
>an inoffensive gray.

But our baby girl
loves books. We can't
keep her away from them.

At the library on 52nd Street
we pick up books about black kids
and learn that black kids are mostly boys.
At the branch on Rittenhouse Square
we discover books about
independent, capable little girls
who happen to be white.

Come to think of it
I never saw myself in any book
and I survived—
but that was thirty years ago.

We did find one book
(not in the library)
where one parent is black and the other white
like us
(of course,
they were of opposite sexes. . .
still happily married. . .
and both sets of grandparents were still speaking. . .).

Downtown, there is
one gay bookstore
where we may not be able to
take the kid any more.
The government wants to
improve
our obscenity laws.

They can try, but
some things they can't deny.
Wherever she finds it
she'll piece together
some kind of identity—
figure it out
whatever way she can.
She's smart.
She'll put it together.

The Survivors

Caeia March

As unexpected as a rainbow in a puddle, the question came at me. He was in the bath at the time. In my bathroom. He's eleven. With hazel eyes and honey hair. He was just visiting. Usually he lives with his dad.

"Mum, why exactly did you leave my dad?"

Honest. Direct. Appropriate. My skull reverberating with three words from my first-ever assertiveness workshop. Sausages. Beans. Chips. Three things on the shopping list for lunch. Laughing. Flowing. Water. Three concepts from my bathroom.

Nine items: scattered then like colors across a pool table by the straight-lined finely timed cue from my elder son. I imagined him there, at some later grown-up stage, concentrating, aiming for the center of the triangle on the green baize as accurately as his words struck the center of the pink triangle I wore.

The colors rolled, hit the edges, bouncing from each other and disappearing into pockets.

How do you explain to the son of an oh-so-gentle father about the price of compulsory heterosexuality?

These days I love to laugh. I think I've done more laughing since I've been a dyke than in the whole twelve years of marriage before that. How to keep my son whole without belittling his dad?

"There are some people you love," I said, "but you find out that you can't live with them."

My child likes his body. He's free with it. Soaps himself all over and still enjoys squirty bottles and bubbles in the water. At night he sometimes sleeps with blue-and-white ted. Football Ted. But in school he's beginning to notice girls and is being trained to be a het. The worst insult he calls his younger brother is *stupid pufter* [faggot], which he learned at school.

"Don't you EVER use that word as an insult in my flat," I yelled.

What will I feel in the future if he brings home his girlfriends and I like them and they like me and I'm glad they like him, but all the time I recognize that without him they could be loving each other?

On the other hand, I may become the mother of a gay man who needs my support as a member of an oppressed minority, even though he is separated from me by his gender and his choices. I would be his mother, yet I left him with his father when I started to choose women.

This child was a Christmas present in 1974. But children are not like puppies that you can take to the dogs' home or dump on Wimbledon Common amongst the Wombles when you grow tired or change your mind. I remember the first bathtimes. The curly arms and legs. The huge unfocused vulnerable eyes. A laughing closeness. A bond of erotic joy. Splashing and freedom and nakedness. I looked into the eyes of that baby and saw a person. A mind that might love colors, shapes, and words. An intellect capable of creating kisses, pictures, poems, spaceships, and missiles. I wasn't a feminist then. I didn't know any women who called themselves lesbians. When I did meet some three years later, I was curious, scared, and troubled. I didn't sit next to them—just in case.

After Roger came out of the bathroom, he played a game of Smugglers with his brother, Tom, and Trish and me. She bought it for his birthday in the hope he'd enjoy breaking rules.

He makes rules to keep himself safe. I did that as a child. I had to touch all four walls of a strange room before I felt secure. I also said a spell, though I called it a prayer, before I dared sit on the toilet in the old vicarage that my friend's dad told me was haunted. If I said "Jesus will take care of me" three times before I sat, then the ghost that lived down the loo wouldn't reach up and grab me.

The weight of Roger's rules on Tom, who is nine, presses him down to thumb-size, and since Tom wants to be a giant, this isn't simple. We dealt the Smugglers cards and began.

They have to sleep on my front room floor. Each morning we roll up the beds before we can begin. I cannot have more access because I haven't got the space. I cannot get more space because I haven't got more access. Sunshine is parks and petrol or fares, and drinks and hamburgers and debates about money. Rain is museums and petrol or fares, or canasta and mah jong and Scrabble. I ought to buy Monopoly because it lasts five hours.

On the boys' last visit, we went up the Thames on a boat. We were just watching the sun on the waves when we reached Cuckold's Corner. The boatman said the men used to pay one penny to have their wives tied to a stool and ducked in the river. He said the practice had unfortunately been stopped.

Among the four Smugglers in my front room, Roger declared the whisky, the crown jewels, and the two watches—and won his round.

When a woman leaps through the window of a glass house into the open air, there is left behind her the sharp, jagged edges that tear at the children's flesh, and there are, in the shaggy carpet, shards of glass that will easily become embedded in their bare feet. But if she is to survive, she needs time to attend her own tourniquets.

"Mum, if you could choose to have girls instead of boys, what would you choose?"

Why did Tom ask me that in rush hour at an amber traffic light? Deal with clutch, gears, brake. Stall for time.

"I've got you two and that's fine by me. You can't know what a baby's going to be. Well, I mean, they can test the fluid these days around the baby to see if it's already a boy or girl, can't they, but that's when it's already growing in the mum's womb. You two are what's been born. I know who you are, so how could I possibly choose different now?"

"Stands to reason," said Roger.

As far as I know I'm not on file as a lesbian in their school. So they are free of the psychiatrists' labels if they do something wrong or don't achieve good grades. (What does achieve mean?) I go to the parents' evenings with their dad, and I play the role of separate but equal. I take off my badges, my silver pendant, and my ring from my small finger. I take my hands out of my pockets, adjust my walk, modify how I sit and talk, and I choose my colors with care. None of those stripey feminist sweaters or garish pink socks. I won't wear a dress because I'd feel I was going in drag. I fix my smile, lower my shoulders so that I look relaxed, and I keep it up for a whole two hours.

I have a bath where I let out the weeping when I return.

Tom failed to declare the camera and the brandy, then tried to tell us he hadn't smuggled them. Roger flung his cards on the table in disgust.

"You see. I can't even trust him when he's supposed to be cheating." Roger wept huge drops, without rainbows.

They come every three weeks, which is as much as they and I can cope with of the waiting, preparing to meet, meeting, and saying good-bye again until the next time. To regulate the intensity, they use escape techniques like the tele in my bedroom, and I use my writing in the the kitchen. Or we all make cakes, which they both love, to take home to dad, and we can hide as separate individuals while working with our hands.

Sometimes Tom wants to see my guilt. He stands there like a young patriarch, an infant king in embroidered robes, demanding my obedience to his whims.

"I'm not coming to your flat ever again. I'm not ever ever coming to see you."

"That's a pity, Tom. I'll miss you. Now are you going to change that shirt so that you can come and look for Legos in Smiths'?"

"That's bribery."

"Bribery's if I want something. What I'm saying is that if you want to go out with me, you need a clean shirt without your dinner down the front. You asked me to take you shopping."

"If you go now, you won't be able to double-lock the front door because I'll be here inside."

"Yes. That's right. I won't. So we might all get burgled, mightn't we, and that's just too bad, because Roger and I are ready and we are going now. So are you changing your shirt and coming?"

"No. I won't. You're mean."

"I'll wait three minutes down in the car, then I'm driving off. O.K.?"

He stayed enthroned in the armchair, crown slightly toppled. I fretted silently there and back in case he'd taken revenge by setting the chip pan alight or flooding the bath. When we arrived home, he was calmly engrossed in a book.

Later, Roger stayed with Trish while Tom and I went for a walk. We held hands through the azaleas and played tiptoes through the tulips singing loudly. We hardly spoke. Just sang it all out of us, improvising and skipping. That night he came and hugged me.

"You know about today," he said, "well, I'm sorry."

He read beside me for half an hour and slept soundly in the front room till eight next morning.

The grief over access is not mine alone. It is also my mother and father's grief. They, too, are members of a minority group. Dad was a working-class priest on a minimum income in a northern mining town. My mother used to say that if you stuck a goat on a table wearing a red rosette, she and all the others would vote for it in preference to the Tories. The minority went to church on Sundays, then to the pub with a thirst after righteousness. We could dance and sing and play tennis and anything so long as we went to church first. But anything meant after marriage, and marriage is heterosexual.

They taught me my politics, and now they pay their price. They have watched me become a marxist, an antiracist (it was always a white goat), a feminist, and a lesbian. They say they love me, but their eyes are a mirror of the law courts. Their minority has visible royal patronage.

Just as they were about to retire, with both daughters married and their future organized around four grandchildren, I became a dyke.

"We all have women friends," said Mum. "You always did do things in extremes."

"If you would just talk to an expert, dear," said Dad.

Two years later, they fear what they call my corrupting influence upon their grandchildren. My father wrote: "This cannot be the atmosphere for training youngsters toward a married relationship when they become heterosexual adults." And then, although I felt that new skin had grown since I leapt through the window and had healed fresh, clean, and whole, his words pulled the elastoplasts off my bare arms, ripping away the hairs, revealing some splinters still buried in the tissues.

My mother's ancestors were working people on a gaelic island where homosexuality is still illegal and lesbianism invisible.

I will teach my sons their gaelic heritage. I'd like them to see the cliffs with the seabirds' swooping feathered flight on feathered skies; to look out across the Atlantic and image that the oceans last forever; to hear the lilt and songs of the language which are there today in the voices; to ask why there are matriarchal dragons carved there on runic crosses; and to hear the stories of the raw demands of the sea for generations back into the times of myth when the faeries wove green lace across the terminal moraines of the glaciers.

But if my sons are to be survivors, they may need to face the contradiction that in the land where their mother was born, there is a hill down which, in earlier times, she would have been rolled in a spiked barrel for rejecting heterosexuality and the Christian church.

Man Child:
A Black Lesbian-Feminist's Response
Audre Lorde

This is not a theoretical discussion of Lesbian Mothers and their Sons, nor a how-to article. It is an attempt to scrutinize and share some pieces of that common history belonging to my son and to me. I have two children: a fifteen-and-a-half-year-old daughter Beth, and a fourteen-year-old son Jonathan. This is the way it was/is with me and Jonathan, and I leave the theory to another time and person. This is one woman's telling.

I have no golden message about the raising of sons for other lesbian mothers, no secret to transpose your questions into certain light. I have my own ways of rewording those same questions, hoping we will all come to speak those questions and pieces of our lives we need to share. We are women making contact within ourselves and with each other across the restrictions of a printed page, bent upon the use of our own/one another's knowledge.

The truest direction comes from inside. I give the most strength to my children by being willing to look within myself, and by being honest with them about what I find there, without expecting a response beyond their years. In this way they begin to learn to look beyond their own fears.

All our children are outriders for a queendom not yet assured.

My adolescent son's growing sexuality is a conscious dynamic between Jonathan and me. It would be presumptuous of me to discuss Jonathan's sexuality here, except to state my belief that whomever he chooses to explore this area with, his choices will be nonoppressive, joyful, and deeply felt from within, places of growth.

One of the difficulties in writing this piece has been temporal; this is the summer when Jonathan is becoming a man, physically. And our sons must become men—such men as we hope our daughters, born and unborn, will be pleased to live among. Our sons will not grow into women. Their way is more difficult than that of our daughters, for they must move away from us, without us. Hopefully, our sons have what they have learned from us, and a howness to forge it into their own image.

Our daughters have us, for measure or rebellion or outline or dream; but the sons of lesbians have to make their own definitions of self as men. This is both power and vulnerability. The sons of lesbians have the advantage of our blueprints for survival, but they must take what we know and transpose it into their own maleness. May the goddess be kind to my son, Jonathan. Recently I have met young Black men about whom I am pleased to say that their future and their visions, as well as their concerns within the present, intersect more closely with Jonathan's than do my own. I have shared vision with these men as well as temporal strategies for our survivals and I appreciate the spaces in which we could sit down together. Some of these men I met at the First Annual Conference of Third World Lesbians and Gays held in Washington D.C. in October, 1979. I have met others in different places and do not know how they identify themselves sexually. Some of these men are raising families alone. Some have adopted sons. They are Black men who dream and who act and who own their feelings, questioning. It is heartening to know our sons do not step out alone.

When Jonathan makes me angriest, I always say he is bringing out the testosterone in me. What I mean is that he is representing some piece of myself as a woman that I am reluctant to acknowledge or explore. For instance, what does *acting like a man* mean? For me, what I reject? For Jonathan, what he is trying to redefine?

Raising Black children—female and male—in the mouth of a racist, sexist, suicidal dragon is perilous and chancy. If they cannot love and resist at the same time, they will probably not survive. And in order to survive they must let go. This is what mothers teach—love, survival—that is, self-definition and letting go. For each of these, the ability to feel strongly and to recognize those feelings is central: how to feel love, how to neither discount fear nor be overwhelmed by it, how to enjoy feeling deeply.

I wish to raise a Black man who will not be destroyed by, nor settle for, those corruptions called *power* by the white fathers who mean his destruction as surely as they mean mine. I wish to raise a Black man who will recognize that the legitimate objects of his hostility are not women, but the particulars of a structure that programs him to fear and despise women as well as his own Black self.

For me, this task begins with teaching my son that I do not exist to do his feeling for him.

Men who are afraid to feel must keep women around to do their feeling for them while dismissing us for the same supposedly inferior capacity to feel deeply. But in this way also, men deny themselves their own essential humanity, becoming trapped in dependency and fear.

As a Black woman committed to a liveable future, and as a mother loving and raising a boy who will become a man, I must examine all my possibilities of being within such a destructive system.

Jonathan was three-and-a-half when Frances, my lover, and I met; he was seven when we all began to live together permanently. From the start, Frances' and my insistence that there be no secrets in our household about the fact that we were lesbians has been the source of problems and strengths for both children. In the beginning, this insistence grew out of the knowledge, on both our parts, that whatever was hidden out of fear could always be used either against the children or ourselves—one imperfect but useful argument for honesty. The knowledge of fear can help make us free.

> *for the embattled*
> *there is no place*
> *that cannot be*
> *home*
> *nor is.**

For survival, Black children in america must be raised to be warriors. For survival, they must also be raised to recognize the enemy's many faces. Black children of lesbian couples have an advantage because they learn, very early, that oppression comes in many different forms, none of which have anything to do with their own worth.

To help give me perspective, I remember that for years, in the namecalling at school, boys shouted at Jonathan not—"Your mother's a lesbian"—but rather—"Your mother's a nigger."

When Jonathan was eight years old and in the third grade, we moved, and he went to a new school where his life was hellish as the new boy on the block. He did not like to play rough games. He did not like to fight. He did not like to stone dogs. And all this marked him early on as an easy target.

When he came in crying one afternoon, I heard from Beth how the corner bullies were making Jonathan wipe their shoes on the way home whenever Beth wasn't there to fight them off. And when I heard that the ringleader was a little boy in Jonathan's class his own size, an interesting and very disturbing thing happened to me.

My fury at my own long-ago impotence, and my present pain at his suffering, made me start to forget all that I knew about violence and fear, and blaming the victim, I started to hiss at the weeping child. "The next time you come in here crying...," and I suddenly caught myself in horror.

This is the way we allow the destruction of our sons to begin—in the name of protection and to ease our own pain. *My* son get beaten up? I was about to demand that he buy that first lesson in the corruption of power, that might

---

* From "School Note" in *The Black Unicorn* (W. W. Norton and Company, New York, 1978), p. 55.

makes right. I could hear myself beginning to perpetuate the age-old distortions about what strength and bravery really are.

And no, Jonathan didn't have to fight if he didn't want to, but somehow he did have to feel better about not fighting. An old horror rolled over me of being the fat kid who ran away, terrified of getting her glasses broken.

About that time, a very wise woman said to me, "Have you ever told Jonathan that once you used to be afraid, too?"

The idea seemed far-out to me then, but the next time he came in crying and sweaty from having run away again, I could see that he felt shamed at having failed me, or some image he and I had created in his head of mother/woman. This image of woman being able to handle it all was bolstered by the fact that he lived in a household with three strong women, his lesbian parents and his forthright older sister. At home, for Jonathan, power was clearly female.

And because our society teaches us to think in an either/or mode—kill or be killed, dominate or be dominated—this meant that he must either surpass or be lacking. I could see the implications of this line of thought. Consider the two western classic myth/models of mother/son relationships: Jocasta/Oedipus, the son who fucks his mother, and Clytemnestra/Orestes, the son who kills his mother.

It all felt connected to me.

I sat down on the hallway steps and took Jonathan on my lap and wiped his tears. "Did I ever tell you about how I used to be afraid when I was your age?"

I will never forget the look on that little boy's face as I told him the tale of my glasses and my after-school fights. It was a look of relief and total disbelief, all rolled into one.

It is hard for our children to believe that we are not omnipotent as it is for us to know it, as parents. But that knowledge is necessary as the first step in the reassessment of power as something other than might, age, privilege, or the lack of fear. It is an important step for a boy, whose societal destruction begins when he is forced to believe that he can only be strong if he doesn't feel, or if he wins.

I thought about all this one year later when Beth and Jonathan, ten and nine, were asked by an interviewer how they thought they had been affected by being children of a feminist.

Jonathan said he didn't think there was too much in feminism for boys, although it certainly was good to be able to cry if he felt like it and not to have to play football if he didn't want to. I think of this sometimes now when I see him practicing for his Brown Belt in Tae Kwon Do.

The strongest lesson I can teach my son is the same lesson I teach my daughter: how to be who he wishes to be for himself. And the best way

I can do this is to be who I am and hope he will learn from this not how to be me, which is not possible, but how to be himself. And this means how to move to that voice from within himself, rather than to those raucous, persuasive, or threatening voices from outside, pressuring him to be what the world wants him to be.

And that is hard enough.

Jonathan is learning to find within himself some of the different faces of courage and strength, whatever he chooses to call them. Two years ago, when Jonathan was twelve and in the seventh grade, one of his friends at school who had been to the house persisted in calling Frances "the maid." When Jonathan corrected him, the boy then referred to her as "the cleaning woman." Finally Jonathan said, simply, "Frances is not the cleaning woman, she's my mother's lover." Interestingly enough, it is the teachers at this school who still have not recovered from his openness.

Frances and I were considering attending a Lesbian-Feminist conference this summer, when we were notified that no boys over ten were allowed. This presented logistic as well as philosophical problems for us, and we sent the following letter:

Sisters:

Ten years as an interracial lesbian couple has taught us both the dangers of an oversimplified approach to the nature and solutions of any oppression, as well as the danger inherent in an incomplete vision.

Our thirteen-year-old son represents as much hope for our future world as does our fifteen-year-old daughter, and we are not willing to abandon him to the killing streets of New York City while we journey west to help form a Lesbian-Feminist vision of the future world in which we can all survive and flourish. I hope we can continue this dialogue in the near future, as I feel it is important to our vision and our survival.

The question of separatism is by no means simple. I am thankful that one of my children is male, since that helps to keep me honest. Every line I write shrieks there are no easy solutions.

I grew up in largely female environments, and I know how crucial that has been to my own development. I feel the want and need often for the society of women, exclusively. I recognize that our own spaces are essential for developing and recharging.

As a Black woman, I find it necessary to withdraw into all-Black groups at times for exactly the same reasons—differences in stages of development and differences in levels of interaction. Frequently, when speaking with men and white women, I am reminded of how difficult and time-consuming it is to have to reinvent the pencil every time you want to send a message.

But this does not mean that my responsibility for my son's education stops at age ten, any more than it does for my daughter's. However, for each of them, that responsibility does grow less and less as they become more woman and man.

Both Beth and Jonathan need to know what they can share and what they cannot, how they are joined and how they are not. And Frances and I, as grown women and lesbians coming more and more into our power, need to relearn the experience that difference does not have to be threatening.

When I envision the future, I think of the world I crave for my daughters and my sons. It is thinking for survival of the species—thinking for life.

Most likely there will always be women who move with women, women who live with men, men who choose men. I work for a time when women with women, women with men, men with men, all share the work of a world that does not barter bread or self for obedience, nor beauty, nor love. And in that world we will raise our children free to choose how best to fulfill themselves. For we are jointly responsible for the care and raising of the young, since *that* they be raised is a function, ultimately, of the species.

Within that tripartite pattern of relating/existence, the raising of the young will be the joint responsibility of all adults who choose to be associated with children. Obviously, the children raised within each of these three relationships will be different, lending a special savor to that eternal inquiry into how best can we live our lives.

Jonathan was three-and-a-half when Frances and I met. He is now fourteen years old. I feel the living perspective that having lesbian parents has brought to Jonathan is a valuable addition to his human sensitivity.

Jonathan has had the advantage of growing up within a nonsexist relationship, one in which this society's pseudonatural assumptions of ruler/ruled are being challenged. And this is not only because Frances and I are lesbians, for unfortunately there are some lesbians who are still locked into patriarchal patterns of unequal power relationships.

These assumptions of power relationships are being questioned because Frances and I, often painfully and with varying degrees of success, attempt to evaluate and measure over and over again our feelings concerning power, our own and others'. And we explore with care those areas concerning how it is used and expressed between us and between us and the children, openly and otherwise. A good part of our biweekly family meetings are devoted to this exploration.

As parents, Frances and I have given Jonathan our love, our openness, and our dreams to help form his visions. Most importantly, as the son of lesbians, he has had an invaluable model—not only of a relationship—but of relating.

Jonathan is fourteen now. In talking over this paper with him and asking his permission to share some pieces of his life, I asked Jonathan what he felt were the strongest negative and the strongest positive aspects for him in having grown up with lesbian parents.

He said the strongest benefit he felt he had gained was that he knew a lot more about people than most other kids his age that he knew, and that he did not have a lot of hang-ups that some other boys did about men and women.

And the most negative aspect he felt, Jonathan said, was the ridicule he got from some kids with straight parents.

"You mean, from your peers?" I said.

"Oh no," he answered promptly. "My peers know better. I mean other kids."

Waterbabies

Brangwen Griffith

Anne stands at the edge of the field, her thumb poised ready to click off a stopwatch. "Keep running. Keep running, Josh. Just one more lap."

"How did I ever have this child," she asks herself. "This child who looks so much like me?" She searches his body and sees her own long neck, triangular shadows under high cheeks, the odd wide mouth. Dark brown hair straight as southern rain. "He uses his body the way I was told not to," Anne thinks.

She remembers her own body straining, a body growing, a body frozen with contradictions—and Beth, whose body flourished unhampered. "Beth. Beth, I wonder what you would think of me with a son. With Josh...."

"Be careful!" Anne shouts.

"Shit," he says, sliding across a mudpuddle through the grass, scattering dandelion manes in the sun.

She sees her own feet, muddied, on his stretching adolescent legs. "I gave you those feet," she thinks. "I gave you those high arches. So you could dance with them, push off from your precarious place in my life like a hawk after tomorrow's rabbit, so you can catch yourself before you fall when I cannot. They remind me of Beth's," she muses, "as if passed on by some quiet parthenogenesis."

"Here, give me your leg." A massage for his calf, a wiggle of the kneecap, circling thumbs—with pressure—up the thigh.

"Ouch! Fuck, I think I pulled a muscle," he says.

"No. I'd feel something. Come on home, I'll work on it there. Go get your stuff." She shouts across the field, "Normal mothers don't let their kids swear like that, do they?"

"Anne, you're not normal."

"Why? because I'm a les—"

"Mom, don't shout it all over the place!"

Anne remembers another track. She and Beth, seventeen, grinding triangles of gravel under white sneakers. Their strides snapped through brittle air, breaking through old snow blown and frozen across the track. The world

was a ship creaking, wrenching from its moorings, rebounding against py-
lons driven through ice into the rock.

". . .the rule for *piece* and *ceiling*?" Anne gasped.

"*I* before *e* except after *c*," answered Beth, skipping the gravel like stones
across water.

Anne passed through the breath of her answer, not listening. *Beth has
workable legs. If I could sculpt them*, she heaved herself forward, feeling
the thinness of air in her chest, *I'd grind them from riverstone, carve hard-
muscled, lean legs. Fit each flexor, each abductor like Peruvian stone. No
need for mortar, unessential flesh.*

"I have to stop. I'm running out of breath," Anne said.

"Keep walking until you don't feel lightheaded anymore."

Beth's legs did what they were supposed to do. Worked when she wanted
them to. Arms swung in opposition with the progress of her feet. She ran
like the river when it was up—churning, lowering into unfilled space, cutting a straighter channel, rushing toward its source.

Even the cement crumbled underfoot that winter. Long underwear and
lined boots might have been gauze. The river by Anne's house reflected only
grey in its patina, an old and broken mirror too tarnished to catch the sky;
and wild ducks padded over its solid surface, picking up crumbs scattered
by an old couple next door. Every morning they carried a shopping bag to
the riverbank, two penguins in heavy coats with mufflers drawn across the
mouth, bobbing slightly as they tossed out gifts to the river. They, like the
birds they nurtured, seemed mated for life.

"Not like me," Anne told herself, watching their daily movements. She
dreamed of molding mountains of clay with her hands, of sculpting wom-
en's breasts. Women's ribs like lyres, wings rising from naked shoulders,
banners lifting faceted toes off the ground. Of life in a big city where there
would be a view of a different river. "Where no one would care that my
nails are dirty," she said. "And I won't marry, but one day I will find a little
girl with hands that will shape mythological creatures from fallen clay. We'll
go to the park by the river and count the seagulls swarming the boats, count
the time it takes raindrops to crack a mudpuddle. When the thunder starts,
we'll run to a little kitchen filled like a ship's galley for a long journey.

" 'Anne, I'm hungry,' she will say, and I'll peel blood oranges with a knife,
and we'll eat and eat and eat till the juice runs down our chins."

Joshua and his mother argue the relative embarrassment of shouting *lesbian!* across an athletic field. He is seventeen. She told him about her love
for women ten years ago. Ten years of women playing baseball with him,
running with him, throwing football with him, athletes with tenderness, holding their hands to his tears.

"Sometimes I think you would have been happier if I were a girl. Is that true, Anne?" he questions. "Did you really want a girl?"

Anne saw herself at seventeen, standing in front of her English teacher: "If she doesn't pass, they won't let her run. You're the verbal athlete, but she's as good on her feet as you with your words," said Mrs. Wolfe, who was also girls' coach. "It wouldn't hurt you to run with her now and then. Can't read and draw all the time." She believed in filling life with possibility.

Beth, when tutored, was unsettled and confined. "If you sit still and pay attention, I'll run with you," Anne bargained with her. Beth, with her loose athletic clothes and long silences, was a foreigner to Anne. Anne polished words in her head, looking for ones that would open Beth's secrets, that would tell her who she was—what pulses moved Beth's body, stirred the river of her legs, blocked the flow of words.

Beth was a watcher, but still she outran the well-worn phrase.

"I like your feet," she finally said.

"What do you mean *feet?*"

"High arches. They push you off the ground when you want them to."

"I'm not an athlete. Why do I need athlete's feet?"

They laughed like percolating coffee, tumbling into speech.

"What do you want to be when you grow up?"

"An artist. You?"

"To run the 100 in 10."

"What are your parents like?" Anne asked.

"Mom's fat and cooks. Dad's a plumber. They're kind of crude but get along O.K. Yours?"

"My Mom's scared of me being on my own. She wants me to get married. My father wants me to go to college. They don't get along so well."

"Don't you want to get married?" asked Beth.

"No. I want to be famous and live in a big city. You?"

"No. I have nightmares about having babies. I like kids, though."

"Are you a virgin?"

"I don't want someone sticking his thing up me! That's disgusting!"

"I saw my Dad with an erection in the bathroom once. I thought he had some kind of disease. I didn't know what it was till I read a sex book from my parents' room."

"Did the book say anything about women?" asked Beth. "Women who like other women, I mean?"

"Lesbians?"

"What?"

"That's what they're called."

"I never heard that before. Was that in your Mom and Dad's book?"

"No. My father's a psychologist. It was in one of his big reference books."

"What'd it say?"

"Oh, that women want penises. They think they lost theirs. Lesbians are women who want to be men. They're jealous of men."

"Who would want to be a man?"

"What do you mean?"

"Anne, I think I'm queer."

Anne was sliding, the world falling on its side, something was pounding under her chest—

"Have you told anyone else?" she whispered.

"No. If it bothers you, I can get another tutor."

"NO! I didn't mean to shout at you. I don't know what to say. . ." (*Can it be fixed?*) . . . "Could you go to a shrink?"

"There's nothing wrong. Just scared, that's all."

"Let's run."

Joshua waits while Anne dreams, waits for an answer. We are losing each other, she thinks. You are seventeen, about to leave, to go into a world where I can't live. A boy raised among women.

"Josh, I loved being pregnant," she says. "I love you. Not my fantasies."

"Then I'm second-best. Not what you wanted but what you got."

"You're not a booby prize. But that's what you're going to get at this Saturday's meet if you don't go to bed." A tease, a hug for Josh. Better than this tug of war.

"Okay. I love what I got, too, Anne," he says.

"Let him be a little angry," she decides. "Be propelled, helped to leave."

Anne remembered the spring of her seventeenth year and the first track meet she went to with Beth. She remembered how she watched as Beth's body leaped like a clear spring, splashed sand, heaved up a javelin, tossed shotputs like boulders into the stream, flooded past the other runners. Won.

"Thanks for coming," said Beth.

"Will you pose for me sometime?"

Anne's modeling studio was under the house, bisected by insulated pipes. Incandescent lights, cupped by aluminum, were clipped to conduits. This was the spoils of a war between parents and child, the bribe to block rude rejection: Do Not Disturb. This was where Anne grew that spring, turning toward the one small source of natural light, a basement window with a film of rain-washed dirt. Where she lengthened like a hothouse plant left too long in a flat, drawn up by light, by her own idiosyncrasy.

With the sputtering of rainclouds overhead, Beth came to the studio one afternoon, slick with sweat, bringing news of imminent and torrential rain.

"The river's up. Let's go see," she said. She smelled of earth releasing its warmth into the storm-charged air.

"Here, this is for you," Anne said over the sound of the rising river. "I sketched you at the meet a while ago."

"Thanks. Hey, that's really good!"

"Thanks. I want to do more clay. That's why I got the basement room. My parents even paid for classes at the college for a while. I learned lots of things, to mold and cast. . . But they said I couldn't go anymore. My teacher tried to talk to them, but they told him I was too young."

"Why?"

"There were models in the nude."

"Weren't you embarrassed?"

"Sometimes at the men. But the women—round, yearning lines. Like the way their stomachs sit, the way the line of this muscle"—Anne pushed her thumb upward along Beth's leg, closed her palm over Beth's skin—"comes diagonal across your inner thigh."

Beth's leg was not cold retentive rock, but milkweed down, smooth inner pod. "You're still warm from running," Anne said, her eyes darkening with the stormy sky.

"Your eyes are blue," said Beth.

The river crashed through the ice, pounded the banks, was ready to jump.

"Beth," answered Anne.

Together in Anne's basement room, their refuge, they named names and whispered passwords known only among the same tribe. They gathered warmth beneath the skin, sought water for itself, their arms bursting with the river joining underneath—the river they came to know, the river of their thirst. In the sureness of their bodies, in the unimpeded current of muscle and bone they grew from spring into summer. Until Anne's mother found them and sent Anne away. Too late to stop the current.

Yes, I did dream of a daughter, Anne thinks, as the track meet swarms with the parents who come in matched sets with matched younger brothers and sisters, with matched coolers, matched family campers and two-week vacations. *No room for me here,* she reminds herself. Yet, for several years she has taken her turn providing sodas for the team, has cheered for Josh and his friends, fixed potato salad at school picnics. Sometimes with a lover like an aunt or sister. Sometimes not.

Track meets are Anne's time of superficial ordinariness. Alone, just a woman with a son, where Josh's fears of her visibility—static in the background of his love—where this conflict tears out of him with floods of adrenalin.

The prize will help him separate from me, she thinks. *A scholarship. An accolade. He'll win today.*

Unself-consciously poised, he joins the air, the river that carries him downstream, over turbulence, past all obstacles, past the finish line unaware the race is done. And that he has won, that the final ribbon he has broken is a spider's web. A thread Anne has spun from her heart and placed there. A thread she has been spinning for a long time, through the years since she was seventeen, through the years since she saw Beth run like that river, carried by dumb currents, water caught by the stream. He is unaware it hurts when it breaks. That he has won and that his mother and he are not lost, just parted.

The Radical Potential
In Lesbian Mothering Of Daughters
Baba Copper

Radical motherhood. Surely it is a measure of woman's defeat that this phrase
has a self-contradictory ring. The practice of motherhood embodies legitimate power—the power of early childhood socialization and a lifelong position of influence on one's children. Each different culture—the sand mold
in which every individual is cast—is transmitted by women. The process,
if not the goals, of this fundamental source of social cohesion rests uncon-
tested in the hands of women. All that potential, and yet mothers almost
always function, and expect to function, in continual denial of their own
self-interest.

Within the context of female-to-female training in motherhood lies yet
another potential—that of strong, women-come-first female bonding. The
mother who teaches her daughter how to mother could be an alchemist of
culture, vaporizing woman-hating traditions into the gold of feminist change.
Yet mothers do not use their power to commit their daughters to resistance
to patriarchal conformity. The very women who insist that radical feminists
should live their politics question the *political* potential of motherhood. Many
lesbians continue to view motherhood as locked in tradition—an institution
which, even with antisexist reforms, can be of service only to the patriarchy. How can we understand the connection between being a lesbian mother
and radical mothering—motherhood which involves conscious detachment
from much of the programming women carry out, generation to generation, in the service of patriarchy.

I am a lesbian mother to a lesbian daughter. I have moved from traditional to radical feminist lesbian midstream in my mothering process. My two
married daughters reflect the "success" of the patriarchal mothering I did
within a nuclear family; traditional socialization that more or less mirrored
those values and practices my mother used with me. But my midlife switch
has allowed me, as an old lesbian, to explore—in practice as well as theory—
active resistance to the ideology and institutions of heteromotherhood. I am
extending and politicizing my mothering. I am making a connection between
my radicalism and the lesbianism of my daughter.

Recently I sought out other mother/daughter dyads who are both lesbians. In carrying out this search, I discerned a suppressed anxiety surrounding the whole subject, resulting, I suspect, from the "congenital disease"

theory of homosexuality promulgated by psychiatrists, and reinforced by the Gay Rights we-are-just-like-everybody-else defense against homophobia. The relationship my daughter and I share often appears invisible, even to our friends and lovers who see it as apolitical—a personal anomaly, threateningly different. Perhaps lesbians have not yet identified either the goals or the "rules" of heteropatriarchal mothering with sufficient clarity to be able to change them.

Why is there strong support among women for the separation between mothers and adult daughters? Why should they not remain close, expanding their ways of being together into adult-to-adult intimacy which provides mutual support and growth? Surely the separation of the daughter from the mother is not an appropriate expectation to guide the behavior of two lesbians?

A tight mother/adult daughter bonding may be the ultimate patriarchal no-no. Therapists reinforce the definition of female maturity as a woman who has separated from, not bonded with her mother. There are the oft-repeated mother-in-law jokes which pressure married women to discard their mother as ally. Although loving relationships between traditional mothers and their heterosexual daughters are not unknown, most daughters value the distances which their lives have generated away from their mothers. Here is a rule of heteromothering worth breaking.

My lesbian daughter and I are exploring the mined territory of mother/adult daughter bonding. We do so without honor in the lesbian community. She suffers the indignity of derogatory comments from her peers, such as being told to "grow up" when she expresses yearning for my presence. I face the assumptions that my motherhood somehow defines my life, instead of being a small but important part of it.

Yet she and I, as well as other lesbian mothers/lesbian daughters I have questioned, express a high level of satisfaction and pride about the relationship we share. I know that without her support, I could not be nearly as courageous or willful in my pursuit of the mysteries of my aging identity. A realistic response to these postmenopausal days demands that I be militant about my age, and vocal about the prejudice which surrounds it. What if all four of my children were heterosexual! Could my unconventional life choices survive another son-in-law sitting in judgment on his dangerous mother-in-law as he badgers his wife, my daughter, to deny the validity of my feminism or my lesbianism? As one of my married daughters explained to me, "He is doing the best he can, under the circumstances."

If my lesbian daughter gives me magical permission to explore oldwomanhood, I supply her with a supportive continuity of trust and intimacy as she navigates the years of changing partners and careers that often characterize the late twenties. We continue to struggle with the residual power imbalances which linger from our mother/child past. In practical terms, our bonding has translated into some financial interdependency, occasional shared living situations (including two-and-one-half hectic years in a lesbian separatist rural community), traveling together to foreign countries, at least weekly exchanges of the details of our lives. We are, I believe, truly intimates "for keeps."

I do not want to imply that lesbian mother/lesbian daughter relationships are easy. One of my lesbian mother respondents described her relationship with her two lesbian daughters as "passionate, fraught, exciting, compelling." New demands are put upon mother/daughter relations by the heightened awareness of erotic energy between women which lesbians cultivate. The mother may fear that she and her daughter will find themselves being lovers with the same woman, since often they both circulate socially in a relatively small lesbian community. The daughter, tending to ignore the handicap of ageism which diminishes her mother in the sexual marketplace, may feel intimidated in an imagined sexual competition with her. I know one daughter in a very close mother/daughter dyad who came out at sixteen with her mother's lover of that time. Another mother said to me with great feeling, "There is something oppressive about my lover's need to like my daughter and my daughter's need to like my lover." Insecurity in mothers, in daughters, or in lovers, breeds tensions between them. The assumptions of accessibility which play back and forth between lesbian mothers and lesbian daughters may be extremely threatening to lovers.

On the other hand, the daughter of a lesbian may have a great advantage over her heterosisters by being able to learn from loving woman-to-woman interactions as she grows up. Not many daughters learn the "hows" of this liberating knowledge from traditional nuclear families. In my own case, it was only when I broke out of the selflessness of marriage that I was able to demand an *exchange* of nurturing from those around me, including my children. Now, only the daughter who saw me loved by women is able to give as well as take nurturance. Knowing how to nurture the nurturer is the best path out of dependency and the ugly feelings that often accompany feeling dependent. Being validated as equal nurturer by one's mother can be a key factor in female self-esteem.

My own experience, and my learnings from other lesbian mother/lesbian daughter dyads, indicate that something different is happening between lesbians which merits attention. To extend and deepen the mother/daughter bond into adulthood did not seem a radical act to me, until I encountered the degree of opposition and misinterpretation which it evoked in other lesbians. I had assumed we were a threat to men, not to women-loving-women. Now I believe lesbians are fully as prejudiced toward mothers—any mothers—as any other segment of the population. The sooner lesbians detach from the heteromythology which clusters around motherhood, the better.

Although many mothers, hetero and lesbian, diligently study whatever expertise they can find on mothering as their bellies swell, probably half of what they do, once the hectic dance of mothering begins, are repetitions of the mothering they learned at a nonverbal level from their own mothers. Teaching little girls to cater to male supremacy—to serve and submit—have been the basic lessons of female survival. Any woman who is herself adequately socialized by male standards, transmits some of this. Built into these unconscious patterns of communication between mother and daughter is content that lesbians will want to raise to a conscious level and judge with modern, politicized eyes.

Lesbians cannot look for satisfactory guidance from heterofeminists who write books about raising antisexist boys and liberated girls. These children are expected to be high achievers in a man's world without questioning the assumptions underpinning that goal. There is also a great deal of lyrical psychobabble by heterofeminists about the redemption of the human psyche possible through male mothering of infants. Theory needs some basis in evidence. No one has been denying fathers the joys of parenting. Some men have been successful fathers. But for every well-fathered child, there are a million who were conceived irresponsibly or abandoned or raped or physically terrorized or emotionally denied by their fathers. The true circumstances of women and children in the heterofamily are not reflected in the heterofeminist party line, which seems to say: if mothers will encourage little girls to have a demanding career and choose a feminist man who will help her with the babies, then all will be equal between the sexes in the next generation. Unfortunately, the intention that lies behind most decisions to have a baby is the desire to prove the permanency and value of a romantic attachment (half of which end in divorce). The reality which underlies this mythic intention is the disastrous institution of traditional motherhood, in which female children are taught to love everyone but themselves.

There are issues important to lesbian mothers that heterofeminists do not address. First and foremost, we must acknowledge that the mothering of daughters is of primary importance to us. If women come first, then daughters come first. The next step in disengaging motherhood from male definitions is to identify the mother/daughter dyad as *the* evolutionary crucible of society. Any abuse by the adult males of the former family—daughter rape, or battery, or harsh labor exploitation—may diminish female autonomy in that family tree for generations. The mother teaches the next generation of mothers how to mother—how to transmit much of the societal information which humans share at an unconscious level.

What are the hidden agendas built into heteromotherhood that are destructive to females, both daughters and mothers? Is it possible, at this particular herstorical juncture, to successfully enable both boys and girls within the same early behavioral environment? Are there psychological chains between the generations of women, analogous to those created by alcohol or sexual abuse, that pass the damage from mother to daughter—damage done in the name of female survival or being a loving mother or a good wife; damage done during the times of the Burnings, or in concentration or refugee camps, or during other mass atrocities suffered by women; damage done century after century, so that acceptance of those ways became the norm? Radical lesbian analysis of these kinds of questions can help lesbian mothers to: 1) avoid falling into the traps of "naturalness" built around the assumptions, rules, and myths of heteromothering; 2) devise active resistance to the repeated betrayals by mothers of daughters, and daughters of mothers; and 3) identify the inherent and unique benefits of lesbian mothering.

Lesbian mothers are, almost without exception, themselves products of heteromothering. Lesbians raise their children within patriarchy, just like other women. However, the lesbian can make choices in relation to the degree of assimilation of her daughter into patriarchy, choices not possible to the heteromother, if she is willing to raise to a conscious level some of the unconscious roots of female subordination.

All mammals teach appropriate responses of submission to their young. Within the context of the heterosexual tradition from which she sprang, the lesbian mother has learned to communicate to both her boy and girl children her understanding of the current cultural parameters of male entitlement—e.g. the cluster of expectations which surround being a man in a man's world. Since this is never a static body of information—there are infinite variations on male entitlement operative from one family structure to the next, one religion to the next, one ethnic or national group to the next—the child is raised to meet the expectations of the mother. By ten years of age, a daughter has always needed to know the limitations upon her identity which is the other side of the coin of male entitlement. Daughters of sixteen must be prepared to find opportunity and fulfillment within an elaborate system never clearly articulated by anyone. Male entitlement is created by assumptions, mythologized to be natural, justified, universal.

Obviously, the mother is not the only source of this information flow. However, she is the one most strongly motivated to communicate successful manipulation of this hidden system to her daughters, since she herself learned it from her mother *as the key to female survival*. Depending on which culture one looks at, maternal collusion in male entitlement takes various forms: preferring the birth of a son, female infanticide, selective neglect of girl babies which impairs their development, grossly unequal educational opportunities or attention, the sale or exchange of daughters in marriage. Does anyone know how many generations it will take without these practices to erase their psychological scars?

There is no counterpart system of female entitlement—only the obvious sex-segregated labor and sex-differentiated customs that all cultures have. In order to keep patriarchy functioning as a self-sustaining heterosystem, daughters must be taught to mistrust females and to attend/depend on males. Mothers teach daughters, even at a preverbal level, that their instinct of self-preservation is best served by the *absence* of female bonding, the *absence* of female-to-female entitlement. Mothers must also imprint their daughters with allegiance to patriarchal aesthetics. By example, mothers train their daughters to fear female aging, to find continual fault with their own bodies, to believe they must cash in on natural beauty or youth. Teaching daughters to be "attractive" and "successful" has been the innocuous justification for some of the most pernicious betrayals of daughters by mothers: footbinding; physical weakness and mental shallowness; cosmetic surgery and dieting; sexual ignorance; child brides, child prostitution, and child pornography; genital mutilation. Teaching daughters to succeed in the lifelong struggle to assimilate into a manmade hierarchy of female worth has always been a trap.

This subtle process and its woman-hating content is buried in the often harried day-to-day interactions between a mother and her daughters. Radical mothering means involving children in disloyalty to the culture the mother is expected to transmit at the expense of woman-bonding and female empowerment. Excavating the heteromyths buried in the transmitted information of daughter-rearing is the most important work of the lesbian radical mother. These heteromyths embody the unconscious informational chains between the generations of women that lesbians have the potential to break, if they will consciously accept the task.

The fact of lesbian existence as radical lesbians in patriarchy gives their mothering some clear advantages. For instance, lesbian mothers for the most part eschew that bedrock heteromyth which says a child needs a resident father in order to grow up whole. Lesbian mothering can enhance the development of female autonomy and self-love. Lesbian mothers may also have more motivation to imagine what might constitute positive female rights and role expectations for our daughters.

There are also aspects of lesbian radicalism which need to be adapted for lesbian mothers, such as separatism. Few lesbians live or work in a male-free world. Of necessity, even a separatist's daughter will someday have men in her life: how can she best be prepared for this eventuality? First, radical mothers need a new definition of lesbian separatism which takes into account the vulnerability of the children in our community. We cannot afford to pretend that the statistics of incest, rape, battery, and addiction to female-degrading pornography do not apply to the men we all know. I would like to suggest the following: Each adult woman needs to make her own determination as to which males she will allow into her life, as well as the degree of access these males will have to her home and person. However, no woman should assume that the males *she* trusts can be trusted by any other female, including female children, or that another woman should trust them because she does. The presence of males in the life of her female child demands that a radical mother not only live by this maxim, but that she does so openly, with the full and early knowledge of her female child.

If this seems extreme, then the mother should ask, *How much harm does one incident of sexual abuse cause to the trust the child is building toward her world in general, and men in particular?* If it were a serious but avoidable communicable disease which crippled one female out of five, would it be an "acceptable risk"? How does the female child raised in a heterosexual household learn to cede space, body integrity, or verbal perogative to males, even before she is five years old? It seems clear that the daughter of a lesbian who has the opportunity to watch women exchange power, attention, and trust—preferably between as many different kids of women as possible—will learn new ways of being a woman in the world.

Another heteromyth which needs radical defusing is the notion that lesbian mothers must maintain neutrality in relation to the future sexual preference of their daughters. *Sexual preference* is not the issue. The reality underlying the myth is one we all know: female heterosexuality cannot be called a choice when it is compulsory in all cultures, everywhere. But we are lesbian, and it is a fundamental expression of self-love to want our daughters to grow up reflecting our woman-identified choices. Although many heteromothers have tried to force their daughters out of lesbianism, it is hard to imagine a lesbian mother who would deny choice to her daughter.

Radical mothering must also encompass many of the same struggles that conscientious heteromothers face. As all politically committed mothers have discovered, it is not enough to verbalize antiracist, antiageist, antilooksist sentiments to our children. In addition to talk, we must communicate by modeling the behavior we expect in them. This necessitates viewing one's lifestyle not as an extension of who-I-am but of who-I-want-them-to-learn-to-be. No mother succeeds in always being how she wants her children to be, but the radical mother structures her lifestyle so that her child has ample opportunity to see her trying. Lesbians do not hesitate to choose for our daughters when it comes to the prevention of childhood diseases, but we balk at inoculating them against assimilation into heterofeminitiy—into the addictive satisfactions of female normalcy.

We need to make some dramatic changes in the information usually shared with daughters. Daughters have been deprived *by their mothers* of knowledge of their orgasmic potential and the various ways of satisfying it, detailed knowledge of both the history and the current oppression of women worldwide, information about matrifocal civilizations and woman-defined women of the past, and revelations about their mothers' lives and sexuality. This suppression of information is a learned pattern of behavior passed from mother to daughter that teaches mistrust between women. Honor between women starts with honesty and with the determination to empower each other. Our children are the daughters of women who love women over men. Daughters of lesbians, like freedom fighters everywhere, need to be enlisted in infancy, and protected against heterofemininity by words and actions—not for the mother's sake nor for the movement's sake—but for their own psychological well-being.

With my lesbian daughter, I have never asked that perennial lament of motherhood, "Where did I go wrong?" although she and I joke a lot about both her strengths and her weaknesses being my fault. All mothers make a terrible investment in their children. All mothers are brainwashed to believe they are totally responsible for the results. I recognize I have not diminished that heteromyth by the questions I have raised about the goals of lesbian mothering. Nor have I addressed the issues of comothering or group mothering, both of which represent new and important variations on heteromothering that lesbians are exploring. Uninvestigated allegiances and assumptions clutter the actions of all women who mother. Many of them are pivotal to self-hatred and the absence of female bonding. My own experience, and that of the other lesbian mothers I have interviewed, has encouraged me to think that lesbian motherhood has a unique role to play in these areas.

Lesbians are political women, whether or not our politics are radical, or even at an aware level. What all lesbians need is a woman-identified world, in which female self-love is the norm, not the exception. Part of the lesbian image has been to contrast the woman-who-asserts-her-self, the Amazon, as the opposite of the-woman-who-sacrifices-her-self, the Mother. This, like so many binary concepts, is a false division of the possibilities, intended to divide women. True, most lesbians probably will not reproduce or mother, but the lesbian community will continue to include lots of mothers, comothers, and children. True, even the most radical lesbian mothering will include considerable altruism. But it is also true that lesbian mothering embodies a remarkable chance to redesign woman's primary biologically-based role in the service of woman-chosen goals.

Daughters And Mothers

Evelyn Torton Beck

An Autobiographical Sketch (1980)

I have a piece of lesbian history I haven't quite known what to do with. Sometimes you know something is important and ought to be shared, and yet the uncertainty of where you might find the right place to publish it and the fear that it might not be accepted anywhere keeps you from putting it down on paper. This has been true for me and the story I've been carrying around in my head for a long time now.

The story is the story of my life. My life and my daughter's. I am EviB— the lesbian name my lover gave to me. It is a name I especially like, with its warm and playful evocation of Gertrude Stein and Alice B. Toklas. In the name I am both Gertrude and Alice. I am a community woman and a university professor. I am Jewish and a mother. I am a Jewish lesbian who is the mother of a Jewish lesbian. And if the world were a different place, and my mother not so hooked into the patriarchy, I'd be the daughter of a lesbian, too.

It was my mother who taught me to love women. Not by loving me or by encouraging me to love women, but by her own unwitting example—the intense, life-long ties she shared with her women friends. I saw the closeness and the caring, even as she faithfully spouted what she believed to be her truths: Love men, they are our only salvation. Fear men, they are the dangerous enemy. She dreamed of male heroes, yet lived in a safe world of women. In real life, my father provided protection and sustenance. My memory is that other men were there only as essential backdrop and for occasional flirtation.

My daughter was an active lesbian in her teens. I envy her the freedom she took—I did not give it to her. If I had not been so fearful; if I had lived in other times; if my own mother had not been so watchful or so judgmental, especially when I was in my early teens, I'd have been freer to be the lesbian I was. I would not have had to spend long hours in the library agonizing, proving that I wasn't what I feared I was, knew I was, and talked myself out of being—loving women intensely, passionately, often obsessively, yet denying what this meant.

The best friend of my childhood years turned out to be a lesbian. I didn't know it in the years we shared a great passion for our seventh-grade English teacher; saving our money to buy her a costly gold bracelet, planning and writing about it all summer long, she at camp and I at home. (My friend spent twenty years in therapy, she later told me.) When she came out at age fourteen, it was a neighborhood scandal, talked about at length and in detail, at least in my home, primarily by my mother, who seemed to know everything about it. I can no longer clearly differentiate what I knew for myself from what my mother told me, how much my mother really knew from what she made up or guessed. I do remember some fragments.

My friend was involved with an older woman who lived on the next block with another woman. (How old was older? Twenty-five? Thirty-five?) Did my mother really suggest they seduced her? Probably. Were they really gym teachers, or am I making that up? My friend, herself, told me the police frequently bothered them when they were together in the car. Sometimes they were able to use someone's apartment. Did I know what they did? Did I guess or imagine? I distinctly remember one detail. She told me they always need a lot of tissues. I didn't *exactly* know what for, but I've never forgotten that detail either. I must have known something. Sometime later my friend told me her friend had deflowered her and she had bled. I sensed she was proud of this detail, but I'm not sure I believed she was telling me the truth. Did I think she invented these details just for my sake? How much did I really grasp? I myself was still totally sexually inactive at the time (except for masturbation, which I had learned young and liked a great deal and was terribly ashamed of). I disliked intensely what seemed to be the necessary making out at parties and always tried to get out of participating. Usually, I succeeded. At home, over and over again, my mother repeated that my friend was disgusting. What she did was disgusting. When I was disobedient, it was my friend's fault. She was a bad influence. Her mother was a communist, a divorcee who worked outside the home, what else could you expect?

In spite of my mother, we remained friends. A few years later she told me the details of her love affairs with women at college. How her lovers would touch her in the dark in bed, how they would touch her in bed but refuse to kiss her. How they would, in the daylight, withhold their love and pretend they didn't know her. These stories have stayed with me (till now I had no idea how indelibly) for nearly thirty years. I found it hard to understand why these lovers acted so strangely. If either of us had any inkling, we did not say. I doubt that the word *lesbian* ever crossed our lips, even while she was telling me these stories. I only remember clearly that she was badly hurt and terribly confused. We had no analysis, no names, no vocabulary (not in the early fifties on the streets of Brooklyn) with which to talk about women's love for women. The best I could offer her (and this

I did willingly, eagerly) was to listen. In thinking myself back to those years, it dawns upon me that her stories with their muted eroticism must have aroused me then, mildly, as they do now in the retelling. And I feel ashamed at feeling pleasure from what caused her pain. And at my own cowardice.

We've more or less lost touch now, but she was resigned and a little bitter when I last saw her, a few years ago, after a lapse of fifteen years. The long therapy had not erased the hurt. "I am neither," she said, when I asked her if she was still involved with women. "I cannot dissociate women from how bad and crazy I felt all those years." I remembered then how desperately she had tried to make life with a man work for her. More than once she had seriously contemplated marriage, but it never happened. I knew it was all wrong, but never once in the many years we exchanged letters did I dare express my doubt, did I dare say what I knew in my guts to be true: "Why are you trying to be what you are not?" No, I remained silent, foolishly polite, frequently encouraged her in her pursuit of marriage, and was disappointed with her every disappointment. Now she claims to have found peace in withdrawing from sexual intimacy altogether, and I feel angry for her, for myself, for all of us. Of course she is still a lesbian. Has never been anything else. It doesn't seem fair for her to have to believe she is "neither."

In a way, I was luckier. I masked myself in ways that protected. I think if I had come out then, as my friend did, in the late forties, I would be worse than "neither." I feel sure I would have cracked. My mother would have seen to that. She was so relentless, and I so tied to her approval. I fully believed she would lock me up or throw me out (the latter now doesn't seem very likely—she was too fiercely possessive to let me go). Being poor and new immigrants, we did not believe in or have access to psychiatrists. Instead, thinking to save me, she would not have hesitated to destroy me herself. My need for protection was very real, and for a time my mask worked. True, I continued to fall in love with women all my life (I never did outgrow that passion), but I was able to marry a man. And live with him for twenty years. And bear two children, one of whom is now a lesbian and has been since she was thirteen.

It feels hard to have to say I didn't help her become one. No, if truth be told, I'd have stopped her at the time if I could have. I did try. And so did her father. This is the hardest thing to admit, to set down on paper: I tried to keep her from becoming a dyke. I thought it would ruin her life. I really did. We threatened to call the police if she continued to see her lover. (I had no idea then of the power of the law or the enormity of our threats.) I didn't even really believe that they were lovers—my thirteen-year-old child and the twenty-one-year-old woman who was her mentor. I only knew that they loved each other and had made plans to sleep together. We kept them apart (or thought we did).

We joke about it now, she and I. Her friends all told her I must be a closet case to know so much and care so passionately. They were right, of course, but I was exceptionally obtuse. It took me years to really take in the fact that my daughter made love with another woman (not merely love, *sex*), even after she and her second lover had been living together for two years. And sleeping in one bed. And appearing with a group of Jewish lesbians in a protest at Hillel. I was utterly naive and heavily defended. Ridiculously, after I came out, I kept it from my daughter for a whole year (or thought I did). In fact, she knew and the whole community knew. (Was I ashamed to admit how very wrong I had been when she was thirteen?) One of the mothers I had run to in a panic about my daughter was herself the lesbian mother of a lesbian, only I didn't know it at the time, in spite of the fact that she was sharing her life with a woman. I can hardly bring myself to imagine how she experienced our assault; she met it with silence. We wanted her to *do* something, anything, to warn the other parents, to stop the affair. We did manage to call the youth-group parents together; I don't remember how they calmed us down. From the relatively safe distance of a decade, I can almost see the humor of the situation. That the lesbian mother (who is now also a colleague) speaks to me at all often amazes me. We almost never mention those times. I think they embarrass us both.

Today my daughter is twenty-three. That she is a lesbian comforts me. Whatever her struggles, I don't worry she will give her power away to the patriarchy. I trust and respect her and her lover and the many women who are her friends; I count myself among them. We share much these days. I also know that her example paved the way for me. In trying understand her, I found myself facing myself and my marriage. I clearly remember the day when our family shrink (a patriarchal but sensible man who knew she was a lesbian) said of my young teen-age daughter, with particular emphasis on the first and last words, *"She's* O.K., but what about the two of *you?"* That day marked the beginning of my liberation and my slow return to the lesbian self I had abandoned years ago.

Of course it didn't happen all at once. The process was slow, sometimes painful, and helped enormously, crucially, by my growing economic independence. First, I had to free myself from the mask of heterosexuality I had so earnestly assumed. Only then could I begin to explore my love for women. But I was not going to burn all my bridges at once. Comical as it now seems, I prepared the way by systematically announcing my intentions to my heterosexual friends. It worked. Making love with a woman felt like the most natural thing I had ever done. (That still makes me angry, since all my life I had been led to believe the very opposite.)

In one sense, the transition was easy; my emotional life had never ceased to be with women. That fact had caused me some discomfort while I was married, since it did not fit my picture of marriage. (Now and then my husband complained about it, but I didn't admit it to him. It must have made him feel just slightly crazy.) On the whole, it was a problem I could dismiss with relative ease. Some kindly, well-meaning shrink had once told me, in the early years of my marriage, that if I was successful in having orgasms with men, I could not possibly be a lesbian. I'm not so sure how deeply I believed him. It continued to seem strange to me that I always wanted to express my feelings for women by touching them, but I dutifully held back. (I don't think I ever mentioned these details to my shrink, which may have helped him in his diagnosis.) It also seemed odd to me that the only words that seemed accurately to describe certain of my feelings for women were the "inappropriate" words, "I am in love with. . . ." Instinctively, I knew better than to mention these feelings to anyone but my oldest, dearest, most trustworthy, unquestionably heterosexual friend. I don't think she really knew what to make of my confession either, but I know it helped me enormously that she listened and did not say it was a terrible thing. (Very like the role I played in listening to my childhood lesbian friend.) The word *lesbian*, of course, was never mentioned.

Fortunately, I had never fallen in love with my confidante, though I loved her deeply (and still do). No doubt that saved our friendship. I remember how relieved I was (even at age eighteen when we first met) that I did not have "those" feelings for her. I so much wanted to be her friend, and knew from experience how burdensome those feelings could be and how peculiarly they sometimes made me behave. (My passions for women always felt like some dread disease I had contracted and could neither control nor get rid of.) I was terribly ashamed of these feelings and at the same time, treasured them as my most valued possession, my secret source of joy, comfort, and nourishment, right through the years of my marriage.

As I read and reread these pages, I realize how long and cumbersome the process of coming-to-myself has been. I am now forty-six. I came out five years ago. It frightens me to think that without the lesbian/feminist movement, without the example of my own daughter (and other brave women I admire and respect), I might still be in the closet *to myself*, might still believe in the absolute normality of heterosexuality, despite the strong evidence of my own feelings. I ask myself as I read this: Is it possible that without the support of a movement I might never have come out? Merely continued to inexplicably and inappropriately fall in love with women? A part of me believes this could have happened, unless I had ever fallen in love with a woman who knew herself to be a lesbian (and knew me for one too). Or would I have run away from even such an opportunity?

Recently, one of the women I was in love with years ago told me I had once asked her to go to bed when I was still married, and she had refused.

I have absolutely no recollection of such a conversation, but the longing and the desire were certainly there, perhaps for us both; I suspect more was communicated between us than either of us ever acknowledged in words. But as I said before, even as an adult, I was exceedingly naive. She was a painter. I modeled for her, both in the nude and while nursing my son. Over the years she produced hundreds of portraits and sketches of me. In oils, in pencil, in pastel. For hours, each day, for days on end, I sat while she painted and we talked. I understood well what this time meant to me; I never thought to ask what it meant to her. (Perhaps we made love after all, without touching.)

I have no way of knowing what shape my life might have taken without the influence and support of a lesbian/feminist movement. I only know with certainty that the last five years of my life have been for me the most fully lived. The years of greatest growth and deepest opening, of real congruence with myself. And for this richness, this happiness (unexpected, but actively sought for), I am grateful.

I came out to my mother about three years ago. She knew before I told her. (Her antennae are ever up.) In fact, I did not tell her. She asked. The very first thing she wanted to know was which of us was the man, I or my lover? When I told her we were not at all into roles, she was incredulous, particularly about sex. How was it possible, she wanted to know. "Who decides what to do?" She constantly brings up the subject of homosexuality (sometimes playfully) and as constantly puts it down. Just the same, letting her know was the most freeing thing I have ever done for myself. I no longer wait for her approval. She accepts me, as best she can, with some severe reservations—what she refers to as the "big big BUT." Her sense of humor saves her for me. I have come to understand that she is not simply judging me, that she is also jealous—of the obvious closeness with my lover, of the nurturing we give each other. In her ironic vision, she faults our love as a "mutual admiration society." She is slightly peeved. If we can be so gentle and loving to each other, why can't everyone else (in the heterosexual world she knows) be equally so? She says this in tones that could be called accusing. It was not the model for her marriage nor one she ever envisioned. We do not talk well. She has not learned to love me, nor has she ever loved herself. About these things, I am sad.

As for me, in coming out I finally gave birth to the woman I had been carrying for decades. She has learned to love herself as she has allowed herself to love and be loved by another woman. I am glad to share her life. I like her and am glad she finally told her story. My story.

Further Thoughts (1987)

I feel very protective of this essay. It is more private than anything else I have ever published, and exposing it to public view in an anthology likely to have a wide audience makes me feel particularly vulnerable. When it first appeared in 1980, I had not yet fully taken in the fact that if you write something down and send it out for publication, it will, if published, very likely be read. Such "innocence" makes it considerably easier to write of delicate matters in your own voice.

It should not then be surprising that this essay means more to me than any other writing I have produced. Together with the introductory essay to *Nice Jewish Girls: A Lesbian Anthology,** it is implanted in my mind as the very core of my autobiography. In rereading my own words today, I am struck by how deeply I knew and trusted that I could not speak as a mother without speaking almost at the same time, in counterpoint, as a daughter. I still appreciate the way I wove together themes I have since pursued independently in greater depth, but I am amazed at what I did not highlight at all. The fact that I am a Jew is clearly present but not foregrounded; I did not pursue what it meant to be a Jewish daughter and Holocaust survivor, a Jewish lesbian mother of a Jewish lesbian daughter, themes that still wait to be further developed. Nonetheless, it is impossible for me to rewrite this essay today without violating the truths of my life as I understood them at the time. What this essay suggests, but does not analyze, needs to be explored independently. For example, I have only recently begun to deal with the fact that when speaking in a public, nonlesbian forum, I feel a distinct discomfort at revealing that I have a lesbian daughter. This, in spite of the strong comfort this fact gives me in private and in safe (i.e., nonhomophobic) environments. What to do with the filter which makes me see myself as peculiar in the eyes of others? Why should I, for even one minute, have to worry that my family has "gone too far" by containing a lesbian daughter *and* mother? To what extent is this particular fear connected to my own history as a survivor? Who determines the limits of the acceptable? How to combat this defensiveness in myself? How to speak of my lesbian daughter naturally, with ease and pride, the way I now speak easily as a lesbian and a Jew?

My son and his wife recently provided a hopeful counterpoint to this sense of dis-ease. At their wedding this summer, they invited me and my partner, my daughter and her partner, to sit up front with the wedding party, together with the other close relatives. The fact that two of the couples were of the same sex was unmarked in any way, and I felt a good deal of pride that their love for us made it possible for them to refuse to see through any filter but their own.

---

* Persephone Press, 1982, reissued by The Crossing Press (Freedom, CA 95019, 1984)

To return to the past. Some facts in the essay as I wrote it then have changed and can easily be brought up-to-date.

Eight years have gone by. My daughter is now thirty-one, and I have just turned fifty-four. We still have only gingerly discussed the difficult years of her coming out. We are friends, but respectful of the distance we need in order to remain close. I had hoped that the occasion of the republication of this essay might provide an opportunity for us to talk about the past in greater depth, but we seem not to be ready for such intimacy. Yet my daughter appears to take pride in my writing and has willingly given her permission for the inclusion of this essay, which is, after all, as much about her as it is about me. I have never shown it to my mother who, in the intervening years, has learned to love me better, and has allowed her "big big BUT" to undergo some considerable shrinkage. She seems to have made peace with my life in spite of her own determination to resist what could be construed as absolute affirmation. She sees that I am genuinely happy and is happy for me; is finally even proud of my accomplishments.

The friend who claimed that she was "neither" heterosexual nor lesbian has since accepted her lesbian self in more positive ways, though she still lives a heavily closeted life in relative isolation.

My first lesbian lover who named me EviB is now a deep and abiding friend. I have found a life-partner, whose love and trust are the foundation for my life, my loving, and my work in the world.

Working It Out

Here Comes The Sun

Conversation With Julie

Ellen Bass

Julie (age five) and I are in the women's bathroom of Thunder Deli. She is sitting on the toilet pooping. I'm waiting. She smiles and giggles with slight uncertainty, then says, "You're a dyke, aren't you?"

"Yes," I say. "I am. You know what that means don't you?"

"Yes," she says.

"A dyke is a woman who loves women," I say. "A lesbian."

She nods. "And men who love men," she adds.

"Yes," I say. "Men who love men are called gay. Usually *dyke* is used just for women."

"Daddy's gay," Julie offers.

"Oh?" I smile. "What makes you think so?"

"He loves a man. He has a friend he loves."

"Do you know if they are lovers or just good friends?" I ask.

"Probably friends," Julie says.

"I'd guess so," I agree. "Sometimes people use the words *gay* or *lesbian* to mean friends, but usually it means lovers. Like Kate and I are lovers."

"What's *lovers*?" Julie asks finally.

Never in our many conversations about women loving women, men loving men, women loving men, men loving women, conception, pregnancy, labor and birth, birth control and artificial insemination, has she inquired into the matter of lovers.

"Lovers are friends who make love," I begin. "Making love is hugging and kissing and giving each other pleasure with your bodies."

"Can I watch sometime?" she asks simply.

I take in breath. "No," I say simply.

Surprise startles her face. "Do you think Kate would mind?" she asks, incredulous. Julie has known Kate since birth.

"I would mind," I say.

"*You* would?" She is stunned. "But I'm your *daughter*."

I can't help smiling. "You can watch some of making love," I say. "You already do. You've seen us hugging and kissing many times."

She nods.

"But the rest of making love is something that's private between two grown-ups. No one gets to watch. It's something they share just with each other."

"What do you do?" she asks.

"We hug and kiss each other all over. Making love is a way of saying I love you with your body, by giving the person you love pleasure with your body."

Julie's face is flushed with the concentration of pushing poop out. Her eyes water. When I look at her in this state, I feel I am intruding on something intimate and entirely vulnerable. She, however, is unself-conscious.

"Do you get naked?" she asks in a tone of calm interest.

"Yes, we usually get naked."

"Do men get naked too?"

"I think usually."

I decide to make the connection with reproduction. "When men and women make love, sometimes the woman opens her vagina to take in the man's penis. They can make a baby that way.

"When women make love they touch each other all over and kiss each other all over and touch each others' vagina and clitoris to give each other pleasure. Like sometimes you touch your vagina and clitoris and that feels good."

Julie doesn't confirm the good feeling, but says, "I put my finger in my vagina and then smell it. I *love* how my vagina smells."

"I love the smell of vaginas, too," I concur.

"My vagina smells so good," she continues, enthusiastic. "Sometimes I do my finger up and down in my vagina" (she demonstrates here, rubbing her finger lightly between her labia), "to get a lot of smell. Then after I'm done smelling, I wipe my finger on some toilet paper or on the rug—usually on the rug to save trees. Mother Nature likes that."

"Yes," I smile at her. This is not the time to think about the landlady's carpet. Then I say, "Making love is a way that adults say I love you to each other by sharing pleasure. Children and adults say I love you in different ways."

"Yes," Julie says, nodding. "Like when I sit on your lap and you read me a book, that's our way of saying I love you."

"Exactly," I say. "Are you done?"

"Yes," she says, and gets ready to leave.

Coming Out To My Children
Antiga

I thought that I was waiting
until
they could handle it
before telling them.

When I did
both daughters wondered why
it had taken me so long
both sons pretended that
they hadn't heard.

The pain
of the oldest daughter was spoken:
"Mom, I wish you weren't a Lesbian."
The pain
of the youngest son was hidden until
he was hospitalized
so drunk
he could not say his name.
When he could speak
they asked for my phone number
and he answered:
"Don't call her. She's a Lesbian."

Creature From Outer Space
Josephine Simmons

Coming out was extremely difficult. I was living in a small, isolated, youth-oriented, and primarily white town. Black, thirtyish, and a single parent (I recently shed my heterosexual identity along with my wedding band), I'd only met a handful of lesbians in my life, and those only recently. Of these, only three were Black. But they weren't like me: they were masculine, both in attire and affect. I didn't want to be perceived as one of them, so it was easy to deny my lesbianism. I was ashamed of my preference for women, ashamed of being a lesbian; no wonder my daughter had such a difficult time accepting it. How could she when I couldn't. How could she when I lied to her as I lied to myself.

To make it even more confusing, my first lover initially presented a very feminine image. That image changed when we began sharing the same household. Suddenly my lover fancied herself more man than a man. I was "her woman." She began to walk, dress, and act like a man, and with her deep voice, it was sometimes difficult for others to tell who she was.

Sadly, in spite of the image my lover presented, she, too, denied her lesbianism. My daughter hated this woman. We hid the fact that we were lovers from both our children, saying we were best friends.

My daughter was only seven at the time, but at the ripe old age of eight, she asked me if my lover—she refused to use her name—was gay. I said yes she was. Then she asked if that meant I was gay. Being the coward that I was, I responded with an emphatic NO!

The relationship ended, and its abusive nature left some very nasty scars. My daughter, thinking all lesbians were like this one, hated lesbians.

When she was ten, she asked again if I was gay. She had heard some talk. This time, feeling a little more sure of myself, I gave a rather timid yes, and we both quickly dropped the subject. She didn't want to hear it and didn't want anyone else to know, which was fine by me.

Although my ex-husband lived almost three thousand miles away, he somehow managed to poison my daughter's mind about lesbianism. He said some pretty nasty things that she believed. It was then I realized that in order to educate my daughter and help her to understand and cope, I had to first educate myself. I discovered I didn't know what it meant to be a lesbian. And like everyone else who is homophobic, I thought lezzies were sick. I began to read and read and read, everything I could get my hands on. Gradually I became more accepting of myself, saw I had nothing to be

ashamed of, and acknowledged I was emotionally, intellectually, and sexually a lesbian. I started to feel good about myself, and it showed.

Finding information about lesbian mothers was impossible. Surely there
had to be more of us. I only knew one other Black lesbian mother (besides
my ex-lover), but her daughter was so much older than my preteen. In my
search I discovered little support for mothers trying to help their children
cope with mommy's sexuality. Women without children might sympathize,
but they didn't really understand. In fact, I discovered that a lot of nonmothers
didn't want to be in a relationship with someone who was a mother.

During this time, my daughter continued to hide. She continued to deny
my sexuality as I had done for so long. Since I hung out with many women
but wasn't involved with anyone in particular, my daughter didn't have to
accept my sexuality because she didn't have to see it. When friends came
over and cuddled while watching television, my daugher would make comments like, "It's O.K. when they do it. In fact it looks kind of cute, but
I wouldn't like it if my mother did it. Anyway, my mom's not really a lesbian cause she doesn't act like that."

I recognized I still had a lot of work to do. When I fell in love, I knew
I had to start dealing with the issue quickly. I went cold turkey. I sat her
down at McDonalds, where she couldn't make a scene, and told her that
like my friends, I also loved women, that I liked to snuggle and cuddle just
like they did. I told her I was thinking about getting involved with a woman. I assured her I wouldn't make it hard for her, that I wouldn't advertise
it in front of her friends or make a spectacle of myself, but that I would
not deny myself happiness any longer.

She was furious. She said she was leaving in the morning and going to
live with her dad. She looked at me with such hatred, I was almost ready
to rejoin the straight world just so she would look at me with love again.
"I hate you," she said. "I'm not your daughter. I couldn't have been born
by someone like you. I must be like my dad. I don't know what you are.
Yes I do. You must be a creature from outer space."

She wouldn't talk to me for the rest of the evening, and I was beginning
to get scared. I wanted to play the heavy and be an assertive mom. I wasn't
supposed to let her talk to me that way and get away with it. And here I
was listening to those hurtful words. Right or wrong, I felt I had to accept
her feelings about things. Before going to bed she kissed me, and I began
to think maybe things would be all right.

At the end of the summer she dropped the bomb—she wanted to live with
my mother and go to school there. It was traumatic for both of us. My mother
is all right about my sexuality, but her other children, who looked after my
daughter in the evenings, were not. They said awful things to her, and wonder
of wonders, she defended me. After a week of tears, I dragged her back

kicking and screaming. I decided we were going to work this thing out together.

Once school started, it was easier. She discovered several other Black kids in a similar situation and began to create her own support system, a "family" of supportive individuals. So far she has a straight aunt and uncle, a gay uncle, and two lesbian aunts. One day she mentioned that she'd met her friend's "other mother."

It continues to be hard, and we don't talk about it a lot, but she recently offered to babysit so that another woman and I could go out. When I got home she asked, "Do you think she could maybe be one of my aunts? Then her kid could be my first cousin."

I knew things were finally going to be better after she asked me when I was going to get a girlfriend and settle down. She said, "You're getting old Mom, almost thirty-seven, too old to be running the streets like you do. You gotta settle down and find a steady girlfriend so you can stay home." Then she asked if I thought she'd look as good as I do when she gets to be my age. "You know," she said, "I think I'm going to be just like you when I grow up."

Journal Entries

Anonymous

November 19, 1984

I came out to C yesterday. It was one of the hardest things of my whole life. Coming out to one's child is an absolutely wrenching experience. A twelve-year-old just doesn't understand. Doing it was ill-timed and poorly orchestrated since I hadn't planned on it happening then. We had been having a difficult day; she had been cranky all weekend while S was visiting from Brooklyn. Although S had been in our lives for four years, I guess somehow C had not really known what the nature of our relationship was. I thought it was so obvious. I asked C if her being crabby had to do with S being here. She said yes, and then somehow it came around to my wondering if it had to do with the two of us going to the gay bar. She said, "What about the bar?" Then I said, "Like maybe you think I'm gay," and she asked if I was. I thought for only a moment and answered yes. It was an answer that will change my life. I guess I must have wanted to tell her, or why else would I have taken the conversation in that direction.

Nonetheless, what ensued was horrible. She began to cry very hard and insisted I leave her room. Then she refused to talk to me. S and I had been planning to leave for New York City at that point and were bringing C to a friend's house for the weekend. We all sat in the car in deadly silence. C ran from us as soon as the car door was open. Fortunately, she was staying with a good friend whose mother is a counselor. I felt bad leaving her there, and yet I knew I could not be the one to help her with her pain. I tried to console her a number of times, insisting I still loved her and this did not change the nature of our relationship. She would have none of it and just looked away from me and cried. I, too, was crying through most of this. I kept trying to give her a whole rap about not hating me because of my sexual preference, that there was nothing wrong with my choice. Go tell a pubescent girl being gay is O.K. *Lezzie* is one of the epithets in common use in her junior high school. Her own interest in sex and her body is just developing. Throwing this into her life at this stage is particularly difficult.

The drive to Brooklyn was awful. I tried to call her a number of times from the road, but she refused to talk to me. I will be seeing her in a few days when we visit friends in New Jersey. Perhaps there we can try to have a semblance of normality. Poor dear C. She is strong and will survive this, but I have hurt her so. I wish I could be straight and forget being a lesbian.

I wish I could go back to my marriage, my home, and my family. But that is just not possible. It has gone too far; there is no turning back. I have made my choices. Now I am facing the consequences and must live with them.

I hurt. This is so acutely painful. I love her so much and I do not want to hurt her. And yet here I am, the one person who is supposed to protect her from the pain of the world, bringing the pain into her home and life on such an intimate level. If I choose to move to New York to be with S, I am sure C will not come with me, not after this revelation. Life is so difficult. I have so much to lose—my home, my marriage, and now my child. I can't bear all this. My pain is deep, and I am in agony. I have no preparation for this. My parents are dead. I never had to tell them about my lifestyle. But here is my child, vulnerable and alone, and I cannot console her or myself. Will time heal this one too? I can only hope.

November 25, 1984

Well, C's father came out to her, too. How hard for a child to have a lesbian mother and a gay father. My poor dear baby. There is so much pain and so many tears. I am absolutely sick over this. I have a hacking nervous cough and I am anxiety-ridden. What will this do to her? Will she be suicidal? Will she run away? Will she act out? While I was in Brooklyn, C's father tried to console her, and she confronted him directly, asking him if he was gay too? What could he do? He was honest. She has been silent and holed up in her room. When we were in New Jersey, we all put on a good show, acting normally. But we were walking on eggshells with each other. During our time there, one of our friend's kids talked about the local Gay Pride march. He said his parents had gone to it and he had been embarrassed. He said he would have rather stoned people in the parade but couldn't because his parents were there. C concurred and said she would have thrown stones too. It is too much, having one's own child detest me and what I am.

December 12, 1984

C and I had a talk. She knows her dad and I are separating, but she doesn't want to live with either of us. She is so ashamed of who we are. I have to work on instilling pride in her about us. I am not at all ashamed of who I am and wish she could understand and accept. She is begging to go to a boarding school.

January 10, 1985

We have settled into a pattern: I walk on tiptoes and C is always unhappy, surly, and angry. I wish I could help her. She refuses to talk and won't go to a counselor. I suppose she will have to work it out herself. I will do all that I can—reach out, love, support, be there when and if she is ready to talk or just to give her a little hug when she finally lets me. I want to be there for her.

January 16, 1985

So much unhappiness. C cries all the time, hides away in her room and talks about where she could go to live. I am miserable, and her father is despondent. I must work on creating a happier home for my child and myself. I want one with laughter and light, one filled with love. I must try to keep it together, at least for her. I have been a basket case, and then I am gone so long to see S that I am not there for my child. No wonder she wants to escape. C has turned out fine. She is bright and does well in school; she has friends and is popular. As bad as it seems at home, obviously she is trying to be O.K. outside. There have been no major problems, just her obvious pain. How will this ever evolve?

May 14, 1985

We have become civil to one another. We go shopping together and can discuss school. She spends most of her time alone and has developed a better relationship with her dad. I need to back off from her and hope we will work it out. After all, I am her mother for life. Something will have to develop.

July 22, 1985

I am about to move out of my home and my marriage of fifteen years. With this move, I leave my family and the security of the pain. I was reading Liv Ullman's biography the other day, and she said, "During our short time on earth we exercise and follow choices, with all their ambiguities. We learn that little is clear cut, life's most difficult choices seem indistinct. The most profound aspirations have costs as well as benefits. Absolute good and evil may not exist." She is speaking of me and the choice I am making. The costs are great, including the potential loss of my daughter. I am clear that I must live with S. Of that I am certain. And yet as I leave home, family, security, and my child, I feel much like the Tarot card of the Fool—about to jump into the abyss of the unknown. I have to trust my instincts and hope the decisions are right and eventually my daughter will return to me.

August 13, 1985

C tells me she will not stay with me in my new home because I will be living with S. She says she will come to visit and spend the night once in awhile, but not every other week as I had hoped. I have cried a great deal, feel like an absolute failure. I am not the perfect mother I had thought I could be. Is the answer to motherhood fortitude and perseverance? If so, then I will hold on, and we will come through.

September 7, 1985

We have made the move, and I am now living with S. It is wonderful, an absolute honeymoon. We are playing house, and it is our greatest pleasure to be together after so many years of a long-distance relationship. C is being difficult. She refuses to come over, and when I insist, she does so grudgingly. Her father has been good, insisting she see me and supporting us all during this difficult time. He has her a lot of the time, which helps him during his transition, too. We went to see a therapist and worked out an agreement in which she is with him for two weeks and then with me for one. I also see her for lunch and shopping on the off-weekends. It is not ideal or equal, but it is better than I had feared.

May 13, 1986

It has been so long since I have written and since I have been alone with myself. It is unfolding. C has been with us for a week and then two away. She is more civilized and enjoys that we have a house in town. She and S are getting along well, and unless there are other kids around, she can be reasonable and communicative, to a point. It looks like her father will be moving to New Mexico, and C wants to go with him. We adjust to one set of circumstances, and then we must adapt once again, forever changing. Home, family, security, commitment—all are transmutable and fluid. There are no role models for all this. It continues to evolve, and I never know what will happen next.

July 7, 1986

My forty-second birthday. C has been living with us for over a month while her dad goes to New Mexico. She will be leaving by the end of the summer, and I will try to make our time together fun and close. I love her and I will persevere. She is much more friendly and able to be with us, as long as we do not touch in front of her and her friends are kept from the upstairs bedroom. She is still so ashamed. Her friends joke about *fags* and *queers* in front of us, never knowing how S, C, or I are feeling. But I think C is being amazingly flexible. She is here and coping, although she would rather be with her dad and away from our scene altogether.

September 17, 1986

C will be living with us for this year. Her dad did not get an apartment that could accommodate both of them, nor has his job situation been right. We are adapting. Life is quite calm on the surface, although she will not be seen in public with us, nor will she travel or spend time with us if friends are around. But we are together most evenings, watching television, studying, and working together. We share clothes, play with the cats, and chat about our days. It is far better than I could ever have hoped when I first came out to her almost two years ago. She still wants to move to New Mexico if the situation with her father changes. We are all together in the meantime, living in a semblance of peace. There is a powder keg that could explode any minute under it all. But for now, I have my newly created family— my lover, my child, and my home. I am happy.

Homophobia At Home

Baylah Wolfe

Homophobia has been a profound challenge to me, particularly as it manifested itself in my relationships with my two children, Julie and Steve. I came
out as a lesbian twelve years ago, after leaving a white middle-class marriage. Together with Julie and Steve, I lived in a Long Island suburb, and
became a "known" lesbian after appearing on a television program about
lesbian mothers. Because of this exposure, the children experienced varying degrees of homophobia: my lover's fifteen-year-old daughter was physically roughed up, accompanied by taunts of *lezzie* and *queer*; Steve lost a
friend after his friend found out. Mostly the homophobia played itself out
in subtle attitudinal ways. During this time, I did not waver in asserting my
right to be out.

Six years ago, after breaking up with my lover, I planned a move to Brooklyn. Julie and Steve, then fourteen and eleven, were frightened at the prospect
of this move. I tuned in to the fact that they had been through some very
rough years which included the divorce, my coming out crisis, and adjusting to living with my lover and her two children. My heart went out to them,
and I decided to make a compromise. I told them I would keep a low profile
as a lesbian so that they could make new friends without fear of exposure
to homophobia. Since they felt me caring about their feelings, this compromise served to rebuild trust and was a kind of healing between us. I agreed
to restrict lesbian posters to my bedroom. I was discrete in the neighborhood.

Despite all of this, in the four years we had been here, Julie and Steve
still chose to walk ten paces behind me on the street. They rarely brought
friends home. Julie could not look me in the eye at school plays and concerts. They never told any friend, no matter how close, that they had a lesbian mother. Rather than easing up as they became connected in the city,
they seemed more rigid in their homophobia. They slipped into the expectation that I would remain closeted in their presence, although they never
fully trusted that. This provided a false level of sameness for them and in-

creased a painful alienation between us. I ached from their denial of me and my friends.

The Confrontation

One evening two years ago, I could no longer bear my complicity in protecting Julie and Steve's insecurities, their fear of difference. I took a stand. I told Julie I would be happy to attend her high school graduation the following week, but if she wanted me there, I would be wearing a lesbian mother button. During the next few days, Julie, Steve, and I had many painful conversations. Steve, in particular, thought I was being very unfair. I told him I would no longer erase myself, that I planned to wear my lesbian mother button around the neighborhood.

I felt alternately anxious, sad, and strong. I often played Alix Dobkin's song, "A Mother Knows," which is about Alix's love for her daughter and about the work of being a feminist-lesbian mother. This comforted me and challenged Julie. On the night before her graduation, Julie broke down, wept, engaged her courage, and invited me. We were closer to each other than we had been in a long time.

That was the beginning of Julie's facing and feeling the reality of my lesbianism. She began the painful and scary task of unraveling her homophobia and her strong fear of disapproval. Almost immediately, she told two friends that she had a lesbian mother, and she attended her first Gay Pride march wearing a sign which read, I AM THE DAUGHTER OF A LESBIAN DEALING WITH MY HOMOPHOBIA.

Today Julie lives in the Womanist House at her college. She talks openly about her life. She is excited about introducing me to her friends, whether they be straight, lesbian, or exploring. She speaks out against homophobia and is a true ally to lesbians and gay men. She is doing antiracist work and was arrested this year in an action against apartheid. The pain she has experienced has opened her more to herself and to the struggles of other peoples. I have great respect for her.

Steve had a more difficult time. As Julie and I were leaving for her graduation, he said, "I'm going to kill myself." It is excruciating to hear one's child make this statement. I did not think he was literally suicidal at the time, but something in him had to die—some illusion of sameness, some illusion of control. He was so threatened by my refusal to be invisible that he chose to live with his father, a move he had wanted previously but did not know how to actualize. Now he could present his father with a good reason: his mother was flaunting her lesbianism. We each felt separate agonies.

On the evening Steve left, a violent thunderstorm erupted suddenly. I sat at an upstairs window, encircled by loving sisters, as we watched Steve, Julie, and their father make endless trips to the car in the pouring rain, with a fifteen-year accumulation of things. Lightning illuminated their comings and goings. We did not say goodby. My lover told me the storm was an expression of my clarity, anger, and tears.

I wrote Steve a letter a few weeks later, telling him that while I was hurt by his homophobia and how he used it, I respected his decision and wished him well in his new life. I let him know that I would still be there for him, albeit in a different way. Nevertheless he was very distant, and there was a great strain between us that first year.

Now he stays with me two days a week, and while he is still embarrassed by my lesbianism, he is slowly dealing with his homophobia. I am grateful for the movement in our relationship. He knows what my bottom lines are, and I have learned to respect his pace. Recently, he surprised me: he expressed how much he enjoys his time with me now. After searching for what he called the right verb, he said, "It is more healing here. I am more relaxed. I can be myself. We talk about meaningful things." He said all this hesitantly and with a twinkle in his eye, then added, "I can't believe I just said this." He has become introspective, and his growth brings me great joy.

The Role Of A Counterculture Lesbian Mother

So great is the societal dictum that lesbians do not exist—that there is no such thing as a lesbian mother—that even within the gay/lesbian community, while many people take strength from my actions, others are threatened. A couple of lesbian mothers told me, "When children are secure in their own sexual identity, they will be able to deal with having a lesbian mother." I do not deny the kernel of truth in this, but how long would I have to wait? I did not want to be "iced" or closeted at my children's special events. The former happened to a dear lesbian sister at her daughter's wedding.

These critics imply that I was immature or selfish to think of my own needs, or to "push" my sexuality into the lives of my children. Should gay/lesbian activists wait until religious fundamentalists are more secure before insisting on basic civil rights? The answer is no, yet mothers are expected to put ourselves last. Of course, if our children then grow up either selfish or too self-sacrificing, we will be blamed for our martyrdom. It is a painful reality that mothers, both heterosexual and lesbian, are not appreciated for our work. The culture requires great individual sacrifices from its mothers, yet the reward is often blame for whatever goes wrong—blame from the children themselves, blame from the schools, blame from law enforcement agencies, and blame from psychotherapists. In other words, "You are having this problem because of your mother." Mothers are thus robbed of their power. We are used to absorb full responsibility for the development of the next generation in a society riddled with contradictions.

This fuller understanding of the institution of motherhood has opened many channels for me. I have been able to more deeply forgive my own mother for the many real and imagined hurts and resentments I had harbored over the years. This, in turn, has helped me to be easier on myself for the countless times I have hurt Julie and Steve, be it through my own limitations or a conflict in our needs or wills, by asserting my power as an adult.

In the confrontation I had with my children, I acted out of a need to be affirmed in my wholeness as a lesbian mother, but this was not my sole motivation. There is a serious dilemma of parenthood at stake here. Parents are charged not only with the responsibility to feed, clothe, shelter, and love our children, but to transmit cultural values as well. We are supposed to teach our children about "reality." Well, the culture asserts that white is right, that middle class is normative, that male is active and female passive, that mothers provide the nurturing and fathers teach the children about power and how the world works. My very being and many of my values run counter to the dominant culture in general, and to the values of the children's father in particular.

Experiencing oneself as different from the dominant culture is quite difficult for adults, let alone for children. A lesbian mother, with a divergent perspective on reality is not necessarily taken seriously by her children. Julie and Steve's other relatives, their schools, and especially the media, reflect images and values that I resist, albeit with my own contradictions. Until I took a stand, I was either like an ineffectual tape recorder, periodically playing cassettes on sexism, racism, homophobia, and capitalism, or I found myself bullying Julie and Steve verbally in an attempt to jog their narrowness. I have since learned that people cannot be forced into a change of consciousness, no matter how righteous the change.

While I could not convince Julie and Steve to change their attitudes, I could determine how I myself would act. Once again I chose to be public as a lesbian. I disregarded the unwritten rules of motherhood by engaging in an individual act of civil disobedience. In this process I discovered I choose honest relationships with my children above superficial comfort. It is likely that lesbian mothers will feel the painful effects of homophobia acted out by their children, and like night follows day, feminist mothers will feel the sexism that their sons have absorbed. When these "isms" arise in my family, it is my instinct to name and resist them. I would rather grapple with these issues, even if this exposes a deep rift, than live in an illusion of false togetherness.

I am in no way suggesting that my actions be a prototype for others. People move as they will, in their own way, and in their own time—a lesson I am forever relearning. Challenging the norms of this society in a family context can have an explosive and shattering impact. There will be upheavals, at least temporarily. I have had to toughen myself to withstand the consequences that come from taking part in a movement for social change. Lesbian mothers play a hard and socially significant role, especially in light of right-wing efforts to entrench traditional family values. More than ever, we need to support each other, to cry together, to share solutions, and to celebrate passages.

Growing homophobia requires that we reassess the joys and pains of living without heterosexual privilege and how we deal with this difference in our families. As lesbian mothers, we define our lives in our own terms, and this is an invaluable legacy to pass on to both our daughters and sons. While Julie has scars from homophobia, today she is consciously grateful for having a mother who insists on her own existence. That makes everything worthwhile!

Getting Close To My Daughter
Rose

Dealing with our children's hostility toward our lesbianism is no small task. I have two daughters who are now eighteen and nineteen. We are very close, and they are both comfortable with my lesbianism, but it wasn't always that way.

When my younger daughter A turned fourteen, the shit hit the fan. Up until that point, both daughters were fairly quiet about my lesbianism, but then they didn't talk to me about much that was important to them on any subject. I would describe our relationships as cordial, a little distant, and kind of loving. Then I went to a workshop on homophobia. The leader gave us a phrase to use with teen-agers who are making homophobic comments. She suggested saying, "I know two women who are lesbians (or men who are gay), and they are very happy." To use that sentence is to tell the young person that homosexuality is a valid lifestyle without telling them about ourselves.

At the time I was tutoring a fourteen-year-old girl who was constantly talking about women who were "funny." She would say, "I think Ms. so-and-so is funny," or "I saw two women holding hands today and that's really weird." I decided to try out the suggestion made by the leader of the workshop I had just attended. My student started in on her favorite subject. I found myself very nervous. My palms were sweating, and I blurted out, "Oh, I know two women who are lesbians, and they are very happy."

That did it. "UGH, ugh," she said. "That is sick. That is so sick." She was holding onto her stomach as she continued. "That's the most disgusting thing I ever heard. Ugh, ugh, that's disgusting. That's sick. Ugh, ugh, ugh!"

I knew I was on the right track, so I waited for her to calm down and then repeated what I had said. "I know two women who are lesbians, and they are very happy." She started right in again, and we didn't get much studying done that day.

I was telling this story to my lover, and my daughter A was standing with us in the kitchen. After I told the story, I faintly heard A mumble something under her breath. It sounded like she was saying that my student was right. I thought I heard her say, "It really is sick, Mom."

I thought, "At last I have an opening to her feelings," so I said to her, "but I really am happy." That did it. I think my obvious joy in being a lesbian and my lack of concern about my student's response allowed her the safety to let her feelings out.

What I got was a repeat of the session with my student. "You really are sick. You are disgusting, Mom," she said, with all of the appropriate *ughs*.

A had been sitting on a lot of intense feelings and her speaking out in the kitchen was only the beginning. There was lots more to come. When I picked her up from school, she would practically snarl at me. Her lip kind of curled up, and she would say, "You lezzie." Sometimes she would mumble until I reminded her I was really happy, at which point she would shout it at me. Her anger reached such a pitch that she decided to move in with her dad. Both girls had been living half-time with me and half-time with him.

I felt it was important to find ways to remind A that I loved her, so I would do little things for her, like make a special lunch and leave it at her father's before she left for school. One day I saw her walking down the street and offered her a ride. I was heading for the local food co-op. She rode with me, but when I invited her to come in and get some food, she went totally out of control.

She had the biggest outburst I had seen her have. She started yelling at me, "I hate your hippie food store. I hate everything about you. You are disgusting. I can't stand that you are a lesbian and shop at hippie food stores. You are so horrible!" She went on and on hysterically. She jumped out of the car and ran off crying. I tried to find her. I went to her father's house first, then her boyfriend's, then different friends, and the last place I tried was my own home.

I found her at my house in her room, lying on her bed sobbing her eyes out. I lay down next to her, put my arms around her, and told her, "No matter what you say or do, I know how much you love me." That did it. She faced me and took me into her arms, and I found myself sobbing with her. I was weeping because of the depth of her love for me. The moment was very special, and A has never expressed a homophobic feeling since. She moved back in right away, and we are very, very close.

Family Matters:
Mother/Daughter Conversation
Anne Rhodes and Satya Conway-Rhodes

When I think about communicating something about lesbian motherhood and daughterhood, the vastness of my relationship with Satya presses into my mind—the countless details, the moments of rage, those of pure and precious loving, and all the rest, as any mother or any daughter knows, so potent and miraculous, and yet so mundane and ordinary. Finding a way to present all this seemed formidable until we thought of making lists. Sats and I both love lists; we find them irresistible.

So we made up categories that sounded like fun, and we had a great time remembering, moaning about the past, celebrating, and making fun of each other. We had to call Claudia in Virginia to get her additions because she generally remembers more details than we do.

The content of some of these lists is probably not very different from lists that might be compiled by heterosexual mothers and their daughters. There is one difference, however: the distress and ignorance of the heterosexist and homophobic world around us influences our experiences daily and deeply. Life with Satya (and therefore the content of these lists) reflects this reality.

Hi, I'm Satya (otherwise known as Satya Vadia Rhodes-Conway). I'm fifteen. My mother Anne is forty-one, even though she pretends to be fourteen. She's a lesbian. That's what I'm supposed to write about, her being a lesbian. It's really no big deal—just another fact about her. Her being a lesbian in itself has never bothered me. The way other people reacted to it is the problem. So anyway, let me tell you about us. We live in Ithaca, which is a semi-small town with two universities in upstate New York. We live collectively with two other women, and between the four of us, we have five cats. My mother's lover of ten years, Claudia, lives in Virginia, where she's going to architecture school. Annie has other lovers sometimes (like now), but Claudia is the only one who's been my mother. Here are some facts about us:

I'm in tenth grade.
Annie's a professional mime artist.
I go to a public alternative school.
We're vegetarians.
I'm a brown belt in karate.

Annie came out when I was four.
Both of us sing and play piano.
My dad lives in New Jersey.
I spent six months in Israel with Claudia.
Annie and I both love to read. I love fiction, but she prefers nonfiction.
My dad's remarried and has a seven-year-old son.
Annie writes plays. I write poetry.
We are very silly most of the time.
We do almost everything together.
We're actively political around almost every issue you can think of.
We don't have a lot of money.
We're white.
Claude is a Jew and Annie was raised atheist. We celebrate pagan and Jewish holidays.
Annie and my dad were divorced when I was two.
I'm a Scorpio. Annie's a Gemini. Claude's a Cancer.
We share clothes. (What that really means is that I take things out of Annie's closet and she complains about it.)

Ridiculous Things We Do Together

Satya's first year when she couldn't sleep, I'd turn up the rock 'n' roll *loud* in the living room and dance with her in my arms hard and fast, until she clunked.

The three of us playing all kinds of silly games in bed together in the morning, being feisty.

Annie and I ballroom dancing in the kitchen. (Crooning and dipping, me imagining we're Fred Astaire and Fred Astaire, or Ginger Rogers and Ginger Rogers. Who gets to lead?) *(You always lead and you know it.)*

Fireworks in the front yard in November for no reason. *(For every reason.)*

Breaking into song in the middle of conversations, usually '50s songs.

Satya sleeping under a bar table on top of a pile of coats when she was little because I wanted to hear the band.

We're melting the butter for popcorn and Satya notices the pan smoking and says to me, "You've got a fire under you." I glance down at my body and say, "I know." *(I can't believe you're putting this in.)*

Interesting Behaviors We Have Tolerated In Each Other

Satya's *storm cloud* face when she was beginning to get angry. It was usually accompanied by an amazon stance and a raised fist. (This began at age six.)

Satya's *dragon breath* when she was full-blown angry.

Anne and Satya speaking "ubbi-dubbi" so fast that Claudia can't keep up.

Me and Claude speaking Hebrew. (Just about the only thing Anne can say in Hebrew is good night.*)*

My room. It used to be knee-deep, but it's gotten better. (We needed a bulldozer.)

Annie and Claudia talking about their relationship stuff for hours.

Nonmonogamy, particularly when Annie gets involved with women I don't like.

Satya's intense privacy. *(And Annie always has to tell everything about everything to everybody.)*

Anne's need to be outside of conventions.

Sa's "Ribbon Period" when she wore nothing but ribbons, lace, and slips for months.

Sa's "Bride Period" at about age five. *(I absolutely forbid you to put that in.)*

Anne going away on tour performing with Mischief Mime, and Claudia having to be a full-time parent to me.

Satya reading books two or three times over—fiction books!

Claudia's obsessiveness.

Letting the cats eat off our plates.

Karate katas in the living room, complete with kicks, punches, and kiais.

Annie and Claudia needing to almost never live together which meant schlepping over to one another's house constantly.

Times Together That Have Been The Most Fun

Living in Jerusalem.

Hiking in the Uintas in Utah.

Being home together on the weekends doing projects, fixing things, baking.

Visiting New Mexico, the place I lived when I was little, and the clinic where I was born.

Birthdays (very big deals).

Times when something wonderful was going on in Ithaca and Anne and Claude wanted to go but couldn't find child care. So there were always the decisions about whether *one* of us should go and leave the other home with Sa, which made for hard feelings. We'd often decide to both stay home and make it wonderful.

Satya getting her brown belt in karate.

Celebrating solstice with our extended family of women.

Being at women's events and concerts, and feeling the power and validation of loving women.

When I was finally taller than Annie.

People And Things That Have Made It Hard For Us

Fear of Satya's father trying to take custody away from us, which made us scared to share our life with him.

The legal system. (No parental rights for Claudia.)

My dad doesn't approve of the way we live.

Heterosexual assumptions everywhere.

My friends can hardly ever understand who Claudia is and what she means to me.

Lesbians being unaware of mothering issues. (I was worried when Claudia and I first got together that she wouldn't want to be involved with me if I let her see how consuming mothering is.)

The way society doesn't treat me like a full human being because I'm young.

Claudia not being included or counted as mother even by liberals and alternative types who should know better. (Claudia says it's hard to be a lesbian mom, and hard to be a nonbiological parent, but to be both is a lot.)

Relatives not celebrating our family, and not telling their friends.

The neighbor kids yelling lezzie and lez-bean.

The insurance industry.

The medical system.

Narrow definitions of family for family memberships and family discounts.

Lesbians with negative attitudes toward young people. (On an invitation to a lesbian party: No men. No dogs. No children.)

Claude's feeling like Annie's other lovers wanted to take her place in the family, or threatened our unit.

Satya's feeling that some of my other lovers only wanted to befriend or be good to her in order to get closer to me. *(It was true!)*

The myth that two parents are enough. (And if you buy that one. . . .)

Claude is short and looks younger than she is, and she and Satya don't look at all like each other. *(She's your mother?!)*

People And Things That Have Made It Easier For Us

The strong and supportive lesbian community.

All the women (mostly lesbians) we have lived with who were/are my friends and helped take care of me.

My sister, who has completely accepted Claudia as family.

Eventually Claudia's and my parents began to treat us like a unit.

My best friend, Sasha, who doesn't give a damn what people think about lesbians.

My other best friend, whose mom is a lesbian, too, and whose dad is a lot like my dad.

My friends think I have a great mom, that she's fun, and wish they had a mom like mine.

The fact that there are so very few "regular" families any more (i.e., dad works, mom takes care of 2.5 kids).

We know how to make it good for ourselves.

Women's culture: music, theater, art.

Things That Have Been Said To Or About Us

Aren't you worried she'll _____?" (Fill in with the worst damage that could happen to a child.)

Questions about Satya's sexuality (and whether we're brainwashing her.)

"Do you think it's really O.K. for her to know?"

"Are you a lez-bean?"

"There's a hole in that dike. Let's put something in it."

"I can't believe her. Is she really your daughter?"

"I can't believe her. Is she really your mother?"

"I wish I had a mom like her."

"Hey, you need a husband." (To Anne and Claude, arm in arm downtown. Our response: "Eat your heart out. You wish you had it so good.")

From Satya's father: "I have no desire to make Satya suffer by withholding support payments, yet neither have I much enthusiasm to contribute to a style of living and a system of values that I believe will make it very difficult for my daughter to achieve a healthy equilibrium within the culture of which she is a part."

What You Need To Have If You've Got A Lesbian Mom (Anyway, What Helps)

You have to be willing to be different, or at least accept it. You'll never fit into the stereotype of a normal family.

You'll need an inner sense of being O.K. in spite of not being normal. You have to learn to trust yourself.

You always have to think who you can tell and who you can't.

You have to learn to not pay attention to what other people think.

You have to not let what other people do hurt you.

Guts. Nerve. Chutzpah. And be a double Scorpio.

An alternative community.

An open mind.

Open communication with your mom(s).
(Remember, it could happen to anyone.)

What Satya Learned About Life That Kids With Heterosexual Parents Might Have A Harder Time Learning

Values aren't absolute. There's lots of choices, lots of options, more options than most young people think. I learned that there are lots of versions of what's O.K., and the conventional way isn't automatically the best way. I think I have the better deal, 'cause I get to see more options.

Because lesbianism puts us outside the rewarded norms of family and couples, we are more willing to step outside the norm around other issues.

How to have nonmonogamous relationships and survive. *(And not be miserable all the time.)*

How to dance cheek to cheek with your mom.
How to walk into someplace and feel like whatever you do is O.K.
That women can do everything and anything they want.

That women can be powerful, creative, and visionary leaders.

What We Couldn't Do Because We're Lesbians

Nothing. Absolutely nothing.

What We Did Anyway

I took Claudia to my parent/teacher conferences instead of Anne.

We went as a family to the "Family and Spouses Welcome" Christmas party where Claudia worked. ("Oh, I don't think I know you. Who did you come with?")

I went to live with Claudia in Jerusalem while Anne stayed in Ithaca.
The three of us walk, our arms linked together, beaming.
We go to Anne's and Claudia's family events as a unit.

We figure out how to be individuals *and* be a family together; how to balance independence with commitment.

What Satya Gets From Anne

Height (also from my dad, not from Claude).
Believing in myself and trusting my thinking.
Being silly.

Being loud.
Physical affection, and ease in expressing it.
A safe place to try out stuff.
How to keep school in perspective.
Someone to talk to.
The ability to function in chaos.
Love of lists, love of cats, love of paper, love of books.
A bit of philosophical perspective.
Her new white shirt. (And my white scarf!)

What Satya Gets From Claudia

Regularity (allowance on time).
Consistency.
Being on time.
Practical stuff, like baking, fixing the bikes, building.
Stability.
Details taken care of.
Favors, like taxiing me around.
Learning to ride my bike. Probably also learning to drive next year.
Help admitting when I'm wrong.
Full responsibility as a parent in Israel, and when Anne's performing on tour, and when Anne's mother was dying and she had to be in California a lot.

What Anne And Claudia Learned From Satya

We built a real sense of family, based in love, respect, and struggle—a *chosen* family.

If we are honest with her, she can help us.

Everything.

Especially how to be good parents.

When to leave me alone and when to interfere.

She always resisted our ageism and interrupted it whenever she could.

This was written mostly by Satya and me because Claudia isn't much involved in our day-to-day family right now. She needed to go back to school, and Sa and I didn't want to move for four years, so we're enduring a separation. It's hard, always hard to stay connected and still do what we each need for ourselves, but Claudia's commitment to Satya is strong. It has evolved steadily and has grown and deepened with every year, in spite of all kinds of obstacles (a major one being persistent nonmonogamy).

Claudia says this family felt like it was meant to be from the first, and that parenting came easily to her. It certainly has worked for all of us for ten years. I could never have done it as well as I did without Claude, and Satya wouldn't have turned out as swell as she is if it weren't for Claude's loving and consistency in her life. Even now, with contact limited to letters, phone calls, and holidays, Claudia functions as a parent. We talk and make decisions together, and when she comes home, the transition into the family feels seamless. Our futures are linked, the three of us, and that provides a stability for each of us that keeps us strong. That won't ever go away.

It's hard to say how much of my upbringing has to do with Annie being a lesbian, and how much of it has to do with who she is and who I am regardless of who any of us sleeps with. Annie's always taught me to be who I really am, to do what I need to do, to express my emotions, to think clearly, and so much else I can't even begin to write it down. She's taught me all of this just by doing it, and encouraging me to do it if I wanted to. She's been an example for me—and she's the best example anyone could ask for.

Community

We
Are
Family

Mi'ja

Ivette Merced

Sigo sobreviviendo
viviendo más y más
que sobre.
Soy espuma,
ligera agua,
mar de lágrimas.
Como bellas olas,
vengo y también voy.
Es ahora la hora
de venir,
a ser la madre
mi'ja de todas
y de nadie
pero de mí misma.
Pues soy de todas
y de nadie nada.
Espuma, agua, lágrimas,
es que vengo
y también voy
al ritmo del ahora:
la hora de vivir
y volver a nacer.
Ven mi'ja.

I keep on surviving
living more and more
than just surviving.
I am foam,
light water,
an ocean of tears.
As beautiful waves do,
so do I come and also go.
Now is the time
to come
to be the mother
the child of all women
and of none
but myself.
Cause I am of all women
and nothing to no one.
Foam, water, tears,
cause I come
and also go
to the rhythm of the now:
the time to live
and to be reborn.
Come my child.

Translated by Zulma

God Bless The Child

Andrea R. Canaan

In A Letter From A Friend

Joshua is here with us now. We are almost entirely responsible for him. He sees his mother every five weeks and his grandmother keeps him on Thursdays.

Our roommate, and the last of the women who committed with us to care for Joshua, has decided to stop. Her reason is that she recently realized her brothers got all of the attention when they were growing up, and she cannot stand to see Joshua being at the center of things so much.

She also told us she has decided to have a child of her own. She said her child would be different—unselfish, attentive, totally nonaggressive and not demanding. "Sure," I say. "Now, back to Josh...."

My Response

How thankful I am to you for responding to a call from a recovering alcoholic lesbian by agreeing to care for her son. I am grateful you took on such a responsibility, and that you have come to love and care for this young person while still knowing that what he needs and wants most is his mother, as whole and sane as possible.

With A Friend, I Am Planning A Reading

My friend said to me in a by-the-way tone, "Since Fern moves around a lot, maybe you can get child care for her."

Something in me came to full alert. Although what I was hearing had probably always been there, I was only now becoming aware of an undercurrent—intonations, pauses, meanings beyond the usual shorthand spoken between friends. I was afraid of what more I was about to learn of myself and this woman I had come to consider a friend.

"Does the bookstore have child care?" I asked. I did not address the feelings that put me on alert; I was stalling, feeling her out. I thought this a fertile place to start because she volunteered at the bookstore we were about to read in.

She responded that she did not know the child-care policy of the bookstore, but *I* could call and find out. I asked her to call *for me*, as I mumbled I would check my child-care resources and apologized in case I couldn't find anyone.

I remember feeling sensitive and bruised by this exchange. I asked myself later on, of her but not to her, "If you feel you would be uncomfortable at the reading with Fern present, why don't you secure appropriate child care?" I said to myself, in my own defense, "I have no money. I have no phone and no vehicle." I asked my friend in this internal conversation, "Will you pay for a sitter and get Fern there? Will you do this for your comfort or to accommodate your discomfort?"

What I said instead was, "I will see what I can arrange."

I remembered holding this woman in my arms. I sat with her and called up every ounce of compassion, love, and support to protect her while she named her childhood wounds and the sources of her pain. I became all of the me's that could possibly hold the terrors, the angers, the hurts of these namings. I was friend, sister, mother, daughter.

This same friend of mine had shared with me, listened to me, held me. She had heard my agonizing process of excavating my own childhood abuse and how hard it was for me to be a parent alone. I had thought this sharing between us, this holding of each other's hard places, had made her equally invested in the health and welfare of my child, of children. I thought we shared the vision that they would suffer less from the poisonous child- and woman-hatred that had marked both of our childhoods.

A Phone Conversation With This Same Friend

We began to talk about children. I was still bruised and wary. I hoped I could speak my feelings and thoughts directly to her. I still did not have a sitter for the reading. I remember thinking how ironic it was that we were reading "Eye to Eye: Black Women, Hatred, and Anger," by Black lesbian poet/writer and mother, Audre Lorde. That we had committed ourselves to sharing this piece with other Black women, and that we had made this commitment based on our urgent needs to confront, share, and heal the angers between Black women.

My friend talked about how children always wanted "center stage." She told me about inviting her family to holiday dinner and insisting they leave their children at home, and of her definite "choice" not to have children. She went on to say how mothers "allow" their children to take up "too much space."

At that point a rage so large rose inside me, it threatened to render me speechless. I told her bluntly that she had described children as sadists who would grow out of a disgusting and inconvenient phase to become human at some magical point, and mothers as misguided masochists, blaming them for their tortured state as well as their children's behavior.

After this conversation I felt an inconsolable grief. I was washed over with the knowledge that I had betrayed my daughter, bit by bit and time after time, through the years of her precious living. I had betrayed her to lovers, to friends, to cultural, political, and activist coworkers. I had allowed the seepage of child- and mother-hatred to slip unnoticed and unnamed into the bones of my daughter and into the pores of my skin, leaving us both with the crippling effects and yet another unlearning and undoing to effect.

It is hard to accept the fact that the same women who love and nurture me as a lesbian, as a feminist, as a writer, as a Black woman, as a Southerner, fail to acknowledge and support me in the same way as a mother.

I am beginning to feel that few lesbians see me, or any mother, as living her life like a majestic tapestry with motherhood, parenting, and childrearing intricately woven throughout—that a mother can live powerfully and purposefully with her parenting intermixed with her writing, her political and cultural work, and her most intimate relationships.

Much of my energy to be and do comes directly from birthing, nurturing, and preparing a child for her future. Much of my vision derives from those healings and teachings the life I protect gives me.

I made a vow before my daughter was born that I would not allow the lack of a sitter or child care to stop me from attending or participating in women's cultural or political events. Increasingly my daughter has learned to respect adult space. She is growing steadily more responsive, responsible, and accountable regarding adult needs. So I ask myself, what is going on that I feel forced to defend my eight-year-old daughter's childness and my motherness?

A Visit From Another Friend

A friend came over after work to give me messages and to spend some time with me. When she arrived, Fern and I were having what I call a "critical and crucial" discussion about homework. I told my friend I would be with her as soon as we were finished. A few minutes later, she walked into the kitchen where we were and nudged me. Her touch said, "Hurry up. I'm tired and I want to talk to you now!" My immediate internal response was, "What is this? Now I'm the mother of two children?"

I said nothing to her directly. I continued my conversation with Fern. No. That is not quite true. I turned and looked at her. My eyes said patiently, "I'll be with you as soon as possible."

When I finished my talk with Fern, I sat down to visit with my friend. As we talked, Fern came in to ask me about something we had not covered earlier. I told her firmly that I was busy and could not talk to her then. Frustrated and angry, she stormed into her room and began to cry. I ignored her loud wailing. Later I went to Fern to say I was upset with her behavior and I wanted her to respect adult space.

Still later I realized I had not told my friend I wanted her to respect mother and child space, nor did I express my anger and disappointment at her lack of patience, control, and respect.

A Mother On The Edge

It was days before Thanksgiving and only a few weeks before Fern would travel to New Orleans to be with her comother. During the short time before she was to leave, I started to come apart. I began snapping and yelling at her for the smallest things. She cried. I raged. As I escalated, she variously cringed and cried and fought back. Finally, two days in a row, I cursed and hit her.

The first time this happened, I immediately called friends and asked them to help monitor my behavior. I put them on alert that Fern might be in danger because I was feeling so out of control.

I felt horrified. I cried and talked to Fern, apologizing and explaining as honestly as I could. I thought the worst had passed.

The very next day I went out of control again while combing her hair. As I combed, she winced and cried. In total frustration, I threw the brush and comb away violently. They ricocheted inside the tub sounding like gunfire as I shouted at her, "Then don't go to fucking school."

I pulled myself together enough to call a friend who helped me get Fern off to school. She listened to me and then helped me think of how to create separate and safe space for Fern and me. I called other women and finally worked out a complicated plan to get time alone and arrange for Fern to be in a safe and caring place.

Finally I had time to myself. I woke up on a glorious Sunday morning thinking I would be able to sleep late, listen to Gospel and walk to the local lesbian-owned restaurant for coffee.

Before the coffee, I decided to double-check with the woman whose car I had arranged to use to pick Fern up in. When I phoned I found her plans had changed. She would drive me to pick up Fern, but she wanted me to spend the next three hours traveling to where she was in order to give me a ride. If I did what she demanded, I would lose my precious morning.

As I was trying to convince this woman friend to simply pick Fern up for me, I suddenly realized I was no longer speaking to her, but to her lover. I stood on a street corner at a pay phone looking at the receiver in shock. I could not believe I had been switched over to someone else who had nothing to do with this transaction. Her lover said in a very no-nonsense tone that my friend was tired and I should do as she said. "After all," she said, "Fern *is* YOUR child."

I did not think. I did not feel. I simply spent the next five hours getting my daughter home.

It was not until much later that I allowed myself to feel the insult, the discounting by these women I had considered friends; women to whom I had turned for support when I had been feeling desperate and wanted to insure my daughter and myself some safe and separate space.

These same two friends supported my writing and acknowledged it as essential to my survival and my living. They applauded my decision to send my eight-year-old daughter away for the holidays so that I could have "space." I understood then that their support did not come from genuine compassion or mutual care and respect, but from their view of children as unfortunate consequences of male/female coupling; burdens better not seen or heard, a hindrance to women's work and relationships.

A Birthday Party

I was invited to a birthday party. Among the carefully selected guests were three children, all of whom I considered mine. Elana, the celebrant, specifically asked two of my women friends, whom she considered La Familia, to cook dinner and pamper her.

Earlier in the day I sat at my writing table looking for poems that would please her. I stopped to buy a favored scent, a card, and some birthday stickers, knowing I should not spend even this modest amount because we had so little. I did anyway, hoping these small things, bought with care in celebration of her birth, would bring her joy.

We had planned to go to a concert benefiting the children of El Salvador after the dinner. As soon as our children left to get settled at child care, Elana came into the living room with a burst of pent-up energy. It was then that I connected her being in the tiny bathroom for a very long time, my friends who had just left with our children and who had been trying to talk to her through the bathroom door, and this sudden and elated reappearance of hers. "Good, they are gone," she said jubilantly.

I felt like I had been stabbed. I felt like I was in a room filled with white people who had invited some Black people to a cocktail party. When the Black people left, everyone sighed, wrinkled their noses, and fanned the room to get rid of the smell. Somehow they did not realize I, too, was Black, making me not only invisible but a party to the degradation of my own people. What was worse, in this real-life situation, I did not protest, or raise my voice in rage, or leave.

The care and love with which these women had prepared this dinner, the personal sacrifice of precious time and money for tickets, the humble but carefully selected gifts, and the joy, excitement and love of the children were all smashed into nothingness by the cavalier wave of Elana's hand and her hateful words.

I rationalized that it was her birthday, and she did not have to deal with children. But it did not work. She knew that three of us present were mothers; that the two women who cooked and cleaned her house for her birthday were mothers. Our children had probably never even entered her mind.

I felt a little dead, and the concert seemed as empty and meaningless as the rhetoric about support, and community-building, and sensitivity.

After the concert all three children stayed at my house. My friends came to pick their two children up the next morning. This is the gift I gave to them—one mother to another, one friend to another.

That night I cried myself to sleep because I failed again to speak up, to speak out. I realized I had allowed some of the women around me to witness the pain and sometimes the despair of raising children, but they had not seen, or recognized, or believed the joy in this bonding.

I wonder how I can tell these women how much I love and honor their survival, how much I love the lonely, isolated, abused, or happy children they were, but hate the bitter and uncaring adults they have become in their treatment of children and mothers.

God Bless The Child

I feel I have betrayed my daughter because it was not until she quickened in my womb that I became a writer, propelled by wanting to mark the things it would take so long for her to comprehend.

When I became pregnant, I knew myself to be a feminist, a cultural worker, a mental health and political worker. My pregnancy and the subsequent birth of a chocolate woman-child transformed me into an activist feminist, cultural, mental health, and political worker and writer.

I betray my daughter when I give so much of the time and energy that resides in the place from which my mothering comes to women—friends, community, family, lovers—that I often have very little to give to Fern and the other children around me.

I betray my daughter when a friend oppresses us with a less-than-committed extension of a helping hand and I become speechless, when I do not stand up for my daughter or myself. What kind of activist am I? What kind of mother is this that I have become? What kind of Black lesbian-feminist allows this to happen? Who are these women I call *friends?*

It is true that children can be a nuisance and a distraction. It is also true that women have the right to choose to have or not to have children in their lives. It is equally true that we all have children inside of us. We have deep scars from our long trek from birth to adulthood and have an investment in the health and well-being of the child that resides within each of us. Most of women's work and the "movement" is about reclaiming and healing the old wounds and working toward a different future for other women and for ourselves. In this way we all are invested in the children now living and yet to be born. It is our children, biological or not, who teach us the precious art of living and constantly revive in us hope and wonder and laughter and love.

How can I confront my own shortcomings without so beating myself down with guilt and shame that I am overcome by inertia, by silence (which is my most deadly enemy)? How can I speak of these things to women, yet honor their choices and feelings? How can I refuse to continue to have my choices, feelings, and realities discounted, used, abused, and dishonored? How do I survive the critical scrutiny of myself and the other women in my life, recognizing we have wide and varying capabilities, desires, inclinations, and choices concerning young people and motherhood that come out of complex and often painful experiences? At the same time, how do I not see these same women as the source of my isolation and bitter resentment, as the source of the acts of cruelty, insensitivity, and hatred that dot the landscapes of our children's and our own lives? How can I defuse and divert to productive use the rejection, degradation, oppression, devaluation, and the rage and self-hatred I often feel?

How can I honor the commitment of friends, of loved ones, of my comother and others who hold me, who comfort me, who hold children dear and necessary to their own survival—they who understand that loving women means loving all the women we were, could have been, may become, and are becoming, including the mothers who bore us and the children we once were.

How can I bless the love, compassion, patient teaching and the joy my daughter has brought into my living? How can I find the strength and will to continue to speak and speak and speak and banish the crippling silences that have painted our lives with self-hatred?

Now that I have the basic questions before me, I will begin to work on the answers.

Thoughts On Child Care

Kate Hall

I hate to ask
I mean
I'm really sorry
but could you
possibly
well are you
doing anything
please feel free
to say no
if you're busy
doing something
important
or simply having
fun
of course if
you're just not
in the right space
but could you
if it's possible
and you
don't mind

Oh I see
no, no, it's really O.K.
I'm sure I'll get someone
no, no, don't worry
it was only
a thought.

Coming Out Poor
Helen

I need to do some coming out in the lesbian community. I need to come out as a welfare mother. Most of my friends and political allies know that I am a lesbian, that I mother a boy child, that I was a student until last spring, and that I am unemployed.

But there are many friends who have never been to my apartment in subsidized housing. I haven't come out to them as a welfare mother. I'm embarrassed by the filth in the halls and elevators, by the graffiti, by the row of women and children sitting in the lobby because they have nothing better to do, and because they can't stand to stay in their apartments one more minute. Living in my $97/month apartment is the only way I survive on mothers' allowance, but it embarrasses me. I have a couple of these strange, one-sided friendships in which I'm always at her house and she's never at mine.

When I do invite someone over, I always bring her, so I can talk and explain as we ride the elevator up to my home. "The apartments are nice inside. It's just that no one cares about the halls." But in my apartment, too, I'm afraid people will find the furniture tasteless. I don't have enough money to replace the things I bought years ago as a nineteen-year-old bride.

There's some anger in my coming out. I'm fighting the assumption that mothers are not political. That we don't care to get involved.

Every meeting costs two bus tickets and $5 for a babysitter. The latest feminist film or women's concert that everyone "simply has to see" breaks my budget for a month. Lots of lesbians have very little money. But for me, deciding to go to a concert doesn't mean rearranging my priorities; it means not paying the phone bill or eating spaghetti and macaroni more the next week than is good for me or my son.

Some meetings also mean guilt for me. The little boy that my friends think is so cute, pipes up with, "Are you going to another meeting, Mom? Can I come? Do I have to go to the sitter's?" Not always, of course, but often enough.

Lesbian mothers, especially the poor ones, need some recognition of the problems we face. We very often can't afford to be as out as we'd like. Some judges will say that we can love women just as long as we don't flaunt it by going to meetings or demonstrations.

It really isn't that we don't care. So often it is simply too difficult, in so many ways, for us to be a regular member of a committee, or a frequently seen face at events in the lesbian community.

Every coming out also has joy, celebration, and hope. I am glad I now feel strong enough to tell and to show some people I am a lesbian welfare mother. I can foresee some nice times at my place with friends, finally reciprocating all those visits, and not having to pay a sitter to boot.

I hope the lesbian community starts to understand the special problems of mothers, and more than that, offers real help in solving some of them. Many mothers are less involved and less out than they want to be because of the fear of custody hassles, the costs of child care, and the actual time involved in mothering.

But places must be made for us to contribute to the advancement of the lesbian movement in whatever way we are able. After all, what's more political than survival? Who is more revolutionary than those who live in the lifestyle they choose in defiance of patriarchal custom? We want to love women and keep our children, too.

Our Lovers Will Never Be Fathers, But Our Community Can Be Our Family

Lesbian Mothers' Group: Pearl Henderson, Debbie Lubarr, Barbara Neumann, Shirley Royster

We are six lesbian mothers. We are two white women, three Black American women and one West Indian woman, all living in Boston. We range in age from thirty to forty-two. Our children are two to twenty-two years old. One of us is a grandmother. Four of us are writing this article. We have been meeting together for almost a year as a group. In that year, there have been other women who have been in and out of the group. We mainly deal with supporting each other with whatever is going on in our lives. During the early stages of the group, we were very unstructured and often didn't know who would participate from week to week. As we grew to trust each other, the group settled. We meet every two weeks, usually without our kids, although kids are welcome. We meet for two or three hours and generally just go around the room and talk about whatever's happening in each of our lives. We see each other and speak to each other between meetings.

As a group we've dealt with a range of concerns: fathers—in our kids' lives and not in our kids' lives; kids leaving school and leaving home; breaking up with lovers and how that affects our kids; learning parenting skills from each other; being invisible in the broader lesbian community and looking for support there; coming out to our kids; meeting with each other's lovers; reaching out to other lesbian mothers; coparenting. In this article we will address the following: relationships between our children and ourselves, our families' relationships to the lesbian community and to the straight world, secrecy and invisibility, and the value of the group in our lives.

We started meeting in April 1986. We didn't really know each other, but we were drawn together as lesbian mothers. We spent the first few months figuring out what we had in common, defining our roles in the group, deciding how much we could trust each other—but we were all bursting to talk. One thing we found out: very few of us had any support systems in our dual roles as lesbians and mothers.

We had all felt isolated for years within the lesbian community, and now that the lesbian community began to talk about having children, or by what method to conceive, we wanted to say, "Give me a fucking break." We had been doing kids for years and were almost totally invisible as parents to the lesbian community.

My name is Debbie. I am a thirty-six-year old Jewish woman, a lesbian, the mother of a nine-year-old son. I've been in various stages of being out as a lesbian for four years. Two years ago I spent a year of being totally frustrated in dual roles as a lover and as a mother. This last year I have been coming out as a lesbian mother. At times it's been painful, at times joyous, and almost always satisfying. The lesbian mothers' group has been there for support and has made it possible for me to become a lesbian mother.

As I felt more out there as a lesbian mother, I began to feel compelled to identify myself. Mostly this led to countless discussions of two varieties: "Oh, I love kids." Dead silence. Or, "I want to have a baby." I don't want to have either of these conversations again, especially with a woman who hasn't had any relationship to kids since she baby sat as a teen-ager.

My child is a person. If I said to another lesbian, "I have a new lover," I would never get either one of the above responses. You would ask me what she does, who she is, what my dreams and fears are about the relationship. My child is a primary relationship in my life. I've had a relationship with my child longer than any lover. It's a relationship where I am totally committed to working through problems, differences. It's a relationship in which I am challenged to grow, learn, and change, but it's not a relationship I can easily leave, if I can leave at all.

My child is an important focal point in my life. I am a mother because I choose to be a mother and I like the shape that role gives my life. I see the future through the eyes of my child. Sometimes that's scary (what is this world going to be like?), sometimes that gives me incredible hope, and yes, sometimes my child gives me a reason to live, a reason to face another day.

My relationship with my child is a relationship I will have full-time for at least eighteen years; it's a relationship that will be part of my life, in whatever form, forever. It's a loving, caring relationship that is a main focus in my life. My child is a person I usually like a lot. My child is someone I love.

Many of us had to be invisible out of fear of retaliation from social workers, teachers, and fathers. Most of us had our values around honesty, openness, and being proud of who we are, which we taught our kids, but we all knew that they have to hide the fact that their mothers are lesbians. It wasn't something they were taught; all the kids knew it by instinct. People had different ways of coping with it—either by not being out to their kids or by referring to people as "safe." It was important for each of us to hear there were other mothers and kids who experienced this secrecy.

For us, being out is a damned-if-you-do-and-damned-if-you-don't situation. You pay a price for staying in the closet—carrying all the load of having to hide and having your kids dealing with secrecy. But if you're out, you're constantly vulnerable to people making these attacks or taking your kids away. Even if it is not that extreme a threat, everything your kid does is looked at in light of the fact that you are a lesbian. Every problem gets blamed on that. We even do this to ourselves; we internalize this oppression.

My name is Pearl. I think it's important that gay parents have a support system, whether it is family, friends, or a local support group. I feel very fortunate to be associated with the support group I am presently involved in. It gives me the opportunity to vocalize issues on a biweekly basis, problems which I am not able to address with my family because, like most gay parents, problems involving our children are always blamed on our homosexuality.

Recently my seventeen-year-old son dropped out of school. As a parent I was devastated; as a gay parent it made my task even harder. There is so much guilt associated with being a gay parent. At first I was in total shock. Was this the same child who communicated to me on several occasions that he would never quit school because it represented failure? Has he accepted failure? Did I fail? All these questions kept racing in my mind. I was totally confused. Out of that confusion I remembered a special teacher's words which gave me the strength to continue school, and they have become more or less my bible by which I live: "No one ever achieved worthwhile success who did not at one time or other find herself with at least one foot hanging well over the brink of failure." I communicated those words of wisdom to my son, hoping to give him hope to continue his education.

I know how difficult it must be for him. My life at the present time is in turmoil. He doesn't have his own space and must be in a state of confusion. In spite of all of this, I believe that for the past seventeen years I have given unselfishly to my son. Every decision I have made during this time has been with him in mind. I believe it is about time for him to assume some respon-sibility for his own actions. I also believe the only lasting favor the parent can confer upon the child is that of helping the child to help itself. I have accomplished those goals. I have nothing to feel guilty or ashamed about.

My son is back in school, thanks to the support I received from friends, family, and coworkers of my son who unselfishly got involved in a very per-sonal issue and took the time to communicate to him how important it was to continue school. Without their combined effort, it would not have been possible.

Our kids are also invisible. Barbara told the group about an experience she had a couple of years ago: "It was Thanksgiving dinner—all lesbians, and Chris (her son). Neither of us really wanted to be in that situation. But the thought of me and Chris staying home by ourselves on Thanksgiving wasn't very appealing. After dinner we were all sitting in the kitchen talking. Somebody started to say a lot of shit about men. Chris was in the next room and he came in and said something. All the women were apologetic." What's the message for that boy child? "Oh, not you dear, you're all right." How's that child going to be different from those men that were being talked about? Where's that culture to reinforce the nonsexist values we try to teach our children, expecially our boy children? Is there space for our children to explore different values and choose what they need? Is there space for them to grow?

I am Shirley, a Black woman, a mother of two girls, and a lesbian. I am proud of my titles and I try to wear them well.

I have decided to be open about who I am with my children. My oldest daughter has been aware of my being a lesbian most of her life because I came out when she was one year old. My youngest daughter is now beginning to ask questions. She is trying to understand why there's a woman I share my bed with and what that means.

I feel I don't get a lot of support from my Black lesbian sisters. Their comments to me come in the form of, "Girl, it must be hard raising kids," or, "How do you do it?" I smile and say, "Yes, it is hard, but it's not so bad." And I really feel that. It could be more rewarding if my community was more supportive of me and my children. The nonparent sister, in my opinion, sees having to deal with me and my children in a relationship as scary. One-on-one relationships can be hard. With kids, nonparent sisters have to define their role in my family, just as any other person does in my life. I sometime see it as, "Who wants a ready-made family?" Something that men say.

Black lesbian mothers I meet are just like any other parents. We can relate to each other, voice our concerns, express our hopes and dreams for ourselves and our children.

I want my girls to learn about loving and caring relationships. I want them to see examples of this in the lesbian community. In the lesbian community as a whole, I feel my children are not always welcome even when the invitation says they are. Children can be very curious. They can ask questions like, "What is gay? Are you gay? Do you have on boy's shoes? Are you a lesbian like my mother?" I have seen lesbian women very uncomfortable trying to answer these questions coming out of children's mouths. And they sometimes have problems expressing affection to each other with children in the room. I want my girls to learn about loving relationships from my lesbian community, but I question if this will happen. Lesbians exclude boys at certain ages. What will my girls learn from that?

I would like my girls to see boys at lesbian social events. This would make me feel the lesbian community is saying my girls can have choices about their own sexuality. It's important for them to have boyfriends with whom they don't have to hide the fact their mother is a lesbian. And they need this social contact.

I would like to help the lesbian community become more sensitive to the needs of the lesbian mother and work toward really being a community. Some of the ways I see the community being supportive of me as a lesbian mother are to be sensitive to my children's need to be around people who understand the secrecy they live with, to take regular committed responsibility for children, to understand my primary job begins after eight hours at work, to make the effort to include kids at functions, not just by providing child care.

As our children become teen-agers, it is harder and harder for us to spend time doing things with them. That is part of a natural separation process. It's difficult enough without an outside force deciding that at age eight a boy child can no longer be in certain places. As lesbians, we all appreciate women-only space, but we also need lesbian spaces where we are not split up from our families.

Kids learn early on how to push their parents' buttons and make them feel guilty or not normal. For us as lesbian mothers, that guilt was doubled by knowing we would never measure up to the "Brady Bunch," a view our kids have of the perfect family. Even if we are in couples, our lovers will never be fathers. At this point in America, with all these religious right-wing family values pervading the broader culture, it's even worse. Our kids are in the broader culture—they watch TV, go to public schools. As adults, we have certain choices which our kids don't have. We've been through a growing-up process where we have rejected many of society's values and created our own. As Sweet Honey and the Rock sings, "You can house their bodies but not their souls. You can strive to be like them but you cannot make them just like you."

My name is Barbara, and I am the lesbian mother of a sixteen-year-old son, Chris. We live surrounded by books, cats, good kitchen smells, and city noises. Our home also includes my lover of three years. My lover and my son care for and about each other, but don't relate at all as parent and child. One of the problems the three of us grapple with a lot is trying to describe our relationship(s). There doesn't seem to be a language yet invented that reflects our reality. There is tremendous pressure put on us to conform. "If you aren't a nuclear family, then you should at least adopt nuclear family (straight, white, middle-class) values." That's the message we are bombarded with. Even the lesbian community buys into this in ways I can't accept. Many of the lesbian couples now having babies seem to ignore the statistical likelihood that they will one day be single parents. There is a kind of arrogance in this attitude, and I wonder why these women feel they don't have anything to learn from my history, from all of us "invisible" lesbian mothers who have been doing this for years.

I came out when my son was twelve years old. I can't say that was an easy or simple process for either of us. But he has never made me feel I have to choose between his love and acceptance and being a lesbian, even an out lesbian. Actually, Chris brings his friends home a lot, and I feel some of these kids really appreciate being able to participate in our nontraditional family life. They have a chance to see lesbians (and some gay men) as real people instead of the queers they've been taught to fear and avoid. My son once said to me, "If I meet a girl and I want to ask her out because she is really beautiful, I think about whether I'd be comfortable telling her you're a lesbian. If she's the kind of person who couldn't deal with that, then I figure I probably wouldn't want to be involved with her."

Being a lesbian mother means being myself, whole and natural. But the world doesn't want to see me whole. Instead, daily, I am asked to sacrifice my integrity. Lesbianism and motherhood just don't go together in most people's minds—in fact, quite a few people see this as an outright contradiction. They would deny I even exist.

A few days ago I was talking to a woman I work with and had the opportunity to come out to her, in a very direct way, as a lesbian mother. She was asking me if I had any support in dealing with my teen-age son, and I said I was part of a lesbian mothers' group and that was important to me. Her response was, "Oh. . .that must be real different." I asked her what she meant by that. (Being a mother? Being a lesbian? Having a teen-ager? Belonging to a support group?) She stumbled around a little bit and then said, "Well, being a mother of a teen-age son is something. . .but being a lesbian mother. . . . She went on, later in the conversation, to ask me a lot of questions, and I realized how strange and mysterious my ordinary life must seem to some people.

That's why I cherish this group. It's one of the few places where I can be both a lesbian and a mother, where the two aspects of myself are not seen as contradictory. And I feel so proud of us. Being lesbians and raising our kids, day by day creating with them a home, a family, a community that is in contrast to the dominant culture—we are doing something very significant.

So much of the time we are just holding it together. If we can get home from work in time, cook supper, help with homework, and get through the evening without screaming at somebody—even ourselves—we feel like we made it. This is the optimum. We don't have exciting, challenging jobs. We can't devote time every day to personal growth and development. When we go out into the women's community, we feel that lack of openness—we often feel we are boring, that our lives are boring.

The group has secured our identity as lesbian mothers and improved our parenting skills. It was affirming for all of us to hear other lesbian mothers' stories—to feel we are not alone in thinking, "My kid is acting out because I'm a lesbian and my kid hates that"—and to acknowledge with other lesbians the frustrations of being a single parent. The group has helped us realize we are not alone in our struggle to remain who we are. The group has given us support to deal with the heterosexual molding of our kids' lives and of our own.

Postscript

As this article reached its final stage a few events have happened in our lives which prompt us to write this postscript. First, after living and breathing this article in the Fall (1986), we reread it for the first time after two months. We liked it and felt it expresses what was happening at the time. We would not change the article. It is an important marker for us, a synthesis of all our beginning places. Hopefully, it can be that place for other lesbian mothers. But we did want to note that through the support group and the process of doing the article, we have changed and grown. We feel more self-confident. The duality of our roles has significantly decreased, and we realize how important the support of this group has been in our individual lives.

Secondly, three of us have participated in a workshop and a radio show about lesbian mothers for International Women's Day. We realize we are past some of our initial anger and feel much more in a place of doing outreach with other lesbian mothers. We wanted to include an address for lesbian mothers, especially in this area, to contact us. Now that you've heard parts of our stories, we'd love to hear yours. Please contact us through Debbie Lubarr, P.O. Box 103, Jamaica Plain, MA 02130.

Love In Motion

Sue Gambill

I never wanted to be a mother. Then my sister left her two children, and I was presented with circumstances I had never previously desired.

For thirteen years I had traveled about, on my own, in a lifestyle many considered exotic. A small part of my heart yearned for some stability and rootedness, but a larger passion lived within my gypsy soul.

I had left my small, Midwestern hometown at the age of twenty. The new and expansive ideas and possibilities I encountered outside made me immediately aware I did not want to return to that closed and conservative part of the country I had known as a child.

But now, here I am doing these two seemingly impossible things—parenting and living again in Cincinnati, Ohio. I didn't know my lesbian and feminist self was capable of responding to such a challenge. However, it was exactly my lesbian and feminist self that made this response.

For more than a decade I had been working with women—through community organizing, Women's Studies, and with women artists and writers. For eight years I had been out and active in the lesbian community. My concern for women had traveled with me through my various places of residence in Michigan, Portugal, New York, Massachusetts, and Oregon. Could I possibly translate my global concern for women into the more immediate and, in some ways, more intimate involvement with my two nieces and my own mother (with whom the two girls were living)? Of course there were various women's issues affecting this female household of three. But my thoughts were not on them. The question which moved in my heart, seeking an intense and immediate answer, was how could I be committed to women and to a better life and not be willing to be involved with the women of my family? No one asked me to do it, but I knew it was time to return to the place that once had been home.

I was terrified. I was sure it wasn't in my nature to be a mother. Plus, flat, landlocked Ohio (where the majority of the people's responses match the landscape) seemed desolate. Many of my friends thought I was crazy, and most didn't know how to give me support in this move. Some people saw me as dropping out of the "real" struggle—however they were defining *real* and *struggle* at the time. In addition, my worst fear was soon realized: I moved back to this vast stretch of Midwestern land and immediately lost contact with all my coastal friends. Two years later isolation continues to be a major factor, even within the feminist and lesbian community of Cincinnati. It has not been an easy two years. I have not always understood why this particular situation developed for me in my mid-thirties. However, this path I have chosen has always felt right—an intuitive, heartfelt sensation (which often does not sit easily with my intellectual, reasoning self).

The first year back in town I lived with my mother and two nieces in a small suburban house, the kind they put up in the '50s: National Homes, one floor, three bedrooms, carport, quarter acre. Since 1970 the subdivisions have multiplied at an enormous rate, expanding into bigger, split-level houses, and filling a landscape that had once been farm land and woods.

Two months after my arrival I began to feel numb and insane. The television was on constantly. There were no conversations of significance. No one did anything. At the grocery store and the gas stations I'd run into old high school acquaintances who'd never left the area. Surrounded by nearly grown children, they looked worn down and old. When they asked what I'd been doing with my life, the response was a translation between two worlds I felt incapable of making. I experienced this same difficulty with my family. I was a foreigner, alone in a territory that was supposed to be as familiar as my own skin and the rhythm of my voice. It was in this context I tried to actualize what to me felt like a radical and intimate love. In the old days, I would have called it one of those small acts which, when added up, would surely save the world. After two years, however, the reality does not feel radical nor made of love.

The impulse that brought me into all of this was a desire to help one of my two nieces, Carie, who's twelve years old, developmentally handicapped, carrying a lot of emotional baggage because of her mother's desertion, and who was then living in an abusive situation with my mother. I'd also returned because there seemed a strong chance that some day she might define herself as lesbian. It was because of Carie I lived that first year in suburbia, getting my bearings and checking out the possibility of assuming sole and independent responsibility for her. The second year she and I moved to a better school district and lived on our own.

I had been looking forward to this second-year change as a great relief for me—getting some distance from a mother with whom I'd never had a very good relationship. For Carie, the move was to a much better school district (a crucial consideration for a DH student), the opportunity to live with an aunt with whom she'd always wanted to live, and a try at the greater independence and responsibility she seemed to desire. I knew the change would not necessarily be easy for Carie, but our strong bond and her interest in moving made me think it would be much easier than it turned out to be. I came to see how the feelings of desertion that shadow her every move are so crippling they shut out the very love and special attention she wants. We spent an entire school year shuttling back and forth between two households: weekends at my Mom's, school days with me; happiness at the familiar household, depression and lethargy at the new.

Carie's attitude and behavior in her new school improved over 100 percent. She developed many independent living skills and a more responsible attitude in her new living situation. She was determined, however, not to enjoy herself or to make herself a part of this home. Her only desire continues to be to return to live with her grandmother. We've spoken openly about the positives and negatives of each situation, and she's aware of the abuse she has previously experienced there. But it's the familiarity and belonging she wants, and we have not been able to create that in our living together.

There's a possibility that Carie will return to live with my mother. When Carie and I started talking about this, I began to feel like I had failed. Then I went through a stage of anger, resenting that I'd "given up my life" for two years. I've had periods of being afraid she wouldn't be able to return to my mother's and I'd be trapped forever with this moody, unhappy child. And I've also felt some relief and the desire for further relief.

Just last week, Carie went back to my mother's to spend the summer. Suddenly, most evenings are my own. Making dinner for myself, writing, going to the movies or the library are tremendously appreciated activities. I feel like a prisoner who has been freed. I realize now that parenting, taking on the full responsibility for another person, has made me question how the role of parenting could possibly work. Maybe there are people for whom it is natural, but for me it doesn't feel that way. Granted, my particular situation had several complications that probably made it more difficult. Nonetheless, as a writer I have found it impossible to write these past two years. As a person with a reflective, spiritual, artistic, and critical mind and soul, I have found myself mostly numbed out. Like a swimmer who's desperate for air, I've been thrashing about, trying to find a way to survive.

Even though people have said I've done well, I look at my expectations and realize I've fallen quite short. The hardest part to face is that I have not been able to create for Carie a place of love and freedom in which she could feel the acceptance and trust she so desperately needs. I don't know if she will ever have that.

I look at my own self and wonder what I will do if my mother doesn't want Carie year round. For this is a story not just between myself and a child, but also between my mother and me. My mother is sixty-five. She has literally spent her entire life taking care of children: her younger siblings, her stepson who was ten years old at her marriage, her six children, and now her grandchildren. My mother has never been alone, has never taken care of just herself. She is bitter, and her anger comes out indirectly in short, vicious, unpredictable spurts. I don't blame her, and yet I do. She made choices and, at the same time, she was a victim. In my own life, up until two years ago, my sole responsibility had been to myself. My decisions, in the final say, were always my own. Maybe for the first time I am now getting a small taste of what my mother's entire life has been.

The closing of this article is being written in Tallahassee, Florida, where I have taken a new job with Naiad Press. This recent opportunity, and the more recent choice to take it, brought swift changes to my living situation. Within the period of a few days, Carie and my mother had decided to resume living together. Within two weeks Carie's younger sister had moved to Florida with Norma, her other aunt (a change six months in the planning), and Norma's teen-age daughter had moved in with my mother and Carie. A week later my own car was packed and I was on the road south. So the family continues along, not at all in any traditional form, but ever-changing and, hopefully, meeting the needs of everyone involved.

Many friends considered my leaving as my salvation from an unimaginable life of parenting. Other friends saw me as escaping responsibility. My own feelings were not easily defined, fluctuating between relief and guilt, wondering in the late hours of the night if this latest choice was now the right one. I don't really believe the question here is right or wrong, failure or success. The experience has been terrifying and exhilarating, rewarding and disappointing. During these two years many changes have taken place that are of great benefit to everyone involved: Carie developing more independence, my mother realizing she did not want to live alone when she was offered the opportunity, my confirming (what I had expected), that parenting is really foreign to my nature, and, importantly, my securing SSI (Supplemental Security Income) benefits for Carie (after a year-long process of application).

One of my friends thought some mothers might feel angry at my need/ability to walk away. But, after all, I had not really made a choice to be a mother. My choice, and what is most natural to my rhythm, is to be singular in the world. The decision to be with my family the past two years was a choice to engage with them in trying to figure out a difficult situation. I have done that and was lucky the time came when it was possible for me to return again to a life on my own. Being single is as much a choice as being a mother. The crucial thing is the choosing.

There are a lot of feelings to deal with and always the practical consideration of what happens if my mother's age eventually makes it impossible for her to care for Carie. Though the distance has relieved me of day-to-day responsibilities, I again have what is more familiar to my gypsy life—the concerns of long-distance family care. Mobility does not turn off the feelings and responsibility, particularly for me as a lesbian and feminist trying to define and actualize my commitment to this female family.

As lesbians, who are automatically placed on the fringe of society by the choice of our lives, we can bring to parenting and to young children the positive aspects of being on that fringe—of possibility instead of control, acceptance instead of rejection, diversity instead of commercial homogeneity, and, yes, importantly, a world of many families in changing and varied forms, not limited by the term *traditional*. This, then, can be a politics of the heart, the expression of love not as a possession, handed down through the marriage ceremony, but love as a verb in motion, daring the boundaries and stretching each of us to our full possibilities.

Satisfaction In Just This Much

S.S.

When I learned, three years ago, that my then nineteen-year-old son had received severe head injuries because of a drinking driver, at first I felt nothing. I remembered the nightmares of "what if something happens to the kids," but I felt nothing, because I was deeply in shock. My community, my therapist, and my lover quickly rallied around to help me prepare for the drive to the city where my son lay in a coma. I did not know if he would be alive when my lover and I arrived.

My son did live, and more, is a survivor despite the grave consequences of this injury. Where once he jogged five miles daily, today he mostly uses a wheelchair; and we cheer as he makes his way down the hall at home with a pyramid cane. He uses an Epson HX-20 portable computer with speech pak to communicate. At the time of his injury, he had received a near-perfect grade-point average in his university studies and been admitted to the honors program. After an absence of four years, in the fall he will begin attending a college in our area. Brain damage changes almost everything—but not quite all.

As I made my way through the difficult months in which my son lay comatose and then gradually came back into consciousness, I sometimes felt as if I had moved into a steel box held shut by metal straps. There seemed to be no time to think of myself, including my political lesbian self. I worked full-time and commuted weekly between my home and the city where my son was first hospitalized, and then a resident in a rehabilitation institute. It was the dead of winter and driving conditions were dreadful. Appalled by my absences, ambivalent about the attention paid my son, and struggling through her first year of law school, my lover moved out on New Year's Eve, leaving a message with my eldest daughter that she had gone. A week later, my youngest daughter's boyfriend, ostensibly my son's best friend, also "took a walk." The stress was indeed high and costly.

The lesbian community, however, helped see us through this tragedy. Two women, in a relationship of ten years, expected me for dinner every Sunday night as I drove back into town, physically exhausted, shaken by the weather that had pummeled the car, and full of news about minute improvements in my son's circumstances. That this was my son and neither of my daughters was not an issue with them. They took me and mine at face value. I weep as I write, remembering their essential solidarity.

On Tuesday evenings, the two came to my house. At home, this was virtually the only cooking I did. Otherwise I ordered in chicken wings or went out for hamburgers. The end result of stress combined with poor eating habits was, predictably, stomach ulcers—three of them. But, on Tuesday nights, I rubbed garlic, Hungarian paprika and parsley onto olive oil-daubed chicken to gift these beloved friends—and in doing so, also gifted myself.

Help came in a variety of ways. My therapist responded to the difficulties with creativeness. For two weeks running, we had grieving sessions in a carpeted room filled with pillows. Together, we drank endless pots of hot tea. I wept for hours in the arms of lesbian friends who stroked me, brushed my hair, massaged my back. We were none of us afraid to touch each other; and I need this hands-on approach in the midst of an experience that threatened alienation at each turn.

My best friend traveled a long distance repeatedly by train and on arriving, set herself busy defrosting the refrigerator, buying bright oranges, and decking my son's hospital dresser with vivid violet, pink, and yellow tissue paper in still another effort to catch his attention and fancy. She supported us all, equitably and equally.

In came books. By mail, *Onward And Upward In The Garden* by Katharine S. White from my first lover, herself a mother, as were none of my other close friends. After eleven years we had parted ways and become unable to reach out to each other. Here she was with a book that took me to a part of me neglected by now. From a straight friend whose kids mine grew up with came Alice Walker's *The Color Purple*, read on a New Year's Eve, which ripened into greater understanding of and solidarity with others who suffered. This was the right book, and with it my straight friend also acknowledged who I had become in the intervening years. In an acquaintance's hand, also a mother and a lesbian, came May Sarton's *Letters From Maine*, asking, "Who has spoken of the unicorn in old age," and citing for me all the possibilities as clear certainty. Recently, after learning about her stroke, I wrote to Sarton to share our experiences and was moved when she responded to my letter.

On my son's twentieth birthday, Barbara and Anne of Mischief Mime came to the rehabilitation institute to celebrate in a movingly funny flurry of theater. The helium-filled balloons seemed to hold up more than the back of Barbara's pants; and Anne's fairy-godmother wand (which she carried boldly in her hand as she disembarked from the plane that brought her) bouyed and transformed us into something beyond the daily tedium of rehabilitation.

The first weekend we brought my son home we found the house likewise transformed, by the hands of my frequent dinner companions, with balloons and fresh garden flowers. A welcome sign made by the children next door hung from the front door, and a happy birthday sign spanned my son's bedroom doorway. Dinner fragrant with dill awaited us in the kitchen—by virtue of lesbian hands. This was a lively, love-filled home and no somber tomb we returned to.

Thirteen months later my son returned to our city, and in three more months was home to live. Our household nursing staff, paid for by insurance, was almost entirely gay and mostly made up of prior acquaintances and friends. This closeness offered many advantages. After a head injury, an individual may respond most rapidly to familiar cues and persons. My son knew these people, and they poured a seemingly infinite wealth of caring attitudes and ingenious ideas into his recovery. There also was my sexual identification and need for reinforcement and privacy. For months I had effectively belonged to an extended family at the institute—supportive, yes; gay, with but one exception, no. This heterosexual milieu drained part of me. More than once, exhausted and vulnerable, I spoke to my therapist about my wish to live again openly as a lesbian.

There was still a host of issues to deal with. My financial circumstances were grave, as I had spent almost every cent I could get to keep myself on the road. An accountant, another member of the lesbian community, pitched in one year's services "at a discount" (meaning without charge), and kept me from bankruptcy proceedings and in my home. My dinner table friend (she is so much more to me) found me part-time teaching in addition to my full-time appointment, which helped me pay off pressing debts. My lover has returned, and we now have a relationship of five years' duration. This has been a hard but growing time for us. We have *earned* our relationship.

Not long ago, using the pyramid cane, my son walked by himself from his armchair to his bed and has walked the house slowly, deliberately, ever since, without support other than the cane. He and I serve as co-presidents of a large civic organization that works to mitigate the consequences of drinking and driving, and to end them.

No perfect endings are in view. Sometimes we tire; at other times we are elated. Mostly the peaks and valleys of emotion have evened out. Normalcy feels fine. For all that has been lost, a great deal is gained; and we are, in any event, much the same people as before, if deeper and tempered by struggle.

Many are unreceptive to and—unfortunately, I feel sometimes purposefully —ignorant about the needs of differently abled people. This is discouraging, but we face the reality knowing that when we were desperate for help, we were not alone. Partly because of this support we are no longer desperate and again exercise independence. The connections I spent years discovering, and the changes I made from hetero- to homosexuality, have proved to be more than matters of sexual expression, although this too is significant. In assisting my son, my intention was never to sacrifice the self I had forged, and the lesbian community appreciated this fact. These women helped us to create a world that is not yet pervasive in any of our lives, but that was there when we needed it. This is its own brand of politics. There is enormous satisfaction to be found in just this much.

Dear Daniel
Auguste Elliott

There are a few things you should know about your mother. She was beautiful, she was a lesbian, and she nearly died, once, on my living room couch.
The couch was a gaudy, flowered print, mostly in reds and blues. Six feet long, it was the kind of piece I never would have purchased except that I needed a couch and Bessie's son Clyde had one for sale for $25.
I knew she was drawn to the couch because of the huge picture window. The view was magnificent, even in a sporadic rainstorm, looking over what once was the blue lake, now a pasture, to a full range of six thousand-foot mountains. There was a notch in the middle rise where the silhouette of a lone redwood persisted for as long as anyone remembered. I never did put curtains up, just a bamboo shade that glowed golden by the light of the woodstove. From the couch she could see the Mad River outlined—on days like that one, which are neither winter nor spring—by a soft shroud of fog turned mist turned fog again.
She had called me in the morning from Pat's to say she needed some peace and wanted to die. Would I come pick her up?
I was not surprised by either statement. Pat's was a madhouse. Women in and out all hours of the night, music, the constant traffic of the Red Deer Bar and Drive-In, and a steady flow of alcohol and drugs. As far as wanting to die, ever since the last surgery with its chemotherapy and morphine habit, Carla had expressed that sentiment often. In fact, I had heard rumors she was planning a suicide.
Carla and I had two things in common: we were lesbians and we fought hard for other people's rights. We had once made a wonderful team at the Emergency Food Center. I was the diplomatic administrator; she, the defiant welfare rights advocate whose tactics knew no bounds.
She was a fighter, your mama. I remember the first time I met her. She sat in the passenger side of a green Volkswagen bug, with short cropped flaming red hair and one breast. She had just returned from a radical mastectomy and was telling clever Amazon jokes.
As the surgeries progressed and different parts of her were taken to Pathology, she gained a real reputation for harassing nurses. She would enter the floor announcing from the gurney, "I am a *Lesbian* and I want you to know it!" It was said that she threw hospital property at passing medical person-

nel, but I never believed it. Her anger at the nurses was adamantly discussed by counselors and social workers who found the woman and her cancer too disagreeable to talk about.

More than at the nurses, she was angry at the corporate farmers who hired migrant labor at a wage that meant children had to work the fields, as Carla had done for the family to survive, while rivulets of pesticides trickled from rusty barrels into the migrant drinking supply. She was angry at the lawyers and judges who took you away, to live with more "fit" relatives, and who more than once locked her up for being mad and drunk at the same time. She was angry, in a heavy simmering way, at doctors and hospitals that seemed to be taking her body, bit by bit, instead of repairing it.

She wore the mastectomy like a badge, sometimes unconsciously stroking the flat side of her workman's shirt. Next to it, the loose, pendulous breast seemed almost cumbersome.

I had picked her up Saturday evening, and she slept on the couch fully clothed with the stars and the moon. I left the bamboo blind up, but covered her with afghans in my one small effort at nurturance. Her breathing was regular, though I admit to getting up to check her, as with a newborn, when life is so fragile you sometimes wake the babe to be sure it is still breathing.

In the grey morning light, she looked excruciatingly pale and white. I checked her breathing, started a morning fire, and put the kettle on.

The morning was a progression of refusals.

"Have some tea?"

"I made oatmeal pancakes."

"Should I call the doctor?"

"Do you need to pee?"

"Can I call someone?"

"How about some grape juice?"

"Milk?"

"Water?"

"Lunch?"

"Tea?"

All my efforts were greated with a vigorous shake of the head. "No," she kept saying, with all the strength she had left.

By 1:00 p.m. I realized I had been talking to myself for a long time. She had not had anything to eat or drink or say for at least twenty hours, and the sky was not going to clear, or rain. It was the kind of day when great armies of snails would march from nowhere and prove, by devouring every sprout in your half-acre garden, that you had overestimated spring.

I thought of snails to keep the panic down.

The last thing Carla had said to me was, "I just need to rest, here. What ever happens *don't* take me to the hospital. Please!"

I thought of the last time Carla was in the hospital. I was the administrator of a rehabilitation center; she was on disability insurance. I would sneak away three times a week and watch the soaps in her private room. They allowed her a private room, even though Medicare wouldn't pay for it, out of deference to possible roommates who would be offended by her "strong language."

Some days she would be in horrible pain, twitching from side to side. The first few times I rang for help, only to be told she was on as high a morphine dosage as was safe, and there was nothing else to be done. I thought how, if she had been the visitor and I the patient, there would have been hell to pay at that nurses' station.

Other days, she was in a stupor, barely able to recognize me, drugged and dying—I was sure of it.

"Please," she had said, "don't take me to the hospital."

By 2:00 p.m. her breathing was shallow, her lips parched. The only movement she made was to spill a glass of water I put to her lips.

My panic surfaced. Did she really want to die? Could I let her die here in my living room?

She began to mumble incoherently. Leaning over her, all I could make out was your name, over and over, "Daniel, Daniel, Daniel."

Whether the decision was hers or mine or someone else's, it was made. I called the Sheriff's Department and found that the Rescue Team would take thirty minutes to reach us. My truck could make the trip to town in twenty. I filled the cab with pillows and an afghan. Mr. Moon from across the tracks was home, and together we half-dragged, half-carried her over the graveled walk. Her 180 pounds surprised me; she had become so frail in my eyes.

I drove quickly and efficiently. She mumbled words I could not make out, and thank god, the emergency entrance was clear. The doctors said she was severely dehydrated, on the edge of a coma, and, of course, dying of cancer. They reprimanded me for not bringing her in sooner and asked if she had any family. I said she had a son and that I would try to reach him.

People tell me the two of you were together those last two years she lived; that the family agreed to let you come live with her; that it was a remarkably painless remission; and that the end came quickly.

She may be gone. But the days stay with me, the power of your name, whispered through parched lips and fog, turning to mist then turning to fog again.

Into The Future

There's A Long Road Ahead Of Us

Turning The Beat Around: Lesbian Parenting 1986

Audre Lorde

These days it seems like everywhere I turn somebody is either having a baby or talking about having a baby, and on one level that feels quite benign because I love babies. At the same time, I can't help asking myself what it means in terms of where we are as a country, as well as where we are as people of Color within a white racist system. And when infants begin to appear with noticeable regularity within the Gay and Lesbian community, I find this occurrence even more worthy of close and unsentimental scrutiny.

We are Lesbians and Gays of Color surviving in a country that defines human—when it concerns itself with the question at all—as straight and white. We are Gays and Lesbians of Color at a time in that country's history when its domestic and international policies, as well as its posture toward those developing nations with which we share heritage, are so reactionary that self-preservation demands we involve ourselves actively in those policies and postures. And we must have some input and effect upon those policies if we are ever to take a responsible place within the international community of peoples of Color, a human community which includes two-thirds of the world's population. It is a time when the increase in conservatism upon every front affecting our lives as people of Color is oppressively obvious, from the recent appointment of a Supreme Court Chief Justice in flagrant disregard of his history of racial intolerance, to the largely unprotested rise in racial stereotypes and demeaning images saturating our popular media—radio, television, videos, movies, music.

We are Gays and Lesbians of Color at a time when the advent of a new and uncontrolled disease has carved wrenching inroads into the ranks of our comrades, our lovers, our friends. And the connection between these two facts—the rise in social and political conservatism and the appearance of what has become known in the general public's mind as the *gay* disease, AIDS—has not been sufficiently scrutinized. But we certainly see their unholy wedding in the increase of sanctioned and self-righteous acts of heterosexism and homophobia, from queer-bashing in our streets to the legal invasion of our bedrooms. Should we miss these connections between racism and homophobia, we are also asked to believe that this monstrously convenient disease—and I use *convenient* here in the sense of *convenient for*

Talk delivered at the Hunter College Lesbian and Gay Community Center Forum on Lesbian and Gay Parents of Color *extermination*—originated spontaneously and mysteriously in Africa. Yet, for all the public hysteria surrounding AIDS, almost nothing is heard of the growing incidence of CAIDS—along the Mexican border, in the Near East and in the other areas of industrial imperialism. Chemically Acquired Immune Deficiency Syndrome is an industrial disease caused by prolonged exposure to trichloroethylene. TCE is a chemical in wholesale use in the electronic sweatshops of the world, where workers are primarily people of Color, in Malaysia, Sri Lanka, the Philippines, and Mexico.

It is a time when we, Lesbians and Gays of Color, cannot ignore our position as citizens of a country that stands on the wrong side of every liberation struggle on this globe; a country that publicly condones and connives with the most vicious and systematic program for genocide since Nazi Germany—apartheid South Africa.

How do we raise children to deal with these realities? For if we do not, we only disarm them, send them out into the jaws of the dragon unprepared. If we raise our children in the absence of an accurate picture of the world as we know it, then we blunt their most effective weapons for survival and growth, as well as their motivation for social change.

We are Gays and Lesbians of Color in a time when race-war is being fought in a small Idaho town, Coeur D'Alene. It is a time when the lynching of two Black people in California within twenty miles of each other is called nonracial and coincidental by the local media. One of the two victims was a Black Gay man, Timothy Lee; the other was a Black woman reporter investigating his death, Jacqueline Peters.

It is a time when local and national funds for day care and other programs which offer help to poor and working-class families are being cut, a time when even the definition of family is growing more and more restrictive.

But we are having babies! And I say, thank the goddess. As members of ethnic and racial communities historically under siege, every Gay and Lesbian of Color knows deep down inside that the question of children is not merely an academic one, nor do our children represent a theoretical hold upon some vague immortality. Our parents are examples of survival as a living pursuit, and no matter how different from them we may now find ourselves, we have built their example into our definitions of self—which is why we can be here tonight, naming ourselves. We know that all our work upon this planet is not going to be done in our lifetimes, and maybe not even in our children's lifetimes. But if we do what we came to do, our children will carry it on through their own living. And if we can keep this earth spinning and remain upon it long enough, the future belongs to us and our children because we are fashioning it with a vision rooted in human possibility and growth, a vision that does not shrivel before adversity.

There are those who say the urge to have children is a reaction to encroaching despair, a last desperate outcry before the leap into the void. I disagree. I believe that raising children is one way of participating in the future, in social change. On the other hand, it would be dangerous as well as sentimental to think that childrearing alone is enough to bring about a liveable future in the absence of any definition of that future. For unless we develop some cohesive vision of that world in which we hope these children will participate, and some sense of our own responsibilities in the shaping of that world, we will only raise new performers in the master's sorry drama.

So what does this all have to do with Lesbian parenting? Well, when I talk about mothering, I do so with an urgency born of my consciousness as a Lesbian and a Black African Caribbean american woman staked out in white racist sexist homophobic america.

I gave birth to two children. I have a daughter and a son. The memory of their childhood years, storms and all, remains a joy to me. Those years were the most chaotic as well as the most creative of my life. Raising two children together with my lover, Frances, balancing the intracacies of relationship within that four-person interracial family, taught me invaluable measurements for my self, my capacities, my real agendas. It gave me tangible and sometimes painful lessons about difference, about power, and about purpose.

We were a Black and a white Lesbian in our forties, raising two Black children. Making do was not going to be a safe way to live our lives, nor was pretense, nor euphemism. *Lesbian* is a name for women who love each other. *Black* means of African ancestry. Our lives would never be simple. We had to learn and to teach what works when we lived, always, with a cautionary awareness of the social forces aligned against us—at the same time there was laundry to be done, dental appointments to be kept, and no you can't watch cartoons because we think they rot your feelings and we pay the electricity.

I knew, for example, that the rage I felt and kept carefully under lock and key would one day be matched by a similar rage in my children: the rage of Black survival within the daily trivializations of white racism. I had to discover ways to own and use that rage if I was to teach them how to own and use theirs, so that we did not wind up torturing ourselves by turning our rage against each other. It was not restraint I had to learn, but ways to use my rage to fuel actions, actions that could alter the very circumstances of oppression feeding my rage.

Screaming at my daughter's childish banter instead of standing up to a racist bus driver was misplacing my anger, making her its innocent victim. Getting a migraine headache instead of injecting my Black woman's voice into the smug whiteness of a Women's Studies meeting was swallowing that anger, turning it against myself. Neither one of these actions offered solutions I wanted to give my children for dealing with relationships or racism. Learning to recognize and label my angers, and to put them where they belonged in some effective way, became crucial—not only for my own survival, but also for my children's. So that when I was justifiably angry with one of them—and no one short of sainthood can live around growing children and not get angry at one time or another—I could express the anger appropriate to the situation and not have that anger magnified and distorted by all my other unexpressed and unused furies. I was not always successful in achieving that distinction, but trying kept me conscious of the difference.

If I could not learn to handle my anger, how could I expect the children to learn to handle theirs in some constructive way—not deny it or hide it or self-destruct upon it? As a Black Lesbian mother I came to realize I could not afford the energy drains of denial and still be open to my own growth. And if we do not grow with our children, they cannot learn.

That was a long and sometimes arduous journey toward self-possession. And that journey was sweetened by an increasing ability to stretch far beyond what I had previously thought possible—in understanding, in seeing common events in a new perspective, in trusting my own perceptions. It was an exciting journey, sweetened also by the sounds of their laughter in the street and the endearing beauty of the bodies of children sleeping. My daughter and my son made issues of survival daily questions, the answers to which had to be scrutinized as well as practiced. And what our children learned about using their own power and difference within our family, I hope they will someday use to save the world. I can hope for no less. I know that I am constantly learning from them. Still.

Like getting used to looking up instead of down. How looking up all the time gives you a slight ache in the back of the neck. Jonathan, at seventeen, asking, "Hey Ma, how come you never hit us until we were bigger'n you?" At that moment realizing I guess I never hit my kids when they were little for the same reason my father never hit me: because we were afraid that our rage at the world in which we lived might leak out to contaminate and destroy someone we loved. But my father never learned to express his anger beyond imaginary conversations behind closed doors. Instead, he stoppered it, denying me his image, and he died of inchoate rage at fifty-one. My mother, on the other hand, would beat me until she wept from weariness. But it was not me, the overly rambunctious child, who sold her rotting food and spat upon her and her children in the street.

Frances and I wanted the children to know who we were and who they were, and that we were proud of them and of ourselves, and we hoped they would be proud of themselves and of us, too. But I remember Beth's fifteen-year-old angry coolness: "You think just because you're lesbians you're so different from the rest of them, but you're not, you're just like all the other parents. . . ." Then she launched into a fairly accurate record of our disciplines, our demands, our errors.

What I remember most of all now is that we were not just like all the other parents. Our family was not just like all the other families. That did not keep us from being a family any more than our being Lesbians kept Frances and me from being parents. But we did not have to be just like all the rest in order to be valid. We were an interracial Lesbian family with radical parents in the most conservative borough of New York City. Exploring the meaning of those differences kept us all stretching and learning, and we used that exploration to get us from Friday to Thursday, from toothache through homework to who was going to babysit when we both worked late and did Frances go to PTA meetings.

There are certain basic requirements of any child—food, clothing, shelter, love. So what makes our children different? We do. Gays and Lesbians of Color are different because we are embattled by reason of our sexuality and our Color, and if there is any lesson we must teach our children, it is that difference is a creative force for change, that survival and struggle for the future is not a theoretical issue. It is the very texture of our lives, just as revolution is the texture of the lives of the children who stuff their pockets with stones in Soweto and quickstep all the way to Johannesburg to fall in the streets from tear gas and rubber bullets in front of Anglo-American Corporation. Those children did not choose to die little heroes. They did not ask their mothers and fathers for permission to run in the streets and die. They do it because somewhere their parents gave them an example of what can be paid for survival, and these children carry on the same work by redefining their roles in an inhuman environment.

The children of Lesbians of Color did not choose their Color nor their mamas. But these are the facts of their lives, and the power as well as the peril of these realities must not be hidden from them as they seek self-definition.

And yes, sometimes our daughter and son did pay a price for our insisting upon the articulation of our differences—political, racial, sexual. That is difficult for me to say, because it hurts to raise your children knowing they may be sacrificed to your vision, your beliefs. But as children of Color, Lesbian parents or no, our children are programmed to be sacrifices to the vision of white racist profit-oriented sexist homophobic america, and that we cannot allow. So if we must raise our children to be warriors rather than cannon fodder, at least let us be very clear in what war we are fighting and what inevitable shape victory will wear. Then our children will choose their own battles.

Lesbians and Gays of Color and the children of Lesbians and Gays of Color are in the forefront of every struggle for human dignity in this country today, and that is not by accident. At the same time, we must remember when they are children that they are children, and need love, protection, and direction. From the beginning, Frances and I tried to teach the children that they each had a right to define herself and himself and to feel his own and her own feelings. They also had to take responsibility for the actions which arose out of those feelings. In order to do this teaching, we had to make sure that Beth and Jonathan had access to information from which to form those definitions—true information, no matter how uncomfortable it might be for us. We also had to provide them with sufficient space within which to feel anger, fear, rebellion, joy.

We were very lucky to have the love and support of other Lesbians, most of whom did not have children of their own, but who loved us and our son and daughter. That support was particularly important at those times when some apparently insurmountable breech left us feeling isolated and alone as Lesbian parents. Another source of support and connection came from other Black women who were raising children alone. Even so, there were times when it seemed to Frances and me that we would not survive neighborhood disapproval, a double case of chickenpox, or escalating teen-age rebellion. It is really scary when your children take what they have learned about self-assertion and nonviolent power and decide to test it in confrontations with you. But that is a necessary part of learning themselves, and the primary question is, have they learned to use it well?

Our daughter and son are in their twenties now. They are both warriors, and the battlefields shift: the war is the same. It stretches from the brothels of Southeast Asia to the blood-ridden alleys of Capetown to the incinerated Lesbian in Berlin to Michael Stewart's purloined eyes and grandmother Eleanor Bumpurs shot dead in the projects of New York. It stretches from the classroom where our daughter teaches Black and Latino third graders to chant, "I am somebody beautiful," to the college campus where our son replaced the Stars and Stripes with the flag of South Africa to protest his school's refusal to divest. They are in the process of choosing their own weapons, and no doubt some of those weapons will feel completely alien to me. Yet I trust them, deeply, because they were raised to be their own woman, their own man, in struggle, and in the service of all of our futures.

Lesbian Mothers:
A Lesbian-Feminist Perspective
On Research

Sandra Pollack

Many recent studies suggest that lesbian mothers are just like other mothers. While this might seem reassuring at first glance, such a conclusion is dangerous. It makes us once more invisible, and it obscures the radical alternative lesbian lives can model. Uncritical acceptance of such research also may lead us to the false conclusion that we will be accepted by the larger society because we have some of the same problems and concerns as other mothers. Research which focuses on the ways lesbians and their children resemble heterosexual mothers and their children may be important as part of courtroom strategy, but it negates the healthy and positive characteristics unique to lesbian parenting.

This paper will evaluate the direction of the growing body of research on lesbian mothers, assess its strengths, and identify some potential dangers it poses to lesbians and feminists.

The studies often start out with some variation of, "To many, being a lesbian and being a mother seem like contradictions." This recurring statement is important to remember since it is the common public assumption. Researchers who want to show that lesbian motherhood is not a contradiction often unconsciously validate this form of argument by replacing the assumption that "lesbians are not mothers" with the assumption that "lesbians are not different." This has led to the promotion of the belief that "we are all alike," i.e., just like straight mothers.

Early research on sexual practices, etiology, and "cures," combined with a view of sexual preference as immutable, defined the lesbian mother out of existence. Our lives were invisible. Before 1970, lesbian mothers were virtually invisible in the research on homosexuality, in the early research in Women's Studies, and in the literature on mothering.

In 1977 I was shocked into recognizing my own complicity in this process. A woman I worked with in organizing for the New York Women's Studies Association asked me incredulously, "You are a mother?" While I had been open about being a lesbian during the two years of our work together, I had never mentioned my children. Suddenly I became conscious of being a "closet mother." I asked others in the room whether they had children and discovered two other lesbian mothers. Why hadn't we spoken about our children and the ways we combine the various activities in our lives? I thought of all the years as a wife when mothering was all I was expected to talk about. In mixed social situations my conversations were almost always about "the children," and for many years I thought I had nothing else to discuss except my two daughters. Now it seemed I had unconsciously stopped talking about children. The time had come to acknowledge them—not as a way of claiming my identity and worth as before, but to better understand the impact of raising children as a lesbian in a patriarchal society.

The fact that we have been ignored in research, and that we, at times, have colluded in that invisibility, adds to the difficulty of knowing just how large the number of lesbian mothers really is. In spite of this, several researchers have estimated that ten to twenty percent of adult women are lesbians, and that twenty to thirty percent of lesbians are mothers, a total of three to four million lesbian mothers in the United States. Many might be more open if the legal system were not so weighted against them.[1] As economic heads of households, lesbian parents also often remain in the closet because they cannot afford to risk their jobs.

We begin to break that pattern of invisibility as we define ourselves. When we consciously claim the label of *lesbian* and of *parent*, we assume the power to decide what we want them to mean in our lives. This self-definition and empowerment should anchor future research and legal defense strategies.

The homophobia that pervades our society exhibits itself in a myriad of myths about lesbian parents—i.e., lesbians will molest children, the children will grow up to be homosexuals, lesbians will engage in sexual activity in front of their children, the children will develop psychological problems and be stigmatized and ridiculed by society. Nowhere does this homophobia allow for the recognition that lesbian parenting can be a healthy, wholesome experience for adults and children.

Lesbian Mothers And The Law

One of the most publicized lesbian mother custody battles was that of Mary Jo Risher. The 1975 case was covered by the mass media and turned into a prime-time television movie. In a comprehensive summary of this case, Lindsay Van Gelder showed that public sympathy was aroused (perhaps for the first time) when people saw how a thirty-nine-year-old Texas mother lost custody of her nine-year-old son, despite the fact that she was a college graduate, nurse, a former Baptist Sunday school teacher, a PTA President, and a Chaplain of the Order of the Eastern Star who had been living for the past three years in a stable commited relationship with her lover.[2]

Feminist and civil rights groups rallied behind what seemed like the ideal case. Both women had good jobs; they were solid members of their community. There was no question of alcoholism or drugs. They didn't go to the bars. They saw themselves as a family with two adults and three children (two boys from Mary Jo's previous marriage and one daughter from her lover Ann's previous marriage). They were each other's insurance beneficiaries, had joint checking accounts, co-owned property. The life Mary Jo and Ann lived was "straight" in most ways except that they were two women loving each other. According to several psychologists, Mary Jo's son had an "exceptionally loving, stable family life." However, as one juror said, "We are taking him out of a good home to put him in a better one."[3]

Remarried Douglas Risher now had a new baby and a "full-time" wife to stay home with the children. One of Doug Risher's witnesses was a social worker who felt that nine-year-old Richard would be better off in a home "where the mother didn't work." Douglas and his wife could provide the proper father and mother image. This image was more important than the fact that Douglas Risher had a record of drunk driving, had broken Mary Jo's nose, had been accused of getting a nineteen-year-old woman pregnant, and had paid for her abortion. The older son, Jimmy, rewarded with a new car from his father, testified he was ashamed of his mother's lesbianism and wanted to spare his younger brother that embarrassment. This embarrassment was not evident in Richard's statement, which was that he wanted to stay with the two women.[4]

The mass media coverage of this case may have caused some people to feel sorry for Mary Jo when she was ordered to give up her son on Christmas morning, but it barely began to challenge the assumption that the straight nuclear family is best. The question was never whether or not Mary Jo was a good mother; Mary Jo as a *lesbian* mother was on trial.

The Risher case is an important example of the futility of seeking safety in the argument that we are "all really the same"—that lesbian mothers and straight mothers are not so different after all. Even when our lives are superficially similar, the threat we present to patriarchal institutions is undiminished.

Lesbian mothers have always raised children in our society, but this fact has only recently come to the attention of the courts. With the consciousness stimulated by the women's liberation and gay liberation movements, more and more women are insisting on their right to be what they are: lesbians *and* mothers.

While there have been some lesbian mother court victories,[5] the overwhelming fear among lesbian mothers is that they will lose their children. That fear is based on reality. In a contested custody case, the courts will, in most instances, believe the mother is an unfit parent because she is a lesbian. Going to court is also an enormous psychological, emotional, and financial drain. An average contested case costs $10,000, and can cost as much as $50,000.⁶ And custody cases can always be reopened. The homophobic nature of the courts is shown in the child custody orders which grant the homosexual parent custody but include provisions that she is not permitted to live with a lover.⁷ One can never really feel safe as a lesbian mother.

Judges at times exhibit a voyeurism that belies their claim to objectivity. Such an attitude was evidenced in my own protracted custody case when my ex-husband's lawyer was describing a visit his client made to my house when my lover had been visiting me for the weekend. As the lawyer was reciting the events, the judge burst out with, "Where were they (the adult women) and what were they wearing?" What assumptions did this judge have about homosexuals? Was he assuming we were probably in bed or parading around naked? Would he ask those questions about a heterosexual man or woman? To have to explain that we were sitting in the living room wearing ordinary clothing, that my daughters and my lover's daughter were watching TV, was an insult to our dignity. Yet lesbian mothers are frequently abused in this way. For too many people, the word *lesbian* or *homosexual* only conjures up images of sex.

In the words of another judge, "Ma'am, will you explain to the Court exactly what occurs—we talk here generally of a homosexual act. Just what does this entail? What do you do?" And again later, the same judge asked if there was "any potential that the lesbian mother might 'use' her child in sexual activity."⁸

Given the realities that many lesbian mother custody cases are lost, that the legal system is homophobic, and that court battles are long and expensive, the focus on research that will help the lesbian parent in court is understandable. This research has thus been largely a reaction—an attempt to answer the fears and myths perpetuated by the very homophobic society we must now try to convince.

The fact that a mother is a lesbian is often so startling and offensive to a judge's value system that once this issue is brought into the case, it is omnipresent in the judge's mind. Hitchens and Price argue that this problem should be dealt with directly by the mother's attorney, who should know the prejudices to be countered and the evidence to be used. The custody outcome, they state, depends more on the beliefs and attitudes of the judge about homosexuality than on the specific facts of the case. Court transcripts reveal three erroneous assumptions commonly held by judges and mental health professionals called in to testify.⁹

The first has to do with the sexual behavior of lesbians. Lesbians are assumed to be promiscuous, liable to sexually harm the children, and sexually maladjusted. Allowing the mother to be both with her lover and her children would result, therefore, in undesirable sexual behavior. The myth that lesbians molest their children needs to be countered by expert witnesses who can show that incest or child molestation within the family primarily involves fathers and/or stepfathers and their daughters.

The second wrong assumption is that children of gay parents will grow up to be gay or will have confused sex-role identification. The courts need to be educated on the sex-role development of children and on how social values are learned in this society. Hitchens and Price suggest bringing in witnesses to discuss research on the origins of homosexuality, none of which has indicated any specific causative factor. All research also points out that most lesbians had heterosexual parents.

The third mistaken assumption is that the child could be socially stigmatized and seriously harmed if the mother's lesbianism is widely known. If this is true, it is certainly an example of blaming the victim for the society's ills. The belief that the children will be socially damaged should be countered by showing that, like children of a different race or religion from others in the neighborhood, the child raised in a lesbian home can, in fact, gain inner strength from this experience.

Expert testimony directed at countering these myths rather than focusing only on the general stability of the mother and the mother's parenting ability appears to be essential.

Comparison Studies: Are We All Alike?

Most studies comparing lesbian and straight families have shown few differences. This simply means that according to these researchers, neither lesbians nor their children have pathological problems that are very different from those of heterosexual single mothers.[10] My concern centers on the underlying assumption that the lesbian mother should be judged on how well she compares to the heterosexual norm.

Demonstrating that we are the "same" may be useful as a legal strategy, but these comparison studies often overlook serious questions, and therefore, present skewed results. For example, to study the ways lesbians and straight mothers rely on relationships with kin, particularly in child care and holiday celebrations, one must also ask questions related to the realities of lesbian life. Do lesbians go home for the holidays alone or with their lovers? Are children free to talk about the women in their mother's life when they are with relatives? What is the relationship between disclosure and employment for lesbian parents?

While the daily lives of both groups of mothers have many similarities, the specifics of the household must be examined to really find out about raising a child in this setting. Are lesbian posters, books, and records around as freely as heterosexual materials would be? Can lesbian conversations take place as freely as heterosexual conversations? Probing these areas will uncover differences that mark lesbian lives more deeply than questions about whom they can turn to for child care, or how to cope with the low salaries all women receive, or the fact that few women get adequate financial support from ex-husbands.

We also need research which looks at court-order decisions and the ways disclosure affects our relationships, our living, and our employment situations. There is clearly a difference in the way lesbian and heterosexual women take charge of and plan for their futures—be it in home ownership, self-employment, or life-long planning.[11]

So, too, when we show lesbian and straight mothers functioning as caregivers, the myth that heterosexual mothers are more child-oriented than lesbian mothers comes under serious challenge.[12] These differences, rather than the similarities, must be emphasized both in court and in the larger world to show the benefits of lesbian parenting and to reinforce a positive self-image among lesbian mothers.

Sex Roles Of Children

A number of the comparison studies focus on the sex roles of children. Again, my reservation is the underlying assumption that there are appropriate sex roles for boys and girls. What these studies really examine is whether the children conform to acceptable societal norms. Yet this very assumption of appropriate roles is what feminists are committed to eliminating. The consequences of not conforming weigh heavily, however.

In the Mary Jo Risher case, much was made of the apparent heterosexual orientation of the children. Ann's daughter, Judie Ann, was described as an "especially pretty child, very charming (who) espouses a traditional feminine role." Mary Jo's son, Richard, said he wanted to be a policeman. Despite all this backward bending, even the slightest deviations were seized upon. Apparently Mary Jo allowed Richard to appear at the psychologist's office "wearing unsuitable clothing"—a YWCA T-shirt and a jacket that belonged to Judie Ann. Upon cross-examination, the psychologist acknowledged that since Richard was taking a gym course at the Y, the shirt was hardly high drag.[13] No matter, Mary Jo was a lesbian and therefore should be more sensitive to Richard's appearance.

Researchers often feel it necessary to show that the children are "all right," that they are not contaminated by lesbianism, and that they will grow up to be "proper boys and girls." Kirkpatrick tested children (ages five to twelve) and concluded that the gender development of the children of heterosexual and homosexual mothers was not identifiably different.[14] While we might use these studies as a courtroom tactic because the children "do just fine," we must remain aware of the acceptance of sex-role stereotyping on which such an argument is based.

Our strategies would be very different if we chose to emphasize the value of the independent model provided by lesbians.[15] Dorothy Riddle says it strongly: "Rather than posing a menace to children, gays may actually facilitate important developmental learning. . .children have the possibility of learning that it is possible to resist traditional sex-role socialization. . . . Children become exposed to the concept of cultural and individual diversity as positive rather than threatening."[16]

Having gays as open role models for children is beneficial to the children, to the breakdown of sexism and sex-role stereotyping, and to the elimination of negative societal attitudes towards homosexuality. Fear of homosexuality is most strongly correlated with a commitment to traditional sex roles and traditional attitudes toward women.[17]

Studies that look at the actual lives of the children of lesbians may be more useful than those focusing on sex-role identities. Karen Gail Lewis encouraged children of lesbians to talk about how their mother's lifestyles have influenced their lives. She identified three areas that caused the children concern: (1) disclosure—the way the mother's sexual identity is revealed is often overlaid with secrecy, half-truths, ambiguity, and avoidance; (2) the lack of support systems for the children—there is a need for peer groups to gain support, security, and to demystify the "secret"; and (3) denial of ambivalence toward the mother—children need to be provided with ways to explore feelings of anger, hurt, and grief. Lewis concludes that "the children do want to be accepting of their mother's lifestyles, and. . .the gay community and the therapeutic community owe it to the children to provide the opportunity for them to work towards a realistic assessment and acceptance of their feelings."[18]

Lewis raises an important point rarely addressed by the research: the possible benefits of being a child of a lesbian mother. The children of lesbians may become aware (perhaps more so than other children) of their responsibility for themselves and their own choices. What counts, according to Lewis, is not the sexual preference of the adults, but their love, concern, responsibility, and maturity in helping their children become self-reliant and self-assured. This message should be repeated frequently in the courts.

We should be seeking ways to redirect the research so that our objective is not simply to prove the homogeneity of lesbian and straight parents (and their children), but to illustrate the advantages of lesbian parenting in ways that can be used successfully in the courts. We need to convince the courts that the child's interests are often best served by living with a lesbian parent who can be open rather than leading a double and secret life.

We must also make the courts realize that concern over the absence of a male model is a bogus issue. The problem often is not the lack of a male presence, but the lack of a male income. A lesbian parent who can live openly, and who can share income and household expenses with other women, has a better chance of maintaining a standard of living that is beneficial for the child.

Directions for new research are indicated by the questions asked at lesbian parent workshops. Women say they want a stop to the neutralizing of their lives. They want to portray the positive aspects and specialness. They want research on the relationship of adolescents to lesbian mothers, as there is little in the adolescent literature that pertains to them. They are concerned with the role of coparents and with how to provide their children with skills to counter homophobia. They want help in developing groups for children. They want to know how to get support for lesbians choosing to have children via artificial insemination and how to better validate lesbians who do not live with their children. They want to find ways to recognize second-generation lesbians and gay men, individuals whose lives are often kept invisible because their existence feeds into the homophobic fear that children will turn out gay.

These concerns raised by lesbians indicate we are at a crossroads. It is within our grasp to redirect and refocus the research to more truly reflect the empowering directions of our lives as lesbian parents.

Notes

1. For various estimates of numbers see Nan Hunter and Nancy Polikoff, "Custody Rights of Lesbian Mothers: Legal Theory and Litigation Strategy." Vol 25, *Buffalo Law Review* (1976), p. 691: Del Martin and Phylis Lyon, *Lesbian/Woman* (New York: Bantam, 1972); and "The Avowed Lesbian Mother and Her Right to Child Custody," 12 *San Diego Law Review* 799 (1975).

2. Lindsay Van Gelder, "Lesbian Custody: A Tragic Day in Court," *MS.*, Sept. 1976, pp. 72-3.

3. Ibid., p. 72.

4. Ibid., p. 73.

5. See Armanini v. Armanini, 5 Family L. Rptr. 2501 (N.Y. Sup. Ct. 1979); Medeiros v. Medeiros, 8 Family L. Rptr. 2372 (Vt. Super. Ct. 1982); Miller v. Miller, 405 Mich. Rptr. 809 (1979); Schuster v. Schuster and Isaacson v. Isaacson, 585 P. 2d 130 (Wash. Sup. Ct. 1978) as reported in Basile, *Women's Rights Law Reporter*, 1974.

6. "Lesbian Mothers Fight Back," *Quest*, Vol. 5, No. 1 (Summer 1979), p. 64.

7. R.A. Basile, "Lesbian Mothers," *Women's Rights Law Reporter*, Vol. 2, No. 2 (Dec. 1974), p. 3.

8. Donna Hitchens and Barbara Price, "Trial Strategy in Lesbian Mother Custody Cases: The Use of Expert Testimony," 9 *Golden Gate Univ. Law Review* (1978-9), p. 453.

9. Ibid., p. 451.

10. For comparison studies see Golombok, Spencer, and Rutter, "Children in Lesbian Single Parent Households: Psychosexual and Psychiatric Appraisal," *Journal of Child Psychology*

and Allied Disciplines, Vol. 24, No. 4 (Oct. 1983), pp. 551-572; Ellen Lewin and Terrie A. Lyons, "Everything in Its Place: The Co-Existence of Lesbianism and Motherhood," in *Homosexuality*, William Paul et. al. (Beverly Hills: Sage Publications, 1982), p. 250; Kirkpatrick, Smith, and Roy, "Lesbian Mothers and their Children: A Comparative Study," *Journal of Orthopsychiatry*, Vol. 51 (1981), pp. 545-551.

11. See for example Mildred Pagelow, "Heterosexual and Lesbian Single Mothers: A Comparison of Problems, Coping, and Solutions," *Journal of Homosexuality*, Vol. 5, No. 3 (1980), pp. 189-203.

12. Judith Ann Miller, R. Brooke Jacobson, and Harry J. Bigner, "The Child's Home Environment for Lesbian vs. Heterosexual Mothers: A Neglected Area of Research," *Journal of Homosexuality*, Vol. 7, No. 1 (1981), pp. 49-56.

13. Van Gelder, p. 73.

14. Kirkpatrick.

15. See for example Berzins, Willing, and Wetter, "A New Measure of Psychological Androgyny" (1978); J. H. Hopkins, "The Lesbian Personality" (1969) as quoted in Riddle, "Relating to Children: Gays as Role Models," Vol. 34, No. 3, *Journal of Social Issues* (1978), pp. 39-50.

16. Riddle, p. 53.

17. See for example A. P. MacDonald, "Homophobia: Its Roots and Meanings," (1976), C. L. Montgomery and Burgoon, "An Experimental Study of the Interactive Effects of Sex and Androgyny on Attitude Change," (1977) as quoted in Riddle.

18. Karen Gail Lewis, "Children of Lesbians: Their Point of View," *Social Work* (May 1980) pp. 198-203.

Lesbian Mothers, Lesbian Families: Legal Obstacles, Legal Challenges
Nancy D. Polikoff

This coming week, two women in San Francisco will enter a courtroom as open lesbians and ask a judge to grant their petition to adopt a child together.[1] The California Department of Social Services has already recommended the adoption be granted. The proposed new birth certificate submitted by the Department of Social Services has *mother* and *father* crossed out and instead reads *parent one* and *parent two*. For the first time, a court may confer upon a lesbian couple the legal status of joint motherhood.[2]

I would like to use the occasion of this historic event to reflect on several separate but related issues relevant to lesbian and gay parents, our legal advocates, and the larger community of which we are a part. I am still in the process of developing and refining my ideas on these topics. I share them with you in this unfinished form.

The legal system is not friendly to lesbians and gay men. We have lost more battles in the courts than we have won, and things are likely to get worse, not better.[3] While no formula will guarantee victory in courtroom custody disputes involving lesbian mothers or gay fathers, one thing is clear: the more we appear to be part of the mainstream, with midle-class values, middle-of-the-road political beliefs, repressed sexuality, and sex-role stereotyped behavior, the more likely we are to keep custody of our children. On the other hand, communal childrearing arrangements, radical feminist activism, sexual experimentation—these choices are all predictably fatal to any custody action. The courtroom is no place in which to affirm our pride in our lesbian sexuality, or to advocate alternative childrearing designed to produce strong, independent women.

A lesbian mother must portray herself as being as close to the All-American norm as possible—the spitting image of her ideal heterosexual counterpart—and preferably asexual. Only then does she stand a chance of retaining custody. The necessity of assuming a role that contradicts her identity has important consequences, both for the lesbian mother and for her lawyer.

The toll on the client is obviously enormous. She is forced to deny any price in her lesbianism, any solidarity with other lesbians; she may even be compelled to deny or alter her sexual relationships. There is no guarantee that, at the end of this ordeal, she will be allowed to keep her children.

The complicity of lesbian and gay lawyers in this system has its own effects. When we construct courtroom scenarios that deny our differences from heterosexual society, we quickly forget that our strength and our promise are rooted in those very differences. For example, a study comparing heterosexual and lesbian mothers concluded that the two groups have similar sex-role behavior and attitudes toward ideal child behavior.[4] My immediate response as a lawyer was to be elated—one more piece of evidence to help convince a judge that our clients are not really "different" kinds of mothers at all.

But as a lesbian, a feminist, and a mother with a vision of an entirely different way of raising our children, I was horrified. I am not pleased to discover that my lesbian sisters pose no threat to the perpetuation of patriarchal childrearing. As a lawyer, I worry that my role within the system of adjudicating custody rights has a conservatizing effect on all gay and lesbian people. It is hard to maintain a clear vision of lesbian/gay/feminist/socialist/antiracist social change while constantly asserting an image as mainstream as possible of the life of a lesbian mother and her children in the courtroom. Similarly, it is hard to be committed to the development of sexual diversity while adopting the courtroom strategy, effective when custody of older children is at stake, of offering scientific proof that sexual orientation is immutably determined by the age of five.

As lawyers we must respond to this predicament. I suggest two possibilities. First, we can support our clients' most progressive political awareness even as we build an acceptable courtroom demeanor. Our clients should clearly see that it is not we who make unreasonable and repressive demands of them, and that we, too, are actors playing a role.

Second, we attorneys need to develop and strengthen a radical vision that will not be extinguished in the painful process of negotiating through a hostile system. Perhaps we should consider taking affirmative steps in some arena other than lesbian mother litigation. We certainly must recognize that assessing the political value of lesbian mother litigation is a complex matter. It is wrong for society to deny lesbian mothers their children, and it is right to oppose that effect of homophobia. But when we constantly assert in the public arena that we will raise our children to be heterosexual, and that we will protect them from manifestations of our sexuality and from the larger lesbian and gay community, we lose something that affects all lesbians and gay men. We essentially concede it is preferable to be heterosexual, thereby foreclosing an assertion of pride and of the positive value in homosexuality.

A lesbian mother emerging from a heterosexual relationship and facing a custody dispute is in a *defensive* posture. I contrast this with lesbians choosing to have children in lesbian families. This is an *offensive* step. It opens the possibility of affirmation, rather than denial, of our differences from the heterosexual norm. However, it brings its own legal and political risks. For the past year and a half, I have been talking and writing about the political significance of lesbians choosing to have children. My questions about lesbian motherhood are intended to expose any potentially negative political effects of this choice of lifestyle. I have criticized the perspective suggesting that the choices involved are purely personal,[5] and the failure of many to place lesbians choosing motherhood in the context of a fiercely pronatalist period.[6] I have asked whether we—including myself—have chosen to have children as a retreat from the political to the personal, from the public to the private; whether having children reflects a desire to fit into mainstream society, arising after personal traumas and political differences shattered naive beliefs in building the lesbian alternative community.[7] I have defended, and encouraged other mothers to defend, the right and the value of lesbians choosing *not* to have children and choosing *not* to fight for custody of children born of heterosexual marriages.[8] I have urged lesbian mothers not to see themselves as having more in common with heterosexual mothers than they have with lesbians who have no children.[9] I have also urged them to resist, in every conceivable forum, the presumption of heterosexuality that attaches to motherhood. I have asked others to examine, as I continue to examine, how the institution of motherhood functions to maintain and promote patriarchy. I have argued that our lesbianism, by itself, does not negate or transform that institution.[10]

I believe that all these points are still valid and will bear repetition and refinement. But having made them, I will move on to examine the positive political value of lesbians choosing motherhood, and the challenge to lesbian and gay lawyers of fitting our families within the existing legal system.

I began this presentation by talking about a lesbian couple gaining legal recognition as comothers. Despite their success, legal recognition of our families will remain the exception rather than the rule. Therefore, I would like to discuss briefly the legal status of most lesbians raising children together.

The system confers great power on the legal mother, whether biological or adoptive. Her lover, regardless of her role within the family, can be easily disenfranchised. Lawyers serving lesbian and gay clients can expect to face requests for representation when these comothering relationships dissolve. To protect the status and interests of the unrecognized mother, we should consider both litigation and legislative strategies.

We must remember that out efforts are not made in a vacuum, but rather in the context of the developing law of custodial rights. For example, as we think about obtaining legal rights for unrecognized lesbian mothers, it is tempting to argue for expanded rights for nonparents. However, we must bear in mind that if we ask judges to stretch case law and statutes to reach such a result, those very interpretations may be used against lesbians and political or nontraditional heterosexual women in other cases.

Already, under current law, many nonparents—usually grandparents—have successfully obtained custody from lesbian mothers.[11] Under the prevailing "best interest of the child" standard, nonparents have an easier time obtaining custody than they would under a standard reflecting strong parental preference. Advocates for lesbian mothers in custody disputes have long recognized the importance of a strong preference for parents over nonparents. Such a standard would require clear and convincing evidence that the parent is unfit before a nonparent could be awarded custody.

The theory of psychological parenthood[12] may be useful in assessing which of two parents with equal legal rights should get custody. However, the same theory has been used against mothers, mostly poor ones, who require the extensive assistance of relatives, friends, or even babysitters, and who subsequently lose custody to someone who is designated the "psychological parent."[13] Extending the theory increases the likelihood that a lesbian mother will lose custody of her children. The potential for misuse is frightening.

How do we fit our families into an alien legal framework structured to preserve and perpetuate patriarchy? In the present system, known sperm donors who originally intend to remain unidentified and uninvolved can later change their minds and gain full parental rights.[14] A minimally involved father of a child raised by a lesbian couple will almost certainly obtain custody if the legal mother dies. Under the law, after all, he is the sole surviving parent.

The answer—simpler to describe than to realize—lies in the recognition of legal parenthood for both mothers. The adoption laws of some states may be interpreted to permit adoption without automatically extinguishing the biological mother's rights.[15] In those states, before sympathetic judges, there may be room to take the offensive and gain this legal recognition. In most states, legislative change will be the only recourse, an unlikely occurrence at present. But perhaps we need to put it on our public agenda now, and dig in for a struggle that may extend beyond our lifetimes.

It is not only because I believe both mothers should have equal rights upon the dissolution of their relationship that I consider legal recognition important. I am also profoundly concerned with issues of power within our relationships and in the transmission of values to our children.

Fundamental to lesbian/gay relationships is a potential equalization of power more difficult to achieve in a heterosexual context. Numerous factors come into play in any specific relationship, including class of origin, race, financial or vocational differences, and the internal dynamics of roles, expectations, sexual fantasy, and sexual practice. In this context, we do not know whether the different legal status which each woman has in relation to the child in a lesbian family has significant ramifications. It would be highly unusual to find a biological mother willing to relinquish all her legal parental rights so that her lover could adopt their child. To me, this predictable reluctance is a clue that legal status means something to the couple and does affect their relationship.

We know that children are sensitive to emotional undercurrents and non-verbal communications in their environments. If the difference in legal status affects the adults, it may affect the child as well. This phenomenon is significant because the emergence of lesbian families provides a unique opportunity in history to raise children in a home with two parents of potentially equal power. The opportunity to grow up observing such equality in the home could have a lasting impact on children in lesbian families, and we need to embrace that possibility. If legal inequality diminishes or eliminates the experience of equal power within the home, we are missing the chance to make what might be our biggest contribution to future generations.

I believe, therefore, that the equal rights approach is essential because of its impact on both the adult relationship and the children. However, it is far from a perfect solution. What happens if two legally equal mothers split up? Conflicts will probably be resolved in our court system according to the cardinal unwritten principle governing custody disputes between lesbian mothers and straight fathers: that mainstream, conventional, nonthreatening values are more likely to prevail. The political activist, the outspoken sexual outlaw, the proud lesbian, and the butch will all lose. The mother who goes straight will win. And the parent with access to more money may exploit that fact to the fullest. The concept of equal rights, without control over its application, is form without substance.

I am now watching close friends who have raised a child together for more than three years begin to break up. I am worried about the extent to which the legally recognized mother will respect the relationship between her ex-lover and the child. In private conversations I have been extolling the equal rights theory, even though it is not, of course, a legal reality. Recently, as I privately defended the right of the mother with no legal access to frequent overnight visitation, someone asked how I would feel if this comother went straight and exposed the child to her heterosexual relationship. I was taken aback. Surely it is a destructive and offensive message to a child raised in a lesbian relationship if one mother later rejects lesbianism. I would rather not have this child, or any of our children, exposed to such a phenomenon.

The person suggesting this hypothetical then stated she would be happy if the legal mother had the right to curtail visitation under those circumstances. I countered by saying that if the legal mother could not be stopped from exposing the child to heterosexuality or any other adverse influence, then the other mother had to have the same rights. Better to save some of the children, and equal rights be damned, was the reply I received.

It may be the lawyer in me that clings so tenaciously to equal rights theory, in spite of its shortcomings as applied. More likely, it is my concern for equal power within our ongoing relationships that compels me to fight for legal recognition of our families.

The strength and value to all lesbians of some lesbians choosing to have children is that we mothers are pushed to be out to the world, that we challenge at home and in public the transmission of patriarchal values, and that we offer the opportunity to explore the significance of equal power between two mothers. In our time, we may be able to offer our children significantly different models from those that are patriarchal, because we can build a community of lesbian families that will include substantial numbers of women who have chosen motherhood outside the context of heterosexuality. Realization of this potential depends on our resistance to the pressure to blend our families and our community into mainstream heterosexual society. We must evaluate the role of the legal definition of *family* in furthering or undermining our goals.

I would like to close by discussing the impact the AIDS crisis has on lesbians and lesbian mothers. I have come to appreciate the extent to which AIDS is a lesbian issue in the context of lesbian mother custody disputes. I offer two stories. Last year I happened to be speaking to a West Virginia Supreme Court Justice. In West Virginia, the primary caretaker parent within a marriage is entitled to custody upon divorce unless proven unfit.[16] I asked the Justice whether a lesbian mother would be considered unfit under his state's standard. His first response was: "We don't have much of that around here." His second statement was: "We have to rethink our opinions on that since the coming of AIDS."

In a second instance, a custodial father refused to permit the noncustodial lesbian mother to exercise Christmas visitation with her son, as she had done for over ten years. He gave as his reason the fear that the boy would contract AIDS. Although the case was ultimately settled without a court hearing, the mother was forced to retain an attorney and convince the father's attorney that his position was not supportable.[17]

As these stories demonstrate, homophobia generated by the AIDS crisis strikes lesbians as well as gay men. But lesbians are affected in other ways as well. Never has gay male sexuality been so visible in mainstream culture. Reference to gay men and AIDS in the media is an almost daily occurrence. This new prominence for male homosexuality means that only lesbian sexuality remains in the closet. We are *less* visible than ever, except as targets of homophobia, now that our gay brothers are attracting so much attention.

If this invisibility contributes to the decision of many lesbians to work on AIDS-related issues, it has ironic consequences: lesbians are no more recognized as AIDS workers than we are in the mainstream. Further, we must not let our desire to make our sexuality visible lead us to focus on finding a lesbian mode of AIDS transmission, or on encouraging HIV testing[18] of lesbians. AIDS is relevant to lesbians, but it does not raise precisely the same issues for us as it does for gay men. We should fight the homophobia that AIDS engenders, and we have a right to be recognized for our work. But we also need to affirm our sexuality outside the context of the AIDS crisis.

In this time of increased repression, when the opposition finds AIDS a ready excuse and when we are so frequently on the defensive, it is imperative to the lifeline of our community that we seek positive measures to strengthen our culture. Forthright discussion and analysis of our sexuality, along the lines of the work of Carole Vance[19] and others, is one such measure. Politically conscious lesbian families is another.

Notes

1. This presentation was delivered on February 22, 1986.

2. The joint adoption was granted. In re N.L.D. and D.J.H., No. 17945, slip op. (Cal. Super. Ct. Feb. 24, 1986). Information on other cases involving adoption by the two same sex parents is available from the Lesbian Rights Project, 1370 Mission Street, 4th Floor, San Francisco, CA 94103.

3. For a review of appelate case law, see Sheppard, "Lesbian Mothers II: Long Night's Journey Into Day," Vol. 8, *Women's Rts. L. Rep.* (1985), p. 219. See also Bowers v. Hardwick, 106 S. Ct. 2841 (1986).

4. S. Kweskin and A. Cook, "Heterosexual and Homosexual Mothers' Self-described Sex-role Behavior and Ideal and Sex-role Behavior in Children," Vol. 8, *Sex Roles* (1982), p. 967.

5. N. Polikoff, "Lesbians Choosing Children: The Personal Is Political Revisited," in *Politics of the Heart: A Lesbian Parenting Anthology.*

6. I use the term pronatalism to characterize a system of beliefs which explicitly values childbearing and simultaneously devalues and discourages the option of not bearing children. Reflections of contemporary pronatalism include the hostility to abortion and the recurring media depictions of successful working women who become mothers in their thirties and then explicitly or implicitly reject the value of their previous accomplishments.

7. Polikoff.

8. Ibid.

9. Ibid.

10. Ibid.

11. N. Hunter and N. Polikoff, "Custody Rights of Lesbian Mothers: Legal Theory and Litigation Strategy," Vol. 25, *Buffalo L. Rev.* (1976), pp. 691, 705-11.

12. J. Goldstein, A. Freud, and A. J. Solnit, *Beyond The Best Interest Of The Child* (1979). The authors define a psychological parent as "one who, on a continuing, day to day basis, through interaction, companionship, interplay, and mutuality, fulfills the child's psychological needs for a parent, as well as the child's physical needs. The psychological parent may be a biological, adoptive, foster, or common-law parent, or any person." p. 98.

13. See generally Martin v. Sand, 8 Fam. L. Rep. (BNA) 2272 (Del. Fam. Ct. Feb. 22, 1982) (homemaker assigned to help family after mother suffered injuries in car accident began keeping child with her and was later awarded custody as psychological parent); Painter v. Bannister, 258 Iowa 1390, 140 N.W. 2d 152, 158 (1966) (father who sent son temporarily to his

maternal grandparents after the mother's death lost custody to the grandparents); Mansukhani v. Pailing, 318 N.W. 2d 748, 753 (N.D. 1982) (mother who intended to take children back after finding a job lost custody to grandparents).

14. Jhordan C. v. Mary K., 12 Fam. L. Rep. (BNA) 1330 (Cal. Ct. App. 1986).

15. See, e.g., In re A.D.L., No. 1 JU-85-25 P/A, slip op. (1st Jud. Dis. Alaska Aug. 9, 1985) (copy in possession of the author). Adoption statutes customarily envision two sets of circumstances in which adoptions may take place. In the first, where one biological parent has died or consented to the adoption, a stepparent may adopt the child when he or she marries the other biological parent. In this situation, the stepparent simply acquires the legal status of the absent parent. Lesbians cannot legally marry, and thus cannot take advantage of the statutory provision for stepparent adoption. In the second situation, a child can become part of a new family; adoption extinguishes the rights of the biological parents, in order to protect the stability of the new family unit. The language of these statutes is mandatory. See D.C. Code s+ 16-312(a) (Michie 1981) ("All rights and duties. . .between the adoptee, his natural parents, their issue, collateral relatives, and so forth, are cut off, except that when one of the natural parents is the spouse of the adoptor, the rights and relations as between adoptee, that natural parent, and his parents and collateral relatives. . .are in no wise altered."). To accomplish an adoption whereby a lesbian partner became a second mother, the court would have to waive the operation of the statute. The court in A.D.L. accepted such an argument.

16. Garska v. McCoy, 278 S.E. 2d 357 (W.Va. 1981).

17. Telephone conversation with the mother.

18. The test which is currently available determines whether there are antibodies to the virus associated with AIDS in the blood. It is therefore an appropriate device for blood screening. However, a positive test result does not predict whether the individual will ever become sick. Selvyn, "AIDS: What Is Now Known," *Hospital Practices*, May 15, 1986, pp. 67-8.

19. C. Vance, *Pleasure and Danger* (1984).

To Live Outside The Law
You Must Be Honest:
A Flommy Looks At Lesbian Parenting
Jan Clausen

When it comes to parenting, I consider myself a hopeless amateur, a fact that's made me hesitate a good deal in thinking about what to say here today, even though I'm excited and pleased to have the chance to put together some of the scattered thoughts about lesbian parenting which have occurred to me over the years. My primary self-chosen identity is that of a writer, an identity that has frequently conflicted with the demands of childrearing. *Writer* is something I think I'm really good at, at least part of the time, whereas *parent* is something I think I do O.K.

And yet: I'm a writer who, much to her own surprise, has often been drawn to use fiction as a way of exploring some of what goes on between lesbian parents and their children. I've also been, for more than ten years now, a live in, "nonbiological" parent, or coparent (in our household we like to use the word *flommy* instead, since it makes me sound less like I'm made out of Teflon). I have shared daily life with my lover's daughter, have fought with her, laughed with her, traveled with her, worried about her after-school whereabouts and her migraine headaches and her TV and sugar consumption, attended karate demonstrations and open school nights and swim meets. I've watched her grow from a scrawny, barely articulate preschooler into a poised high school sophomore who towers over me—and if only she had *my* genes, I joke, her size would be more appropriate.

For me, being a parent has had more positives than negatives. It helps that I really *like* this child I'm raising—which I consider to be largely a matter of good fortune, since at bottom I'm pessimistic about exactly how much control parents have over how their kids turn out. As the years have gone by, I've come to feel much more secure in my role as this weird, socially

---

Keynote delivered at "Mother's Courage: Lesbians Creating a Parenting Community," Albany, New York, April 5, 1986.

invisible person, a flommy; much more at home in the solidity of Anna's and my ongoing, daily connection to one another—a history that no law court, no "natural" father, and no context of conventional public assumptions about the sanctity of blood ties could now erase. My lover and I and our child, all three of us, have somehow made our chosen family work. It provides us with emotional and material supports that are sometimes strikingly different from, sometimes frankly reminiscent of, the supports to be found in other types of families.

And yet my enormous ambivalence about parenthood—about the role of *mother*, no matter what name it wears—has never gone away. Every time I think I've resolved "all that" (after all, I've helped raise one child nearly to adulthood, and I'm quite clear in my mind that I don't want to have a baby or take such major responsibility for a young child again), some situation arises which shows me just how complicated my feelings still are. *Other* women, I tend to assume, are sure of what they're doing—especially those who are just now becoming parents. *I'm* the only one who doesn't have it all together. (Last week, for instance, I was enormously relieved when a close friend of mine who inseminated last fall and is expecting her baby in the summer mentioned her ongoing ambivalence about what she was getting into. Though I knew her so well and had watched her difficult decision-making process, I'd somehow managed to decide that now that she was pregnant, she must be well on the road to being the "good" parent I think I ought to be—one who nurtures spontaneously and without second thoughts.)

The fact is that parenthood has given rise to some of the most painful emotional and practical dilemmas I've encountered in the course of my complicated efforts to figure out some tolerable way of living as a woman. There's a part of me that perceives the work of caring for children as a trap, a fatal diversion from the rest of the work I want to do in this world: the work of disciplined fantasy that is writing, the work of understanding that leads to political analysis, the work of taking care of my lover and my other adult friends, the work of getting together in activist settings to change social conditions on this planet.

I've observed similar contradictory feelings in most of the lesbians I know who've had kids for a while now, especially biological mothers who've been parenting for ten or fifteen years already. For some, their struggle both to meet their kids' needs and to have full adult lives, which include every important lesbian activity from torrid sex to political organizing, has made it just too difficult even to talk about lesbian parenting at conferences like this one. (*My* feelings about being a mother are simply not fit to be spoken in public, a friend of mine said when she heard I was doing this talk.) And then there are the lesbians who do not live with their children, who've lost them in custody battles or backed down from custody battles or decided early on that it was better for their kids to be reared by someone else. Lesbians who gave infants up for adoption, lesbians who had kids who died, lesbians who were flommies like me and lost touch with the kids they loved when they broke up with the mother. As much as any other role we ever find ourselves in, parenting points up the contradictions of being female, and being lesbian parents doesn't mean that we sidestep those contradictions. Far from it.

This morning the main thing I want to do is to think about lesbian parenting as a place where promising opportunities for women and their children intersect with ancient problems, where real freedom exists in a complicated tension with hoary stereotypes about our "place" as females. In other words, what Adrienne Rich called the *institution* of motherhood is going to haunt lesbians' efforts at redefining our relationships to children, not only because of what society requires, but sometimes because of what we expect of ourselves.

I think it's especially important to look at this intersection of opportunities and pitfalls now that larger numbers of lesbians seem to be having babies or actively seeking out parenting relationships—the phenomenon vulgarly referred to as the "lesbian baby boom." I'm not sure the actual numbers of mothers and coparents are radically different from what they were ten years ago, for example, but the atmosphere clearly has changed. Having a baby is now an accepted activity in many lesbian-feminist circles, where back then it was something you'd done when you were straight, like shaving your legs or performing fellatio, only motherhood had longer-term consequences. Then lesbian custody fights were the big parenting issue; though they haven't gone away, more publicity is now given to topics like donor insemination. The lesbian mothers of ten years ago were frequently viewed by the childfree as martyrs to women's condition, in line with the early feminist criticism of social definitions of motherhood. And coparents were even less well-understood, scarcely perceived to exist by the women's community, let alone the straight world.

The new focus on lesbian parenting issues clearly has the potential to help create a more supportive atmosphere in which to raise children—or to be a child oneself. But at the same time, it involves the danger that we may be trying to reinvent the wheel: either by forgetting that there's already a long history of lesbian parenting which we need to look at, or by assuming that we have it within our power to create a brave new world of lesbian childrearing immune to the problems and disappointments traditional mothers have faced. At times I've been concerned about what I perceive to be an intense focus on deciding whether and how to have children, with a lack of equivalent attention to the array of puzzling issues that like in wait for lesbian parents a little further down the road. (To pick one woefully underexamined topic: what happens when coparents break up?) I'm reminded of those civil disobedience training sessions that anticipate every conceivable thing that could happen in the half hour between sitting down in front of the nuke plant and being popped into the police van, but say not a word about what to expect when you find yourself in jail or prison for two weeks.

Besides being aware of the parenting experience of other generations of lesbians, I think that before we speak of creating a parenting community, we must examine how our individual ideas about being parents, and our daily experience of living with children, differ according to our identities and backgrounds—the specific oppression we face and the specific strengths we have that grow out of our memories of the people who raised us. To put this in the words of a Black friend of mine: "Black children are still being shot down in the streets in this country. That's something Black lesbians have to discuss when we talk about parenting."

For some of us, having kids is intimately bound up with survival issues, as it is for this friend; as it is for those Jewish women who feel a direct link between the Holocaust and their desire to raise a new generation of Jewish children; or for those Native Americans for whom the genocide of white rule makes parenting a crucial act of resistance. For a working-class lesbian who plans to have a baby by herself, economic realities and hence the entire experience are going to be worlds apart from those of the middle-class professional couple who have a baby together. For me, whose college-educated mother never worked for wages while I was at home, my assumptions about what a mother is "supposed" to do differ in crucial aspects from those of women who held jobs to help support the family. Growing up, I saw my mother as a kind of privileged servant, and it was a role I knew I wanted no part of in my own adult life.

All of these variations and many more exist among lesbians, including lesbians who don't think of themselves as feminists and would never come to a conference like this. In deliberately building a lesbian parenting community, we not only have to be prepared to explore the meaning of these differences, but to identify ways in which specific forms of oppression selectively target parents and kids. And then we have to be prepared for yet another struggle, both in our own circles and the society at large, to make the necessary changes. (Here, of course, the burden of commitment is largely on women with more relative privilege. Those with less have no choice about the daily fight they wage.) Otherwise, lesbian parenting becomes yet another private enterprise, and the self-defined "lesbian parenting community" is likely to be one of shared advantage.

I want to speak briefly about some of the ways it's been for me in my time as a flommy, because I'm especially concerned that in a context where the realities of all forms of lesbian parenting have been insufficiently discussed, the experience of coparenting has been particularly neglected. Coparenting highlights very sharply what I call the basically "outlaw" character of all lesbian—and gay—family situations. If lesbian mothers are not supposed to exist (since everyone knows queers can't reproduce themselves), then a comother or nonbiological parent is doubly a nonperson: she lacks the blood bond to her child which our society considers so vital that it will occasionally concede even dykes can care about the kids we birth. Audre Lorde has written of a school friend of her son's who insisted on referring to Audre's lover as "the maid"; I know I've been in countless situations where I felt Anna's and my relationship was either not seen or completely misjudged. Because of our own frequently confused feelings, our ambiguous standing with our lovers' children, coparents have sometimes had a hard time discussing our situations even amongst ourselves. A group rather oppressively titled Lovers of Lesbian Mothers which was formed by the New York City-based Dykes and Tykes in the mid-seventies, only succeeded in attracting three flommies—one of whom immediately dropped out, leaving me and another woman to be a support group of two.

When I began to write down what I wanted to say about my personal experience, I was taken aback by how many painful memories surfaced. My first three or four years as a flommy were especially difficult. It was hard to fit myself into an already established mother-child system, even though my lover welcomed the presence of another adult and genuinely tried her best to share the parenting with me on an equal basis—a willingness, I believe, that was absolutely essential to whatever success we had later. What made things doubly difficult was the fact that often I wasn't sure whether I *wanted* to fit in.

It was hard to be with a young child who was frequently miserable, even when her misery had little to do with me. I remember years of violent tantrums that turned our apartment into a battlefield, engulfing every room so that there was no room apart, no DMZ to retreat to. I remember the guilty anger with which I responded, sometimes hitting, more often imposing a mature, abstract punishment like taking away TV-watching time that nevertheless left me feeling like an ogre. I remember the discomfort of doubting whether there'd ever be room for *anybody's* needs—mine, my lover's, our child's. I remember the awful nagging worry—maybe Anna won't be O.K.—and it's a terrible thing to worry that a child isn't going to be O.K. I remember just wanting to withdraw, find my own separate space, but knowing that to do that would be to make myself even more of an outsider, and so choosing to stay. I remember, when I stayed, the intense anger I felt at my lover's ex-husband, our child's father, the man who was not, as I was, a participant in her daily life, but who was besides her mother *the* socially recognized parent, the one who had a legal right to her I could never claim. (A worst-case scenario based on that circumstance became the plot of my novel, *Sinking, Stealing*.)

Ours was certainly not a well-thought-out, neatly planned arrangement. I still tease my lover about how one time very early in our relationship when I asked her about me and Anna, she replied, "Oh, I wouldn't worry about it—she'll probably just want you to read her a few bedtime stories once in a while." Yet gradually we all three developed an intense loyalty to one another. As my lover and I like to say, "We stuck together through thin and thin." And certainly there are moments in both parents' and children's lives when *thin* seems to follow *thin* interminably. Interestingly, we still seem to work better as a series of pairs than as a threesome; when we're all together, there's too much of a chance one person will feel left out.

With Anna I finally feel I have a secure place as someone who is a very unique relative: clearly, to us both, not her mother, even though I connect so many of my parental feelings to what I know of motherhood; certainly not a father-substitute, and not a stepparent, for I'm replacing no one—I'm the only flommy she's ever had. The fact that she and her mother are Jewish and I am not underscores the chosen nature of our family. Dealing with that difference has meant hard work and some painful moments, but a great deal of growth for me as well.

And now, just when I feel more comfortable than ever with my family setting, and when, at the same time, I'm looking forward to the freedom of ceasing to be responsible for the care and feeding of a resident daughter, parenting has suddenly become a hot topic in the lesbian community. And it's not simply that a younger generation of lesbians has decided they want to do what I did and build a life with kids. So many of my peers, women from their mid-thirties on up into their forties are deciding to have babies, or at any rate investing a lot of energy in contemplating that possibility. And though sometimes I feel excited by what this means for individuals among my friends, and have even begun to look forward to the possibility of being an "aunt" to one close friend's child in a way I never felt I was to my blood sister's little boy, I also have a lot of negative reactions: fear of being abandoned by specific women as they immerse themselves in the demanding, absorbing world of early childhood; fear of finding myself trapped in a community where my emancipation from the need to locate a babysitter is meaningless because everyone else is home with the kids.

Most interesting and most painful is a totally irrational feeling of betrayal: I thought other lesbians were with me in the decision not to give birth, in that defiance of our expected womanly role—and now here these new lesbian mothers go, showing me up, *proving* that the fact I'm a dyke is no excuse for my failure to have a baby. The nerve is such a sensitive one that in examining my reactions I'm sometimes reminded of the gay/straight split of the early seventies. Such, I fear, is the power of the entrenched social institutions that have traditionally defined us as women to come between sisters.

As I've said, I think many longtime biological mothers are even warier than I am about the positive potential of lesbian parenting. Some are angry that there was so little support from the feminist community when they themselves were raising small children, yet now they're expected to attend a baby shower every week. Some fear that interest in children is becoming a substitute for political activism, or at best that many lesbians who are new to parenting have an unrealistic notion of the extent of the contradictions between an activist way of life and the needs of infants and toddlers. Some separatists have gone so far as to pen furious manifestoes listing fifteen reasons why any lesbian who dares to have a kid is a traitor to the Lesbian Nation.

Which only indicates once again what an incredibly charged topic motherhood is for rebellious women (and as lesbians, we're rebellious almost by definition). The consequent conflicts certainly won't be resolved with manifestoes, any more than were earlier controversies over everything from the length of our hair to monogamy vs. nonmonogamy to our lovemaking techniques to whether or not we ought to be doing political work with men. We don't move by rules; we move toward what we love. We don't have kids or not have them for political reasons. Having kids, being with kids, looking toward a new generation, is part of being human, and in one sense I think the current public and publicized interest in having babies is another way the lesbian-feminist community has of stretching into a new-found sense of its rights to the full range of human and female experience.

Yet I think there are some important questions to be raised about this community trend. The flyer for this conference inquires under a workshop heading: "Does having children and building a family provide a feeling of connectedness that is missing in the women's community?" I would add to that: are we somehow trying to compensate for the failure of the women's movement to change the world in all the ways we so desperately need it to change? Feminism, the gay movement, Third World communities, poor and working-class people, all have sustained enormous setbacks in the 1980s. Of course many of us haven't stopped fighting, no matter what the media thinks, but the temptation is certainly there to turn to more private, seemingly more controllable spheres of activity. Which leads me to pose the question: if there were more hands cradling rocks (to borrow the title of a poetry collection Rita Mae Brown published eons ago, before her novels started selling in airport newsstands), would there be fewer hands rocking cradles?

As lesbians, we're not necessarily immune to the oldest trap there is—the false consolation of motherhood, the notion that women can be compensated for our lack of power and standing in the adult world by the supposed influence we exert over our children's development. I think we have to be very cold-eyed and clear-headed about just how much control over kids' lives we really do have, particularly in this society. I believe that to be a parent requires the performance of that strange act of faith that's referred to in Christian scripture as "casting your bread upon the waters." You hope it will come back increased, but for all you know it might not come back at all, or it might be a soggy, inedible mess. At least as lesbians we're more likely to be alive to the possibility our children will grow up straight, reversing our sexual choices. And in that, perhaps we have an important advantage over many traditional parents. From the very beginning we know it's going to be about difference as well as sameness.

The reality is that society brings home to us its most painful contradictions, not only through our internal experience of parenting, but through the experience of our children. I think of racism, of class: in my case, for instance, the experience of living on a mostly-Black Brooklyn block with a small white girlchild; wondering, when she was bullied by an older Black boy next door, how do I try to protect her and help her sort this out in a way that lets her be angry at being terrorized by this kid without attaching that anger to Black people in general; how to make sure she doesn't distort the social reality entirely, misunderstanding the power of her skin color inside her real feelings of powerlessness; how to give weight to his gender-based privilege *and* his probable racial motivation.

Or how about the choices regarding schools: public schools, yes, but what did this supposedly egalitarian choice teach in the long run, given the realities of tracking in the New York City public school system? Though Anna's junior high was statistically thoroughly integrated, in fact *her* classes were heavily white middle-class; her high school amounts to a fairly exclusive prep school within the public education system. And anti-Semitism: the twinge I've sometimes felt reading about Hitler's Europe—they'd have done this to *my* kid, and how could I have protected her? And sexism, and homophobia, and certainly economics—an issue I think lesbians interested in parenting need to discuss in far greater depth, especially in light of the many grim statistics about poverty in female-headed households. The reality is that we have to ask ourselves, not simply how will we take care of the kids *and* go to the meetings and demos too, but how will we take care of the kids and go to the meetings and demos *and* hold down a job that will support everybody in the family at the pittance most women make for most of the work we do? Is parenting a luxury affordable only by lesbians with professional incomes?

And on top of all that, what about war and peace? Will there even *be* a world for our kids to grow up in?

This litany, I know, is overwhelming. I'm certainly not saying I think little kids should be dragged to meetings every night of the week, and of course there will be plenty of times for many lesbian parents when macro-level political concerns get tabled for long stretches. But I would like to suggest that the questions I've raised imply an opportunity as well as a burden. For one thing, they bring us smack up against some of the early-seventies women's movement agendas that are still waiting to be addressed: the need for good, affordable day care; welfare rights issues; the high rate of teen-age pregnancy that, especially in Black and Latino communities, turns the lives of so many very young women into a day-in, day-out battle for the bare minimums of survival. I believe we need to start thinking and talking about those issues we have in common with straight women, as well as those that uniquely affect us as lesbian parents.

When I told a friend I was thinking of titling this talk "To Live Outside the Law You Must Be Honest," she wanted to know why. In closing, I want to offer an answer. First of all, as lesbian parents even more so than simply as lesbian women, I believe we are all fundamentally outlaws. That doesn't mean we all realize the full radical potential of our outsider status all the time, and it certainly doesn't mean the *law*—informal social law or the law of the court system—falls with equal weight on each one of us: other forms of privilege, other aspects of oppression are crucial. It does mean that we are doubly in defiance of the general society's prescriptions for what we should be. We're not supposed to be dykes, and if we are dykes, we're certainly not supposed to have families. Our involvement with children mixes up their categories too much. It's as confusing as the involvement of many religious Nicaraguans with that country's revolutionary process: for a reactionary, the only thing to say about that puzzling circumstance is that Sandinista priests and nuns are not real priests and nuns. By the same token, the heterosexual reactionaries would have it that lesbian mothers are not real mothers, children of lesbian mothers are completely invisible as such, and flommies don't even exist. Like open, unashamed lesbian and gay sexuality, our chosen lesbian families call into question some terribly basic assumptions about who's important to whom, and why.

So that's the outlaw part, and considering what the laws are, I'm proud to be outside them. The honesty part is about what you do with where you find yourself. To live outside the law is to live without a script, without preformulated rules for being with other people. Living that way requires being clear about feelings, both good and bad feelings. It also requires a finely tuned awareness of the contours of the country that surrounds you.

Being an outlaw doesn't mean being a law unto yourself. It doesn't mean the luxury of being able to retreat to a safe corner, a cozy community, and forget the rest of the world. And our kids are a constant reminder of that.

If escapism ever tempts us, they will be right there to bring us back home. Kids live on the block; they ride the school bus; they play in the street, in the woods, in the vacant lots with all the neighbor kids. Abstractions rarely impress them. Daily experience marks them deeply. Along with our love for them as who they uniquely are, I believe the process of our daily struggles as women who still intend to change the world is the greatest gift we lesbian parents can give our children.

References On Lesbian Parenting

Publications And Visuals

Abbitt, Diane and Bobbie Bennett. "Being a Lesbian Mother." In *Positively Gay*. Betty Berzon and Robert Leighton, Millbrae, CA: Celestial Arts, 1979, pp. 123-129.

Action for Lesbian Parents. *The Guide to Gay Custody*. London: The Action, 1977.

Adair, Nancy and Casey Adair. "Pam and Rusty." In *Word Is Out: Stories of Some of Our Lives*. Nancy Adair and Casey Adair, New York: New Glide Publications, 1978, pp. 43-54.

Ager, Susan. "Gay Parenting: Can Love Conquer All?" San Jose *Mercury-News*, November 28, 1982.

Alternative Conceptions [video]. Women Make Movies, 225 Lafayette St., New York, NY 10012, (212) 925-0606, 1985.

Armanno, Benna F. "The Lesbian Mother: Her Right to Child Custody." *Golden Gate Law Review*, Vol. 4, Fall 1973, pp. 1-18.

Arthur, Christine and Katherine English. "An Expert Testifies in a Lesbian Parenting Custody Case." Lesbian and Gay Parenting Project, English and Metcalf, 408 SW 2nd, Portland, OR 97204.

Artificial Insemination: An Alternative Conception. Lesbian Health Information Project, San Francisco Women's Center, 3543 18th St., San Francisco, CA 94110, 1979.

Azalea: A Magazine by Third World Lesbians. Vol. 3, No. 1 (Issue on Third World Lesbian Mothers), 1979/80.

Baetz, Ruth. "Children." In *Lesbian Crossroads: Personal Stories of Lesbian Struggles and Triumphs*. Ruth Baetz, New York: Morrow, 1980, pp. 187-206.

Barnet, Alison. "Lesbians Choosing Children." *Bay Windows* (Boston), Vol. 2, No. 1, January 5-18, 1974.

Basile, R. A. "Lesbian Mothers I." *Women's Rights Law Reporter*, Vol. 2, December 1974, pp. 3-18.

Beck, Evelyn Torton. "The Motherhood That Dare Not Speak Its Name." *Women's Studies Quarterly*, Vol.11, No. 4, Winter 1983.

Berzon, Betty. "Sharing Your Lesbian Identity with Your Children: A Case for Openness." In *Our Right to Love: A Lesbian Resource Book*. Ginny Vida, Englewood Cliffs, New Jersey: Prentice-Hall, 1978, pp. 69-74.

"Bezio v. Patenaude: The Coming Out Custody Controversy of Lesbian Mothers in Court." *New England Law Review*, Vol. 16, 1981, p. 331.

Biren, Joan E. "Darquita and Denyata" [photograph]. In *Eye to Eye: Portraits of Lesbians*. Joan E. Biren, Washington, DC: Glad Hag Books, 1977, p. 73.

Biren, Joan E. "Melanie, Lynne, Susie and Janice" [photograph]. In *Eye to Eye: Portraits of Lesbians*. Joan E. Biren, Washington, DC: Glad Hag Books, 1977, p. 25.

Budd, Sharon. "Proud Lesbian Motherhood." In *The Lesbian Path*. Margaret Cruikshank, Monterey, CA: Angel Press, 1980, pp. 163-170.

Chesler, Phyllis. *Mothers On Trial: The Battle for Children and Custody*. New York: McGraw-Hill, 1986 (hard cover); Seattle: Seal Press, 1987 (softcover), pp. 118-129.

"Children in Gay Families: An Investigation of Services." *The Homosexual Counseling Journal*, Vol. 3, No. 2, April 1976.

Choosing Children [motion picture]. Cambridge, MA: Cambridge Documentary Films, P. O. Box 385, Cambridge, MA 02139.

Clausen, Jan. *Mother, Sister, Daughter, Lover.* Freedom, CA: Crossing Press, 1980.

Clausen, Jan. *Sinking, Stealing.* Freedom, CA: Crossing Press, 1985.

Cummings, Judith. "Homosexual Views Adoption Approval as Victory." New York *Times*, January 10, 1983.

Curry, Hayden and Denis Clifford. *A Legal Guide for Lesbian and Gay Couples.* Reading, MA: Addison-Wesley, 1980.

"Custody: Lesbian Mothers in the Courts." *Gonzaga Law Review*, Vol. 16, 1980, p. 147.

"Custody and Homosexual Parents." *Women's Rights Law Reporter*, Vol. 2, December 1974, pp. 11-18.

Cutler, Wendy. "Institutionalized Heterosexism: The Social and Legal Aspects of Lesbian Parenting and Child Custody." Unpublished paper (University of California, Santa Cruz, CA), 1982.

Cutler, Wendy, Yasmin A. Sayyed, and Jeanne Vaughn. *Lesbian Parenting and Child Custody Struggles: Community Organizing and Legal Defense Networks.* Santa Cruz, CA: Susan Parker Defense Committee. 524-C Ocean View Ave., Santa Cruz, CA 95062, 1982.

Davies, Rosalie C. "The Impact of the Lesbian Mother's Legal Position on the Counseling Situation." Women's Resource Series, 613 Lombard St., Philadelphia, PA 19147, 1978.

Davies, Rosalie C. *Motherright and the Lesbian.* Custody Action for Lesbian Mothers (CALM), Box 281, Narberth, PA 19072, 1979.

Davies, Rosalie C. "Representing the Lesbian Mother." *Family Advocate*, Vol. 1, 1979, p. 21.

Dejanikus, Tacie. "The Politics of Lesbians Choosing Motherhood." *off our backs* (Washington, DC), December 1984, p. 20.

Devine, Andrea. "CLUM Supports Rights of Lesbian Parents." *The Docket*, Civil Liberties Union of Massachusetts, Vol. 13, No. 3, August 1983.

Di Bella, G. "Family Psychotherapy with the Homosexual Family: A Community Psychiatry Approach to Homosexuality." *Community Mental Health Journal*, Vol. 15, 1979, p. 41.

Dormont, Paul. "The Homosexual Parent." *Sexual Medicine Today*, October 1978.

Eiduson, B. and J. Alexander. "The Role of Children in Alternative Family Styles." *Journal of Social Issues*, No. 34, 1978.

Ferris, Kathryn. "Child Custody and the Lesbian Mother: An Annotated Bibliography." *Resources for Feminist Research-Documentation sur la Recherche feministe*, Vol.12, No. 1, (The Lesbian Issue-Etre Lesbienne), March 1983, pp. 106-109.

Gantz, Joe. *Whose Child Cries: Children of Gay Parents Talk About Their Lives.* Rolling Hills Estates, CA: Jalmar Press, 1983.

"The Gay Family." In *The Rights of Gay People.* E. Carrington Boggan and others, New York: Avon, 1981, pp. 103-115.

"The Gay Parent: A Special Custody Case." *Oregon State Bar Bulletin Forum*, Vol. 1, 1979.

Gibson, Clifford Gay, with cooperation from Mary Jo Risher. *By Her Own Admission: A Lesbian Mother's Fight to Keep Her Son.* New York: Doubleday, 1977.

Godley, Elizabeth. "Lesbian Mothers: Living a Lie—Or Living in Fear." *Vancouver Sun*, May 26, 1981, sec. B, p. 3.

Golombok, Spencer and Rutter. "Children in Lesbian Single-Parent Households: Psychosexual and Psychiatric Appraisal." *Journal of Child Psychology and Allied Disciplines*, Vol. 124, No. 4, October 1983, pp. 551-572.

Goodman, Bernice. *The Lesbian: A Celebration of Difference.* Brooklyn, New York: Out & Out Books, 476 Second St., Brooklyn, NY 11215, 1977.

Goodman, Bernice. "The Lesbian Mother." *American Journal of Orthopsychiatry*, Vol. 43, March 1973, pp. 283-284.

Goodman, Bernice. "Some Mothers Are Lesbians." In *Women's Issues and Social Work Practice.* Ed. Elaine Norman and Arlene Mancuso, Itasca, IL: F.E. Peacock Publishers, 1980, pp. 153-181.

Goodman, Ellen. "Homosexuality of a Parent: A New Issue in Custody Disputes." *Monash University Law Review*, Vol. 5, 1979, p. 305.

Green, Richard. "The Best Interests of the Child with a Lesbian Mother." *Bulletin of the American Academy of Psychiatry and the Law*, Vol. 10, No. 1, 1982, pp. 7-15.

Green, Richard. "Sexual Identity of 37 Children Raised by Homosexual or Trans-sexual Parents." *American Journal of Psychiatry*, Vol. 135, 1978, p. 692.

Gunther, Catherine. "Gay Dads and Gay Moms: The Parents Are Alright." Baltimore *City Paper*, July 13, 1979.

Hall, Marny. "Lesbian Families: Cultural and Clinical Issues." *Social Work*, Vol. 23. No. 5, September 1978, pp. 380-385.

Hanscombe, Gillian E. and Jackie Forster. *Rocking the Cradle: Lesbian Mothers: A Challenge in Family Living.* Boston: Alyson Publications, 1981.

Harris, Barbara S. "Lesbian Mother Child Custody: Legal and Psychiatric Aspects." *Bulletin of the American Academy of Psychology and the Law*, Vol. 5, 1977, p. 75.

Hart, H. (chairperson). *Families and Children of Gays: Final Report of the Task Force on Sexual Preference.* Salem, OR: State of Oregon Dept. of Human Resources, 1978.

Herman, Ellen. "Lesbians and Kids: Community We Create." *Gay Community News* (Boston, MA), May 24, 1986.

Hidalgo, Hilda, Travis L. Peterson, and Natalie Jane Woodman. *Lesbian and Gay Issues: A Resource Manual for Social Workers.* Silver Spring, MD: National Association of Social Workers, 1985.

Hitchens, Donna J. "Donor Insemination: A Legal Summary." *Update*, Lambda Legal Defense and Education Fund, September 1984.

Hitchens, Donna J. *Lesbian Mother Litigation Manual.* Lesbian Rights Project, 1370 Mission St., 4th Floor, San Francisco, CA 94103, 1982.

Hitchens, Donna J. "Social Attitudes, Legal Standards, and Personal Trauma in Child Custody Cases." *Journal of Homosexuality*, Vol. 5, No. 1-2, 1979, pp. 89-96.

Hitchens, Donna J., D. Martin and M. Morgan. "An Alternative View to Child Custody: When One Parent Is a Homosexual." *Conciliation Courts Review*, Vol. 17, 1979, p. 27.

Hitchens, Donna J., D. Martin and M. Morgan. "Child Custody and the Homosexual Parent." *The Judges Journal*, Vol. 18, 1979, p. 33.

Hitchens, Donna J. and Barbara Price. "Trial Strategy in Lesbian Mother Custody Cases: The Use of Expert Testimony." *Golden Gate Law Review*, Vol. 9, 1978/79, p. 451.

Hitchens, Donna J. and Ann G. Thomas. *Lesbian Mothers and Their Children: An Annotated Bibliography of Legal and Psychological Materials.* San Francisco: Lesbian Rights Project, 1370 Mission St., 4th Floor, San Francisco, CA 94103, 1983.

Hoeffer, Beverly. "Children's Acquisition of Sex-Role Behavior in Lesbian-Mother Families." *American Journal of Orthopsychiatry*, Vol. 51, July 1981, pp. 536-544.

Hornstein, Francis. "Children by Donor Insemination: A New Choice for Lesbians." In *Test-Tube Women: What Future for Motherhood*. Rita Arditti, Renate Duelli Klein, and Shelley Minden. London: Pandora Press, 1985, pp. 373-381.

"Homosexual Parent in Custody Disputes." *Queen's Law Journal*, Vol. 5, 1980, p. 199.

Hunter, Nan D. and Nancy D. Polikoff. "Custody Rights of Lesbian Mothers: Legal Theory and Litigation Strategy." *Buffalo Law Review*, Vol. 25, 1976, pp. 691-733.

In the Best Interests of the Children [motion picture/video]. Berkeley, CA: Iris Films, Box 5353, Berkeley, CA 94705, 1977.

Jullion, Jeanne. *Long Way Home: The Odyssey of a Lesbian Mother and Her Children*. Pittsburgh, PA: Cleis Press, 1985.

Kirkpatrick, Martha, Ron Roy and Catherine Smith. "A New Look at Lesbian Mothers." *Human Behavior*, Vol. 5, No. 8, August 1976.

Kirkpatrick, Martha, Catherine Smith, and Ron Roy. "Lesbian Mothers and Their Children: A Comparative Survey." *American Journal of Orthopsychiatry*, Vol. 51, July 1981, pp. 545-551.

Klaitch, Dolores. "Parents Who Are Gay." *New Times*, Vol. 7, No. 2, July 23, 1976, pp. 34-42.

Klein, C. "Homosexual Parents." In *The Single Parent Experience*. New York: Avon, 1973.

Klein, Renate Duelli. "Doing It Ourselves: Self-Insemination." In *Test-Tube Women: What Future for Motherhood*. Rita Arditti, Renate Duelli Klein, and Shelley Minden. London: Pandora Press, 1985, pp. 382-390.

Klemesrud, Judy. "Lesbians Who Try to Be Good Mothers." New York *Times*, January 31, 1973.

Krieger, Susan. "Mothers and Children." In *The Mirror Dance: Identity in a Women's Community*. Philadelphia, PA: Temple University Press, 1983, pp. 111-124.

Labor More Than Once [video]. Women Make Movies, 225 Lafayette St., New York, NY 10012, (212) 925-0606.

Lanser, Susan Sniader. "Breaking the Waters: The Mother As Lesbian." In *Interdisciplinary and Cross-Cultural Aspects of Motherhood*, Vol. 1 of *Proceedings of the Motherhood Symposia*, Madison, WI: University of Wisconsin, Madison, 1980, pp. 57-72.

Larkin, Mary Ann. "Coping Alone: Gay Parents and Children." *The Hill Rag* (Washington, DC), April 1, 1980.

"Lesbian Families" *Matrix Women's Newsmagazine* (Santa Cruz, CA), June 1986.

"Lesbian Foster Parents Used in Jersey." *New York Times*, 129, November 27, 1979, p. B2, col. 1.

Lesbian Mothers [videotape]. Vancouver, British Columbia, Canada: Amelia Productions, 1981.

"Lesbian Mothers and Custody." *Resources for Feminist Research-Documentation sur la Recherche féministe*, Vol, 12, No. 1, (The Lesbian Issue-Etre Lesbienne), March 1983, pp. 98-99.

"Lesbian Mothers Fight Back." *Quest*, Vol. 5, No. 1, Summer 1979, pp. 54-74.

Lesbian Mothers Networker. Berkeley, CA: Pacific Center for Human Growth, P.O. Box 908, Berkeley, CA 94701.

"Lesbians and Children: Three Impressions." *Sojourner* (Boston, MA) July 1986, p. 6.

Levy, Eileen. "Coping with Stress: Resources Utilized by Lesbian Mothers in a Heterosexist, Patriarchal Society." In *Constructing Mothers: The Impact of Children on Women*, Vol. 3 of *Proceedings of the Motherhood Symposia*, Madison, WI: University of Wisconsin, Madison, 1982.

Lewin, Ellen. "Lesbianism and Motherhood: Implications for Child Custody." *Human Organization*, Vol. 40, No. 1, 1981.

Lewin, Ellen and Terrie Lyons. "Everything in Its Place: The Co-existence of Lesbianism and Motherhood." In *Homosexuality*. W. Paul and others, Beverly Hills, CA: Sage Publications, 1982.

Lewin, Ellen and Terrie Lyons. "Lesbians and Heterosexual Mothers." Paper presented at American Psychological Association Meeting, New York, September 1979.

Lewin, Ellen and Terrie Lyons. "Psychological Status of Children in Lesbian Mother Families." Paper presented at American Orthopsychiatric Association Meeting, Toronto, April, 1980.

Lewis, Karen Gail. "Children of Lesbians: Their Point of View." *Social Work*, Vol. 25, No. 3, May 1980, pp. 198-203.

Lewis, Sasha Gregory. *Sunday's Women: A Report on Lesbian Life Today.* Boston: Beacon Press, 1979.

Linscott, Gillian. "Lesbian Mother Wins Custody of Twins." *The Guardian*, November 5, 1976.

Loshak, David. "Ban on Artificial Insemination for Lesbians Rejected." London *Daily Telegraph*, June 27, 1978.

Lyons, Terrie. "Lesbian Mothers' Custody Fears." In *Women Changing Therapy*, Robbins and Siegel, New York: Haworth Press, 1983, pp. 231-239.

MacAdams, Lewis. "Kramer vs. Kramer with a Twist." *L.A. Weekly*, November 26-December 2, 1982.

Macklin, E. and R. Rubins. *Contemporary Families and Alternative Lifestyles.* Beverly Hills, CA: Sage Publications, 1983.

Maddox, Brenda. "Homosexual Parents." *Psychology Today*, February 1982, pp. 66-69.

Maddox, Brenda. "In Front of the Children." In *Married and Gay: An Intimate Look at a Different Relationship*, Brenda Maddox, New York: Harcourt, Brace, Jovanovich, 1982, pp. 133-151.

Mandel, Jane Barclay and others. "The Lesbian Parent: Comparison of Heterosexual and Homosexual Mothers and Their Children." Paper presented at American Psychological Association Annual Meeting, New York, September 1979.

Martin, Del and Phyllis Lyon. "Lesbian Mothers." *Ms.*, Vol. 2, No. 4, 1973, pp. 78-80.

Martin, Del and Phyllis Lyon. "Lesbians Are Mothers Too." *Lesbian/Woman*, San Francisco, CA: Glide Publications, 1972, pp. 140-176.

Mattie, D. Pat. "No Name He Can Say." In *The Lesbian Path*. Margaret Cruikshank, Monterey, CA: Angel Press, 1980, pp. 171-175.

Mayadas, L. and W. Duehn. "Children in Gay Families: An Investigation of Services." *Homosexual Counseling Journal*, Vol. 3, No. 2, 1976.

Mehren, Elizabeth. "Lesbian Mothers: Two New Studies Shatter Stereotypes." Los Angeles *Times*, 102, June 1, 1983, section V, p. 1, col. 1.

Miller, J., R. Jacobsen and J. Bigner. "The Child's Home Environment for Lesbian Versus Heterosexual Mothers." *Journal of Homosexuality*, Vol. 7, No. 1, 1981, pp. 49-56.

Moira, Fran. "Lesbian Self-Insemination: Life Without Father." *off our backs*, January 1982.

Mom's Apple Pie: Lesbian Mothers' National Defense Fund Newsletter. Seattle, WA: Lesbian Mothers' National Defense Fund, P.O. Box 21567, Seattle, WA 98111.

Moses, A. Elfin and Robert O. Hawkins, Jr. *Counseling Lesbian Women and Gay Men: A Life-Issues Approach*. St. Louis: C.V. Mosby, 1982.

Mother's Day [videotape]. Vancouver, British Columbia, Canada: Amelia Productions, 1980.

Mucklow, B. and K. Phelan. "Lesbian and Traditional Mothers' Responses to Adult Response to Child Behavior and Self-Concept." *Psychological Reports*, Vol. 44, 1979, p. 880.

National Gay Task Force. *Gay Parents Support Packet: Resources for Lesbian Mothers/Gay Fathers*. New York: National Gay Task Force, 80 Fifth Ave., New York, NY 10011.

Not All Parents Are Straight [video/film]. Full Frame Productions, 363 Brannan St., San Francisco, CA 94109. (415) 546-0155, 1987.

"Oregon Task Force on Sexual Preference Preliminary Report." *Sexual Law Reporter*, Vol. 3, 1977, p. 46.

Osman, Shelomo. "My Stepfather Is a She." *Family Process*, Vol. 11, 1972, pp. 209-218.

Pagelow, Mildred. "Heterosexual and Lesbian Single Mothers: A Comparison of Problems, Coping, and Solutions." *Journal of Homosexuality*, Vol. 5, No. 3, 1980, pp. 189-204.

Pagelow, Mildred. "Lesbian Mothers." Paper presented at American Sociological Association Meeting, New York, 1976.

Payne, A. "The Law and the Problem Parent: Custody and Parental Rights of Homosexual, Mentally Retarded, Mentally Ill, and Incarcerated Parents." *Journal of Family Law*, Vol. 16, 1977, p. 797.

Pegesser, L. "Theoretical Bases for Research on the Acquisition of Social Roles by Children of Lesbian Mothers." *Journal of Homosexuality*, Vol. 5, No. 3, 1980, pp. 177-188.

Pies, Cheri. *Considering Parenthood: A Workbook for Lesbians*. San Francisco: Spinsters Ink, 1985.

Pogrebin, Letty Cottin. *Growing Up Free: Raising Your Child in the '80s*. New York: Bantam, 1981.

Pogrebin, Letty Cottin. "The Secret Fear That Keeps Us from Raising Free Children." *Ms.*, October 1980.

Pratt, Minnie Bruce. "In Which I Weep Like Niobe." In *The Lesbian Path*. Margaret Cruikshank, Monterey, CA: Angel Press, 1980, pp. 156-162.

Rafkin, Louise. *Different Daughters: A Book by Mothers of Lesbians*. Pittsburg, PA: Cleis Press, 1987.

Rees, Richard L. "A Comparison of Children of Lesbian and Single Heterosexual Mothers on Three Measures of Socialization." *Dissertation Abstracts International*, 1979.

Rich, Adrienne. *Of Woman Born: Motherhood As Experience and Institution*. Tenth Anniversary Edition. New York: W. W. Norton, 1986.

Richardson, Diane. "Do Lesbians Make Good Parents?" *Community Care*, August 2, 1978, pp. 16-17.

Riddle, Dorothy I. "Relating to Children: Gays as Role Models." *Journal of Social Issues*, Vol. 34, No. 3, 1978, pp. 38-58.

Riddle, Dorothy I. and Maria de Lourdes Arguelles. "Children of Gay Parents: Homophobia's Victims." In *Children of Separation and Divorce*. Abott and Stuart, Van Nostrand, 1981.

Riley, Marilyn. "The Avowed Lesbian Mother and Her Right to Child Custody: A Constitutional Challenge That Can No Longer Be Denied." *San Diego Law Review*, Vol. 12, No. 4, June 1975, pp. 799-864.

Rivera, Rhonda R. "Our Straight-Laced Judges: The Legal Position of Homosexual Persons in the United States." *Hastings Law Journal*, Vol. 30, 1979, p. 799.

Saffron, Lisa. *Getting Pregnant Our Own Way: A Guide to Alternative Insemination.* Women's Health Information Centre. London, England, 1986.

Sands, Mimee. *We Are Family: Parenting and Foster Parenting in Gay Families* [video]. Contact WGBN-TV Boston.

San Francisco Bay Area National Lawyers Guild, Anti-Sexism Committee. *A Gay Parent's Legal Guide to Child Custody.* San Francisco: The Guild, 558 Capp St., San Francisco, CA 94110, 1978.

Sandy and Madeleine's Family [motion picture]. San Francisco, CA: Multi-Media Resource Center, 340 Jones St., Box 439E, San Francisco, CA 94102.

Schulenburg, Joy A. *Gay Parenting.* Garden City, New York: Anchor Books, 1985.

Schuster, S. L. *Love Is for All.* Mountlake Terrace, WA: Schuster-Isaacson Family Productions, P.O. Box 82, Mountlake Terrace, WA 98043, 1974.

Severance, Jane. *When Megan Went Away.* North Carolina: Lollipop Power, P.O. Box 1171, Chapel Hill, NC 27514.

"Sharing Your Lesbian Lifestyle with Your Children." In *Our Right to Love: A Lesbian Resource Book.* Ginny Vida. Englewood Cliffs, New Jersey: Prentice-Hall, 1978.

Sheppard. "Lesbian Mothers II: Long Night's Journey Into Day." Vol. 8 *Women's Rights Law Reporter*, Vol. 8, 1985.

Shipp, E. R. "A Lesbian Who Won a Child Custody Battle." New York *Times*, September 5, 1980.

Stein, Terry S. and Carol J. Cohen. *Contemporary Perspectives on Psychotherapy with Lesbians and Gay Men.* New York: Plenum Medical Book Co., 1986.

Steinhorn, Audrey I. "Lesbian Mothers." *Women and Therapy*, Vol. 1, Winter 1982, pp. 35-48.

Stevens, Mary. "Lesbian Mothers in Transition." In *Our Right to Love: A Lesbian Resource Book.* Ginny Vida, Englewood Cliffs, New Jersey: Prentice-Hall, 1978, pp. 207-210.

Stewart, Pearl. "Lesbian's Suit for Visiting Rights." San Francisco *Chronicle*, April 23, 1983.

Sutton, Stuart. "The Lesbian Family: Rights in Conflict under the Uniform Parentage Act." *Golden Gate Law Review*, 10, 1980, p. 1007.

Taylor, Sheila Ortiz. *Faultlines.* Tallahasee, FL: Naiad Press, 1982.

Telfer, Judie. "Artificial Insemination Available, Quietly, to Lesbians in Bay Area." San Jose *Mercury-News*, December 17, 1978.

Van Gelder, Lindsay. "Lesbian Custody: A Tragic Day in Court." *Ms.*, Vol. 5, September 1976, pp. 72-73.

Wolf, Deborah Goleman. "Lesbian Mothers." In *The Lesbian Community*, Deborah Goleman Wolf, Berkeley, CA: University of California Press, 1980, pp. 136-165.

Wolfe, Susan J. "Jewish Lesbian Mother." In *Nice Jewish Girls: A Lesbian Anthology.* Evelyn Torton Beck, Persephone Press, 1982, pp. 164-173.

Woodman, Natalie Jane and Harry R. Lenna. *Counseling with Gay Men and Women: A Guide for Facilitating Positive Life-Styles.* San Francisco: Jossey-Bass, 1980.

Wyland, Francie. *Motherhood, Lesbians, and Child Custody.* Toronto: Wages Due Lesbians, P.O. Box 38, Station E, Toronto, Ontario, Canada, 1977.

Wysor, Bettie. "Lesbian Mothers." In *The Lesbian Myth*, Bettie Wysor, New York: Random House, 1974, pp. 326-363.

Organizations

Boys of Lesbian Mothers, 935 W. Broadway, Eugene, OR 97402.

Children of Gays/Lesbians, 8306 Wilshire Blvd., No. 222, Beverly Hills, CA 90211. (213) 738-1008.

Children of Lesbians and Gays, c/o Noel Maze, P.O. Box 12501, Fort Wayne, IN 46863.

Custody Action for Lesbian Mothers (CALM), Box 281, Narberth, PA 19072. (215) 667-7508.

Families and Friends of Gays and Lesbians, 5336 N.E. 184th St., Seattle, WA 98155. (206) 363-2762.

Gay Parents Legal Research Group, Box 1723, Lynwood, WA 98036.

Lambda Legal Defense and Education Fund, 132 W. 43rd St., New York, NY 10036. (212) 944-9488.

Lesbian and Gay Parent Project, 21 Bay St., Cambridge, MA 02139. (617) 492-2655.

Lesbian Health Information Project, c/o San Francisco Women's Center, 3543 18th St., San Francisco, CA 94110.

Lesbian Herstory Archives, P.O. Box 1258, New York, NY 10116. (212) 874-7232.

Lesbian Mothers Defense Fund, Box 38, Station E, Toronto, Ontario, Canada M6H 4E1.

Lesbian Mothers Support Group, c/o Lesbian Resource Center, 713 Monroe Ave., Rochester, NY 14607. (716) 244-8640.

Lesbian Rights Project, 1370 Mission St., 4th Floor, San Francisco, CA 94103.

Mountain Meadow Country Experience, 3736 Kenawha St. N.W., Washington, DC 20015. [A summer camp for children of lesbian mothers.]

National Federation of Parents and Friends of Gays, 5715 16th St. N.W., Washington, DC 20011. (202) 726-3322.

National Gay/Lesbian Task Force, NGLTF, 1517 U St. N.W., Washington, DC 20009.

National Lawyer's Guild, Gay Caucus, 558 Capp St., San Francisco, CA 94110. (415) 285-5066.

National Lawyer's Guild, Gay Rights Task Force, 835 Broadway, New York, NY 10003. (212) 260-1360.

National Organization for Women, Lesbian Mothers Support Group, Box 40982, Memphis, TN 38104. (901) 458-1661.

National Organization for Women, Lesbian Task Force, Box 1404, Sacramento, CA 95807. (916) 443-3470.

Parents and Friends of Lesbians and Gays, P.O. Box 24565, Los Angeles, CA 90024. (213) 472-8952.

SIGMA (Spouses in a Gay Marriage), P.O. Box 262, Pella, IA 50219. [Use only initials on envelopes.]

Contributor Notes

Anonymous is sorry that conditions in our society are such that making her identity known would create problems for her child. When she is not struggling with mothering, she works as a psychotherapist and college professor in a small university town. She also revels in creating a new social order within the confines of her home. Her politics are in her heart.

Antiga is a feminist writer, artist, educator, singer, and workshop creator. Her writing and art have appeared in many feminist publications. Her book of poetry and art, *What Can I Learn?* (Mary Lee George), is an intriguing invitation to enjoy life as one learns. (Available from Sisters, P.O. Box 6513, Minneapolis, Minnesota 55406, $6.25)

Ellen Bass has published many books of poetry including *Our Stunning Harvest*. She is coeditor of *I Never Told Anyone*, and is coauthor (with Laura Davis) of a book for survivors on the process of healing from child sexual abuse, forthcoming from Harper & Row (1988). She has one eight-year-old daughter, Sara, and is hoping to have another child soon.

Evelyn Torton Beck, scholar/teacher/activist, is currently Director of the Women's Studies Program at the University of Maryland, College Park, Maryland. She is the editor of *Nice Jewish Girls: A Lesbian Anthology* (1982); *The Prism Of Sex: Essays In The Sociology of Knowledge* (1979); and author of *Kafka And The Yiddish Theatre; Its Impact On His Work* (1971). She has translated stories from the Yiddish of I.B. Singer and has written in the areas of Jewish Women's Studies, lesbian studies, anti-Semitism in the Women's Movement, and feminist critiques of Kafka and Singer. She is currently putting together a collection of her essays, speeches, and autobiographical writings.

Becky Birtha is a Black feminist writer whose work has appeared in many periodicals and anthologies, including *Home Girls*, *Lesbian Poetry*, *The Things That Divide Us*, and *Hear The Silence*. A collection of her stories, *For Nights Like This One: Stories Of Loving Women*, has been published by Frog in the Well, and her new book, *Lovers' Choice*, by Seal Press. She is a lesbian godmother.

Beth Brant (*Degonwadonti*) is a Bay of Quinte Mohawk, member of the Turtle Clan. She is cofounder of Turtle Grandmother, an archive and library of information about North American Indian women, and the editor of *A Gathering Of Spirit* (Sinister Wisdom Books), an anthology of American Indian women's writing. Her own collection, *Mohawk Trail*, was published by Firebrand Books in 1985. She lives in Detroit with her lover of twelve years, Denise.

Elly Bulkin was a founding editor (1976-84) of *Conditions*, a feminist magazine of writing by women with an emphasis on writing by lesbians. She edited *Lesbian Fiction* and coedited, with Joan Larkin, *Lesbian Poetry*, two anthologies (Gay Presses of New York). With Minnie Bruce Pratt and Barbara Smith, she coauthored *Yours In Struggle: Three Feminist Perspectives On Anti-Semitism And Racism* (Firebrand Books). Most recently, she helped put together "Coming Out, Coming Home: Lesbian And Gay Jews And The Jewish Community," a New Jewish Agenda National Feminist Task Force pamphlet. For more than a dozen years, she and Jan Clausen have coparented their daughter, Anna.

Andrea R. Canaan, thirty-six, is a Black Southern lesbian-feminist, co-mother, poet and writer. Living in Oakland, California when "God Bless The Child" was written, she has since moved to New Orleans, Louisiana, her original home.

Jan Clausen is a poet, fiction writer, and critic who lives with her family in Brooklyn, New York. Her first novel, *Sinking, Stealing*, deals with lesbian parenting. She is at work on a second, *The Prosperine Papers*, and is active in the Central America solidarity movement.

Baba Copper is an artist, writer, and Crone Futurist.

Rosalie G. Davies was the founder of CALM (Custody Action for Lesbian Mothers). She is a feminist attorney in private practice, advocating women's rights. She had published and spoken widely on a variety of feminist and lesbian issues and is currently at work with her life-partner on a lesbian adventure novel.

Jiivanii J. Dent lives in New Mexico with her mate and their child.

Auguste Elliott lives on a 120-acre farm, where she plans to grow herbs and become a great storyteller.

Sue Gambill is a writer presently working on a novel about the 1980s, American culture, and her love of Portugal. She also has a collection of short stories in progress.

Rocky Gámez was born and raised in the Lower Rio Grande Valley of Texas, the location of most of her Gloria stories. She is presently living in the Bay Area of San Francisco.

Pamela Gray is a Jewish lesbian writer living in Oakland. Her work appears in *New Lesbian Writing* and *Women-Identified Women*. The early struggles of comotherhood seem far behind her now. Andrew continues to be a source of light, joy, and inspiration in her life.

Brangwen Griffith is a writer living in Western Massachusetts. She contributes to several publications. She is a poet and has just completed a book that records the anecdotes and stories of African Americans facing terminal cancer.

Marilyn Hacker is the author of *Love, Death, And The Changing Of The Seasons* (Arbor House, 1986), *Assumptions* (Knopf, 1985), *Taking Notice* (Knopf, 1980), *Separations* (Knopf, 1976), and *Presentation Piece* (Viking, 1974). She lives in New York City and Paris with her daugher, Iva. She was editor of the feminist literary magazine *13th Moon* from 1982 through 1986.

Rachel Hallenback has worked with young people in a variety of capacities, including counselor and teacher. She helped raise the daughter of a friend for five years before the birth of her own daughter. She and Nancy have been lovers for five years.

Kate Hall is English, white, working-class, and forty-two. She lives with her teen-age daughter, Amy, and sundry animals, in London. She writes, draws, and paints in between life-in-general and work. She teaches dance and writing and is a therapist. She came out in 1978 and is still celebrating.

Kate Hill lives in Santa Cruz with her lover of five years and their four-year-old and five-week-old sons.

Kendall is an actress, teacher, writer, and scholar whose ruling obsession this year is British women playwrights ca. 1696-1915. Her other obsessions include women's theater reflecting subculture or ethnicity; yoga; tai chi; friendships; and biographies, autobiographies, and personal writings of lesbians and other women.

Irena Klepfisz was born in Poland in 1941 and came to the U.S. at the age of eight. Jewish lesbian/feminist activist and poet, she has taught Yiddish, creative writing, and women's studies and has led workshops on Jewish identity, Yiddish women's literature, anti-Semitism, and homophobia. A founder of *Conditions* magazine, she is also the author of a collection of poetry, *Keeper Of Accounts* (Sinister Wisdom Books), and *Different Enclosures: The Poetry And Prose Of Irena Klepfisz* (Onlywomen Press). Most recently, she coedited with Melanie Kaye/Kantrowitz *The Tribe Of Dina: A Jewish Women's Anthology* (Sinister Wisdom Books). She is on the staff of the Adult Degree Program at Vermont College and is working on translations of Yiddish women writers.

Lesbian Mothers' Group: We are four lesbian mothers. Our names are **Shirley, Barbara, Pearl,** and **Debbie.** The group has been on-going since April 1986. As we sat down to write this article we had no set pattern or focus except that we wanted our stories told. We brainstormed, taped our stories, wrote them, and read them to each other and our friends. We hope you can hear our voices in this article.

Audre Lorde is a Black Lesbian mother, cancer survivor, poet, and author of twelve books. A new collection of her essays, *A Burst Of Light*, will be published by Firebrand Books in 1988.

Caeia March was born in the Isle of Man in 1946 of white working-class parents. She studied at London University and became a social studies teacher. She left her marriage in October 1980 when she came out as a lesbian, and now lives in London near her two sons (15 and 13). She works as a clerk to pay the rent and teaches creative writing in adult education.

Ivette Merced is a lesbiana puertorriqueña. She is the daughter of a woman-loving woman. Her struggle is to free herself and others of negative labels. She writes in her mother tongue as a means of self-preservation.

Jennifer Meyer is a free-lance technical writer. She lives in Santa Cruz, California with her lover and their sons, their golden retriever and three cats. Since 1977, she has spent much of her free time working on a local feminist newspaper.

Marilyn Murphy is an Irish-Italian, catholic-raised, working-class, middle-aged Lesbian-Feminist who has been an activist, organizer, teacher, and writer for the Women's Liberation Movement since 1969.

Sue Overstreet lives, plays, works, and dreams in Indianapolis with her two daughters, Jennifer and Sara, her friend, lover and partner, Judy, and the keeper of their hearth—Isaac Louise. Never before published, she has been a sporadic "closet" writer, journaling her way through life.

Pat Parker has published five books of poetry. Her latest is *Jonestown & Other Madness* (Firebrand Books). She is a director of the Oakland Feminist Women's Health Center and lives in Pleasant Hill, California with her lover and children.

Sherri Paris has her Ph.D. in Philosophy and divides her time between teaching and political activism. Currently she teaches writing at the University of California at Santa Cruz. She has published stories, articles, and poetry. She resides in Santa Cruz with her lover and her lover's ten-year-old daughter.

Nancy D. Polikoff has written about legal issues of lesbian mothers for more than a decade. She was a founding member of the Washington, D.C. Feminist Law Collective, has worked as a staff attorney for the Women's Legal Defense Fund, and has taught both law school and university courses on Family Law and Women and the Law. She has been a member of a lesbian mothers' group for five years and is the comother of a four-year-old daughter, Elena Marya Herbert Polikoff.

Sandra Pollack is thrilled to see this anthology published. She has been wanting to help put together such a book for years. Feminist organizer, teacher, and researcher, she is Professor of English and Coordinator of the Women's Studies Program at Tompkins Cortland Community College in upstate New York. She is the coeditor (with Charlotte Bunch) of *Learning Our Way: Essays In Feminist Education*. Both her daughters are now adults. She and her partner of six years are currently learning how to garden together.

Minnie Bruce Pratt was born and raised in Alabama and now lives in Washington, D.C. She has published two books of poetry, *The Sound Of One Fork* and *We Say We Love Each Other* (Spinsters/Aunt Lute). She coauthored, with Elly Bulkin and Barbara Smith, *Yours In Struggle: Three Feminist Perspectives On Anti-Semitism and Racism* (Firebrand). She is the mother of two teen-aged sons.

Faith Reboin began writing fiction when she was twelve, was a mother at eighteen, came out as a lesbian when she was thirty, became a grandmother at thirty-nine, and got clean and sober at forty. That chronology encompasses what are still her greatest passions.

Anne Rhodes is a performing artist (Mischief Mime Co.), works in the Institutes for the Arts in Education, is writing several plays, and also leads workshops on oppression issues.

Satya Conway-Rhodes lives with her mother, five cats, and two other women in Ithaca, New York. She attends the Alternative Community School, sings and plays piano, leads workshops on oppression issues, and has her brown belt in karate.

Robyn K. Roberts lives in Santa Cruz, California with her partner and two children. In the year 1987 she hopes to have a child through alternative insemination. She also hopes to move to the country, do a long backpack, and finish her work toward her Family and Child Counseling license. Currently she cofacilitates groups for incest survivors and counsels lesbian families. She writes on the side and truly loves her life.

S.S. is a feminist scholar and activist, herbalist and poet.

Teya Schaffer is a feminist writing, loving, and mothering in Oakland, California. Her works have appeared in *Sinister Wisdom, Common Lives/Lesbian Lives, Shmate*, and *off our backs*.

Mab Segrest is the author of *Living In A House I Do Not Own* (Night Heron Press, 1982) and *My Mama's Dead Squirrel: Lesbian Essays On Southern Culture* (Firebrand, 1985). She is presently coordinator of North Carolinians Against Racist and Religious Violence. She is coparent, with her lover Barbara and her friend David, of Annie Elizabeth Culbertson-Jolly Segrest.

Martha Shelley, born in Brooklyn, became a gay activist, poet, essayist, hitchhiker, hellraiser, comother and martial arts student. She is now living in Oakland and working on a mysterious novel. Her two books, *Crossing The DMZ* and *Lovers And Mothers*, can be obtained through Sefir Publishing, 729 55th St., Oakland, California 94609.

Ann Allen Shockley is the author of *Loving Her, Say Jesus And Come To Me*, and *The Black And White Of It*, all recently reissued by Naiad Press.

Josephine Simmons was born November 9, 1949 in Philadelphia. She graduated from Pennsylvania State University and is currently working on a Master's degree at Ithaca College. She and her daughter live in Ithaca, New York.

Toni Tortorilla is a Transformational counselor by profession, specializing in the development of self-loving attitudes, integrating spirituality and empowering the Self. In her free time she is an avid journal keeper and writer. She enjoys traveling, envisioning, partnering, playing with her daughter, and being a parent. She is a Sagittarius.

Lucia Valeska says that "ten-plus years later my/our children (19, 21, and 23) are doing great and all three are outspoken in their thanks for having had such an 'unusual growing up.' I've served three years as Co-Director and then Executive Director of the National Gay Task Force (1979-82) and currently reside with yet another lover in Albuquerque, New Mexico, working in PR and freelance writing. And Yes, I'm Still. . . ."

Jeanne Vaughn is a thirty-three-year-old lesbian and the mother of a seventeen-year-old son. She is a graduate student in Latin American literature at San Jose State University.

Carolyn Kott Washburne is a free-lance writer who lives in Milwaukee, Wisconsin. Formerly a social worker, she now writes full-time. Her publishing credits include two books on marriage and divorce published by Charles Scribner's Sons and magazine articles in a variety of publications including *MS*, *Mademoiselle*, *Vegetarian Times*, and *Teen*. She also teaches writing at the University of Wisconsin-Milwaukee.

Minna F. Weinstein, formerly professor of history and currently an academic administrator, has published on sixteenth- and seventeenth-century women's history and various issues in higher education. She is currently at work with her life-partner on a lesbian novel.

Baylah Wolfe is a feminist lesbian, a mother, a Jew, an activist, a social therapist, a writer, a witch. A cornerstone of her work is the search for, and intensification of, contradictions and conflicts in the service of empowerment and social change.

Susan J. Wolfe is Professor of English at the University of South Dakota, where she teaches linguistics and women's studies. Coeditor of *The Coming Out Stories*, she has also written on the relationship between language, gender, and society. Her son lives with his father.

Nancy Zook frequently speaks to college classes and other groups about alternative parenting. She works with pregnant teens and is also a birth educator. She and Rachel have been lovers for over five years.

Zulma was born and raised in Puerto Rico, married to an American, and converted to Judaism while pregnant with her only child. She divorced to be true to her lesbianism, latent since early childhood. Her daughter, then eleven, chose to stay (at first) with her father. These poems reflect the difficult period following the divorce.

Other titles from Firebrand Books include:

Dykes To Watch Out For, Cartoons by Alison Bechdel/$6.95

Getting Home Alive by Aurora Levins Morales and Rosario Morales/$8.95

Good Enough To Eat, A Novel by Lesléa Newman/$8.95

Jonestown & Other Madness, Poetry by Pat Parker/$5.95

The Land Of Look Behind, Prose and Poetry by Michelle Cliff/$6.95

Living As A Lesbian, Poetry by Cheryl Clarke/$6.95

Making It, A Woman's Guide to Sex in the Age of AIDS by Cindy Patton and Janis Kelly/$3.95

Mohawk Trail by Beth Brant (*Degonwadonti*)/$6.95

Moll Cutpurse, A Novel by Ellen Galford/$7.95

The Monarchs Are Flying, A Novel by Marion Foster/$8.95

My Mama's Dead Squirrel, Lesbian Essays on Southern Culture by Mab Segrest/$8.95

A Restricted Country by Joan Nestle/$8.95

Sanctuary, A Journey by Judith McDaniel/$7.95

Shoulders, A Novel by Georgia Cotrell/$8.95

The Sun Is Not Merciful, Short Stories by Anna Lee Walters/$6.95

Tender Warriors, A Novel by Rachel Guido deVries/$7.95

This Is About Incest by Margaret Randall/$7.95

The Threshing Floor, Short Stories by Barbara Burford/$7.95

The Women Who Hate Me, Poetry by Dorothy Allison/$5.95

Words To The Wise, A Writer's Guide to Feminist and Lesbian Periodicals & Publishers by Andrea Fleck Clardy/$3.95

Yours In Struggle, Three Feminist Perspectives on Anti-Semitism and Racism by Elly Bulkin, Minnie Bruce Pratt, and Barbara Smith/$7.95

You can buy Firebrand titles at your bookstore, or order them directly from the publisher (141 The Commons, Ithaca, New York 14850, 607-272-0000).

Please include $1.50 shipping for the first book and $.50 for each additional book.

A free catalog is available on request.